Brotherhood of Railroad Trainmen

Rates of Pay and Regulations governing Employees

in Train and Yard Service on the principal Railroads of the United States, Canada

and Mexico

Brotherhood of Railroad Trainmen

Rates of Pay and Regulations governing Employees
in Train and Yard Service on the principal Railroads of the United States, Canada and Mexico

ISBN/EAN: 9783337188535

Printed in Europe, USA, Canada, Australia, Japan

Cover: Foto ©ninafisch / pixelio.de

More available books at **www.hansebooks.com**

RATES OF PAY

AND

REGULATIONS GOVERNING EMPLOYES

IN

TRAIN AND YARD SERVICE

Compliments . . . . .
   GRAND LODGE BROTHERHOOD OF RAILROAD TRAINMEN.
 W. A. SHEAHAN,   S. E. WILKINSON,
  Grand Sec'y & Treas.   Grand Master.

S. E. WILKINSON, *Grand Master,*
W. A. SHEAHAN, *Grand Sec'y & Treas.,*
  BROTHERHOOD OF RAILROAD TRAINMEN.

GALESBURG, ILLINOIS.
BROTHERHOOD STEAM PRINT.
1892.

RATES OF PAY

AND

REGULATIONS GOVERNING EMPLOYES

IN

TRAIN AND YARD SERVICE

ON THE

PRINCIPAL RAILROADS

OF THE

UNITED STATES, CANADA AND MEXICO.

COLLECTED AND COMPILED BY
S. E. WILKINSON, *Grand Master*,
W. A. SHEAHAN, *Grand Sec'y & Treas.*,
BROTHERHOOD OF RAILROAD TRAINMEN..
lf

GALESBURG, ILLINOIS.
BROTHERHOOD STEAM PRINT.
1892.

NOTICE!

The aim of the compilers of this work has been to make it as complete as possible, and to that end the management of all principal railroads have been requested to furnish copies of their regulations governing employes in train and yard service, and the rates of pay, etc. As shown by the contents, many of the leading lines have complied with the request; others have refused to give for publication the information asked, while a few have ignored the request.

This work is gotten out by the Brotherhood of Railroad Trainmen at considerable expense, not as an advertisement, nor with the hopes of realizing a money profit therefrom, but as a book of reference for the enlightenment of its members, and we believe it will be found a valuable book for managers and their superintendents.

Supplements to this work will be issued from time to time as important changes in rates, etc., shall make it necessary.

A limited number of copies of this work can be supplied to those wanting them at $2.00 per copy. Address:

GRAND LODGE, BROTHERHOOD OF RAILROAD TRAINMEN,
Drawer A, Galesburg, Ill.

ADDISON & PENNSYLVANIA RAILWAY.

Passenger Conductors, $75.00 per month.
Freight Conductors, $65.00 per month.
Switchmen, $40.00 per month.
Passenger Brakemen, $45.00 per month.
Freight Brakemen, $40.00 per month.
The freight crews make from 82 to 95 miles per day only.
May 14th, 1892. FRANK M. BAKER, General Superintendent.

ANNAPOLIS & BALTIMORE SHORT LINE RAILROAD.

We pay $80.00 per month for Conductors and Engineers of passenger trains, and $70.00 per month for freight trains; $1.50 per day to Baggagemen, Brakemen and Firemen; $1.00 to $1.50 per day for Yardmen and Switchmen. Our road is short and the runs easy. C. A. COOMBS,
May 12th, 1892. Managing Director.

ATCHISON, TOPEKA & SANTA FE RAILROAD.

PASSENGER SERVICE.

ON RUNS EXCEEDING 4,000 MILES PER CALENDAR MO.				ON RUNS LESS THAN 4,000 MILES PER CALENDAR MO.			
DIVISION.	Cond's	Br'k'n.	REMARKS.	DIVISION.	Cond's	Br'k'n.	REMARKS.
Chicago	$125 00	$60 00		Chicago	$100 00	$55 00	
Eastern	125 00	60 00		Eastern	100 00	55 00	
Middle	125 00	60 00		Middle	100 00	55 00	
Southern Kas	125 00	60 00		Southern Kas	100 00	55 00	
Southern	125 00	60 00		Southern	100 00	55 00	
Panhandle	125 00	60 00		Panhandle	100 00	55 00	
Western	125 00 / 130 00	60 00 / 70 00	East of La Junta. West of La Junta.	Western	100 00 / 105 00	55 00 / 65 00	East of La Junta. West of La Junta.
New Mexico	130 00	70 00		New Mexico	105 00	65 00	
Rio Grande	130 00	70 00		Rio Grande	105 00	65 00	

FREIGHT SERVICE.

LOCAL AND MIXED.				THROUGH AND IRREGULAR.			
DIVISION.	PER MONTH.		REMARKS.	DIVISION.	PER MILE.		REMARKS.
	Cond's	Br'k'n.			Cond's	Br'k'n.	
Chicago	$90 00	$60 00		Chicago	3 cts.	2 cts.	
Eastern	90 00	60 00		Eastern	3 cts.	2 cts.	
Middle	90 00	60 00		Middle	3 cts.	2 cts.	
Southern Kas	90 00	60 00		Southern Kas	3 cts.	2 cts.	
Southern	90 00	60 00		Southern	3 cts.	2 cts.	
Panhandle	90 00	60 00		Panhandle	3 cts.	2 cts.	
Western	95 00	65 00		Western	3 cts.	2 cts.	East of La Junta.
New Mexico				" "	3½ cts.	2½ cts.	West of La Junta.
Rio Grande				New Mexico	3½ cts.	2½ cts.	La Junta to Raton.
				" "	3½ cts.	2½ cts.	Raton to Las Vegas.
				" "	3½ cts.	2½ cts.	Las Vegas to Albuquerque.
				Rio Grande	3½ cts.	2½ cts.	

NOTE.—While three crews run the locals between Dodge City and La Junta, and three crews between La Junta and Denver, $110.00 per month for Conductors and $75.00 per month for Brakemen will be allowed.

Twenty-six or twenty-seven days per calendar month will constitute a month's work in local or mixed service.

ATCHISON, TOPEKA & SANTA FE RAILWAY.

BRANCH LINES.—LOCAL OR MIXED TRAINS.

BRANCH.	Cond's.	Brakem'n
M. A. & B.	$ 100 00	$ 65 00
Osage City	100 00	65 00
Independence	100 00	65 00
Benedict	100 00	65 00
Englewood	105 00	65 00
Strong City	100 00	65 00
Salina	100 00	65 00
Barnard	100 00	65 00
Hutchinson	100 00	65 00
Great Bend	100 00	65 00
Rockvale	100 00	70 00
Canon City	100 00	70 00
Starkville	100 00	70 00
Blossburg	100 00	70 00
Magdalena	105 00	70 00
Carthage	105 00	70 00
Lake Valley	105 00	70 00

NOTE.—Twenty-six or twenty-seven days shall constitute a month's work except on Osage City, Salina, Barnard, Carthage and Lake Valley Branches, which shall be at above rates per calendar month. This Schedule is subject to revision on Canon City Branch should switch engines be employed at Canon City or Florence.

WORK TRAIN SERVICE.

DIVISION.	Cond's.	Brakem'n	REMARKS.
Chicago	$ 90 00	$ 60 00	
Eastern	90 00	60 00	
Middle	90 00	60 00	
Southern Kansas	90 00	60 00	
Southern	90 00	60 00	
Panhandle	90 00	60 00	
Western	{ 90 00 / 97 50	{ 60 00 / 67 50	East of La Junta. West of La Junta.
New Mexico	100 00	70 00	
Rio Grande	100 00	70 00	

Twenty six or twenty-seven days per calendar month will constitute a month's work in Work Train Service.
Twelve hours or less to constitute a day's work. When conductors act as foremen, twenty dollars extra per month to be paid.

Rules, 1. On all freight runs of 100 miles or less, requiring more than ten hours to make the run, overtime will be paid at the rate of ten miles per hour for trainmen. On all freight runs exceeding 100 miles, trainmen will be paid overtime for all time used to complete the trip in excess of an average speed of 10 miles per hour at the above rates. Ten hours shall constitute a day's work for conductors and brakemen in freight service.

2. Conductors and brakemen in Freight Service, when making doubles, only the single of which is less than 100 miles and the double more than 100 miles, will be allowed 200 miles should the double consume to exceed 16 hours.

3. When crews of through or local freight, or mixed freight trains are required to do switching service at terminal or division stations, they will be paid extra for such service at the rate of 10 miles per hour for conductors and brakemen; less than thirty minutes not to be counted; thirty minutes and over and less than one hour will be computed one hour, except that on runs which consume less than 10 hours, no extra switching service will be allowed until the total time used in making the run exceeds 10 hours.

4. Short runs or turn-arounds made within 24 hours, where mileage is less than 100 miles, will be allowed 100 miles.

5. Crews in charge of helper engines between Glorieta and Lamy, conductors will be paid $100 per month, brakemen $70 per month, 12 hours to constitute a day's work; overtime after twelve hours, conductors 35 cents per hour, brakemen 25 cents per hour.

6. Freight Train Crews will be allowed regular freight rate for handling passenger trains or passenger equipment.

7. Freight or Passenger crews making extra trips, in addition to their regular assigned runs, will be allowed extra time upon the basis of pay allowed other crews in similar service, except as provided in Article 6.

8. Trainmen required to remain on duty over thirty minutes with their trains after arriving at a Main Line Terminal Station, shall be paid at the rate of 10 miles per hour.

9. Crews paid on basis of calendar month will not have their pay reduced on account of National Holidays, in case their train does not run.

10. In computing overtime no fraction of an hour less than thirty minutes will be counted. Thirty minutes or over will be counted one hour.

11. Crews dead-heading under orders will be paid one-half their regular rates, provided that crews dead-heading perform no other service on that date, shall be paid full rates for 100 miles.

12. Crews not assigned to regular runs will be run first in first out. In ordering crews, when dead-heading is required, the second crew will run the train, the first crew dead-heading. The dead-head crew being ahead of the crew with whom they dead head on reaching the terminal of the run.

13. Pilots on Raton Mountain and on other helper service will receive $75 per calendar month; twelve hours constituting a day's work; overtime at 25 cents per hour after twelve hours. Other Pilots to receive Conductor's pay according to the Division on which they are employed.

14. Where crews are compelled to double hills, such crews will be allowed the extra mileage made; for example if a hill is five miles long, an allowance of ten miles in addition to the length of the run will be allowed.

15. Trainmen will be notified when time is not allowed as per trip report.

16. Main line trainmen will be called at division or terminal stations by train caller, who will be provided with a book in which the men called shall enter their names, together with the time they are called. The district within which trainmen will be called will be established by the Division Superintendent. The working time of all trainmen will commence within one hour after they have signed Caller's book.

17. A crew called for any train that does not go out will be paid at overtime rates at 10 miles per hour, until released, and stand first out; except that a crew held over five hours for a train that does not run shall be paid one day and go behind other crews at that point. Under this article, when a trainman signs the caller's book for the subsequent train, he shall be released from the first train.

18. Any trainman after a continous service of 16 hours or more, shall, upon a written or telegraphic notice, upon Trainmaster or Division Superintendent be entitled to eight hours rest before he is again called for service, except in cases of wrecks, washouts or snow blockades, and provided also, that such notice is given prior to or at expiration of any run. Following crews will have the right to run around any crew laying over for rest.

19. Crews will not be released between terminal points.

20. When crews run over more than one Division the assignment of crews to the through runs will be made as near as practicable on the basis of mileage on each Division.

21. No more men shall be employed in the service than is necessary to do the work and earn a reasonable average monthly compensation. Whenever, in the judgment of the trainmen, there are too many crews, a committee of trainmen in good standing employed on the Division may call the attention of the Trainmaster or Superintendent to such surplus of men, when the matter will be fully investigated, and if conditions are found to warrant it, a reduction in force will be made, such reduction to be made in the order of promotion. Nothing in this article, however, shall prevent the Division Superintendent from increasing or decreasing forces at his discretion. Every employe should understand that it is his privilege and duty to make written appeal to his Division Superintendent whenever by promotion, reduction or assignment, he deems an injustice has been done him.

22. Trainmen attending Court at the request of an official of the company will be paid at the same rate they would have been entitled to had they remained on their run, and if away from their home station, in addition thereto their legitimate expenses.

23. When a change of division or train runs require trainmen to change their place of residence, they will be furnished free transportation for their families and household goods to their new place of residence.

24. In line of promotion, two brakemen will be promoted from rank of brakemen, according to age on respective divisions, and their ability to assume the duties of conductor. For every two Brakemen so promoted, one Conductor may be hired or promoted from the ranks of Brakemen regardless of age in service. Any Conductor so hired or promoted shall have had at least one year's experience on a steam surface railroad, as conductor, and shall be required to pass such examination as the rules of the Company require. The rights of all Conductors and Brakemen shall date from the time they enter the continuous service of the Company.

25. When a conductor or brakeman is suspended, he shall be notified in writing the day his suspension takes place, and it shall plainly state the length of time suspended, and for what cause.

26. When trainmen leave the service of the Company, they shall be given letters stating time of service, in what capacity employed and cause for leaving the service; the said letters to be given within a reasonable time provided they have worked on the division 90 days or more; said letters to be signed and stamped by the Superintendent of the Division

27. All employes will be regarded as in line of promotion, dependent upon the

faithful discharge of duties, capacity for increased responsibility, and term of service. Superintendents are keeping a record of the employes on their respective divisions, in which is entered their merits, demerits and term of service. Upon such record promotions will be based.

28. The assignment of trainmen will be made in accordance with the judgment of the Division Superintendent, according to the provisions of Articles 24 and 27.

29. Conductors and Brakemen will not be dismissed or suspended from the Company's service without just cause. In case of suspension or dismissal, if any employe thinks his sentence unjust, he shall have the right within ten days to refer his case by written statement to the Division Superintendent. Within ten days of the receipt of this notice his case shall have a thorough investigation by the proper officer of the Railroad Company, at which he may be present if he so desires, and also be represented by any disinterested employe of his choice. In case he shall not be satisfied with the result of said investigation, he shall have the right to appeal to the General Superintendent and to the General Manager. In case of intoxication or insubordination, dismissal will follow without hearing, as above provided. In case suspension or dismissal is found to be unjust, he shall be reinstated and paid for all time lost.

30. When Conductors or Brakemen leave the service of the Company of their own accord, they shall not be reinstated. Leave of absence will not be granted for more than ninety days except in cases of sickness.

31. All vacancies occuring in baggage runs, not controlled by joint service, shall be filled from the ranks of the eligible and competent Passenger Brakemen, oldest Passenger Brakemen in service to have the preference on all extra or special runs or excursions trains. Where a man is required to take charge of and handle baggage, regular or extra Passenger Brakemen shall perform the service, oldest men to have the preference.

32. When any Passenger or Freight Conductor makes proper objection in writing to the Trainmaster or Superintendent against any Brakeman under his charge, such Brakeman shall be assigned to other service, or dismissed from the service if the circumstances justify.

33. When reasonable notice has been given, members of General Grievance Committee will be granted unlimited leave of absence when on Committee business.

34. Any employe believing himself to be improperly treated under these rules and regulations shall have the right to appeal to the General Superintendent and General Manager.

35. No departure from the provisions of this agreement will be made by any party thereto without reasonable notice of such a desire in writing has been served upon other parties thereto.

The Articles enumerated constitute in their entirety an agreement between the Atchison, Topeka & Santa Fe Railroad Company and its Conductors and Brakemen.

All Schedules, Rules and Regulations previously in effect are null and void.

SWITCHING SERVICE.

At Chicago, Corwith, Joliet, Streator, Chillicothe, Ft. Madison, Marceline, Kansas City, Argentine, Atchison, Topeka, Emporia, Florence, Newton, Hutchinson, Nickerson, Dodge City, La Junta, Pueblo, Denver, Trinidad, Raton, Las Vegas, Albuquerque, San Marcial, Deming, El Paso, Wichita, Arkansas City, Purcell, Wellington, Cherry Vale, Ottawa, Frontenac and Chanute,

Switchmen, days, 25 cents per hour.
Switchmen. nights, 27 cents per hour.
Foremen, days, 27 cents per hour.
Foremen, nights, 29 cents per hour.

Rules. 1. Switching crews shall consist of a Foreman and two Switchmen, except when in the judgment of the Superintendent three men are not necessary to properly handle the business. Nothing in this article shall prevent the Foreman from acting as Yardmaster, should it be decided by the Superintendent that he can perform this service in connection with his other duties.

2. Yardmen will be permited to take their noon or midnight meal hour immediately after 12 o'clock noon or midnight, except in cases of emergency or when it is necessary to vary from the above rule in order to facilitate the movement of trains. Should Yardmen be required to remain on duty for thirty minutes or less after 12 o'clock, they will be paid overtime at the above rate for thirty minutes, and if required to remain on duty over thirty minutes and less than one hour, they will be paid for one hour. The above rule will also apply to Yardmen working from 12 o'clock noon until 12 o'clock midnight, or on any other split trick.

3. Where the work requires two or more engines, the switching service will be devided into tricks of ten hours or more, it being understood that except in cases of emergency, continuous service exceeding fifteen hours will not be required. It is also understood that the division of the twenty-four hours into tricks shall be arranged by

the Division Officials. A Yardman called for any regular trick shall be paid for ten hours, whether work is furnished for the entire time or not, except in case of insubordination or sickness, when he shall be paid only for the time worked. Nothing in this article shall be construed as allowing ten hours for two, three or more hours addition to a regular trick, it being distinctly understood that such addition is to be paid for on the regular hourly basis.

4. Yardmen will not be dismissed or suspended from the Company's service without just cause, and in case of suspension or dismissal, if any employe thinks his treatment unjust, he shall have the right within ten days, to refer his case by written statement to the Division Superintendent, and within ten days of the receipt of this notice, his case shall have thorough investigation by the proper officers of the Railroad Company, at which he may be present, if he so desires, and also be represented by any disinterested employe of his choice. In case he is not satisfied with the result of such investigation, he shall have the right to appeal to the General Superintendent. The decision of the Division Superintendent, however, shall be final unless the employe sees fit to appeal to the General Superintendent, as above provided. Any employe will be dismissed without hearing in cases of intoxication or insubordination.

5. The rights of all Yardmen shall date from the time they enter the continuous service of the Company, and they shall be regarded as in the line of promotion, dependent upon the faithful discharge of duties, capacity for increased responsibility and term of service. Nothing in this article shall prevent Superintendents from employing experienced men should the good of the service require it.

6. All previous Schedules, Rules and Regulations are void.

For Order Railway Conductors:
  A. B. GARRETSON, Grand Senior Conductor.
  H. J. STANLEY, Chairman O. R. C.
For Brotherhood Railroad Trainmen:
  P. H. MORRISSEY, Acting Grand Master.
  R. C. SCOTT, Chairman B. of R. T.

H. R. NICKERSON,
General Superintendent.
Approved: A. A. ROBINSON,
2nd Vice Pres. and Gen. Manager.

April 1st, 1892.

ATLANTIC & PACIFIC RAILROAD COMPANY.—WESTERN DIVISION.

PASSENGER SERVICE.

Passenger Conductors, $130.00 per month. Passenger Brakemen, $75.00 per month. It is understood that while two through trains daily each way are run as at present, there will be six crews for the New Mexico Division, six crews for the Arizona Division, and five crews for the California Division.

FREIGHT SERVICE.

The pay of Freight Conductors will be as follows:

Between Albuquerque and Winslow, $95.00 per month, for 3,000 miles or less, and 3 1-6 cents per mile for all excess mileage.

Between Winslow and Mojave, $105.00 per month, for 3,000 miles or less, and 3¼ cents per mile for all excess mileage.

The pay of Freight Brakemen will be:

Between Albuquerque and Winslow, $70.00 per month, for 3 000 miles or less, and 2¼ cents per mile for all excess mileage.

Between Winslow and Mojave, $80.00 per month, for 3,000 miles or less, and 2¼ cents per mile for all excess mileage.

WORK TRAIN SERVICE.

Work Train Conductors will be paid $100.00 per month.

Work Train Brakemen will be paid $75.00 per month.

26 or 27 days per calendar month will constitute a month's work on work trains, 12 hours or less to constitute a day's work.

Conductor with helper engine between Williams and Ash Fork will be paid $100.00 per calendar month. Twelve (12) hours to constitute a day's work, the hours to be regulated by Division Superintendents. Overtime to be paid as per Article I.

REGULATIONS.

ARTICLE 1. On all freight runs of less than 100 miles requiring more than 10 hours to make the run, over-time will be paid if the hours used on the trip exceed 12 hours, in which case all over-time exceeding 10 hours will be paid at freight rates. On all freight runs exceeding 100 miles, trainmen will be paid overtime for all time used to complete the trip in excess of an average speed of 10 miles per hour at freight rates. On all through freight runs between Winslow and Williams and between Peach Springs and Williams, where Williams is made a divisional terminal, over-time will be paid for all time used to complete the trip in excess of 10 miles per hour.

ART. 2. Trainmen required to remain on duty over 30 minutes with their trains after arriving at a main line terminal station, shall be paid at the rate of 10 miles per hour.

ART. 3. In computing overtime no fraction of an hour less than 30 minutes will be counted. Any fraction of an hour over 30 minutes will be counted an hour.

ART. 4. Any Conductor or Brakeman running less than 100 miles in 24 hours on freight or extra passenger service or special trains will be paid the same as if 100 miles had been run, and in addition for any overtime earned under Article 1.

ART. 5. Freight and passenger crews making extra trips in addition to their regular assigned runs will be allowed extra time upon the basis allowed other crews in similar service.

ART. 6. Crews dead-heading under orders will be paid one-half their regular rates. The first crew out will run dead-head, and the second run the train; the dead-heading crew being first out on reaching terminal of that run.

ART. 7. Crews not assigned to regular runs will be run first in first out.

ART. 8. All trainmen after a continuous service of 16 hours or more, shall, upon a written or telegraphic notice upon Division Superintendent or Trainmaster, be entitled to 8 hours rest before they are again called for service, except in cases of wrecks, washouts or other emergencies, and provided also that where bulletin notice registering their arrival in a call or register book that an entry therein to the effect that 8 hours rest is needed before the signer is able to go on duty again, will be sufficient notice to the Division Official.

ART. 9. Where crews are compelled to double hills as a regular service, such crews will be allowed the extra mileage made: for example, if a hill is 5 miles long, an allowance of 10 miles in addition to the length of the division will be allowed. Mileage for doubling hills under any other circumstances will not be allowed, except at the discretion of the Division Superintendent.

ART. 10. When crews run over more than one division, the assignment of crews to the through runs will be made, as near as practicable, on the basis of mileage on each division.

ART. 11. Trainmen will be called at terminal stations by Train Caller, who will be provided with a book in which the men called will enter their names, together with the time they are called. The district within which the trainmen will be called will be established by the Division Superintendent, but shall not in any case exceed three-quarters of a mile from the calling office. The working time of all trainmen will commence within one hour after they have signed the caller's book.

ART. 12. Trainmen when called, if for any cause or reason other than their own acts, do not go out, if held on duty less than six hours, shall be paid one-half day and stand first out. If held more than six hours, they will be paid one day and go behind other crews at that point.

ART. 13. Trainmen attending court at the request of an official of the Company, will be paid at the same rate they would have been entitled to had they remained on their run, and if away from their home station, in addition thereto their legitimate expenses.

ART. 14. When a change of divisions or train runs require trainmen to change their place of residence, they will be furnished free transportation for their families and household goods to their new place of residence.

ART. 15. Trainmen will be notified when time is not allowed as per trip report.

ART. 16. The assignment of brakemen will be made in accordance with the judgment of the Division Superintendents, subject to the provisions of Article 18.

ART. 17. Conductors or Brakemen will not be dismissed or suspended from the Company's service without just cause. In case of suspension or dismissal, if any employe thinks his dismissal unjust, he shall have the right within 10 days to refer his case by written statement to the Division Superintendent. Within ten days of the receipt of this notice his case shall have a thorough investigation by the proper officers of the railroad company, at which he may be present if he so desires, and also be represented by any disinterested employe of his grade. In case he shall not be satisfied with the result of the investigation, he shall have the right to appeal to the Superintendent Transportation and to the General Manager. In case suspension or dismissal is found to be unjust, he shall be reinstated and paid for all time lost.

ART. 18. All employes will be regarded as in the line of promotion dependent upon the faithful discharge of their duties, capability for increased responsibility, and term of service. Superintendents are keeping a record of the employes on their respective divisions, in which is entered their merits, demerits and term of service. Upon such record promotions will be based. Reduction of forces will be made at the discretion of Division Superintendents in the order of promotion. Every employe should understand that it is his privilege and duty to make written appeals to his Division Superintendent whenever by promotions, reductions or assignments, he deems an injustice has been done him. Any employe will be dismissed without hearing in case of intoxication, insubordination and collisions. Nothing in this article shall be construed as preventing the Company from employing experienced men when they deem that the good of the service requires it.

ART. 19. Any employe believing himself to be improperly treated under these rules and regulations, shall have the right to appeal to the Superintendent Transportation and General Manager.

ART. 20. All schedules, rules and regulations in conflct with these now adopted, are void. No change will be made from these schedules and rules without reasonable notice.

Approved: D. B. ROBINSON, General Manager.   ANDREW SMITH,
Supt. Transportation.

The baggage on our trains is handled by Wells, Fargo & Co.'s Express Messengers; we paying one-half of their salary,   T. R. GABEL,
September 1st, 1890.   General Superintendent.

ATLANTIC & PACIFIC RAILROAD COMPANY.—WESTERN DIVISION.

SWITCHING SERVICE.

Yardmasters, days, $115.00 per month. Yardmasters, nights, $110.00 per month. Foremen, days, 27 cents per hour. Foremen, nights, 29 cents per hour. Switchmen, days, 25 cents an hour. Switchmen, nights, 27 cents per hour.

ARTICLE 1. Foreman of Gallup mine crew shall be paid $100.00 per month; helper, $80.00. Twenty-six and twenty-seven days to constitute a month's work. Twelve hours to constitute a day's work. All over time to be paid at same rates.

ART. 2. The twenty-four hours to be divided into two shifts of 12 hours each. Allowing the hours between 12 o'clock noon and 1 o'clock p. m., and 12 o'clock midnight and 1 o'clock a. m. for meals. No pay shall be allowed for these hours unless Yardmaster notify men that he wants them to report for work before the hour is up, in which case Foremen and Switchmen will be paid for the hours. Important work shall not be neglected at any time.

ART. 3. When Foremen and Switchmen do any work outside of regular yard work they shall be paid extra for such work at the regular hourly basis, which shall not be deducted from their regular shifts unless other men are employed to take their places, and if so the amount paid them to be deducted from the pay of Foremen and Switchmen, whose places they fill. Loading and unloading stock to be considered yard work when in yard limits.

ART. 4. It shall be understood that a yard crew shall consist of a Yardmaster, Foreman and two Switchmen, night and day, respectively, except, at Gallup, days, Peach Springs and Needles, days and nights, where two men and the Yardmaster shall constitute a crew day and night. The man whom the Yardmaster designates as Foreman to be paid 27 cents per hour in day and 29 cents in night yard.

ART. 5. Trainmen have no rights in yard.

ART. 6. That when a man has a regular position in yard and wants to bring his family to his place of employment, he shall be furnished free transportation for his family and household goods over the A. & P. R. R.

ART. 7. That the General Greivance Committee shall consist of a man duly appointed by each yard crew under this agreement.

ART. 8. Members of the General Committee shall be granted unlimited leave of absence when on committee business connected with this schedule only.

ART. 9. When the yard men attend court at the request of an official of the Company they will be paid the same rate of pay they would have been entitled to had they remained at their respective positions, and, if away from their home station, in addition thereto their legitimate expenses.

ART. 10. All men in yard service to be given clearance when leaving the service of the company, such clearance to show length of service and cause of leaving.

ART. 11. That a copy of this agreement shall be kept by Yardmaster or Trainmaster at each yard, and that every man taking employment in any yard specified in this agreement shall read and sign this agreement before he shall be allowed to go to work. That in case of any grievance that such grievance shall be submitted in writing to the General Grievance Committee for adjustment.

ART. 12. That reasonable notice be given members of the General Grievance Committee, and that they shall take such grievance up for adjustment within ten days, and that all honorable means will be used to adjust all trouble.

ART. 13. No departure from the provisions of this agreement will be made by any party thereto without reasonable notice of such a desire in writing has been served upon the parties thereto. The articles enumerated constitute in their entirety an agreement between the Atlantic & Pacific Railroad Company and its Yardmasters and Switchmen specified. All schedules previously in effect are null and void.

Signed: ATLANTIC & PACIFIC RAILROAD COMPANY,
For the Yardmasters, Foremen and Switchmen:
C. C. JONES.
W. H. M'DONALD,
J. C. CASEY,
S. H. CAMPBELL,
JAMES WALSH.

T. R. GABEL,
General Superintendent.
JOHN DENAIR,
Superintendent Transportation.

April 1, 1892.

GULF, COLORADO & SANTA FE RAILWAY.

ARTICLE 1. *Passenger Service.* Regular assigned passenger runs exceeding 4,000 miles per calendar month, Conductors shall receive $125.00; Brakemen $60.00 per month.

Regular assigned passenger runs less than 4,000 miles per calendar month, Conductors shall receive $100.00; Brakemen $55.00 per month.

BRANCH LINES—MIXED RUNS.

Houston Branch, Conductors $100.00; Brakemen $65.00 per calendar month.
Montgomery Branch, Conductors $100.00; Brakemen $65.00 per calendar month.
Honey Grove Branch, Conductors $90.00; Brakemen $60.00 per calendar month.
Weatherford Branch, Conductors $100.00; Brakemen $65.00 per calendar month.

LOCAL FREIGHT SERVICE.

Between Galveston and Sealy, Conductors $90.00; Brakemen $60.00.
Between Sealy and Temple, Conductors $95.00; Brakemen $65.00.
Between Temple and Cleburne, Conductors $90.00; Brakemen $60.00.
Between Cleburne and Gainesville, Conductors $90.00; Brakemen $60.00.
Between Gainesville and Purcell, Conductors $90.00; Brakemen $60.00.
Lampasas Branch, Conductors $90.00; Brakemen $60.00.
Dallas Branch, Conductors $95.00; Brakemen $65.00.

The working days of a calendar month to constitute a month's work, and mileage in excess of 100 miles will be paid for at same rate between Gainesville and Purcell.

WORK TRAIN SERVICE.

Conductors shall receive $90.00; Brakemen $60.00. The working days of a calendar month to constitute a month's work. Twelve hours or less to constitute a day's work. Work train crews to be paid mileage going to or returning from point where work train is located, provided that cars are handled which do not belong in the service in which they have been engaged. Crews assigned to work train service shall be notified of such assignment when called. Where Conductors act as foremen, $20.00 extra per month to be paid.

THROUGH AND IRREGULAR FREIGHT SERVICE.

Conductors shall receive 3 cents and Brakemen 2 cents per mile.

ART. 2. On all freight runs of 100 miles or less requiring more than 10 hours to make the run, overtime will be paid at the rate of 10 miles per hour for trainmen. On all freight runs exceeding 100 miles, trainmen will be paid overtime for all time used to complete the trip in excess of an average speed of 10 miles per hour at the above rates. Ten hours shall constitute a day's work for Conductors and Brakemen in freight service.

ART. 3. Conductors and Brakemen in freight service, when making doubles, only the single of which is less than 100 and the double more than 100 miles, will be allowed 200 miles should the double consume to exceed 16 hours.

ART. 4. When crews of through, local or mixed freight trains are required to do switching service at terminal or division stations, they will be paid extra for such service at a rate of 10 miles per hour for Conductors and Brakemen; less than 30 minutes not to be counted; 30 minutes and over and less than one hour will be computed as one hour. Through freight crews delayed at any point more than one hour loading or unloading stock, loading or unloading material, or required to switch more than one hour at any point will be paid extra for such service at the regular overtime rates. Local crews switching, loading or unloading stock at places where switch engines are usually kept, shall be paid extra for such service at regular overtime rates, provided however, that any time allowed under this article for such extra service will not be computed as overtime at the expiration of the run.

ART. 5. When local freight crews are compelled to sidetrack their trains to do construction work, load or unload material, they will be paid extra for such service at regular overtime rates, regardless of time used in making the trip, it being understood that this service is not to be paid for twice.

ART. 6. Short runs or turn-rounds made within 24 hours, where mileage is less than 100 miles, will be allowed 100 miles.

rews will be allowed regular freight rate for handling passenger
uipment.
r passenger crews making extra trips in addition to their regu-
)e allowed extra time on the basis of pay allowed other crews in
 as is provided in Article 7.
ι required to remain on duty 30 minutes or over with their trains
minal station shall be paid at the rate of 10 miles per hour.
ιid on a basis of a calendar month will not have their pay re-
ational holidays in case their train does not run.
ιting overtime no fraction of an hour less than 30 minutes will
; or over and less than one hour will be counted one hour.
:ad-heading under orders will be paid full time, excepting that
ϱ on passenger trains under orders will be paid half time. Crews
)oses when cabooses are dead-headed.
)t assigned to regular runs will be run first in first out. In order-
eading is required, the second crew will run the train, the first
e dead-head crew being ahead of the crew with whom they are
.ing the terminal of the run.
)g up trains yardmen shall put all air cars on head end of train
en safe.
.s to receive Conductor's pay according to the division on which

rews are compelled to double hills such crews will be allowed the
For example: If a hill is 5 miles long an allowance of 10 miles in
of the run will be allowed.
n will be notified when time is not allowed as per trip report.
e trainmen will be called at Division terminal station by train
·ovided with a book in which the men called shall enter their
he time they are called. The district in which trainmen will be
.ed by the Division Superintendent. Working time of trainmen
ιe hour after they have signed Caller's book unless leaving earlier.
·ainmen are called and for any reason other than their own act
n duty less than 5 hours they will be paid one-half day and stand
e than 5 hours they will be paid one day and go behind other

nman after a continuous service of 16 hours or more shall, upon
ic notice upon Trainmaster or other proper officer, be entitled to
is again called for service, except in case of wrecks and wash-
ιo that such notice is given prior to or at the expiration of any
will have the right to run around any crew laying over for rest.
ιll not be released between terminal points.
men shall be employed in the service than is necessary to do the
nable monthly compensation. Whenever train crews are mak-
:s per month, a committee of trainmen in good standing employed
ιll the attention of the Trainmaster or Superintendent to such
he matter will be fully investigated, and if conditions are found
ion of force will be made, such reduction to be made in the order
in this article, however, shall prevent the Division Superintend-
· reducing forces at his discretion. Every employe should under-
vilege and duty to make written appeal to his Division Superin-
)romotion, reduction or assignment, he deems an injustice has

n attending court at the request of an official of the Company
ιe rate that they would have been entitled to had they remained
·ay from their home station, in addition thereto their legitimate

cabooses and their crews shall not be laid over for the reason
ιave laid off for any cause.
change of Division or train runs require trainmen to change
:e they will be furnished free transportation for their families
) their new place of residence.
of promotion, Brakemen will be promoted from the ranks of
ording to age on respective Divisions and their ability to assume
r; for every two Brakemen so promoted one Conductor may be
n the ranks regardless of age in the service. Any Conductor so
ιll have had at least one year's experience as Conductor on a
 and shall be required to pass such examination as the rules of
 The rights of all Conductors and Brakemen, as such, shall date
ter the continuous freight train service of the Company, it being

understood that a man shall be classed as a Conductor from the date of his assignment as extra Conductor, in accord with the provisions of this Article. In the hiring of Brakemen preference will be given to experienced and competent men.

ART. 27. When a Conductor or Brakeman is suspended he shall be notified in writing the day his suspension shall take place, and it shall plainly state the length of time suspended and for what cause.

ART. 28. When trainmen leave the service of the Company they shall be given letters stating time of service, in what capacity employed and cause for leaving the service, the said letters to be given within a reasonable length of time, provided they have worked on the Division 60 days or more, said letters to be signed and stamped by the Superintendent of the Division.

ART. 29. Conductors and Brakemen will not be dismissed or suspended from the Company's service without just cause. In case of suspension or dismissal, if any employe thinks his sentence unjust he shall have the right within ten days to refer his case by written statement to the Division Superintendent. Within ten days of the receipt of this notice his case shall have a thorough investigation by the proper officer of the Railroad Company, at which he may be present if he so desires, and also be represented by any disinterested employe of his choice. In case he shall not be satisfied with the result of said investigation he shall have the right to appeal to the General Manager. In case of intoxication or insubordination dismissal will follow. In case dismissal or suspension is found to be unjust he shall be re-instated and paid for all time lost.

ART. 30. When Conductors or Brakemen leave the service of the Company of their own accord they shall not be re-instated. Leave of absence will not be granted for more than 60 days, except in case of sickness.

ART. 31. When it shall become necessary for train crews to coal up engines, the crew shall be paid for same at the rate of 30 cents each per engine.

ART. 32. Local crews shall load cotton only at station platform, and then only as many as seven bales at any one station.

ART. 33. When any passenger or freight Conductor makes proper objection in writing to the Trainmaster or Superintendent against any Brakeman under his charge such Brakeman shall be assigned to another crew or dismissed from the service if the circumstances justify. Any Brakeman shall have the privilege of changing from any crew or run on presentation to the Trainmaster of proper reasons therefor, the Trainmaster to decide what constitutes proper reasons.

ART. 34. When reasonable notice has been given, members of Grievance Committees will be granted unlimited leave of absence when on committee business.

ART. 35. Regular assigned runs shall be run by the oldest Conductors and Brakemen, if competent. When vacancies occur in such runs, Conductors and Brakemen entitled to such runs declining to accept them, or having accepted them declining to keep them, shall fall behind the men who take the run in line of promotion.

ART. 36. Extra Conductors who are put back braking on account of dull business or by their own request, shall not lose their rights as Conductors. The oldest extra Conductors will have the privilege of remaining on extra list if they so desire. Any extra Conductor or Brakeman on extra list who in his regular turn shall catch a caboose and crew from which the Conductor or Brakeman has been laid or pulled off, shall hold said caboose and crew until the regular Conductor or Brakeman returns to work. Extra Conductors and Brakemen will be run first in first out.

ART. 37. Trainmen accepting a permanent position in yard service shall have no rights in train service, Brenham and San Angelo excepted; 30 days at one time shall be considered permanent service in yard.

ART. 38. On locals between Cleburne and Gainesville the third Brakeman shall be allowed from July 15th to October 15th of each year until such time as the local business on said Division requires his services continuously. The Brakeman on Weatherford Branch trains required to handle mail or baggage shall receive $5.00 per month in addition to regular Brakeman's salary on same run.

ART. 39. The Articles enumerated constitute in their entirety an agreement between the Gulf, Colorado & Santa Fe Railway Company and its Conductors and Brakemen. All rules and regulations previously in effect are null and void. No departure from the provisions of this agreement will be made by any party thereto without 30 days notice of such a desire in writing has been served upon either party thereto.

Signed: GULF, COLORADO & SANTA FE RAILWAY CO.
For the Order of Railway Conductors: C. O. WHEELER,
    A. B. GARRETSON, Grand Senior Conductor.   General Manager
    J. A. WILSON, General Chairman O. R. C.   S. K. WHEELER,
For the Brotherhood of Railroad Trainmen: Superintendent Transportation
    P. H. MORRISSEY, Acting Grand Master.
    O. W. BETTS, Chairman General Grievance Committee B. of R. T.
July 15th, 1892.

ST. LOUIS & SAN FRANCISCO RAILWAY.

The following will be the established schedule of rate of wages and regulations to govern Trainmen on this Company's lines after this date.

1. In the employment of Conductors and Brakemen, Division Superintendents are instructed to employ none but sober, reliable and competent men, and all such employees will be directly responsible to and subject to the orders of the Division Trainmasters and Division Superintendents at all times and in all matters pertaining to their duties. Division Superintendents will keep a record of the employes on their respective divisions in which is entered their merits, demerits and term of service.

2. Wages of Passenger Conductors shall remain as at present. Wages of Main Line Passenger Baggagemen $65.00 per month; Passenger Brakemen $60.00 per month. Wages of Branch Passenger Baggagemen and Brakemen remain as at present.

3. Conductors and Brakemen on through freight trains will be paid three (3) and two (2) cents per mile respectively for all runs of 100 miles or more; runs of less than 100 miles to be paid as 100 miles.

4. Wages of Main Line Local Freight crews shall be, Conductors $90.00 per month; Brakemen $60.00 per month. 26 or 27 days shall constitute a month, except on runs where three local crews are allowed, which shall be at above rates per calendar month.

5. Local Divisions. Each Freight Division east of Springfield 3 local crews; Springfield and Monett 2; Monett and Neodesha 3; Neodesha and Burrton 3; Monett and Chester 2; Chester and Talihina 2; Talihina and Paris 2.

6. It is understood that road between St. Louis and Monett, Monett and Paris, and Monett and Burrton, be considered as main line, all other portions as branch.

7. For all Freight Conductors and Brakemen employed by the month—except as provided for in paragraph 4—26 and 27 days shall be rated as full month, and fractional time as parts of a month shall be paid as so many 26ths of a month.

8. Twelve hours shall constitute a day's work on construction or work trains. Conductor $3.00, Brakemen $2.00. Overtime will be paid at thirty and twenty cents per hour.

9. Wages for Conductors and Brakemen on branch freight and mixed trains shall remain as at present.

10. For running special passenger and excursion trains, Conductors and Brakemen will be paid as follows: Conductors for runs of 125 miles or less $3.25 per day. For runs of more than 125 miles 2½ cents per mile. Brakemen on same basis $2.00 per day and 1½ cents per mile.

11. Overtime and excess mileage. On all freight runs which may require more than 10 hours time, overtime will be paid for all time used in making any trip in excess of 10 hours after deducting one hour for delayed time. For example: runs of 100 miles or less overtime will be be paid for all time used in excess of 11 hours at 30 and 20 cents per hour. On a run of 150 miles Conductors and Brakemen will be paid 3 and 2 cents per mile for 150 miles run, and in addition thereto for all overtime made in excess of 16 hours at the rate of 30 and 20 cents per hour.

12. Freight Conductors and Brakemen required to remain on duty with their train after arrival at terminal stations 30 minutes or more shall be paid therefor as overtime on basis of 10 miles per hour, provided the whole time exceeds 10 hours.

13. All overtime made by Freight Conductors and Brakemen shall be paid 30 and 20 cents per hour. When time is not allowed as per time slip, Conductors will be notified at once. In computing overtime no fraction of an hour less than 30 minutes shall be counted, but all overtime of 30 minutes or over and less than one hour shall be counted one hour.

14. On all turn-arounds where mileage exceeds 100 miles, actual mileage will govern.

15. Conductors and Brakemen attending court at request of an official of the Company will be paid the same rate they would have been entitled to had they remained on their run, and if away from their home station in addition thereto their legitimate expenses.

16. When a change of Division or train runs require Trainmen to change their place of residence, they will be furnished free transportation for their family and household goods to their new place of residence.

17. A crew called for any train that does not run will be paid at overtime rates at 10 miles per hour until released, and stand first out, except that a crew held over 6 hours for the train that does not run shall be paid one day and go behind other crews at that point.

18. Main line crews will be called at division or terminal stations by a Caller, who will be provided with a book in which the men called enter their names together with time they are called. The pay of Trainmen shall begin from the time the train is ordered for. The district within which Trainmen will be called will be established by Division Superintendent.

19. Freight crews required to do switching service at terminal or divison stations will be paid extra for such service at rate of 10 miles per hour for Conductors and Brakemen; less than 30 minutes not to be counted; thirty minutes and over, and less than one hour will be computed one hour.

20. Crews dead-heading under orders with caboose shall be paid 3 and 2 cents per mile respectively, and in ordering crews, second crew shall run the train, first crew dead-heading and shall stand first out on reaching terminal. Crews dead-heading on passenger trains shall receive half regular rate for actual mileage.

21. Crews not assigned to regular runs will run first in first out.

22. Crews compelled to double bill will be paid for the actual extra mileage made.

23. After continuous service of 16 hours or more, Trainmen shall be entitled to and allowed eight hours rest before being called to go out, except in cases of wrecks, wash-outs, or similar emergencies, provided telegraphic or written notice is given Trainmaster or Division Superintendent prior to or at expiration of any run. Following crews will have the right to run around any crew laying over for rest.

24. Conductors and Brakemen will not be dismissed or suspended from the Company's service without just cause. In case of dismissal or suspension, if any employe thinks his sentence unjust he shall have the right, within ten days, to refer his case by written statement to Division Superintendent. Within ten days of the receipt of this notice his case shall have a thorough investigation by the proper officers of the company at which he may be present, if he so desires, and also be represented by any disinterested employe of his choice. In case he shall not be satisfied with the result of said investigation he shall have the right to appeal to General Superintendent and General Manager. In case suspension or dismissal is found to be unjust, he shall be reinstated and paid half time for all time lost on said account. In case of intoxication or insubordination, dismissal will follow without hearing as above provided.

25. All Conductors and Brakemen shall be considered in line of promotion according to their term of service, dependent on their good conduct and ability, except that the Company reserves the right to employ additional Conductors and Brakemen when the good of the service demands it.

26. Whenever additional Conductors are required in the passenger service, promotion will be made from the ranks of freight Conductors, it being understood that the rule to be generally pursued does not permit of transferring an employe from one division to another to the detriment of the division employes.

27. All vacancies occurring in baggage runs not controlled by joint service shall be filled from the ranks of eligible and competent Passenger Brakemen, oldest Brakeman in passenger service to have preference dependent on his good conduct and ability. The same rule to apply in transferring from one division to another as in article 26.

28. No more men shall be employed in the service than is necessary to do the work and earn a reasonable average monthly compensation. Whenever in the judgment of the Trainmen there are too many crews, a committee of Trainmen in good standing employed on the division may call the attention of the Trainmaster or Superintendent to such surplus of men, when the matter will be fully investigated and if Division Superintendent finds condition to warrant it, a reduction in force will be made, such reduction to be made in order of promotion.

29. Any Conductor or Brakeman leaving the employ of this Company will at his request be given a letter by his Division Superintendent stating his term of service, capacities in which employed, and whether he has been discharged or left the service of his own accord. If discharged, such letter shall state the reasons.

30. Any employe believing himself to be improperly treated under these rules and regulations shall have the right to appeal to the General Superintendent and General Manager.

31. No departure from the provisions of this Schedule will be made by any party thereto without reasonable notice of such a desire in writing has been served upon other parties thereto.

32. A copy of this Schedule will be furnished to all Division Superintendents and Trainmasters, and the same shall be accessible to any employe who may desire to see it.

J. R. WENTWORTH, Gen. Supt.   Approved: H. L. MORRILL,
E. AKERS, Chairman O. R. C.   2d Vice-Pres. & Gen. Manager.
M. C. COSTELLO, Chairman B. of R. T.   April 1st, 1892.

CIRCULAR.—SWITCHING SERVICE.

From and after May 1st, 1890, and until further notice, Division Superintendents will be governed by the following basis of wages for Switchmen:

$2.50 per day for day Switchmen and $2.70 per day for night Switchmen. Day Foremen $2.70 per day; night Foremen $2.90 per day. Ten hours to constitute a day's work, but no extra time to be allowed unless the service rendered exceeds ten hours and thirty minutes, and when it exceeds ten hours and thirty minutes all overtime above ten hours will be paid for at the rate of 25 cents per hour for day work, and 27 cents per hour for night work. So far as possible, the hours of duty shall be so arranged as to avoid overtime. The number and grade of men to be employed for one tour of duty for each engine to be governed at all times by the necessities of the service, under the judgment of the Superintendents as approved by the General Manager.

The utmost economy, consistent with the exigencies of the service and the protection of the Company's interests, must be observed at all times.

Approved:

H. L. MORRILL,
2d Vice-Prest. and Gen'l. Manager.
May 5th, 1890.

F. E. MERRILL,
Gen'l. Superintendent.

COLORADO MIDLAND RAILWAY.—FIRST DIVISION.

ARTICLE 1. SECTION 1. Passenger crews will be paid at the rate of—Conductors $130, and Brakemen $85 per month, on runs consisting of mountain and valley mileage and on runs consisting of valley mileage only, Conductors $125, and Brakemen $70 per month.

SEC. 2. Crews on suburban trains, making one round trip per day between Colorado Springs and Florissant or intermediate points, will receive valley mileage pay. When more than one trip is made, Conductors will receive $130 and Brakemen $80 per month.

ART. 2. SEC. 1. When suburban train crews make more than one round trip per day, Yardmen will take the backover train to and from Colorado Springs, morning and evening, if yard crew is on duty at Colorado City.

SEC. 2. Services rendered by assigned crews, outside of their regular runs, will be paid extra at the regular rates for class of service performed.

ART. 3. SEC. 1. Freight crews on First Division will be paid at the rate of—Conductors 4.4 cents per mile, and Brakemen 3.3 cents per mile.

SEC. 2. Fifty miles will be allowed for the following round trip runs: Colorado Springs or Colorado City to Mile Post No. 24, and including all intermediate points and spurs; Leadville or Arkansas Junction to Mile Post No. 113, and including all intermediate points and spurs. Fifty miles additional will be allowed when crews are required to do the work at the Quarry Spur, on one of the above named trips.

SEC. 3. On fifty mile trips, crews will stand first out on their arrival.

SEC. 4. One hundred miles will be allowed for the following round trip runs: Colorado Springs or Colorado City to Mile Post No. 25, and including all intermediate points and spurs to Mile Post No. 50; Leadville or Arkansas Junction to Mile Post No. 88 and including all intermediate points and spurs to Mile Post No. 113.

SEC. 5. Crews shall receive actual mileage for all short doubles on the road.

SEC. 6. The crew known as Florissant Hill Crew will receive—Conductors $115, and Brakemen $80 per month; over time as per Section 1, Article 4, after 12 hours.

SEC. 7. Work train and wrecking crews will be paid at the rate of—Conductors $115, and Brakemen $75 per month; and over time, after 12 hours, Conductors 35 cents, and Brakemen 25 cents per hour. Calendar working days in a month to constitute a month's work. When a crew is ordered for work train service, five hours or less will constitute one-half day's work; over five hours, one day. Should a crew be ordered to move at night, outside their working hours, they will be paid regular mileage. Regular mileage will also be paid to or from their work if commercial freight is hauled. Freight crews in snow plow or flanger service will receive freight train schedule pay.

SEC. 8. Freight crews running special or excursion trains will receive 100 miles for ten hours or less, at the rate paid in freight service; over time as per Section 1, Article 4. Should such a trip consume five hours or less, crews may be used for other short trips, time not to exceed ten hours altogether, for this daily rate. Actual freight train mileage will be allowed when 100 miles is exceeded. When First Division crews run over Second Division, the pay schedule of that Division will apply.

ART. 4. SEC. 1. Overtime will be paid at the rate of—Conductors 40 cents per hour, and Brakemen 30 cents per hour. In computing overtime, fractions of an hour less than 30 minutes will not be counted; 30 minutes or over will be counted one hour.

SEC. 2. Overtime for special excursion and all freight trains will be computed on a basis of 12 miles per hour, unless otherwise provided for herein.

SEC. 3. When crews coal engines by hand, they will be allowed one hour overtime.

SEC. 4. When crews go beyond Mile Post 50 and turn, it will be considered a continuous trip. Overtime will commence, on trips Colorado City to Spinney and return, after ten hours have been consumed.

SEC. 5. When dead-head service is required, the first crew out will dead-head, and the second crew will run the train. Upon reaching terminal points, the dead-head crew will stand first out. Full time will be allowed for dead-heading. Individuals dead-heading on passenger trains will be paid one-half time.

SEC. 6. The oldest extra Conductor and the oldest extra Brakeman will stand first out. When they are unable to go out on the run, the next oldest Conductor or Brakeman available will be used.

SEC. 7. Eastern terminal for First Division freight crews will be at Colorado Springs or Colorado City. Western terminal at Leadville, whether reached via High Line or Cut-off.

SEC. 8. Allowance for short, extra or special and other runs not provided for in schedule, and for extraordinary delays, will be made by the Superintendent, on a fair and equitable basis, consistent with the general plan herein given.

ART. 5. SEC. 1. A Caller will be stationed at terminals, who will call trainmen for service when needed. They will be provided with a book giving the names of the crews, and the number or kind of train for which they are wanted, in which book trainmen will sign their names and enter the time of call. The pay of the crew will begin from the time the train is ordered, leaving time of train not to exceed one and one-half hours as nearly as practicable from the time the crew have signed the Caller's book. Limit of calling crews, three-quarters of a mile from yard, Colorado City, and to Fifth street, West Colorado Springs. Callers will not be allowed to call men in saloons.

SEC. 2. Trainmen who are called and report for duty, and whose services are not required on account of the abandonment of train, or other causes other than their own acts, will stand first out on unassigned runs and will be allowed 50 miles.

SEC. 3. Trainmen, after continuous service, shall not be required to go out when they need rest. Of this each man will judge for himself, but must give notice to Trainmaster or Superintendent in sufficient time to avoid delays, and will be entitled to eight hours rest before being again called for service, except in case of wrecks, washouts, or other emergencies.

SEC. 4. Trainmen will be notified when time is not allowed as per trip reports.

SEC. 5. The oldest Conductor or Brakeman will have preference of runs in his class, merit being equal. Of this the Superintendent is to be the judge.

SEC. 6. Trainmen attending court at the request of an officer of the Company will be paid the same rate they would have been entitled to had they remained on their runs, and if away from home, in addition their legitimate expenses.

SEC. 7. When a change of Division or train run requires men to change their places of residence, they will be furnished free transportation for families and household goods.

SEC. 8. When Conductors or Brakemen leave the service of the Company of their own accord they will not be re-instated. Leave of absence will not be granted for more than 90 days, except in case of sickness.

SEC. 9. When any passenger or freight Conductor makes proper objection, in writing, to the Trainmaster or Superintendent, against any Brakeman under his charge, such Brakeman will be assigned to other service, or dismissed from the service, as the circumstances justify.

SEC. 10. In case a Conductor or Brakeman believes his discharge or suspension to be unjust, he shall have the right to within ten days make a statement of the facts in the premises, and submit same to the Superintendent, and at the same time designate any employe of the Colorado Midland Railway, of his class on the same Division, who, with the Superintendent, will investigate the case in question. If at all practicable, such investigation will be made within five days from the receipt of the statement of the employe. In case the discharge or suspension is decided to be unjust, he shall be re-instated and paid for all time lost on such account. If dismissed, employe, upon request, will be given a letter stating cause of dismissal. Exceptions will be made to this in cases of intoxication or insubordination, in which case no investigation will be made.

SEC. 11. In the event of any charges being made against any trainman, an investigation shall be commenced within a period of ten (10) days, whenever it is at all reasonable and practicable to do so.

SEC. 12. Yard employes and passenger Brakemen can claim no rights in freight service, and vice versa. In case of emergency, extra freight men may work in yard, not to exceed ten days at any one time.

SEC. 13. No more crews will be kept in service than are necessary to move the business with promptness and certainty. When crews are laid off on account of dullness of business, it will be done in the order of their employment or promotion, beginning with Conductors or Brakemen last promoted or employed.

SEC. 14. In line of promotion, two Brakemen will be promoted from the ranks of Brakemen, according to age and their ability to assume the duties of Conductor. For every two Brakemen so promoted, one Conductor may be hired or promoted from the ranks of Brakemen, regardless of age in the service. Any Conductor so hired or promoted shall have had at least one year's experience on steam surface railroad as Conductor, and shall be required to pass such examination as the rules of the Company require. Conductors in the ranks who are qualified, will have preference over men who are not in the service of the Company. The Conductor so hired shall go to the foot of extra Conductors' list. The rights of all Conductors and Brakemen shall date from the time they enter the service of the Company as such. No Brakeman will stand in line of promotion unless he has had at least two years' experience as a freight Brakeman.

SEC. 15. Freight crews will run first in first out, except assigned crews.

SEC. 16. It is to be understood, by both the employer and employes, that the list of Conductors is not to be altered from what it was January 1st, 1892. All the provisions of this agreement are to apply to the future.

SEC. 17. No departure from the provisions of this agreement will be made by either party, except after 30 days notice of such a desire, in writing, has been served upon the parties hereto.

The Articles enumerated above constitute, in their entirety, an agreement between the Colorado Midland Railway Company and its Conductors and Brakemen on the First Division. All schedules, rules and regulations previously in effect are null and void.

COLORADO MIDLAND RAILWAY COMPANY.

GEO. A. BRIGGS,
E. C. WALDON,
E. M. HARNER,
JAS. DELANEY,
GEO. A. PERRY,
CHAS. MEEHAN,
Committee for B. R. T.
June 3, 1892.

Approved:

W. J. LAWRENCE,
Superintendent.
H. COLLBRAN,
General Manager.

COLORADO MIDLAND RAILWAY.—SECOND DIVISION.

Between Leadville and Aspen Junction, 62 miles—Conductors (trip rate), $4.00; Brakemen, $3.00. Overtime when 7 hours has been exceeded 30 minutes.

Between Leadville and Aspen, 81 miles—Conductors (trip rate), $4.75; Brakemen, $3.55. Overtime when 9 hours and 30 minutes has been exceeded 30 minutes.

Between Leadville and Cardiffs 82 miles—Conductors (trip rate), $4.68; Brakemen, $3.51. Overtime when 9 hours has been exceeded 30 minutes.

Between Leadville and Newcastle, 98 miles—Conductors (trip rate), $5.22; Brakemen, $3.91. Overtime when 10 hours has been exceeded 30 minutes.

Between Aspen Junction and Grand Junction, 113 miles—Conductors (trip rate), $3.82; Brakemen, $2.86. Overtime when 7 hours and 30 minutes has been exceeded 30 minutes.

Between Newcastle and Grand Junction, 77 miles—Conductors (trip rate), $2.60; Brakemen. $1.95. Overtime when 5 hours has been exceeded 30 minutes.

Between Leadville and Ruedi, 47 miles—Conductors (trip rate), $4.00; Brakemen, $3.00. Overtime, between Leadville and Ruedi, when 7 hours has been exceeded 30 minutes.

Between Leadville and Sellar (round trip), 61 miles—Conductors (trip rate), $4.00; Brakemen, $3.00. Overtime when 7 hours has been exceeded 30 minutes.

1. On local freight train run between Leadville and Aspen Junction crews will be allowed: Conductors, $115.00, and Brakemen, $86.25, for the calendar working days the month, and overtime when 8 hours and 30 minutes has been exceeded 30 minutes. in

2. On Jerome Park Coal Branch, Conductor in charge, $125.00 per calendar month; other Conductors, $115.00 per calendar month; Brakemen, $86.25 per calendar month. Overtime for all hours on duty in excess of 12 hours per day.

3. Crew on run between Aspen Junction and New Castle will be allowed: Conductor, $125.00; Brakemen, $93.75 per calendar month of 12 hours or less per day. If this run is changed so as to require only 10 hours per day, or if the crew is relieved from doing switching at New Castle, the regular monthly rate of $115.00 and $86.25 will apply. In the respective cases hours in excess of 12 and 10 will be paid extra at regular overtime rate.

4. All other assigned runs: Conductors, $115.00; Brakemen, $86.25, and overtime for all hours on duty in excess of 10 hours in any one day.

5. Overtime at the rate of 35 and 25 cents per hour, for Conductors and Brakemen respectively.

6. Services rendered by assigned crews outside their regular run will be paid extra at regular rates for class of service performed.

7. Crews will not be assigned to runs except where the assigned rate equals or exceeds the trip rates for same run. Crews assigned to runs for which a trip rate has been established, will be allowed overtime at same rate fixed in trip rate. On other assigned runs not specified, overtime will be allowed when schedule time has been exceeded one hour.

8. On all turn-around trips, where crews do their own turning, time so consumed will be paid for at overtime rates.

9. Freight or mixed runs not provided for in this schedule will be paid for at the rate of $4.00 per day for Conductors and $3.00 per day for Brakemen; 10 hours per day to constitute a day's work. One-half day will be allowed for 5 hours or less. Mileage rates on the district on which the runs are made will be allowed when they exceed the daily rate. This daily rate will apply to snow plow and flanger service, except between points where trip rates are established.

10. Work train crews will be paid at the rate of: Conductors, $115.00, and Brakmen, 86.25 per month, and overtime after 12 hours. Calendar working days in a month to constitute a month's work. When a crew is ordered for work train service, 5 hours or less will constitute one-half day's work. Over 5 hours and less than 12, one day. Should a crew be ordered to move at night outside of their working hours they will be paid regular mileage therefor.

11. Overtime for extra freight trains will be computed as for regular service, namely: If in local work, the time will be the same as for local trains of that district: if through trains, the time will be computed as for regular through runs.

12. One hour overtime will be allowed freight train crews when they coal engines by hand.

13. All train crews, except assigned crews, will run first in, first out.

14. In all cases of computing overtime, fractions of an hour less than 30 minutes will not be counted; fractions of an hour 30 minutes or over will be counted a full hour.

15. When dead-head service is required the first crew out will dead-head, and upon reaching terminal points the dead-head crew will be out ahead of the crew with which it dead-headed.

16. Crews dead-heading under orders will be paid full time. Individuals dead-heading on passenger trains under orders will be paid one-half time.

17. Freight trainmen living within three-fourths of a mile of yard will be called at main division terminals, as nearly as practicable, one hour before leaving time of the train for which they are called, by a Train Caller, who will be provided with a book in which will be entered the train called for and leaving time of same. Men called will sign this book, entering the time called. The time of men will begin at time set for departure of their train' unless they leave earlier.

18. Trainmen who are called and report for duty and are not required for any cause other than their own acts, will be allowed one-half day and stand first out. This rule not to interfere with assigned crews.

19. Trainmen, after continuous service, shall not be required to go out when they need rest. Of this man will judge for himself, but must give written or telegraphic notice in sufficient time to avoid delays, to the Trainmaster or Superintendent, and will be entitled to eight hours' rest before being again called for service, except in case of wrecks, washouts or similar emergencies.

20. Trainmen attending court at the request of an officer of the Company will be paid the same amount they would have been entitled to had they remained on their runs, and, if away from home, in addition their legitimate expenses.

21. When a change of division of train runs requires men to change their place of residence, they will be furnished free transportation for their families and household goods.

22. The oldest Conductor or Brakeman shall have preference of runs in his class, merit being equal; of this the superintendent is to be judge.

23. Conductors will be promptly notified in writing of any errors discovered or corrections made in their time slips.

24. In case a Conductor or Brakemen believes discharge or suspension to be unjust, he shall have a right to within 10 days make out a written statement of the facts in the premises and submit the same to his Superintendent, and at the same time designate any employe of the Colorado Midland Railway of his class on the same division, who, with the Superintendent, shall investigate the case in question, and when at all practicable such investigation shall be made within five days from date of receipt of the statement of the employe. In case the discharge or suspension is decided to have been unjust, he shall be reinstated and paid for all the time lost on such account. If dismissed, employe upon request will be given letter stating cause of dismissal; exception to this rule in cases of intoxication or insubordination, in which cases no investigation will be held.

25. All employes will be regarded in line of promotion dependent upon the faithful discharge of their duties, capacity for increased responsibility, and term of serice, merit being equal, of which the Superintendent is to be judge, except in filling vacancies in the ranks of freight Conductors; for every two men promoted from the ranks one Conductor may be hired as a Conductor, or promoted from the ranks regardless of age in service provided he has had at least one year of actual experience as a Conductor. In filling vacancies in the ranks of through passenger Conductors, as soon as

practicable, the number of First and Second Division men employed as through passenger Conductors, will be made equal, and thereafter this equality will be observed by the promotion of Second division men to fill the vacancies caused by the retirement of Second Division men. Yard employes can claim no rights in road service, and vice versa.

26. No more crews will be kept in service than are necessary to move the business with promptness and certainty. When crews are laid off on account of dullness of business, it will be done in order of dates of their employment, beginning with the Conductors and Brakemen last employed.

27. No departure from the provisions of this agreement will be made by any party thereto except after thirty days notice of such a desire, in writing, has been served upon the other parties thereto.

28. The articles enumerated herein constitute, in their entirety, an agreement between the Company and its Second Division Freight Conductors and Brakemen, and all schedules, rules and regulations previously in effect, and in conflict herewith, are by this agreement abolished.

COLORADO MIDLAND RAILWAY COMPANY.
For the Order of Railway Conductors: W. J. LAWRENCE,
  E. E. CLARK, Grand Chief Conductor.   Superintendent.
For the Brotherhood of Railroad Trainmen: E. W. SELLS,
  T. T. SLATTERY, Second Vice Grand Master.   Secretary and Auditor.
REV. E. S. RALSTON, as Fifth Arbitrator.
December 1, 1891.

SUPPLEMENT TO A. T. & S. F. SCHEDULE.

A. B. Garretson, Grand Senior Conductor O. R. C., and P. H. Morrissey, 1st Vice Grand Master B. of R. T.:

GENTLEMEN: In connection with our proposed schedule of rates and regulations to take effect April 1st, there were certain matters agreed upon which are not mentioned in said schedule, of which the following is a memorandum: Two Brakemen are to be placed on through passenger trains between Chicago and Kansas City. The present mileage limit of passenger crews now running over 4,000 miles per month is not to be increased, except in case of fast runs and then in accordance with the conditions of the schedule. On the Rio Grande Division, passenger crews are to run between Albuquerque and El Paso, instead of Silver City, and the necessary number of crews to handle the business will be placed on the run between Rincon and Silver City. Brakemen on Chanute extension, passenger train, will receive $60.00 per month. Western Division passenger crews running between Denver and Cooledge to receive highest rate of pay. Freight runs, Topeka to St. Joseph, to be paid on mileage basis. Present conditions relative to coaling engines by trainmen to remain in force until other satisfactory arrangements can be made, Strong City Branch, Topeka and Kansas City and Kansas City and Emporia Branch local passenger crews to receive $125.00 and $60.00 per month. Passenger crews who are now by reason of long runs and continuous service, granted an occasional day or Sunday off, will receive same consideration. Pay of men on Arkansas City, Purcell local freight not to be reduced by reason of this schedule, so long as run remains as it now is. It should be also understood that in cases of breach of trust, where the general officers are satisfied beyond a doubt that trainmen are dishonest, they reserve the right to dismiss said trainmen from the service without formal investigation as provided for in above mentioned schedule. Should the general or division officers of your orders question the justice of such dismissal, the management will endeavor to satisfy them that such action is justified.

Accepted for the O. R. C.:   Yours truly,
  A. B. GARRETSON, G. S. C.   H. R. NICKERSON,
Accepted for the B. of R. T.:   General Superintendent.
  P. H. MORRISSEY, Acting Grand Master.
March 7th, 1892.

ATLANTIC & DANVILLE RAILWAY.

Passenger Conductors $2.75 per day; way freight Conductors $3.00 per day; through freight Conductors $2.50 per day; extra freight Conductors $2.50 per day, 12 hours; yard Conductors $2.50 per day, 12 hours; Brakemen, road or yard, $1.50 per day, 12 hours; train Baggagemasters $40.00 per month; also paid by Southern Express Company.
                                      G. M. HUGHES, General Manager.

BALTIMORE & LEHIGH RAILROAD COMPANY.

Passenger Conductors $2.00 per day; freight Conductors $60.00 per month; Baggagemen $1.60, and freight and passenger Brakemen $1.50 per day. We have no Switchmen. W. R. CRUMPTON, General Manager.
May 16, 1892.

BALTIMORE & OHIO R. R.—PHILADELPHIA AND MAIN STEM DIVISIONS.

ARTICLE I.

	Yard Conductors.	Yard Brakemen.
Philadelphia, per day	$2 50	$1 90
Wilmington, per day	2 50	1 90
Canton, per day	2 50	1 80
Baltimore, per day	2 50	1 80
Washington, D. C., per day	2 50	1 80
Brunswick, per day	2 50	1 80
Martinsburg, per day	2 50	1 80
Cumberland, per day	2 50	1 80
Keyser and Piedmont, per day	2 50	1 80
Grafton, per day	2 50	1 80
Parkersburg, per day	2 50	1 80

Philadelphia Division. ART. 2. One Conductor and three Brakemen to constitute a crew on all the yard engines on the Philadelphia Division, except Piers 40 and 62, at Philadelphia.

First Division. ART. 3. One Conductor and two Brakemen to constitute a crew on all yard engines, day shift, in Camden yard. Night crews to remain as heretofore. Locust Point, Mt. Clare and Washington yards to remain as heretofore.

Second Division. ART. 4. Brunswick and Cumberland yard crews to remain as heretofore.

Third Division. ART. 5. One Conductor and three Brakemen to constitute a crew in Keyser yard. Grafton yard crews to remain as heretofore.

Fourth Division. ART. 6. One Conductor and three Brakemen to constitute a crew in Benwood yard. One Conductor and two Brakemen to constitute a crew on passenger shift in Wheeling yard. One Conductor and three Brakemen to constitute a crew on all other engines Wheeling yard.

Fifth Division. ART. 7. One Conductor and two Brakemen to constitute a crew in Parkersburg yard.

Pittsburgh Division. ART. 8. In Glenwood yard, one Conductor and three Brakemen to constitute a crew on shop yard shift, if, in the judgment of the Superintendent, this is necessary. All other crews to remain as heretofore.

ART. 9. Twelve hours to constitute a day's work: over six hours and less than twelve shall be considered full twelve hours; pay to be received accordingly. All under six hours, pay to be received for one-half day.

ART. 10. That yard men can claim no rights on road, and road men can claim no rights in yard service.

ROAD SERVICE.

Philadelphia Division. ARTICLE 1. SECTION 1. Passenger Brakemen on Philadelphia Division to be paid: Local runs, $49.00 per month; Division runs, $50.00 per month. Baggagemasters, local runs, $52.50 per month. No Baggagemaster or Brakeman to be reduced who receives over this amount. Baggagemasters on trains 122, 123, 128 and 129, trains 504 and 513, will receive $60.00 per month.

SEC. 2. Freight Conductors to receive $2.75 per day; freight Brakemen, $1.85.

Main Stem Division. SEC. 3. Passenger Brakemen on trains 13 and 16 to receive $1.65 per day. Passenger Brakemen on trains 14 and 15 to receive $50.00 per month. Baggagemasters on trains 13 and 16 to receive $52.50 per month. Baggagemasters on trains 14 and 15 to receive $52.50 per month.

SEC. 4. On way trains specifically, Conductors will receive $90.00 per month; Brakemen, $60.00 per month.

Baltimore Division. Freight Conductors, 1st class, on First Division between Baltimore and Brunswick, to receive $2.35 per day; 2nd class, $2.00 per day. Freight Brakemen, 1st class, $1.55 per day; 2nd class, $1.35 per day.

Second Division. Freight Conductors, 1st class, $2.85 per day; 2nd class, $2.50 per day. Freight Brakemen, 1st class, $1.90 per day; 2nd class, $1.70 per day.

Valley Division. Freight Conductors and Brakemen to receive the same rate as Second Division.

Parkersburg and Wheeling Division. Freight Conductors and Brakemen to receive the same rate as Second Division.

Pittsburgh Division. Conductors between Wheeling and Pittsburg, $2.75 per day; Brakemen, $1.80 per day. Conductors between Benwood and Pittsburgh, $2.85 per day; Brakemen, $1.85 per day. Conductors, Western District, $3.50 per day: Brakemen, $2.30 per day. Conductors, Eastern District, $2.85 per day; Brakemen, $1.85 per day.

ART. 2. SEC. 1. All freight Conductors and Brakemen shall receive 22 cents and 15 cents per hour, respectively, for all time over twelve hours, time to commence one hour after being called. Overtime shall not begin until after the expiration of 35 minutes in addition thereto, which 35 minutes shall be reckoned as one hour.

SEC. 2. The classification of all freight trainmen will be reduced from one year to six months.

Philadelphia Division: ART. 3. SECTION 1. One Conductor and two Brakemen to constitute a crew on all through freight runs, Philadelphia Division.

First Division. SEC. 2. One Conductor and two Brakemen on all freight runs on First Division and Branches. That when road crews are required to work in yard, they shall receive road pay for same. That all crews shall run first in and first out from Riverside and Brunswick, same as now.

ART. 4. SECTION 1. Conductors, Baggagemasters and Brakemen dead-heading on Company's business will receive half pay at regular rates.

SEC. 2. Conductors, Baggagemasters and Brakemen attending court as witnesses for the Company will receive regular rates per day.

SEC. 3. When Conductors, Brakemen and Baggagemasters are called for a run and the train is afterward abandoned, they will receive one-fourth of a day and remain first out.

ART. 5. SECTION 1. Conductors and Brakemen reaching a terminal after a continuous service of 16 hours, will be entitled to eight hours rest before being again called to go out, except in case of emergency.

ART. 6. SECTION 1. In case any Conductor, Baggagemaster or Brakeman shall be aggrieved by his treatment, or by any decision of the Division Superintendent, he shall have the right to appeal his case to the higher officials.

SEC. 2. Conductors, Baggagemasters and Brakemen suspended will be given a hearing at the earliest possible date, ordinarily within seven days, and notified promptly of the result of the investigation, and if Conductors, Baggagemasters and Brakemen thus suspended are exonerated from blame, they will be paid for all time lost in excess of five days at regular rates.

ART. 7. SECTION 1. Vacancies in the passenger service will, as a rule, be filled from the freight service, and, all things being equal, the oldest man in freight service will be given the preference.

SEC. 2. That the trains be made up in the yards with a sufficient number of good brakes on rear of train to insure safety.

SEC. 3. The right of Brakemen shall date from first day of their continuous service.

SEC. 4. That all irregularities brought to the notice of the officers will be adjusted promptly.

SEC. 5. Trainmen and yardmen will be in line of promotion; those longest in service, all things being equal, shall have preference. When trainmen and yardmen voluntarily leave the service to engage in other business or work on other roads, and who may subsequently be employed on this road, shall rank as new men. Those discharged from the service and reinstated within less than six months shall not lose their seniority. If reinstated after a longer period than six months, they shall rank as new men.

SEC. 6. Trainmen and yardmen will be suspended or discharged from the service of the Company for good and sufficient cause. Intemperance, incompetency, habitual neglect of duty, gross violation of rules or orders, dishonesty or insubordination, will be sufficient cause for suspension or removal.

TRANS OHIO DIVISION.

STATEMENT OF WAGES PAID TRAINMEN, YARDMEN, SWITCHMEN, ETC.

LOCATION.	POSITION.	RATE.	
Trans. Ohio Division	Conductors, Passenger	$ 09.2	Per Mile.
Trans. Ohio Division	Conductors, Passenger	100 00	Per Month.
Ohio Division	Conductors, Passenger	50 00	Per Month.
Trans. Ohio Division	Conductors, Freight	03.5	Per Mile.
Trans. Ohio Division	Conductors, Freight	03	Per Mile.
Trans. Ohio Division	Conductors, Work Train	3 00	Per Day.

BALTIMORE & OHIO RAILWAY.

TRANS OHIO DIVISION.—STATEMENT OF WAGES PAID—CONTINUED.

LOCATION.	POSITION.		RATE.
Ohio Division	Train Baggage Masters	01.3	Per Mile.
Ohio Division	Train Baggage Masters	65 00	Per Month.
Ohio Division	Train Baggage Masters	36 00	Per Month.
Akron & Chicago Division	Train Baggage Masters	01.2	Per Mile.
Akron & Chicago Division	Train Baggage Masters	60 00	Per Month.
Akron & Chicago Division	Train Baggage Masters	50	Per Trip Acct. Express.
Trans. Ohio Division	Brakemen, Passenger	01.1	Per Mile.
Trans. Ohio Division	Brakemen, Passenger	50 00	Per Month.
Trans. Ohio Division	Brakemen, Freight	02.5	Per Mile.
Trans. Ohio Division	Brakemen, Freight	02	Per Mile.
Trans. Ohio Division	Brakemen, Work Train	2 00	Per Day.
Trans. Ohio Division	Train Porters	35 00	Per Month.
Bellaire, Ohio	Agent and Yard Master	115 00	Per Month.
Bellaire, Ohio	Yard Master	90 00	Per Month.
Bellaire, Ohio	Yard Master	80 00	Per Month.
Bellaire, Ohio	Yard Conductors	2 88	Per Day.
Bellaire, Ohio	Yard Conductors	2 76	Per Day.
Bellaire, Ohio	Yard Brakemen	2 22	Per Day.
Bellaire, Ohio	Yard Brakemen	2 10	Per Day.
Bellaire, Ohio	Yard Enginemen	2 90	Per Day.
Bellaire, Ohio	Yard Firemen	1 75	Per Day.
Bellaire Ohio	Switch Tender	45 00	Per Month.
Bellaire, Ohio	Switch Tender	40 00	Per Month.
Cambridge, Ohio	Yard Conductors	2 25	Per Day.
Cambridge, Ohio	Yard Brakemen	1 95	Per Day.
Cambridge, Ohio	Yard Enginemen	2 75	Per Day.
Cambridge, Ohio	Yard Firemen	1 50	Per Day.
Zanesville, Ohio	Yard Master	78 00	Per Month.
Zanesville, Ohio	Yard Conductors	2 35	Per Day.
Zanesville, Ohio	Yard Brakemen	2 10	Per Day.
Zanesville, Ohio	Yard Brakemen	2 00	Per Day.
Zanesville, Ohio	Yard Enginemen	2 75	Per Day.
Zanesville, Ohio	Yard Firemen	1 50	Per Day.
Newark, Ohio	Yard Master	125 00	Per Month.
Newark, Ohio	Yard Master	90 00	Per Month.
Newark, Ohio	Yard Conductors	85 00	Per Month.
Newark, Ohio	Yard Conductors	2 88	Per Day.
Newark, Ohio	Yard Conductors	2 76	Per Day.
Newark, Ohio	Yard Brakemen	2 22	Per Day.
Newark, Ohio	Yard Brakemen	2 10	Per Day.
Newark, Ohio	Yard Enginemen	2 90	Per Day.
Newark, Ohio	Yard Firemen	1 75	Per Day.
Newark, Ohio	Switch Tender	2 10	Per Day.
Newark, Ohio	Switch Tender	1 98	Per Day.
Columbus, Ohio	Yard Master	100 00	Per Month.
Columbus, Ohio	Yard Master	90 00	Per Month.
Columbus, Ohio	Yard Conductors	2 88	Per Day.
Columbus, Ohio	Yard Conductors	2 76	Per Day.
Columbus, Ohio	Yard Brakemen	2 22	Per Day.
Columbus, Ohio	Yard Brakemen	2 10	Per Day.
Columbus, Ohio	Yard Enginemen	2 75	Per Day.
Columbus, Ohio	Yard Firemen	1 50	Per Day.
Shawnee, Ohio	Yard Master	90 00	Per Month.
Shawnee, Ohio	Yard Conductors	2 25	Per Day.
Shawnee, Ohio	Yard Brakemen	1 95	Per Day.
Shawnee, Ohio	Yard Enginemen	2 90	Per Day.
Shawnee, Ohio	Yard Firemen	1 75	Per Day.
Mansfield, Ohio	Yard Master	65 00	Per Month.
Mansfield, Ohio	Yard Brakemen	1 95	Per Day.
Mansfield, Ohio	Yard Enginemen	2 90	Per Day.
Mansfield, Ohio	Yard Firemen	1 75	Per Day.
Chicago Junction, Ohio	Yard Master	100 00	Per Month.
Chicago Junction, Ohio	Yard Master	90 00	Per Month.
Chicago Junction, Ohio	Yard Conductor	2 88	Per Day.
Chicago Junction, Ohio	Yard Conductor	2 76	Per Day.
Chicago Junction, Ohio	Yard Brakemen	2 22	Per Day.
Chicago Junction, Ohio	Yard Brakemen	2 10	Per Day.
Chicago Junction, Ohio	Yard Enginemen	2 90	Per Day.
Chicago Junction, Ohio	Yard Firemen	2 75	Per Day.
Sandusky, Ohio	Yard Master	83 35	Per Month.
Sandusky, Ohio	Yard Conductors	2 25	Per Day.
Sandusky, Ohio	Yard Brakemen	1 95	Per Day.
Sandusky, Ohio	Yard Enginemen	2 90	Per Day.
Sandusky, Ohio	Yard Firemen	1 75	Per Day.
P. & W. Junction, Ohio	Yard Master	30 00	Per Month.
P. & W. Junction, Ohio	Yard Master	25 00	Per Month.
Fostoria, Ohio	Yard Conductors	2 25	Per Day.
Fostoria, Ohio	Yard Brakemen	1 95	Per Day.
Fostoria, Ohio	Yard Enginemen	2 90	Per Day.
Fostoria, Ohio	Yard Firemen	1 75	Per Day.
North Baltimore Ohio	Yard Conductor	75 00	Per Month.
North Baltimore, Ohio	Yard Brakemen	1 95	Per Day.
North Baltimore, Ohio	Yard Enginemen	2 75	Per Day.
North Baltimore, Ohio	Yard Firemen	1 75	Per Day.
Garrett, Indiana	General Yard Master	100 00	Per Month.
Garrett, Indiana	Yard Master	90 00	Per Month

TRANS OHIO DIVISION.—STATEMENT OF WAGES PAID.—CONTINUED.

LOCATION.	POSITION.	RATE.	
Garrett, Indiana	Yard Conductors	2 88	Per Day.
Garrett, Indiana	Yard Conductors	2 76	Per Day.
Garrett, Indiana	Yard Brakemen	2 22	Per Day.
Garrett, Indiana	Yard Brakemen	2 10	Per Day.
Garrett, Indiana	Yard Enginemen	2 90	Per Day.
Garrett, Indiana	Yard Firemen	1 75	Per Day.
South Chicago, Illinois	General Yard Master	125 00	Per Month.
South Chicago, Illinois	Yard Master	100 00	Per Month.
South Chicago, Illinois	Yard Master	90 00	Per Month.
South Chicago, Illinois	Switch Tenders	40 00	Per Month.
South Chicago, Illinois	Switch Tenders	45 00	Per Month.
South Chicago, Illinois	Yard Conductors	75 00	Per Month. } Working
South Chicago, Illinois	Yard Conductors	70 00	Per Month. } days
South Chicago, Illinois	Yard Brakemen	70 00	Per Month. } to the
South Chicago, Illinois	Yard Brakemen	65 00	Per Month. } month.
South Chicago, Illinois	Yard Enginemen	3 00	Per Day.
South Chicago, Illinois	Yard Enginemen	2 75	Per Day.
South Chicago, Illinois	Yard Firemen	1 85	Per Day.

ALFRED WALTER,
General Superintendent Lines East of Ohio River.
Approved: J. T. ODELL,
February 1, 1892. General Manager.

The following rates of pay for trainmen on the Pittsburg & Western Division, Baltimore & Ohio Railroad:

Passenger Service: ARTICLE 1. On runs whose monthly mileage aggregate 4,000 miles and do not exceed 5,000 miles, Conductors will be paid $100.00 per month; Baggagemen, $65.00 per month, and Brakemen, $55.00 per month. Mileage made in excess of $5,000 miles in any one month will be paid extra at the rate of 2 1-5 cents per mile for Conductors. 1 1-5 cents per mile for Baggagemen and 1 1-10 cents per mile for Brakemen. Allegheny to Akron and Zelienople runs to be paid as runs of over 4,000 miles. Runs whose monthly mileage is less than 4,000 miles will be paid, Conductors, $90.00 per month, Baggagemen, $60.00 per month, and Brakemen, $50.00 per month, except the Butler and Callery Junction to be paid $3.25 per day for Conductors; $65.00 per month for Baggagemen, and $1 90 per day for Brakemen.

Local Freight: ART. 2. In local freight service Conductors will be paid 3¼ cents per mile and Brakemen 2¼ cents per mile; Flagmen 15 cents per day more than Brakemen's pay. All runs of less than 100 miles will be allowed 100 miles, except that on Callery Junction and Butler local pay will be, Conductor, $3.00 per day; Flagmen, $2.20 per day, and Brakemen, $2.10 per day. Twelve hours or less, two round trips or less, to constitute a day; necessary shifting to be done at each end of the run.

Through Freight: ART. 3. In through freight service the following rates per trip will be allowed: Between Willow Grove and New Castle Junction, round trip, Conductors, $4.10; Flagmen, $2.85; Brakemen, $2.75. Between New Castle Junction and Akron Junction, Conductors, $3.00; Flagmen, $2.10; Brakemen. $2.00 Painesville and P. P. & F. Junction, round trip, Conductors, $3.00; Flagmen, $2.10; Brakemen, $2.00. Painesville and New Castle Junction, Conductors, $3.00; Flagmen, $2.10; Brakemen, $2.00. P. P. & F. Junction to Akron Junction, round trip, Conductors, $3.00; Flagmen, $2.10; Brakemen, $2.00. Willow Grove to Akron Junction, Conductors, $4.00; Flagmen, $2.70; Brakemen, $2.60. Willow Grove to P. P. & F. Junction, Conductors, $3.25; Flagmen, $2.25; Brakemen, $2.15. New Castle Junction to P. P. & F. Junction, round trip, Conductors, $3.00; Flagmen, $2.10; Brakemen, $2.00. Between Butler and Foxburg, round trip, Conductors, $3.00; Brakemen, $2.00. Foxburg to Clarion Junction. round trip, Conductors, $2.00; Brakemen, $1.50. Round trips provided for in this article will be computed as continuous trips. Overtime as per Rule 2. Kane and Ormsby Junction Branch, Conductors, $3.00 per day; Brakemen, $2.00. Foxburg and Clarion, including branch work as at present, Conductor, $3.00; Brakemen, $2.00. Duck Run Shift, Conductors $3.00; Flagmen, $2.10; Brakemen, $2.00 per day.

Work and Wrecking Service: ART. 4. Conductors, $3.00 and Brakemen, $2 00 per day of 12 hours or less; all over 12 hours will be paid extra as overtime.

Pay Car and Special Trains: ART. 5. Conductors, $3.25; Brakemen, $2.00 per day.

RULES.

1. All freight crews will consist of a Conductor, Flagman and two Brakemen, except local freight and work train which will consist as follows: Local freight—Conductor, three Brakemen and Flagman, except on Butler local, crew will consist of a Conductor, Flagman and two Brakemen. Work train will consist of a Conductor and two Brakeman.

2. Overtime will be allowed trainmen for all time on duty in excess of 12 hours at the rate of 30 cents per hour for Conductors, and Flagmen and Brakemen 20 cents per

hour. Overtime will not begin until after the expiration of 35 minutes, which 35 minutes is to be reckoned as one hour.

3. Other runs not herein provided for will be paid for as follows: Conductors, 30 cents, Flagmen and Brakemen 20 cents per hour with a minimum of 5 hours.

4. In filling vacancies in the ranks of Freight Conductors all Brakemen will be considered in the line of promotion according to their age in the service and their ability to assume the responsibility of a Conductor, except that three Brakemen will be first promoted and then one experienced Conductor will be hired as a Conductor. A Conductor so hired will take his place at the foot of the list of extra Conductors and may be used temporarily as extra Brakeman, pending vacancies to be filled as Conductor.

5. Crews not assigned to regular runs will run first in first out, except crews coming in not having made at least 12 hours to stand first out ahead of all crews not called.

6. Freight crews dead-heading under orders on freight will receive full freight rates, and on passenger will receive half freight rates. When running light they shall receive full time of such schedules as they may represent. If running extra they shall be paid full freight rates.

7. When Conductors and Brakemen are called to go out and report for duty and are not needed they shall receive 30 cents and 20 cents per hour, respectively, for the time held, with a minimum of a quarter of a day, and shall stand first out.

8. All instructions given to Freight or Passenger Conductors by Trainmasters and Yard Dispatchers relative to the movement of trains or disposition of cars will be given in writing.

9. At all terminals and intermediate points through freight crews will not be required to make up trains or do switching. When used to do this work Conductors shall receive 30 cents and Brakemen and Flagmen 20 cents per hour.

10. If a Trainman is discharged from the service of the Company he shall forfeit all rights previously held unless he is reinstated within six months. In event of a reinstatement the same shall be bulletined for the information of the employes. If a Trainman leaves the service of his own accord, he shall rank as a new man if re-employed.

11. For attending court or appearing before proper persons to give evidence when notified to do so by the proper officers of the Company, Trainmen having regular runs whereby they are required to lose time will be paid for the time they lose at the regular rates. Trainmen not on regular runs will be paid at their regular rates for each calendar day during their absence.

12. Trainmen will not be dismissed or suspended from the service of the Company (except a temporary suspension pending an investigation,) without a fair and impartial trial before a board of inquiry composed of at least three men. Ordinarily this trial will be held within seven days after date of occurrence. Conductors and Brakemen will be notified promptly of the result of the investigation. When suspended for over five days and subsequently exonerated from blame by the board of inquiry, they shall be paid regular wages per day for the time lost in excess of five days.

13. In case any Conductor or Brakeman shall be aggrieved by his treatment or by any decision of the Division Superintendent, he shall have the right to appeal his case to the higher officials.

14. Trainmen living within one mile of terminals shall be called as near as practicable one hour before the time the train is due to leave by a Caller who will be provided with a book in which the men called will enter their names and the time they are called. Time will begin at the time designated in Caller's book for the departure of a train.

15. All Conductors will be considered in the line of promotion according to the time of continuous service, good conduct and ability. When additional Conductors are required in the passenger service, promotions will be made from the ranks of Freight Conductors, as above.

16. When a Traiman is required to change his run and by so doing is obliged to move his family and household goods, they shall be moved free of charge upon application.

17. When the freight traffic on any portion of the road is so light that all the crews in the service are not able to make reasonable wages, crews shall be suspended beginning with the youngest men in the service until the crews remaining are able to make reasonable wages. Any Conductor suspended from service under this rule will be given preference as a Brakeman and will retain his rights as a Conductor and will be placed on his run when the freight traffic requires an increase of crews.

18. Trainmen reaching terminal stations after continuous service of 16 hours or more will be entitled to 8 hours rest and not be required to go out except in cases of wreck or extreme emergency.

19. Trainmen will be notified in writing when time is not allowed as per time slip and reasons given for not allowing same.

20. Trainmen leaving the service of this Company will be given letters stating time of service, in what capacity employed and cause for leaving the service. These letters shall be signed by the proper officers.

Accepted for the Order Railway Conductors: J. V. PATTON,
E. E. CLARK.   General Superintendent.
W. H. BUDD.

Accepted for the Brotherhood of Railroad Trainmen:
S. E. WILKINSON.
E. J. TRACY.

The following rates of pay for Yardmen on the Pittsburg & Western Division, B. & O. R. R., and rules governing the same will take effect June 1st, 1892.

At Allegheny, Butler, New Castle Junction, Youngstown, P. P. & F. Junction, Painesville, Akron Junction, day Conductors, $2.88 per day; day Brakemen, $2.16 per day. Night Conductors, $3.00 per day; and Night Brakemen, $2.23 per day. 12 hours or less to constitute a day's work. All hours in excess of 12 to be paid pro rata. Same rules will apply to yard service as are agreed upon for train service where they apply.

Accepted for the Brotherhood of Railroad Trainmen: J. V. PATTON,
S. E. WILKINSON.   General Superintendent.
E. J. TRACY.
June 1st, 1892.

BALTIMORE & OHIO SOUTHWESTERN RAILROAD COMPANY.

Amended agreement between the Baltimore & Ohio Southwestern Railroad Company and its Engineers and Firemen, in effect July 1, 1890. The same to remain in force until annulled by mutual consent.

ART. 1. Engineers running passenger trains will receive $3.50 per day. Over 50 miles or less than 100 miles to constitute a day's work; 50 miles or less to constitute half a day's work; and are to be paid 3¼ cents per mile for all over 100 miles. Engineers running on freight trains with new eight-wheel Brooks engines, 18x24 cylinder, are to receive $3.75 per day. Engineers running on freight trains with all other eight-wheel engines, are to receive $3.50 per day. Engineers running on freight trains with all ten-wheel engines, are to receive $4.00 per day; 10 hours, or upwards of 50 miles and less than 100 miles, to constitute a day's work: five hours, or 50 miles or less, to constitute half a day's work. Overtime in excess of 10 hours will be computed at the rate of 35 cents an hour. All mileage in excess of 100 miles will be paid for at the same rate per mile as for less than 100 miles. Engineers running on local freight trains between Cincinnati and Chillicothe, and between Chillicothe and Parkersburg, will be paid at the same rate per day as when on through freight, and local runs between the points named will be computed as one and one-quarter days. Twelve hours to constitute a day's work; 35 cents per hour to be paid for all time in excess of 12 hours.

ART. 2. Engineers running helpers, construction or work engines, to receive $3.50 per day, and 30 cents per hour for all over 12 hours, the Company to furnish a suitable man to watch the engine outside of working hours, or pay the Engineer or Fireman $1.40 per day for attending to that duty.

ART. 3. Engineers running engines light will be paid three-fourths the amount they would receive for hauling a train.

ART. 4. Engineers running engines in Cincinnati yard will receive $3.00 per day. Firemen on engines in Cincinnati yard will receive $1.70 per day; 10 hours to constitute a day's work; all time in excess of 10 hours to be paid pro rata. Engineers running engines in the east yard at Chillicothe will receive $2.50 per day; Firemen on engines in the east yard at Chillicothe will receive $1.60 per day. Engineers running engines in the west yard at Chillicothe will receive $2.75 per day; Firemen on engines in the west yard at Chillicothe will receive $1.60 per day. Twelve hours to constitute a day's work, and all time in excess of 12 hours to be paid pro rata.

ART. 5. Promoted Firemen shall be termed second-class Engineers and shall receive $2.75 per day for the first six months and $3.00 per day for the second six months; and after having had one year's experience as road engineers, shall be entitled to receive first-class pay. Overtime and mileage in excess of 100 miles shall be computed at these rates and in the same manner as mentioned in Art. 1.

ART. 6. Engineers dead-heading to any point to take charge of an engine or other property belonging to the Company shall be paid at the rate of 1¼ cents per mile, and Firemen one-half this amount.

ART. 7. Engineers or Firemen serving as witnesses, or on other business for the Company, are to be paid $3.50 and $1.75 per calendar day.

ART. 8. Engineers are to report all delayed time on their trip reports, and must be particular to give all the facts necessary to a clear understanding; said report to be sufficient evidence for the allowance of said extra time if found to correspond with the caller's book and the train-dispatcher's register.

ART. 9. Firemen running on passenger trains to receive $1.75 per day; 100 miles to constitute a day's work, and are to be paid 1¾ cents per mile for all over that distance. Firemen running on freight trains with new eight-wheel Brooks engines, 18x24 cylinder, are to receive $1.90 per day. Firemen running on freight trains with all other eight-wheel engines are to receive $1.75 per day. Firemen running on freight trains with all ten-wheel engines are to receive $2.00 per day. Ten hours, or upwards of 50 and less than 100 miles, to constitute a day's work; five hours, or less than 50 miles, to constitute half a day's work. Overtime in excess of 10 hours will be computed at the rate of 17½ cents per hour. All mileage in excess of 100 miles to be paid for at the same rate as for less than 100 miles.

ART. 10. The caller to be furnished a book and call the Engineers not more than one hour before leaving time, said book to be signed by the Engineer, and his time to commence at the time specified for him to leave, and if the train is delayed in starting or annulled, he shall be paid at the rate of 35 cents an hour until relieved from duty.

ART. 11. Engineers will not be required to do any more work on their engines while in the shop than has been customary.

ART. 12. When Engineers arrive at the engine house in Cincinnati or Parkersburg they will be relieved from duty and called for return trip, and their time commence as per Art. 10.

ART. 13. Engineers and Firemen making round trips between Chillicothe and Hamden are to receive three-fifths of a day and at the rate of 35 and 17½ cents per hour for all time in excess of six hours.

ART. 14. Engineers and Firemen to be allowed one day for making the round trip between Cincinnati and Midland City, and at the rate of 35 and 17½ cents for all over 10 hours.

ART. 15. Engineers to be paid 3 cents per mile and Firemen 1¾ cents per mile for running accommodation trains between Chillicothe and Hillsboro.

ART. 16. Engineers running on Portsmouth Division to receive $3.50 per day and 35 cents per hour for all over 12 hours. Firemen running on Portsmouth Division to receive $1.75 per day and 17½ cents an hour for all over 12 hours.

ART. 17. When Engineers and Firemen are called at Cincinnati to go out, they are to be notified within 30 minutes after reporting as to whether they will be needed. If required to wait longer than 30 minutes and the train is annulled, they will be paid at the rate of 35 and 17½ cents per hour for all time so held in excess of the 30 minutes.

ART. 18. No fines shall be imposed on Engineers or Firemen for damage to Company's property or rolling stock; but if such damage occurs and it is found, upon examination that Engineers or Firemen are at fault for such damage, they shall be suspended or dismissed from the service, as the case may seem to require.

ART. 19. Commencing with the date of this amended agreement, Engineers and Firemen are to be promoted in accordance with their age on the road, the oldest man being given the preference when in every respect competent.

ART. 20. Engineers and Firemen who may be suspended from any cause will be given a hearing within a reasonable time, and will be notified promptly of the result of the investigation. In case the Engineer or Fireman suspended is found to be innocent, he shall be paid half time for the calendar time he has lost.

ART. 21. These articles of agreement shall not affect the pay of the Engineers who are getting more than $3.50 per day for running accommodation trains less than 100 miles per day, nor those who are getting more than $3.50 per day for running local freight trains, who, however, are to receive at the rate of 35 cents per hour for all time in excess of 12 hour per day.

I. G. RAWN,
General Superintendent.

Approved:
W. W. PEABODY, Vice President.

Committee of Engineers—G. W. CUTTER, J. R. WALTERS, W. B. GALIVAN, J. N. KNOPP, W. S. CRYDER, M. H. PURSELL.

Committee of Firemen—SINNET BARKER, GEORGE KRICK, J. W. RUMPF, T. J. GALLAGHER.

Articles of agreement between the Baltimore & Ohio Southwestern Railroad Company and its Conductors and Brakemen; in effect July 1, 1890. The same to remain in force until annulled by mutual consent.

ART. 1. Conductors running on passenger trains between Cincinnati and Parkersburg, Cincinnati and Chillicothe, Chillicothe and Parkersburg, are to receive $100.00 per month; fractional parts of a month to be paid at the same rate. Conductors on local passenger trains between Cincinnati and Blanchester are to be paid at the rate of $85.00 per month and $3.00 per day for Sunday work. Conductors running on passenger trains on the Hillsboro Division are to receive $85.00 per month. Conductors running on passenger and mixed trains on the Portsmouth Division are to receive $90.00 per month.

ART. 2. Conductors running on through freight trains with eight-wheel engines will receive $2.75 per day; Brakemen running on through freight trains with eight-wheel engines will receive $1.75 per day. Conductors running on through freight trains with ten-wheel engines will receive $3.00 per day; Brakemen running on through freight trains with ten-wheel engines will receive $2.00 per day. Ten hours, or upward of 50 and less than 100 miles, to constitute a day's work, and five hours, or 50 miles or less, to constitute half a day's work. Overtime in excess of 10 hours will be computed at the rate of 27½ and 17½ cents per hour, respectively. All mileage in excess of 100 miles will be paid for at the same rate per mile as for less than 100 miles. Local freight Conductors running between Cincinnati and Chillicothe, and Chillicothe and Parkersburg, are to receive $3.50 per day; Brakemen running on local freight trains between Cincinnati and Chillicothe, and Chillicothe and Parkersburg, are to receive $2.40 per day. Twelve hours to constitute a day's work. Over 12 hours to be computed at the rate of 30 and 20 cents per hour, respectively. Conductors running on local freight trains on the Hillsboro and Portsmouth Divisions are to receive $2.90 per day; Brakemen running on local freight trains on the Hillsboro and Portsmouth Divisions to receive $1.90 per day. Twelve hours to constitute a day's work. Overtime to be computed at the rate of 27½ and 17½ cents per hour, respectively.

ART. 3. Conductors of helping engines are to receive $70.00 per month; Brakemen of helping engines are to receive $1.75 per day; fractional parts of a month to be paid at the same rate.

ART. 4. Conductors of work trains to receive $2.90 per day; Brakemen of work trains are to receive $1.90 per day. Twelve hours, or over six hours, to constitute a day's work; less than six hours to constitute half a day's work. All time in excess of 12 hours to be computed at the rate of 27½ and 17½ cents per hour, respectively.

ART. 5. Conductors and Brakemen called to go to wrecks or wash-outs will be allowed 30 and 20 cents per hour, respectively, for the time on duty.

ART. 6. Conductors of coal and ore trains will be allowed $2.00 per day; Brakemen of coal and ore trains will be allowed $1.90 per day. Twelve hours to constitute a day's work. Overtime to be at the rate of 27½ and 17½ cents an hour, respectively.

ART. 7. In computing overtime it is understood that fractions of an hour less than 30 minutes will not be counted; 30 minutes or over will be counted a full hour.

ART. 8. When Conductors and Brakemen are called to go out, their time will commence at the time specified for them to leave, and if the train is annulled they will be paid at the rate of 27½ and 17½ cents per hour, respectively, until notified that such train is annulled, or until they are relieved from duty.

ART. 9. Conductors and Brakemen dead-heading to any point on the Company's business shall be paid one-half their regular rate.

ART. 10. Conductors and Brakemen called to attend court as witnesses on the part of the Railroad Company, will be paid $2.75 and $1.75, per calendar day, respectively.

ART. 11. Conductors and Brakemen running light engines, or engines with only caboose attached, will be paid three-fourths of their regular rates.

ART. 12. Promoted Brakemen will be termed second-class Conductors and will receive $2.50 per day for the first six months, $2.75 per day for the second six months, commencing from the date of promotion, and after the second six months they will receive rate of first-class Conductor.

ART. 13. Commencing with the date of this agreement, Conductors and Brakemen are to be promoted in accordance with their age on the road, the oldest man to be given preference when in every respect competent. Promotion to the position of passenger or freight Conductor will be confined to men in train service.

ART. 14. When freight traffic is light and it is necessary to reduce the number of freight crews in order to allow Conductors and Brakemen to make reasonable wages, the Conductors of crews thus taken off shall be given preference as Brakemen, until such time as the increase of business warrants their being reinstated as Conductors.

ART. 15. Conductors and Brakemen reaching terminal points after continuous service of 16 hours or more shall be entitled to eight hours' rest before being again required to go out, excepting in case of wreck or extreme emergency.

ART. 16. Conductors and Brakemen suspended will be given a hearing within a reasonable time and notified promptly of the result of the investigation, and if Conductors or Brakemen thus suspended are found to be not guilty they will be paid one-half time for calendar time thus lost.

ART. 17. Any Conductor or Brakemen feeling that justice has not been done him in a decision rendered by the Superintendent, will have the right of appeal to the General Superintendent.

ART. 18. No fines shall be imposed upon Conductors or Brakemen for damage to Company's property or rolling stock; but if such damage occurs and it is found that the

Conductor or Brakeman is at fault for such damage he shall be suspended or dismissed the service, as the case may seem to require.

Approved:
W. W. PEABODY, Vice President.

I. G. RAWN,
General Superintendent.

Committee of Conductors—O. T. DEWEY, THOS. A. BROWN, JOHN KOPP, WM. R. BROWN, PAT DORSEY, P. M'GINTY.
Committee of Brakemen—CON DEVERS. JOHN SHAFFER, WALTER HALL, WALTER WILT, C. E. SCHENCK, J. TOUHY.
May 12, 1892.

BENNINGTON & RUTLAND RAILWAY.

Conductors, $75.00; Baggagemen, $45.00; Brakemen, $40.00; Switchmen and Yardmen, $40.00.
May 10, 1892.

E. D. BENNETT,
Superintendent.

BOSTON & MAINE RAILROAD.

Passenger Conductors, from $65 to $100 per month, according to location. Baggagemasters, from $45 to $55 per month. Brakemen, from $40 to $50 per month. Freight Conductors, from $55 to $78 per month. Brakemen, from $40 to $52 per month. Yard Conductors, from $55 to $70 per month. Yard Brakemen, from $40 to $52 per month. Yard Switchmen, from $40 to $60 per month.

May 16, 1892.

D. W. SANBORN,
General Superintendent.

THE CALUMET & BLUE ISLAND RAILWAY COMPANY.

Freight Conductors, 3 cents per mile. Freight Brakemen, 2 cents per mile.
Yardmen—Head Switchmen, $2.90 per day, 10 hours. First Helper, $2.70 per day, 10 hours. Second Helper, $2.50 per day, 10 hours. Overtime and delayed time by men on road and in yards allowed for in accordance with regular Chicago scale governing such matters.

May 13, 1892.

W. G. BRIMSON,
President and General Manager.

CANADIAN PACIFIC RAILWAY COMPANY.—PACIFIC DIVISION.

Passenger—Main Line: Crews assigned to passenger runs will be paid for 4,600 miles or over, as follows: Conductors, $105.00 per month; Baggagemen, $63.00 per month; Brakemen, $63.00 per month.

Passenger—Branch Lines: Conductors, $90.00 per month; Baggagemen, $60.00 per month; Brakemen, $60.00 per month.

Mixed Trains: Conductors, $90.00 per month; Baggagemen, $60.00 per month; Brakemen, $60.00 per month.

Freight Trains: Crews on all freight trains will be paid as follows: Conductors, $3.04 per 100 miles; Brakemen, $2.18 per 100 miles.

These rates to be applied to present constructive mileage on Selkirk Section only, viz.: 120 miles, subject to revision if Canmore Section is included in Pacific Division.

On and after April 1, 1893, freight Conductors to receive $3.15 per 100 miles.

Eleven hours or 100 miles to constitute a day's work in road service. Overtime after 11 hours to be paid for at schedule rates. This time to count from time-bill time, or the hour at which train is ordered: the time of finishing a trip when Conductor registers. Conductors and Trainmen on passenger or freight trains, when held at or between stations for construction or work train service on work train orders from dispatcher, will be paid extra for such work at schedule rates in addition to mileage, 30 minutes or more to count as one hour.

Work Trains: Crews on work trains will be paid as follows: Conductors, $90.00 per month; Brakemen, $70.00 per month. Twenty-six or the calendar working days of a month to constitute one month. Twelve hours or less to constitute a day's work. Overtime to be paid for at the same rate. Above work train rates and conditions will apply to trains on snow service on Selkirk Section with the guarantee of a full month's pay each month, viz.: $90 per month for Conductors and $70 for Brakemen. Trainmen ordered out on occasional short runs of less than 100 miles, shall be allowed one day's pay, but may be held for service to the extent of 11 hours, said hours not to run beyond midnight. When work trains are required to run 40 miles or more to and from their work or wood trains over a division, mileage at schedule rates will be allowed.

Schedule Rates for Yardmen and Rules Governing Same: All engine foremen and helpers emloyed at Vancouver will be paid as follows: Foremen, $2.80 per day; helpers, $2.50 per day; Yardmaster at Revelstoke, $80.00 per month; Night Yardman, $65.00 per month. Twelve hours or less to constitute a day's work. Overtime to be paid for at the same rate.

1. Trainmen will be called as nearly as practicable in time to be on duty 30 minutes at least before leaving time of the train. Caller to be furnished with a book on which is registered time train is ordered to leave, and in which trainmen will sign their names.

2. When trainmen appear for duty and are not required, they will be allowed one-fourth of a day, or 25 miles and will stand first out. All cases of greater delay than 25 miles to be settled on their merits.

3. Trainmen dead-heading on passenger trains will be paid at passenger train rates. Trainmen dead-heading on freight trains with their cabooses will be paid full rates. The first crew out will run dead-head and the second run the train; the dead-heading crew will be the first out of these crews on reaching terminal station.

4. Trainmen held off on Company's business will receive pay at their schedule rates, and reasonable expenses when away from home. If attending court, witness fees to go to Company.

5. Swithing at terminal and turn-around points and at Mission Junction to be paid for at 25 cents an hour for Conductors and 17 cents per hour for Brakemen. All work not in excess of 30 minutes to go to the Compauy, all over 30 minutes to be counted one hour. No switching time will be allowed except on certificate on form 748, signed by agent at station where work is done.

6. The right to regular runs and to promotion will be governed by merit, ability and seniority. Everything being equal, the trainmen longest in the service will have preference, provided they have passed the required examinations. Freight Conductors, when adapted to passenger service, will be promoted to passenger trains according to ability and age of continuous service on their respective divisions. The question of ability and adaptation to be determined by the Superintendent. The rating of of a Conductor as such will begin from the time he is first regularly given a caboose. Occasional trips in an emergency will not be counted.

7. Assistant superintendents will so regulate the number of crews that the trainmen will make fair average wages during slack seasons.

8. In cases of breach of discipline, as a general rule, parties implicated will be notified in writing within 10 days after the occurrence of the decision arrived at. Should any Trainman or Yardman think he has been unjustly dealt with, he may send a written statement of the facts to the Assistant Superintendent, when the case will be reinvestigated and a decision will be given within five days; and if the party interested still considers he has not received justice, he may appeal to the General Superintendent.

9. Conductors shall not be required to take out a Brakeman whom they know to be incompent more than one round trip after they have reported inability of Brakeman in writing to the Superintendent.

10. Freight Trainmen will be run, first in, first out of terminal stations.

11. Trainmen leaving the service shall be given a letter stating the time and capacity of service in which employed, said letter to be given as early as practicable after application.

12. Freight Trainmen running passenger trains will be paid passenger train rates, except when the hand brakes have to be used, in which case they will be paid freight train rates.

13. When there is a grade on any section over which the regular load cannot be taken without doubling, or where the regular load sheet is exceeded by order of the of the train dispatcher, the mileage for doubling to be allowed; all other cases to be settled on their merits.

14. When work trains are put on they will be given to junior Conductors, if the superintendent considers them competent.

15. Time slips will be returned to Conductors for correction when not honored.

16. Brakemen to be promoted to Conductors under their Assistant Superintendents, as per Article 6.

17. All previous schedules are void.

April 1, 1892.

H. ABBOTT,
General Superintendent.

CANADIAN PACIFIC RAILWAY COMPANY.—WESTERN DIVISION.

Passenger—Main Line: Crews assigned to passenger runs will be paid for 4,600 miles or over as follows: Conductors, $100.00 per month; Baggagemen. $60.00 per month; Brakemen, $55.00 per month. The five crews running between Winnipeg and Fort William and the crew between Banff and Donald to be paid $100 per month.

Passenger—Branch Line: Conductors, $90.00 per month; Baggagemen, $60.00 per month; Brakemen, $55.00 per month.

Mixed Trains: Conductors, $90.00 per month; Baggagemen, $60.00 per month; Brakemen, $60.00 per month.

Freight Trains: Crews on all freight trains will be paid as follows: Conductors, $2.90 per 100 miles; Brakemen. $2.07 per 100 miles.

On and after April 1st, 1893, freight Conductors to receive $3.00 per 100 miles.

Eleven hours or 100 miles shall constitute a day's work in road service. Overtime after eleven hours to be paid for at schedule rates. This time to count from time bill time or the hour at which train is ordered, the time of finishing trip when Conductor registers.

Work Trains: Crews on work trains will be paid as follows: Conductors, $90.00 per month: Rrakemen, $70.00. Twenty-six days or the callendar working days of a month to constitute one month. Twelve hours or less to constitnte a day's work. Overtime to be paid for at the same rate.

Trainmen ordered out on occasional short runs of less than one hundred miles shall be allowed one day's pay, but may be held for service to the extent of eleven hours, said hours not to run beyond midnight.

ARTICLE 1. Trainmen will be called as nearly as practicable in time to be on duty thirty minutes at least before leaving time of train. Caller to be furnished with a book on which is registered time train is ordered to leave, and in which trainmen will sign their names.

ART. 2. When trainmen appear for duty and are not required, they will be allowed one-fourth of a day or twenty-five miles, and will stand first out. All cases of greater delay thrn twenty-five miles to be settled on their merits.

ART. 3. Trainmen dead-heading on passenger trains will be paid at passenger train rates. Trainmen dead-heading on freight trains with their cabooses will be paid full rates. The first crew out will run dead-head and the second run the train; the dead-heading crew will be the first out of those crews on reaching terminal station.

ART. 4. Trainmen held off on Company's business will receive pay at their schedule rates and reasonable expenses when away from home. If attending court, witness fees to go to Company.

ART. 5. Switching at terminal and turn-around points to be paid for at twenty-five cents per hour for Conductors and seventeen cents per hour for brakemen. All work not in excess of thirty minutes to go to the Company; all over thirty minutes to be counted one hour. No switching time will be allowed except on certificate on forms 748, signed by agent at station where work is done.

ART. 6. The right to regular runs and to promotion will be governed by merit, ability and seniority. Everything being equal, the trainmen longest in the service will have preference, provided they have passed the required examinations. Freight Conductors, when adapted to passenger service, will be promoted to passenger trains according to ability and age of continuous service on their respective divisions. The question of ability and adaptation to be determined by Superintendent. The rating of a Conductor as such will begin from the time he is first regularly given a caboose. Occasional trips in an emergency will not be counted.

ART. 7. Assistant Superintendents will so regulate the number of crews that all trainmen will make fair average wages during the slack seasons.

ART. 8. In case of breach of discipline as a general rule, parties implicated will be notified, in writing, witin ten days after the occurrence of the decision arrived at. Should any trainman or yardman think he has been unjustly dealt with, he may send a written statement of the fact to the Assistant Superintendent, when the case will be re-investigated and a decision given within five days, and if the party interested still considers he has not received justice, he may appeal to the General Superintendent.

ART. 9. Conductors shall not be required to take out a brakeman whom they know to be incompetent more than one round trip after they have reported inability of Brakeman in writing to Superintendent.

ART. 10. Freight Trainmen will be run first in, first out of terminal stations.

ART. 11. Trainmen leaving the service shall be given a letter stating the time and capacity of service in which employed, said letter to be given as early as practicable after application.

ART. 12. Freight Trainmen running passenger trains will be paid passenger train rates, except when the hand brakes have to be used, in which case they will be paid freight train rates.

ART. 13. When there is a grade on any section over which the regular load cannot be taken without doubling, or where the regular load sheet is exceeded by order of the Train Dispatcher, the mileage for doubling to be allowed, all other cases to be settled on their merits.

ART. 14. When work trains are put on, they will be given to junior Conductors, if the Superintendent considers them competent.

ART. 15. Time slips will be returned to Conductors for correction when not honored.

ART. 16. Brakemen to be promoted to Conductors under their Assistant Superintendent as per Article 6.

ART. 17. All previous schedules are void.

In effect April 1, 1892,
W. WHYTE,
General Superintendent.

Accepted for the O. R. C.—E. E. CLARK, Grand Chief Conductor; W. G. NIBLOCK, Chairman. Accepted for the B. of R. T.—S. E. WILKINSON, Grand Master; F. GARNHAM, Chairman.

Schedule of rates for Yardmen and rules governing the same: All engine Foremen and Helpers at Fort William, Rat Portage and Winnipeg will be paid as follows: Foremen, $2.80 per day; Helpers, $2.50 per day Twelve hours or less to constitute a day's work. Overtime to be paid for at same rate.

In effect April 1, 1892.
W. WHYTE,
Accepted for the B. of R. T.,
General Superintendent.
S. E. WILKINSON, Grand Master.
F. GARNHAM, Chairman.

THE CENTRAL RAILROAD OF NEW JERSEY AND LEASED LINES.

Passenger Conductors from $3.00 to $3.25 per day. We also have a number paid by the month ranging from $85.00 to $91.25 per month Train Baggagemen, $2.10 to $2.25 per day. Some are paid by the month ranging for through runs $55.00 per month; locals, $50.00 per month. All Passenger Brakemen $1.80 per day, and a few long runs $2.00 per day. Freight Brakemen, $1.83 to $2.25 per day according to trip. Yard Drillers, $1.83 per day of 11 hours, and $2.00 per day of 12 hours.

May 16, 1892.
J. H. OLHAUSEN, General Superintendent.

CHARLESTON, CINCINNATI & CHICAGO RAILROAD.

Passenger Conductors, $75.00 per month. Passenger Brakemen, $1.25 per day. Train Baggagemen, $45.00 per month. Freight Conductors, $70.00 per month. Freight Brakemen, $1.25 per day. Switchmen are paid same as Brakemen.

May 25, 1892.
C. M. WARD, General Manager.

CHESAPEAKE & OHIO RAILWAY COMPANY.

ARTICLE I.—PASSENGER SERVICE.

	Conduct'r	Brak'man	Bag'gemn
Through passenger (regular trips) per month..........................	$112 00	$60 00	$70 00
Local passenger (regular trips) per month...............................	107 00	55 00	60 00

Except through Brakemen on Huntington Division will be paid $65.00 per month. Other exceptions as follows: Washington Division, present passenger rates will remain in force. Richmond Division, trains 31 and 32 between Richmond and Doswell, including other passenger service of 100 miles or less if performed within 12 hours, Conductor $90 00; Baggageman or Brakeman $55.00 per month. Big Sandy Division, Warm Springs Valley, Lexington, (Va.) and Craig Valley branches, Passenger and Freight Conductors, $90.00; Baggagemen, $60.00; Brakemen, $55.00 per month. Amounts paid by Express Company to Baggagemen to be deducted.

FREIGHT SERVICE.

RUNS.	MILES.	SERVICE.	RATE PER TRIP.	
			Conduct'r.	Brak'men
PENINSULA DIVISION.				
Richmond to Newport News and Ft. Monroe..........	95	Local freight....	$3 50	$2 40
Richmond to Newport News...............................	75	Through freight	2 50	1 65
RICHMOND DIVISION.				
Clifton Forge to Staunton or Brand and return.......	112	Through freight.	3 40	2 25
Richmond to Charlottesville................................	96	Through freight.	2 90	1 95
Richmond to Charlottesville................................	96	Local freight....	3 50	2 40
Richmond to Gordonsville and return, (12 hours) ..	150	Through freight.	4 35	2 90
Charlottesville to Clifton Forge...........................	96	Through freight.	2 90	1 95
Charlottesville to Clifton Forge...........................	96	Local freight....	3 50	2 40
Local freight to work between Clifton Forge and Craigsville, (12 hours)		Local freight....	3 50	2 40

CHESAPEAKE & OHIO RAILWAY.

FREIGHT SERVICE.—CONTINUED.

RUNS.	MILES.	SERVICE.	RATE PER TRIP. Conduct'r	Brak'men
WASHINGTON DIVISION.				
*Charlottesville to Washington	115	Through freight	3 00	2 00
JAMES RIVER DIVISION.				
Richmond to Gladstone	119	Through freight	3 30	2 20
Richmond to Arvonia	71	Local freight	3 50	2 40
Bremo to Lynchburg	80	Local freight	3 50	2 40
Gladstone to Clifton Forge	111	Through freight	3 15	2 10
Lynchburg to Clifton Forge (12 hours)	84	Through freight	2 75	1 85
Clifton Forge to Balcony Falls and return	111	Through freight	3 15	2 10
Lynchburg to Clifton Forge	84	Local freight	3 50	2 40
HUNTINGTON DIVISION.				
Clifton Forge to Hinton	80	Through freight	2 90	1 95
Clifton Forge to Hinton	80	Local freight	3 50	2 40
Clifton Forge to Alleghany and return	60	Through freight	2 70	1 80
Hinton to Alleghany and return	102	Through freight	3 25	2 15
Alleghany to Ronceverte and return, (in connection with through trip)	34	Through freight	1 00	70
Hinton to Handley	72	Through freight	2 50	1 70
Hinton to Handley	72	Local freight	3 50	2 40
Hinton to Sewell, Thurmond or Quinnimont and return, (10 hours)	78	Through freight	2 50	1 70
Hinton to H. Nest and return, (12 hours)	102	Through freight	3 00	2 00
Handley to Russell	95	Through freight	3 00	2 00
Handley to Huntington	74	Through freight	2 50	1 70
Handley to Huntington	74	Local freight	3 50	2 40
Huntington to Russell and return	41	Local freight	3 50	2 40
Huntington to Russell and return, (9 trips)	82	Through freight	3 00	2 00
Huntington to Lewis and return	74	Through freight	2 50	1 70
Russell to Lewis and return, (12 hours)	114	Through freight	3 30	2 20
CINCINNATI DIVISION.				
Russell to Covington	139	Through freight	4 00	2 80
Russell to Covington, (3 crews)	139	Local freight	3 50	2 50
LEXINGTON DIVISION.				
Huntington to Lexington	140	Through freight	4 00	2 65
Ashland to Lexington	124	Through freight	3 50	2 35
Kilgore to Lexington	111	Through freight	3 20	2 15
Denton to Lexington	103	Through freight	3 00	2 00
Lexington to Olive Hill and return	168	Through freight	4 85	3 25
Morehead to Lexington and return	132	Through freight	3 80	2 55
Ashland to Morehead and return	116	Through freight	3 35	2 25
Ashland to Midland		Local freight	3 50	2 40
Midland to Lexington		Local freight	3 50	2 40

*If trains go to yards beyond Washington, Conductors receive 35 cents and Brakemen 25 cents extra.

ART. 2. Short freight runs not provided for in Article 1 will be paid for as follows: Service of two hours or 25 miles or less, one-fourth day, and stand first out; over two hours or 25 miles and not exceeding six hours or 50 miles, one-half day; over six hours or 50 miles and less than 100 miles, full day, at the trip rate paid on the district where the service is performed. Article 5 will govern hours of service in excess of six hours. Conductors and trainmen going over road with an engine as a light section of a passenger train to move a passenger train in opposite direction, if they run full length of the passenger division, will be paid passenger rates, otherwise, freight rates. If running light to move a freight train in opposite direction, will be paid freight rates. When dead-heading with caboose on freight train, full freight rates will be paid. When dead-heading on passenger trains by orders, one-half rates, according to service, will be paid. It being optional with the freight men as to whether they will go with caboose on freight train, or in coach on passenger train, provided it does not interfere with the business of the road. When through freight trains on the Richmond Division are run from Mineral City to the pyrites mines, or when through or local freights are required to make a trip on the Kinniconnick Branch, Cincinnati Division, the additional mileage made will be allowed at the rate per mile paid for through trip.

ART. 3. Conductors and Brakemen when temporarily assigned to work trains or other special service, or when engaged in hauling ballast long distances, will be paid regular freight rates. Conductors and Brakemen of wrecking trains will be paid as per Article 2, except that they will not be paid for time laid up for rest.

ART. 4. Conductors and trainmen when attending court by order of the Company, will be allowed $3.00 and $2.00 per day, respectively, and $1.00 per day for living expenses. In addition to this, all necessary railroad fare and carriage hire.

ART. 5. Freight Conductors and Brakemen will be paid at the rate of 27 cents and 18 cents per hour, respectively, for delays on the road exceeding the limit of service on each district, which is as follows: Peninsula Division, local and through freight, 9 hours. Richmond Division, (each district,) through freight, 10 hours, local freight, 12 hours. James River Division, (each district,) local and through freight, 12 hours. Washington Division, through freight, 12 hours. Huntington Division, Greenbrier district, local and through freight, 12 hours. New River and Kanawha districts, through freight, 10 hours, local freight, 12 hours. Cincinnati Division, local and through freight, 12 hours. Lexington and Big Sandy Divisions, local and through freight, 12 hours. Delayed time under 30 minutes not to be counted; 30 minutes and over to be computed as a full hour. Time to be computed from one hour after signing Caller's book, or from the time stated in the Caller's book for the train to leave, (unless leaving earlier) to the time of arrival at terminal. Passenger Conductors and trainmen will be allowed delayed time when the schedule time of the train has been exceeded two hours or more, at the rate of 27 cents and 18 cents per hour, respectively, for each hour or fractional part over 30 minutes, including the first two hours.

ART. 6. If the Yardmaster at a terminal point does not relieve a freight crew on arrival, and the latter cannot clear the main track with their train within 30 minutes after arrival, they will be paid, respectively, 27 and 18 cents per hour or fractional part thereof, for the time they are delayed beyond 30 minutes; this to be reported as yard delay, without reference to the time consumed in making the trip.

ART. 7. Freight Conductors and Brakemen will be called, as nearly as possible, one hour before the leaving time of their train, within the hours and limits and under the regulations already in effect. The Caller will be furnished with a book which must show the train for which the men are called, and the time expected to leave. Book must be signed by person called, showing time called. A Conductor or Brakeman failing to properly respond after having been called and signed book, will be suspended or dismissed at the discretion of the Superintendent or Trainmaster. When Conductors and trainmen are called to go out, and the train is afterwards annulled, or they are not needed, they will be paid, respectively, 27 and 18 cents per hour, computing the time from one hour after they are called, until they are notified of the annullment of the train, or relieved from duty. In every case they will receive at least one hour's pay, if they have reported at the yard office or registering place. Conductors and trainmen thus called will stand first out, provided it does not interfere with men who have regular runs. Conductors and trainmen will not be required to double out after making a trip, unless they consider that they are competent to go, or have had at least eight hours rest.

ART. 8. Conductors and trainmen who have served the longest on any division or district of the road shall, if other things are equal, be given preference of runs on that division or district, except that men assigned to any division prior to July 1st, 1892, shall not be affected. The right to promotion will be governed by merit, ability and seniority, other things being equal, the men longest in the service on the division shall have preference. No more Conductors or trainmen will be assigned to runs than are necessary to do the work, and when necessary to reduce the force in order to allow the men to make reasonable wages, a sufficient number of crews will be taken off, commencing with the youngest in the service on each district. Conductors thus reduced will be employed as Brakemen in preference to younger Brakemen in the service, and will retain their right for promotion if competent and worthy.

ART. 9. No fines will be imposed upon Conductors and trainmen for damage caused by their negligence, but suspension or dismissal will be adopted, as the case may seem to require.

ART. 10. Conductors and Brakemen will, if they consider their punishment unjust, have the right of appeal from the decision of the division officers, to the General Manager, through the Division Superintendent; the appeal to be acted upon promptly. Should the Conductor or trainman desire it, he can select a Conductor or trainman who is employed on the same division to be present at the investigation. Conductors and trainmen who may be suspended will be given a hearing by the Trainmaster within seven days, and will be notified promptly of the result of the investigation. If suspension is the punishment, it shall date from the day taken off for investigation. In case the Conductor or trainman suspended, is found to be innocent, he will be paid half-time for the time lost.

ART. 11. In case a difference of opinion as to the construction of this agreement, should arise between the Conductors and trainmen and the division officers, a written statement of the questions at issue must be submitted to the General Manager, through the Division Superintendent, for his construction.

ART. 12. This agreement supersedes all previous agreements.

ART. 13. The articles enumerated constitute in their entirety an agreement between the Chesapeake and Ohio Railway Company and its Conductors and trainmen. No departure from the provisions of this agreement will be made for any party thereto

without a reasonable notice of such a desire in writing is served upon the other party thereto. CHESAPEAKE & OHIO RAILWAY CO.
For the Order Railway Conductors: By GEO. W. STEVENS,
A. B. GARRETSON, Grand Senior Conductor. General Manager.
T. H. WALL, General Chairman.
For the Brotherhood of Railroad Trainmen:
P. H. MORRISSEY, Acting Grand Master.
A. C. HARRISON, Chairman General Grievance Committee.
July 1st, 1892.

CHICAGO & ALTON RAILROAD COMPANY.

ARTICLE 1. No through freight Conductor's pay shall be less than $1.50 for 50 miles or less, and $3.00 for any run of over 50 miles and less than 100, when no other mileage is made the same day, the day to begin and end at midnight. All over 100 miles to be paid for at the rate of 3 cents per mile. No through freight Brakeman's pay shall be less than $1.00 for any run of 50 miles or less, nor less than $2.00 for any run of over 50 miles and less than 100—when no additional mileage is made that day—the day to begin and end at midnight. All over 100 miles shall be paid for at the rate of 2 cents per mile.

ART. 2. Freight trains doing wrecking and construction work, the Conductor and Brakemen thereof shall have pay for the time actually at such work, when schedule time is exceeded by one hour; the schedule time to be considered at the rate of 10 miles per hour; Conductors to receive 30 cents per hour for such wrecking and construction work, and Brakemen 20 cents per hour.

ART. 3. Way freight Conductors shall receive $80.00 per month, and Brakemen $55.00 per month. No overtime will be allowed. Trips made on layover days, or Sundays, will be paid as per Articles 1 and 2.

ART. 4. On regular construction or ballast trains, Conductors shall receive $78.00, and Brakemen $52.00 per month. Twenty-six days to constitute a month and 12 hours or less to constitute a day's work. No loss of time when the crew is held for service.

ART. 5. Conductors or Brakemen dead-heading to a point to take charge of a train, or dead-heading from a point to which they have taken a train, when acting under orders from officers of the Company, shall be paid as prescribed in Article 1.

ART. 6. Any Conductor or Brakeman piloting a train or engine to any point, shall be paid as prescribed in Article 1, except that a Brakeman acting as Conductor in piloting shall receive Conductor's pay.

ART. 7. In case of freight trains doubling hills, Conductors shall receive 3 cents, and Brakemen 2 cents per mile for the same.

ART. 8. All Conductors and Brakemen called as witnesses for the Company, shall receive, for Conductors, $3.00; and for Brakemen, $2.00 per day and expenses.

ART. 9. All the yardmen at Slater, Roodhouse and Alton, shall be paid at the present monthly rates, 26 days to constitute a month's work; additional days to be paid on the same basis.

ART. 10. Passenger Conductors and Brakemen making extra time will be paid for the same.

ART. 11. A caller shall be employed by the Company both day and night at Brighton Park, Bloomington, Roodhouse and Slater.

ART. 12. The right to regular runs and promotion will be governed by merit, ability and seniority. Everthing being equal, Conductor, Brakeman or Yardman longest in the service will have preference, the superintendent to be the judge as to qualifications. Nothing in this article shall be construed as preventing the Company from employing experienced men from other roads when the good of the service requires it.

ART. 13. Unless leave of absence for a definite time is given, Conductors, Brakemen and Yardmen leaving the service of the Company to engage in other business, or to work on other roads, and who shall, subsequently, be re-employed by the Company, shall rank as new men.

ART. 14. No Conductor, Brakeman or Yardman shall be suspended or dismissed without just cause. In case of suspension or dismissal, if he thinks his sentence unjust, his case shall have a thorough investigation by the proper officers, at which he may be present, if he so desire. Any such investigation shall be made within 10 days from the date of notice in writing of his desire for further investigation, and if found unjustly suspended or dismissed, he shall be reinstated and paid full time while so out of service.

ART. 15. It is the rule and intention of the Company to run through freight crews first in, first out; but circumstances may arise where this should be changed, and the Company reserves the right to do so. For instance, we may deem it advisable to run certain crews upon certain designated trains—and we must be at liberty to arrange such matters for the best interests of the Company.

ART. 16. The rate contained in this schedule, and the rules relating thereto, shall not be changed, in any case, without the mutual consent of both parties to this agreement.
T. M. BATES,
Superintendent of Transportation.
Approved: C. H. CHAPPELL,
May 26, 1890.   General Manager.

CHICAGO & ALTON RAILROAD COMPANY.

The following amendments are made to rules dated May 26, 1890, governing the compensation of trainmen on the Chicago & Alton Railroad:

Amendment to ARTICLE 1. No through freight Conductor's pay shall be less than $3.00 for any run less than 100 miles; all over 100 miles shall be paid at the rate of 3 cents per mile. The day to begin and end at midnight. No through freight Brakeman's pay shall be less than $2.00 for any run not less than 100 miles; all over 100 miles shall be paid at the rate of 2 cents per mile. The day to begin and end at midnight.

Amendment to ART. 3. Way freight Conductors shall receive $85.00 per month, and Brakemen $60.00 per month. No overtime will be allowed. Trips made on layover days or Sundays will be paid for as per Articles 1 and 2.
T. M. BATES,
Superintendent of Transportation.
Approved: C. H. CHAPPELL,
December 1, 1891.   General Manager.

We are now paying passenger Conductor on through runs, $120.00 per month; on branch runs, $100.00 per month; all passenger Brakemen, $55.00 per month; train Baggagemen are paid $50.00, $55.00, $58.00 and $60.00, according to the work on the runs.
J. H. WOOD,
May 17, 1892.   General Manager's Assistant.

CHICAGO & EASTERN ILLINOIS RAILROAD COMPANY AND OPERATING CHICAGO & INDIANA COAL RAILWAY.

The following rules will govern the employment and compensation of Trainmen on the Chicago & Eastern Illinois Railroad, effective February 1, 1892, and until July 15, 1892:

Through Passenger Runs: Conductors, $100.00 per month; Baggagemen, $57.50 per month; Baggagemen joint with express company, $60.00 per month; passenger Brakemen $47.50 per month. Crews assigned to regular runs will be paid extra for any service performed outside of their regular runs at the regular rates for the class of service performed.

Short Passenger Runs: Watseka and Terre Haute, Conductors, $90.00; Brakemen, $50.00 per month. St. Louis Division, Conductors, $90.00; Brakemen, $50.00 per month. Suburban, including Momence and Chicago, Conductors, $90.00 per month; Brakemen, $52.50 per month, and Flagmen, $45.00 per month.

Local Freight Runs: Danville and Chicago, Conductors, $85.00 per month; two Brakemen, each $57.50, one Brakeman to act as Foreman, $58.50 per month. Chicago and Momence local, Conductors, $80.00; three Brakemen, $57.50, each, per month. Danville and Terre Haute local, Conductors. $80.00 per month; two Brakemen, each $55.00 per month, one Brakeman to act as Foreman, $56.00. St. Louis Division local, Conductors, $80.00 per month; Brakemen, $55.00 per month, each. Cissna Park, Conductors, $75.00 per month; two Brakemen, $50 per month, each. Extra road service rendered by local train crews shall pe paid for at the regular rate for the class of service performed.

Through Freight Runs: On all through runs of 100 miles or more, Conductors shall receive 2.9 and Brakemen 1.9 cents per mile for the entire distance run. All coal runs between Danville and Grape Creek shall receive, Conductors, $75.00 per month and Brakemen, $55.00 per month. Freight trains will be allowed three Brakemen when the work requires it. The superintendent of transportation or trainmaster to be the one to decide when this is necessary. Through freight runs on the Terre Haute Division to be based as follows: Danville to Terre Haute and return and Danville to Brazil and return, to constitute a trip same as through freight on longer divisions, and based on 12 hours for a day's work. Conductors to receive 2.9 cents per mile and Brakemen, 1.9 cents per mile. Where trains are run from Danville to Terre Haute and return or

Danville to Brazil and return—one way local and return on through freight—time to be computed on a basis of 13 hours: on the same runs where trains are run both ways as local freight, time to be computed on the basis of 14 hours, and overtime to be allowed at the rate of 25 cents an hour for Conductors, and 15 cents an hour for Brakemen, after 12 hours on through freight, 13 hours on local and through freight, and 14 hours on local freight.

[NOTE.—Freight Conductors promoted from Brakemen shall receive 2-10 of a cent per mile less than regular rates for the first year's service.]

Work Trains: Conductors of work trains shall receive $3.00 per day, and Brakemen $2.00 per day.

Crews Running Light: Crews running light shall receive two-thirds of regular through freight pay.

Pilots: Conductors piloting engines over the road shall receive freight Conductor's pay for such service.

Overtime: All over 12 hours on through freight trains or work trains, and 14 hours on local freight trains, will be paid for as overtime at the rate of 25 cents per hour for Conductors, and 15 cents per hour for Brakemen, provided that such overtime is not the fault of such Conductor or Brakeman. Trainmen required to remain on duty after arrival at terminal stations will be allowed yard delay time for all such time on duty. Fractions of an hour less than 35 minutes will not be counted; over 35 minutes and less than 60 minutes to be counted an hour.

Dead-Head Trips: Freight crews required to make dead-head trips shall receive one-half the rate for the class of service which requires such dead-head trip.

Crews Attending Court: Trainmen attending court on the Company's business will be allowed regular pay.

Rest: Trainmen, after a continuous service of 16 hours or more, shall take sufficient rest before they are again called for service, except in case of wrecks or similar emergencies. Trainmen living within one mile of yard offices should be called to go out as near as practicable two hours before the time they are expected to leave, the caller to have a book in which the trainmen shall register their names and the time called. Any Conductor or Brakeman failing to respond after thus being called shall be liable to suspension or discharge, as the general superintendent or superintendent of transportation may determine. Their time will begin two hours after they sign the caller's book, unless they go on duty sooner. When trainmen are called for a train, and the said train is afterward annulled, the Conductor and Brakemen shall receive 25 cents per hour and the Brakemen 15 cents an hour for the time held, and shall stand first out. Trainmen will be notified when time is not allowed, as per time slip, and of the reason why it was not allowed.

Trainmen Taken off Run: If a trainman is relieved from duty for any cause, he shall be granted a thorough investigation, hearing and decision within five days, at which investigation he shall have the right to be present and to have another Conductor or Brakeman, as the case may be, of his selection, to appear and speak for him, and shall have the right to appeal from the local to the general officers of the road, and a decision in five days after presenting his appeal, and, in case such decision is not made within five days on such appeal, one-half pay shall begin and continue until such decision is made.

Promotions: Trainmen will be in the line of promotion according to their time of service, dependent upon their general good conduct, faithful discharge of their duties, and their ability to assume increased responsibilities, the superintendent of transportation to be judge of such qualification. Promotion in the train service to be confined to the ranks of train employes as above. When practicable, Conductors and Brakemen will be assigned to regular runs; on all freight trains, except local freight trains, they will run first in, first out, unless the service requires it otherwise. The right to regular runs will be governed by merit, ability and seniority. Everything being equal, the Conductor and Brakeman longest in faithful service will have the preference.

Turnaround between Chicago and Momence will be paid: Conductors, first class, $3.50, second class, $3.25; Brakemen, $2.30 per round trip, overtime to be allowed after six hours each way. Short runs not otherwise specified, where mileage is 50 miles or less, will be allowed 50 miles; over 50 miles and less than 100 miles to be allowed 100 miles, provided no other mileage is made on that same day. If aggregate mileage made on any one day equals or exceeds 100 miles, actual mileage will govern. Dates to begin and end at midnight, and each trip to date from starting time. When the freight traffic is so light that the crews in service are not able to make reasonable wages, crews will be taken off, beginning with the youngest men, until the crews left in service are able to make reasonable wages. Conductors taken off under this rule will be given preference as Brakemen, and again placed on their runs when business demands an increase of crews.

In connection with the schedule agreed upon and effective February 1, 1892, it is further agreed that on July 15, 1892, the same shall be revised, and if the committee desire audience with the officers at that time the same shall be held, the Company to pay the necessary expenses of the committee. It is further agreed that the schedule as amended and revised on July 15, 1892, shall provide that the rates of pay to the local freight Conductors shall be made uniformly $85.00 per month, and local freight Brakemen $57.50 per month. The rates of pay to through freight trainmen will be made 2.95 cents and 1.95 cents per mile, respectively, for Conductors and Brakemen, and that the rates for overtime shall be 29¼ and 19¼ cents per hour, respectively. On July 15, 1892, the agreement shall be made to stand for one year. On July 15, 1893, the standard rate of 3 and 2 cents per mile, and of 30 and 20 cents per hour for overtime, respectively, for Conductors and Brakemen, will be established. It is further agreed that on July 15, 1892, the pay of Conductors of suburban trains will be made $95.00 per month, and the pay of Conductors on Grape Creek run will be made $80.00 per month.

CHARLES H. ROCKWELL, General Superintendent.
E. E. CLARK, Grand Chief Conductor. Approved: GEO. W. SAUL, President
WM. BELL, Chairman.   Chicago & Eastern Illinois Railroad Company.
  For Order of Railway Conductors.
S. E. WILKINSON, Grand Master.
C. J. KNIERIM, Chairman.
  For the Brotherhood of Railroad Trainmen.

CHICAGO & WESTERN INDIANA RAILROAD COMPANY AND BELT RAILWAY COMPANY OF CHICAGO.

We pay our Switchmen the Chicago standard wages. All trainmen who run over the Chicago & Western Indiana tracks are employed by, and paid by, our several tenant companies.

B. THOMAS,
May 14, 1892.   President and General Manager.

CHICAGO & NORTHWESTERN COMPANY.—PASSENGER SERVICE.

RUNS.		Monthly Mileage.	Cnductors per Month.	Brakemen per Month.	B'g gemen per Month.
FROM	TO				
GALENA DIVISION.					
Chicago	Clinton	5708	$120 00	$50 00	$65 00
do	do	4281	120 00	50 00	65 00
do	do	3729	110 00	50 00	55 00
do	Rockford	5017	110 00	50 00	50 00
do	Lake Geneva	4126	100 00	50 00	50 00
do	do	4644	110 00	50 00	55 00
do	Crystal Lake	3627	100 00	50 00	60 00
do	Elgin	2311	100 00	50 00	55 00
do	Freeport-Maywood	3357	100 00	50 00	{ 4—55 00 { 2—37 50
do	Turner-Maywood	2940	100 00	50 00	55 00
do	do do	2290	100 00	50 00	50 00
do	Belvidere	4223	100 00	50 00	55 00
do	Maywood	1810	100 00	50 00	50 00
do	Aurora-Maywood	2510	100 00	50 00	27 50
Turner	Sterling	4290	110 00	50 00	60 00
do	Lake Geneva	3144	100 00	50 00	55 00
Spring Valley	Caledonia	4644	100 00	50 00	32 50
St. Charles	Geneva-Aurora	2322	100 00	50 00	50 00
Cortland	Sycamore-DeKalb	1620	50 00	40 00	40 00
WISCONSIN DIVISION.					
Chicago	Ft. Howard	5267	120 00	50 00	65 00
do	Milwaukee	5270	120 00	50 00	{ 1—60 00 { 1—55 00
do	do	4590	120 00	50 00	{ 1—55 00 { 1—60 00
do	Elroy	4964	120 00	50 00	65 00
do	Ft. Howard	4060	110 00	50 00	55 00
do	Harvard	4146	110 00	50 00	65 00
do	do	3906	110 00	50 00	55 00
do	Janesville	4920	110 00	50 00	65 00
Milwaukee	Fon du Lac	3418	110 00	50 00	55 00
do	Appleton	6200	110 00	50 00	55 00
Janesville	Fon du Lac	4644	100 00	50 00	
Chicago	Kenosha	2775	100 00	50 00	55 00
do	Waukegan	2970	100 00	50 00	50 00

CHICAGO & NORTHWESTERN RAILWAY.

PASSENGER SERVICE.—CONTINUED

FROM	TO	Monthly Mileage.	Cnductors per Month.	Brakemen per Month.	B'g'gemen per Month.
Chicago...	Waukegan......	3780	100 00	50 00	55 00
do	Highland Park........	3138	10. 00	50 00	50 00
do	Winnetka	3435	100 00	50 00	50 00
do	Evanston......	2988	100 00	50 00	50 00
do	Woodstock	3162	100 00	50 00	55 00
do	Barrington.......	3348	100 00	50 00	55 00
do	do	2133	100 00	50 00	50 00
do	Des Plaines........	2619	100 00	50 00	50 00
do	do	2889	10 00	50 00	50 00
Sheboygan...........	Princeton	4212	100 00	50 00	55 00
IOWA DIVISION.					
Clinton....	Boone	4494	120 00	50 00	65 00
Boone	Council Bluffs........	4500	120 00	50 00	65 00
Mo. Valley........	do	2710	100 00	50 00	60 00
Des Moines........	Jewell Junction.....	2520	100 00	50 00	27 50
Clinton............	Anamosa...	2834	100 00	50 00	27 50
PEN. DIVISION.					
Ft. Howard...........	Ishpeming......	5220	120 00	50 00	65 00
Powers...........	Watersmeet-Crystal Falls.......	4060	110 00	50 00	60 00
do	Iron River......	3596	100 00	50 00	55 00
Ft. Howard...........	Menominee............	2652	10. 00	50 00	55 00
MADISON DIVISION.					
Harvard	Winona	5240	120 00	50 00	65 00
Chicago	Elroy.....	4964	120 00	50 00	65 00
Milwaukee...........	Madison	4988	110 00	60 00	65 00
do	do	4278	100 00	50 00	60 00
do	Lancaster........	4512	110 00	50 00	60 00
Galena	do	4304	100 00	50 00	55 00
Afton....	Janesville	3443	100 00	50 00	65 00
DeKalb.........	do	3234	100 00	50 00	55 00
W. & ST. P. DIVISION.					
Tracy	Waterton.......	4815	120 00	50 00	60 00
Tracy	Winona	4763	120 00	50 00	65 00
DAKOTA DIVISION.					
Hawarden	Oakes	4853	120 00	50 00	65 00
Tracy................	Pierre	4420	120 00	5 00	65 00
Brookings...........	Gettysburg....	4264	110 00	50 00	60 00
NORTH IOWA DIVISION.					
Tama......	Hawarden	4277	120 00	50 00	65 00
Jewell Junction.......	Sioux City...........	4656	110 00	50 00	32 50
Carroll	Moville	5258	100 00	50 00	32 50
do	Sioux City.........	3717	100 00	50 00	32 50

Special Rules: When a passenger Conductor is taken off his regular run to run specials, or extras, he shall receive 3 cents per mile for such service. When a passenger Conductor doubles for such Conductor, taken off his regular run, he shall receive such compensation as such Conductor would receive, in addition to his regular salary. No deduction shall be made for any time lost on account of snow blockades and washouts. No privileges now enjoyed by passenger Conductors shall be abrogated. Extra compensation shall be allowed passenger Conductors for all mileage made in excess of that stated above, except on suburban trains and where the mileage is less than 2,600 miles. On divisions where extra passenger Conductors are employed their pay shall be $100.00 per month, and they shall not be called upon to do freight work. Milk Conductors will be paid $55.00 per month.

FREIGHT SERVICE.—CONDUCTORS.

ARTICLE 1. *Rates and Grades:* 1. There shall be two grades of freight Conductors established and the compensation shall be as follows: (a) For the first year's actual service after promotion from a Brakemen, $68.00 per month. (b) For the second year's service and thereafter. $78.00 per month.

2. Conductors of way freight trains will be paid $85.00 for 2,600 miles or less, made in any one month. All mileage made in any one month in excess of 2,600 miles will be paid for extra, at the rate of 3¼ cents per mile.

3. Conductors of work trains will be paid not less than $85.00 per month of 26 days, 10 hours or less to constitute a day's work. All time made in excess of 10 hours will be paid for at the rate of 3¼ cents per mile.

4. The pay of mixed train Conductors will be computed at freight rates.

5. Freight Conductors temporarily in passenger service will be paid freight mileage.

ART. 2. *Rules for Computation:* 1. The monthly compensation is to be based on a mileage of 2,600 miles or 26 days per month, and any excess over this mileage made by freight Conductors will be paid for in the same proportion as the monthly compensation is to 2,600 miles.

2. If the mileage of a freight Conductor falls below 2,600 miles in any one month, and he has been ready for service, losing no time on his own account, in such cases full time for 2,600 miles shall be allowed.

3. The first year's service is to consist of 12 calendar months.

4. Should it become necessary to reduce the force on account of decreased business, and the Conductor still remains in the employ of the Company as Brakeman, his promotion is to date from the time he made his first trip as Conductor, and he shall receive the highest rate paid Brakemen.

5. Freight Conductors will be notified when time is not allowed as per trip report.

ART. 3. *Extra Mileage:* 1. All freight Conductors on regular runs will receive compensation for extra mileage made outside of their regular runs.

2. All runs of less than 100 miles shall be computed as one day's work, provided the men do not go out again the same day, except on branch runs where the mileage is less than 60 miles per day, where the Company reserves the right to make special agreements with its Conductors as to the compensation they shall receive.

3. Where crews are required to double hills, such crews will be allowed the extra mileage made.

ART. 4. *Delayed Time:* 1. Conductors will be called, as nearly as possible, one hour before the leaving time of their trains. They will be paid for all delayed time at terminal stations, provided the delay exceeds one hour. They will also be paid for all delayed time between terminal stations in case of accidents, washouts, snow, or unloading or loading material, provided no claim will be made unless there is a full hour's delay, or if train arrives at its terminal on time.

2. All delayed time will be paid at the rate of 10 miles per hour.

ART. 5. *Dead-Head Time:* 1. Conductors will be allowed 10 miles per hour for dead-heading on passenger trains. All other dead-heading shall be computed as actual miles run.

2. When freight crews and way cars are ordered dead-head, the crews shall accompany their way cars.

3. In ordering crews, the first crew shall run the train, the next crew dead-heading when such service is required, said crew being ahead of the crew with whom they dead-head, on reaching the terminal of that run.

ART. 6. *Switching Service:* 1. If freight Conductors are required to do switching at terminal stations, either before leaving or after arriving at such terminal, they will be paid extra for all such switching at the rate of 10 miles per hour. Less than 45 minutes will not be counted. Forty-five minutes and less than one hour will be counted an hour.

ART. 7. *Discipline:* 1. In case of dismissal or suspension of a Conductor by any one below the Division Superintendent in rank, he shall have the right to appeal to the Division Superintendent for a full and impartial investigation. Should the Division Superintendent fail to adjust the case, the Conductor may appeal to the General Superintendent or General Manager.

2. No fault shall be found with a Conductor who refuses to go out on account of needed rest.

3. When a freight Conductor is taken from his run for an alleged fault, an investigation shall be held ordinarily within three days. Where more than three days elapse he shall, if found innocent, receive pay for all time lost after the third day. No punishment to be fixed without a thorough investigation.

ART. 8. *Conductors Rights and Privileges:* 1. Conductors will be allowed to lay off on account of the sickness of themselves, their families or for other good and sufficient reasons, provided due notice is given to the proper officers, so that their places may be filled with other men.

2. This does not permit Conductors to leave the division on which they are employed without permission from their Superintendent.

3. Any Conductor having been absent to exceed six consecutive months, thereby forfeits all rights with the Company, except in case of sickness or where leave of absence has been granted. No leave of absence shall be granted to exceed one year, nor reinstatements made after one year's continuous absence, except in case of sickness.

4. The rights of a Conductor commence on the day of his promotion, and he shall have the choice of runs to which his age as Conductor entitles him, provided he is intellectually and morally fitted for it in the opinion of his Superintendent.

5. Where passenger crews run over more than one freight division, the oldest freight Conductor on either division will be considered as entitled to promotion to

passenger runs as above. Nothing in this article shall be considered as preventing the Company from employing experienced men when the service requires it.

6. Conductors having charge of trains will be held responsible for their safe management, and shall have the right to place their Brakemen as their best judgment may dictate.

7. When a Conductor leaves one division, of his own accord, to work on another division, he shall be considered as a new employe; but should he be transferred by order of the Company, the same rights he possessed on the first division shall be maintained on his return to the same.

ART. 9. *Calling of Men:* 1. A book shall be kept in the Train Dispatchers office, showing the name of each Conductor and his residence. Superintendents shall agree with their men on certain limits within which men shall be called, to take their trains, where call boys are provided.

2 Call boys shall be provided with a book in which Conductors shall register their names, and the time they are called.

3. Conductors shall also register in a book kept for that purpose in the Train Dispatcher's office, or other designated place, 30 minutes before their trains are due to leave.

ART. 10. *Running of Crews:* 1. On other than assigned runs the crews will run, first in, first out.

FREIGHT SERVICE.—BRAKEMEN.

ARTICLE 1. *Rates and Grades:* 1. There shall be two grades of freight Brakemen established, and the compensation shall be as follows: (a) For the first three months of actual service; $45.00 per month. (b) For all service after three months' service, $52.00 per month.

2. Brakemen on way freight trains will be paid $55.00 for 2,600 miles or less made in any one month. All mileage made in any one month in excess of 2,600 miles will be paid for extra.

3. Brakemen on work trains will be paid not less than $55.00 per month of 26 days, 10 hours or less to constitute a day's work. All time made in excess of 10 hours will be paid for extra.

4. The pay of mixed train Brakemen will be computed at freight rates.

5. Freight Brakemen temporarily in passenger service will be paid freight mileage.

ART. 2. *Rules for Computation:* 1. The monthly compensation is to be based on a mileage of 2,600 miles, or 26 days per month, and any excess over this mileage made by freight Brakemen will be paid for in the same proportion as the monthly compensation is to 2,600 miles.

2. If the mileage of a freight Brakemen falls below 2,600 miles in any one month, and he has been ready for service, losing no time on his own account, in such cases full time for 2,600 miles will be allowed.

3. Brakemen who are laid off owing to decreased business, will be reinstated and hold their rights as per Article 8, provided they report for work when wanted.

4. Freight Brakemen will be notified when time is not allowed as per trip report.

ART. 3. *Extra Mileage:* 1. All freight Brakemen on regular runs will receive compensation for extra mileage made outside of their regular runs.

2. All runs of less than 100 miles will be computed as one day's work, provided the men do not go out again the same day, except on branch runs where the mileage is less than 60 miles per day, where the Company reserves the right to make special agreements with its Brakemen as to the compensation they will receive.

3. Where crews are required to double hills, such crews will be allowed the extra mileage made.

ART. 4. *Delayed Time:* 1. Brakemen will be called, as nearly as possible, one hour before the leaving time of their trains. They will be paid for all delayed time at terminal stations, provided the delay exceeds one hour. They will also be paid for all delayed time betwen terminal stations in case of accidents, washouts, snow, or unloading or loading material, provided no claim will be made unless there is a full hour's delay, or if train arrives at its terminal on time.

2. All delayed time will be paid at the rate of 10 miles per hour.

ART. 5. *Dead-Head Time:* 1. Brakemen will be allowed 10 miles per hour for dead-heading on passenger trains. All other dead-heading will be computed as actual miles run.

2. When freight crews and way-cars are ordered dead-head, the crews will accompany their way-cars.

3. In ordering crews, the first crew will run the train, the next crew dead-heading, when such service is required, said crew being ahead of the crew with whom they dead-head, on reaching the terminal of that run.

ART. 6. *Switching Service:* 1. If freight Brakemen are required to do switching at terminal stations, either before leaving or after arriving at such terminal, they will be paid extra for all such switching at the rate of 10 miles per hour. Less than 45 minutes will not be counted. Forty-five minutes and less than one hour to be counted one hour.

ART. 7. *Discipline:* 1. In case of dismissal or suspension of a Brakeman by anyone below the Division Superintendent in rank, he will have the right to appeal to the Division Superintendent for a full and impartial investigation. Should the Division Superintendent fail to adjust the case, the Brakeman may appeal to the General Superintendent or General Manager.

2. No fault will be found with a Brakeman who refuses to go out on account of needed rest.

3. When a freight Brakeman is taken from his run for an alleged fault, an investigation will be held ordinarily within three days. Where more than three days elapse, he will, if found innocent, receive pay for all time lost after the third day. No punishment to be fixed without a thorough investigation.

ART. 8. *Brakemen's Rights and Privileges:* 1. Brakemen will be allowed to lay off on account of the sickness of themselves, their families or for other good and sufficient reasons, provided due notice is given to the proper officers, so that their places may be filled with other men.

2. This does not permit Brakemen to leave the division on which they are employed without permission from the Superintendent.

3. Any Brakemen having been absent to exceed six consecutive months, thereby forfeits all rights with the Company, except in case of sickness or where leave of absence has been granted. No leave of absence will be granted to exceed one year, nor reinstatements made after one year's continuous absence, except in case of sickness.

4. The rights of a Brakeman commence on the day of his first trip, and he will have the choice of runs to which his age in the service as Brakeman entitles him, merit and competency being equal, in the judgment of the Conductor.

5. The employment of Brakemen is placed in the hands of the Division Superintendents, or their representatives, but Brakemen will, in all cases, be placed as the Conductor's best judgment may dictate.

6. When a Brakeman leaves one division, of his own accord, to work on another division, he will be considered as a new employe, but should he be transferred by order of the Company, the same rights he possessed on the first division will be maintained on his return to the same.

7. If a Brakeman transfers from either the freight or passenger department to the other, he forfeits all rights in the department which he leaves, and will be classed as a new employe, except in case of disability.

8. In examining men on the Book of Rules for promotion to Conductors, the oldest Brakemen must have the preference, merit and competency being equal. The Company reserves the right, however, to hire Conductors outside of the employes of the Company should the service demand it.

ART. 9. *Calling of Men:* A book will be kept in the Train Dispatcher's office, showing the name of each Brakeman and his residence. Superintendents will agree with their men on certain limits within which men will be called to take their trains, where call boys are provided.

2. Call boys will be provided with a book in which Brakemen will register their names and the time they are called.

3. Brakemen will also register in a book kept for that purpose in the Train Dispatcher's office, or other designated place, 30 minutes before their trains are due to leave.

ART. 10. *Running of Crews:* 1. On other than assigned runs the crews will run, first in, first out.

May 6th, 1892.   Approved: S. SANBORN, General Superintendent.
J. M. WHITMAN, General Manager.

SWITCHING SERVICE.

Our more important switching points are divided into two classes. The first-class stations are as follows: Chicago, Milwaukee and Clinton, Iowa. At the first-class stations rate of pay for Switchmen is as follows: Day Foreman, $70.00 per month; Day Helpers, $65.00 per month; Night Foreman, $75.00 per month; Night Helpers, $70.00 per month. Our second-class stations are as follows: Council Bluffs, Boone, Belle Plaine, Tama, Eagle Grove, Belvidere, Janesville, Madison, Baraboo, Winona, Ft. Howard, Iron Mountain, Escanaba and Ishpeming. The rate of pay at the second-class stations is as follows: Day Foreman, $65.00 per month; Day Helpers, $60.00 per month; Night Foreman, $70.00 per month; Night Helpers, $65.00 per month. Ten hours constitute one day's work and 26 days constitute one month's work. Overtime is paid for at a proportionate rate. Crews working from 12 o'clock noon to 12 o'clock midnight receive the stipulated wages for night crews. Day crews and night crews are allowed one hour

CHI., ST. P., MIN. & OMAHA RY.—MIL., LAKE SHORE & WEST. RY.

between 11:30 A. M. and 1:00 P. M. and between 11:30 P. M. and 1:00 A. M. for meals. If the crews are required to work later than 1:00 P. M. or 1:00 A. M., and thereby lose their time for meals, 20 minutes is allowed them for meals, and compensation is allowed for the full hour from which the 20 minutes is lost.

May 6, 1892.
J. M. WHITMAN, General Manager

CHICAGO, ST. PAUL, MINNEAPOLIS & OMAHA RAILWAY COMPANY.

PASSENGER SERVICE.

When a passenger Conductor is taken off his regular run to run specials or extras, he shall receive 3 cents per mile for such service. When a passenger Conductor doubles for another taken off his regular run, he shall receive same compensation as such Conductor would receive in addition to his regular salary. No deduction shall be made for any time lost on account of snow blockades or washouts.

RUNS.		Cond'crs per Month	Br kmen per Month	Bag men per Month
FROM	TO			
EASTERN & NORTHERN DIVISION.				
Minneapolis	Elroy (3-4-5 and 6)	$120 00	$50 00	$65 00
do	Elroy (1 and 2)	120 00	50 00	*65 00
Stillwater	St. Paul	100 00	50 00	55 00
St. Paul	Ellsworth	100 00	50 00	50 00
Merrillan	Marshfield	100 00	50 00	55 00
Menomonie City	Menomonie Junction	83 33	50 00	65 00
Minneapolis	Duluth (61 and 62)	120 00	50 00	60 00
do	Duluth (63 and 64)	110 00	50 00	*60 00
Eau Claire	Ashland	110 00	50 00	60 00
do	Duluth	120 00	50 00	*60 00
Spooner	Ashland	110 00	50 00	*60 00
Eau Claire	Chippewa Falls	83 33	45 00	50 00
Bayfield	Ashland	100 00	50 00	55 00
ST. PAUL & SIOUX CITY DIVISION.				
Minneapolis	Sioux City (1-2-3 and 4)	120 00	50 00	65 00
do	Mankato (5 and 6)	100 00	50 00	60 00
Worthington	Sioux Falls	95 00	50 00	60 00
Heron Lake	Pipestone	85 00	50 00	55 00
Elmore	Lake Crystal	90 00	50 00	55 00
Luverne	Doon	75 00	50 00	50 00
NEBRASKA DIVISION.				
Omaha	Sioux City	110 00	50 00	*$70 00
Bancroft	Omaha	100 00	45 00	
Norfolk	Sioux City	100 00	5 ! 00	*30 00

*One-half paid by Express Company. §Also acts as Baggageman and Expressman on Bancroft trains.

August 18th, 1892.
E. W. WINTER, General Manager.

MILWAUKEE, LAKE SHORE & WESTERN RAILWAY COMPANY.

(1) All freight Conductors will be paid for the first year's service at the rate of $2.70 per day; for all subsequent service $3.00. Freight Brakemen, $2.00 per day. Way freight run between Milwaukee and Kaukauna, Conductors, $3.46 per day; Brakemen, $2.40 per day. Way freight run between Kaukauna and Antigo, Conductors, $3.46 per day; Brakemen, $2.40 per day. Way freight run between Antigo and Watersmeet (including Wolf River Branch), Conductors, $3.30 per day; Brakemen, $2.20 per day. Way freight run between Watersmeet and Ashland, Conductors, $3.46 per day; Brakemen, $2.40 per day. Work train Conductors, not less than $3.25 per day; Brakemen, not less than $2.11 per day. Compensation of Conductors and Brakemen of mixed trains shall be computed at freight rates.

Rules for Computation: (2) The above compensation shall be based upon a mileage of 100 miles per day (except on way freight trains, specifically named above, and work trains). If the mileage of any freight Conductor or Brakeman shall fall below 2,600 miles in any one month, he having been ready for service, losing no time on his own account, in such cases full time for 2,600 miles will be allowed. This, however, will not apply to men on the extra list. It is distinctly understood that no duty time is to be allowed where the mileage of any Conductor or Brakeman exceeds 2,600 miles per month. (Duty time means time allowed for days in which no mileage is made). Over-

MILWAUKEE, LAKE SHORE & WESTERN RAILWAY. 43

time at the rate of 10 miles per hour will be paid at the rates named above, as follows: on way freight runs between Milwaukee and Kaukauna, Kaukauna and Antigo, and Watersmeet and Ashland, after 12 hours. On way freight runs between Antigo and Watersmeet (including Wolf River Branch), after 11 hours. On work trains, after 10 hours. In all other freight service, after 11 hours. In computing overtime, less than 35 minutes will not be counted. Over 35 minutes will be computed as one hour. The first year's service is to consist of 12 calendar months from the date of promotion.

(3) In the event of there being a surplus of Conductors for the service on the road, the older Conductors shall have the preference in employment; competency and ability in the judgment of the Division Superintendent to be considered.

(4) After a Conductor or Brakeman has been called and reports for duty, he shall be paid for all time lost, such time to be not less than one-quarter of a day, and shall be first out.

(5) Freight Conductors will be notified when time is not allowed as per trip slip report.

Extra Mileage: (6) Freight Conductors and Brakemen on regular runs will receive compensation for extra mileage made outside of their regular run.

(7) All runs of less than 100 miles shall be computed as one day's work, provided the men do not go out again the same day, except on branch runs where the mileage is less than 60 miles per day, where the Company reserves the right to make special agreements as to the compensation to be paid.

(8) Where crews are required to double hills such crews shall be allowed the actual mileage made.

(9) Fifty miles will be allowed for the run on ore trains between Ashland and any station on the Iron Range, the same to include making up of trains as at present, and the weighing of ore at Ore Dock Junction.

Delayed Time: (10) All freight Conductors and Brakemen delayed over one hour when starting from terminal station, or getting into yard at terminal station, or delayed on the road by accident, washouts, snow, or loading or unloading material, shall be paid for all time lost at the rate of 10 miles an hour, but no claim shall be made unless there is a delay of a full hour, it being understood that if a train arrives at its division terminal on time no claim for delayed time shall be made or allowed. All delayed time shall be paid for at the rate of 10 miles per hour.

Dead-head Time: (11) Conductors and Brakemen will be allowed 10 miles per hour for dead-heading on passenger trains. All other dead-heading shall be computed as actual miles run. When freight crews and way cars are ordered dead-head, the crews shall accompany their way cars. In ordering crews dead-head, the first crew shall run the train, the next crew dead-heading when such service is required, said crew being ahead of the crew with whom they dead-head on reaching the terminal of that run.

Switching Service: (12) If freight Conductors and Brakemen are required to do switching at terminal stations either before leaving or after arriving at such terminal, they will be paid extra for all such switching at the rate of 10 miles per hour. Less than 35 minutes will not be counted; 35 minutes and less than one hour will be counted one hour.

Discipline: (13) Conductors or Brakemen shall not be suspended or dismissed from service except upon a full investigation by the Superintendent, and such investigation should ordinarily be made within three days of the occurrence causing the investigation. When more than three days have elapsed they shall, if found innocent, receive pay for all time lost after the third day; no punishment to be fixed without a thorough investigation. Any employe suspended or dismissed from the service who may feel that such action was uncalled for, shall have the right of appeal to the General Superintendent and General Manager.

(14) Conductors and Brakemen will not be required to go out when they need rest. They will make their needs known by proper notice in Trainmaster's office before arrival at terminal points. Eight hours will be considered sufficient rest.

Rank and Privileges: (15) The rank of a Conductor shall date from the day of his promotion, and he shall have the choice of any new or vacant run to which his age as Conductor entitles him; competency and ability in the judgment of the Division Superintendent to be considered.

(16) Conductors having charge of trains will be held responsible for their safe management, and will have the right to place their Brakemen as their best judgment may dictate.

(17) Any Conductor having been absent to exceed six consecutive months thereby forfeits all rights with the company, except in case of sickness or where leave of absence has been granted. No leave of absence shall be granted to exceed one year, nor reinstatement made after one year's absence, except, in case of sickness.

(18) Brakemen shall be examined for promotion according to the time of service. In case a Brakeman shall fail to pass examination he shall retain his chance for promotion.

(19) When a Conductor leaves one division of his own accord to work on anoth[er] division he shall be considered a new employe, but should he be transferred by ord[er] of the company the same rank he possessed on the first division shall be maintained his return to the same.

(20) When a Yardmaster or men employed in the yards take service on the ro[ad] as Conductors their rank shall date from the time they were promoted as Conducto[rs] and they shall not be advanced ahead of Conductors who were running previous that time. Conductors entering yard service, however, shall not lose their rank if any time they return to the road service.

Calling of Men: (21) A book shall be kept in the Train Dispatcher's office showi[ng] the name of each Cohductor and Brakeman and his residence. Superintendents w[ill] designate certain limits within which men shall be called to take their trains whe[n] call boys are provided. Call boys shall be provided with a book in which Conduct[ors] and Brakemen shall register their names and the time they are called. Conduct[ors] and Brakemen shall also register in the book kept for that purpose in the Train D[is]patcher's office, or other designated place, 30 minutes before their trains are due leave.

Running of Crews: (22) Conductors will run first in first out, with the excepti[on] of those assigned to regular runs, and shall, so far as practicable, have regular cre[ws] who will run with them. This does not apply to men on the extra list.

GEO. F. BIDWELL, General Superintendent.
Approved: H. F. WHITCOMB, General Manager.
May 1, 1892.

FREMONT, ELKHORN & MISSOURI VALLEY AND SIOUX CITY & PACIF[IC] RAILWAY COMPANY.

The schedule in effect on the Fremont, Elkhorn & Missouri Valley Railway is t[he] same as on the Chicago & Northwestern Railway proper.   H. G. BURT,
May 26, 1892.   General Manager.

CHICAGO, BURLINGTON & QUINCY RAILROAD.

GENERAL RULES GOVERNING TRAIN SERVICE.

1. Regular freight and passenger crews making extra trips will be paid on t[he] basis of the rate fixed for the service performed. Crews running pay train, office specials or inspection trains, to be paid at the rate of 2½ cents per mile for Conducto[rs] and 1¾ cents per mile for Brakeman, with a minimum of $3.00 per day for Conduct[ors] and $2.00 for Brakeman. If crews are laid up for the day they will be paid at the mi[ni]mum rate given above. Living expenses of such crews will be borne by the Compa[ny] as heretofore.

2. Crews regularly assigned to construction trains: Conductors to receive $90 p[er] month; Brakemen, $60; 12 hours or less to constitute a day's work; calendar work[ing] days to be considered a month. Where Conductor acts as Foreman $15 per month ext[ra] will be allowed. All time over 12 hours to be paid extra proportionately.

3. When other than construction trains are ordered to do construction train wor[k] full time will be allowed at the rate of 30 cents per hour for Conductors, and 20 cen[ts] per hour for Brakemen.

4. Crews delayed 1 hour and 35 minutes in starting from or after arrival at t[er]minals, will be paid at the rate of 30 cents per hour for Conductors, and 20 cents p[er] hour for Brakemen, for the full delay, less one hour. In case crews have been call[ed] and afterward notified they are not wanted, the same rule will apply, with a minim[um] of two and one-half hours' pay, and the crew shall stand first out. On all runs of l[ess] than 100 miles requiring more than 10 hours, overtime will be paid if the hours used the trip exceed 11 hours, in which case all overtime exceeding 10 hours will be paid. [On] all runs exceeding 100 miles, trainmen will be paid overtime for all time used to co[m]plete the trip in excess of a rate of speed of 10 miles per hour when over one hour la[te.]

5. Conductors will have the right to object to Brakemen for cause, and when [ob]jections are sustained by facts they will be furnished with other men.

6. It is the rule of the Company to run freight crews first in, first out. This ru[le,] however, cannot be rigidly carried out at all times, and the proper officers of the Co[m]pany will vary from the rule as circumstances require.

7. Trainmen dead-heading over the road on Company business on passenger tra[in] will be paid one-half rates. When dead-heading on freight trains full rates will be [al]lowed. When necessary to dead-head a crew, the first crew will be dead-headed a[nd] the second crew run the train. The crew dead-headed to stand ahead of the crew ru[n]ning the train on arrival at terminal point.

8. When light engines or trains of other companies are run on main line and prin-
)al branches, a Conductor will be sent in charge, when practicable, who will act as
.ot.
9. Should a train be compelled to double a hill, crews will be paid for one hour's
ne at the rate of 30 cents for Conductors and 20 cents for Brakemen.
10. The right to regular runs and promotion will be governed by merit, ability and
niority, everything being equal; the Conductor, Brakemen or Yardman longest in the
rvice will have preference; the Superintendent to be the judge as to qualifications.
,thing in this rule shall be construed to mean that the Company will not employ men
)m other roads when, in the judgment of the officers, it is expedient to do so.
11. No employe will be suspended or discharged without just cause. In case of sus-
nsion or discharge of any employe, except for insubordination or intoxication, he
1y, if he desires, have a thorough investigation by the proper officers. Such desire
all be signified within five days of the date of suspension or discharge, and the inves-
gation shall be begun within ten days from such notice, and proceed with as little in-
rruption as may be until completed. The employe shall have full opportunity to pre-
it his case and to offer testimony. If the suspension or dismissal shall be found to
.ve been without just cause, the employe shall be reinstated and paid full time for
e period out of service.
12. When a Conductor is assigned to a regular passenger run he will not be used
freight or construction service unless in case of necessity.
13. When traffic becomes so light that reasonable monthly wages cannot be made,
e number of crews will be reduced. Other things being equal the youngest men will
laid off, the Superintendent to be the judge as to qualifications. It is the intention
so apportion the crews that they may make approximately 2,600 miles per month.
14. When crews are required to do switching at terminal stations, they will be paid
r such switching at the rate of 30 cents per hour for Conductors and 20 cents for
rakemen after the first 30 minutes, excepting when pay is arranged to include such
itching.
15. Where callers are furnished by the Company and men live within reasonable
nits—to be fixed by the Trainmaster or Superintendent—crews will be called within a
asonable time of the departure of their trains, except in case of emergency. Such
.llers will be provided with a book in which shall be entered the leaving time of the
ains. Men who are so called shall in each instance register their names with the
ne they are called. The above does not include men who are assigned to regular runs
nose trains leave during the day time.
16. If a trip report is incorrect, the trainman will be notified in writing.
17. Trainmen attending court under instructions from the Company will be paid
ll rates for time lost, and living expenses if away from home; the Company to re-
:ive the witness fees.
18. In all the above rules where pay per hour or per day is mentioned, it refers to
en of the first class. A Conductor is of the first class when he has served as such six
onths or over, and a Brakeman is of the first class when he has served as such three
onths or over. Men of the second class to receive $2.70 and $1.80 per day, respectively,
27 cents and 18 cents per hour, respectively.
19. Trainmen and yardmen will not be required to pay fines on account of breakage.

CHICAGO, BURLINGTON & QUINCY RAILWAY.

ILLINOIS LINES.—RATES OF PAY FOR PASSENGER RUNS.

RUNS.		Cond'ctors Rate per Month.	Baggemen Rate per Month.	Collect'rs Rate per Month.
FROM	TO			
Chicago	Burlington	$125 00	$65 00	....
do	do Fast Mail	110 00	......	......
do	Galesburg	125 00	65 00	......
Galesburg	Quincy	125 00	65 00	......
Chicago	Galesburg Local	110 00	60 00	......
do	Mendota Local	100 00	60 00	......
do	Aurora	75 00	45 00	$60 00
(26 round trips per month.)				
do	Aurora	95 00	55 00	70 00
(39 round trips per month.)				
do	Riverside	90 00	60 00	65 00
(130 round trips per month.)				
do	Downer's Grove	75 00	50 00	55 00
(52 round trips per month.)				
do	Downer's Grove	95 00	60 00	65 00
(78 round trips per month.)				
Rockford	Aurora and Forreston	115 00	60 00	
Rochelle	Rockford and return	80 00	60 00	
Sterling	Shabbona and Ottawa and return	105 00	60 00	
Fulton	Mendota and return	90 00	60 00	
Streator	L. V. & N. Jct. and return	80 00	55 00	
Rock Island	Savanna and return (day run)	90 00	50 00	
Galesburg	Rushville and return	100 00	57 00	
do	Peoria and Burlington and Rio	110 00	57 00	
do	Burlington via Galva	110 00	60 00	
Buda	Rushville and return	110 00	60 00	
Quincy	Burlington and return	95 00	60 00	
do	Hannibal	85 00	55 00	
(3 round trips per day.)				
St. Louis	Rock Island	115 00	60 00	......
Beardstown	Rock Island and return	90 00	55 00	......
Rock Island	Savanna and return (night run)	95 00	60 00	......
do	Sterling and return	80 00	60 00	......
Aurora	Streator and return	90 00	55 00	......
Chicago	Savanna, 47 and 48	115 00	......	......
do	Savanna, 49 and 50	105 00	......	......

NOTE.—Baggageman's pay includes amount paid by Express Company.

IOWA LINES.—PASSENGER RUNS.

RUNS.		Cond'ctors Rate per Month.	Baggem'n Rate per Month.	Brak'm er Rate per Month.
FROM	TO			
Burlington	Creston Through	$125 00	......	$50 00
do	do Local	115 00	$65 00	50 00
do	Pacific Junction	115 00	65 00	45 00
do	U. P. Transfer	......	65 00	......
Creston	do	115 00	55 00	50 00
do	St. Joseph joint run	100 00	60 00	50 00
do	*Cumberland and return	......	60 00	......
Albia	Des Moines and return	95 00	60 00	......
Chariton	St. Joseph	105 00	60 00	......
do	*Indianola and return	......	55 00	......
Bethany	St Joseph and return	90 00	50 00	......
Bethany Jct	*Grant City and return	......	50 00	......
Red Oak	Nebraska City and return	95 00	65 00	45 00
Sidney	*Carson and return	......	50 00	....

*Conductors' and Brakemen's pay is shown on way-freight schedule.
NOTE.—Baggagemen's pay includes amount paid by Express Company.

ILLINOIS LINES—Rates of Pay for Way-Freight Runs.

RUNS.		Conductors.	Brakemen.	REMARKS.
FROM	TO	Rate per Month.	Rate per Month.	
Chicago	Aurora and return through freight one way	$95 00	$62 50	Two crews
Aurora	Mendota and return	90 00	60 00	
Galesburg	Mendota	90 00	60 00	
do	Burlington and return	90 00	60 00	
do	Quincy	90 00	60 00	
do	Peoria and return	85 00	55 00	pool w'y frt l way
Buda	Rushville	75 00	50 00	
Galva	Burlington	80 00	55 00	
Burlington	Quincy	80 00	55 00	
Quincy	Louisiana and return	85 00	55 00	
Aurora	Streator	3¼c per mile	2¼c per mile	Actual mileage p'd with thro frts
do	Rockford	80 00	52 00	
do	Savanna	85 00	57 00	
Shabbona	Sterling and return	85 00	55 00	
Paw Paw	Streator and return	85 00	55 00	
Fulton	Mendota and } Pool, three crews Clinton } to run 4 trains	85 00	55 00	
do	Streator	85 00	55 00	
Beardstown	East St. Louis	95 00	65 00	Two crews
do	Monmouth	85 00	55 00	
Monmouth	Rock Island	80 00	52 00	
Rock Island	Sterling and return	85 00	55 00	
Aurora	Turner Junction and Geneva	80 00	50 00	Baggagman is also Brakeman
La Salle	I. V. & M. Junction and return	80 00	50 00	Includes LaSalle & intermediate switching

NOTE.—No overtime to be allowed until schedule time has been exceeded one hour.

IOWA LINES.—Rates of Pay for Way Freight Runs.

RUNS.		Conductors.	Brakemen	REMARKS.
FROM	TO	Rate per Month.	Rate per Month.	
Burlington	Ottumwa	$90 00	$60 00	
Ottumwa	Chariton and return	110 00	73 00	
Chariton	Creston and return	100 00	67 00	Way frt l way
do	St. Joseph	82 00	54 00	
do	Indianola and return	90 00	60 00	Two round trips, rear Brakeman
do	do do		45 00	One round trip, head Brakeman
Creston	Pacific Junction	90 00	60 00	
Albia	Des Moines	80 00	53 00	Way frt l way inclding Albia wrk, 3 crews
Grant City	Bethany Junction and return	80 00	52 00	Way frt, inclding work at termini
Creston	Cumberland and return	80 00	52 00	
do	St. Joseph joint run	88 00	56 00	
Villisca	Bigelow joint run	75 00	50 00	
Red Oak	Nebraska City and return	90 00	60 00	
Sidney	Carson and return	80 00	50 00	
Clarinda	Corning and return, joint run	75 00	50 00	
Red Oak	Griswold	70 00	45 00	Two round trips
Pacific Junction	Council Bluffs	75 00	50 00	2 round trips, pay swtchng rates pr hour for extra service
Villisca	Clarinda and return	75 00	50 00	Incldes all swching at Clarinda and Villisca
Regular Pushing Engines		70 00		Eligble to promotion if qualified

NOTE.—No overtime to be allowed unless schedule time is exceeded one hour.

CHICAGO, BURLINGTON & QUINCY RAILROAD.—RATES OF PAY FOR FREIGHT RUNS OTHER THAN WAY FREIGHTS.

Through freight runs between Chicago and Burlington and intermediate points will be paid at the rate of 2.8 cents per mile for Conductors and 1.9 cents per mile for Brakemen of the first class. Between Galesburg and Streator through, and between Galesburg and Ottumwa through, 2.9 cents per mile for Conductors and 1.95 cents per

BURLINGTON & MISSOURI RIVER RAILWAY IN NEBRASKA.

mile for Brakemen of the first class. Distance between Chicago and Galesburg to be counted 163 miles. On all other runs the pay will be 3 cents per mile for Conductors and 2 cents per mile for Brakemen of the first class. Conductors and Brakemen of the second class will receive 10 per cent. less than the above rates. The above rates apply to all runs except those specified on the way freight schedules.

NOTE.—The rates between Burlington and Chicago are based on the line being double-tracked all the way. The rates between Galesburg and Ottumwa and Galesburg and Streator, are based on the line being partly double-tracked.

Single or turn-around trips of 50 miles or less, when not over six hours is consumed in trip, to be counted as 50 miles, and the crew making such trip shall stand first out on arrival at terminal point. Single or turn around trips of over 50 miles and less than 100 miles, to be counted as 100 miles, provided no more mileage is made in same day. In case other mileage is made in same day and the aggregate is over 100 miles, actual mileage to be allowed. A day is the 24 hours from midnight to midnight; all trips to be credited to the day on which they begin. This Company reserves the right in case of increase in double track or terminal facilities, which enables crews to make better time over such divisions, to equalize the rate per mile accordingly.

ILLINOIS AND IOWA LINES.—PAY OF YARDMEN.

LOCATION.	Day F'remen	Night F'remen	Day Helpers	Night Helpers
Aurora	$65 00	$70 00	$60 00	$60 00
Mendota	65 00	67 00	50 00	55 00
Streator	65 00	70 00	55 00	60 00
Galesburg	65 00	70 00	55 00	60 00
Peoria	65 00		55 00	
Quincy	65 00	70 00	55 00	60 00
Beardstown	60 00	60 00	55 00	55 10
Rock Island	65 00	60 00	55 00	50 00
Burlington	65 00	70 00	55 00	60 00
Ottumwa	65 00	70 00	55 00	60 00
Chariton	65 00	70 00	55 00	60 00
Creston	65 00	70 00	55 00	60 00
Red Oak		70 00	55 00	60 00
Pacific Junction	65 00	70 00	55 00	60 00
Council Bluffs	65 00	70 00	55 00	60 00

Unless otherwise specified the calendar working days of 12 hours to constitute a month, overtime in proportion.

J. D. BESLER,
General Superintendent.
Approved W. F. MERRILL,
August 1, 1892. General Manager.

BURLINGTON & MISSOURI RIVER RAILROAD IN NEBRASKA.

GERERAL RULES GOVERNING TRAIN SERVICE.

1. Regular freight and passenger crews making extra trips will be paid on the basis of the rate fixed for the service performed. Crews running pay train, officers' specials or inspection trains, to be paid at the rate of 2½ cents per mile for Conductor and 1½ cents per mile for Brakeman, with a minimum of $3.00 per day for Conductor and $2.00 for Brakeman. If crews are laid up for a day they will be paid at the minimum rate given above. Living expenses of such crews will be borne by the Company, as heretofore.

2. Crews regularly assigned to construction trains. Conductors to receive $90 per month, Brakemen $60; 12 hours or less to constitute a day's work; calendar working days to be considered a month. Where Conductor acts as foreman $15 per month extra will be allowed. All time over 12 hours to be paid extra proportionately.

3. When other than construction trains are ordered to do construction train work, full time will be allowed at the rate of 30 cents per hour for Conductors, and 20 cents per hour for Brakemen.

4. Crews delayed one hour and thirty-five minutes in starting from or after arrival at terminals, will be paid at the rate of 30 cents per hour for Conductors and 20 cents per hour for Brakemen, for the full delay, less one hour. In case crews have been called and afterward are notified they are not wanted, the same rule will apply with a minimum of two and a half hours' pay, and the crew shall stand first out. On all runs of less than 100 miles requiring more than 10 hours, overtime will be paid if the hours used on the trip exceed 11 hours, in which case all overtime exceeding 10 hours will be paid. On all runs exceeding 100 miles, trainmen will be paid overtime for all time used to complete the trip in excess of a rate of speed of 10 miles per hour when over one (1) hour late.

5. Conductors will have the right to object to Brakemen for cause, and when objections are sustained by facts they will be furnished with other men.
6. It is the rule of the Company to run freight crews "first in first out." This rule, however, cannot be rigidly carried out at all times, and the proper officers of the Company will vary from the rule as circumstances require.
7. Trainmen dead-heading over the road on company business, on passenger trains, will be paid one-half rates. When dead-heading on freight trains, full rates will be allowed. When necessary to dead-head a crew, the first crew will be dead-headed and the second crew run the train. The crew dead-headed to stand ahead of the crew running the train on arrival at terminal point.
8. When light engines, or trains of other companies are run on main line and principal branches, a Conductor will be sent in charge, when practicable, who will act as pilot.
9. Should a train be compelled to double a hill, crews will be paid for one hour's time at the rate of 30 cents for Conductor and 20 cents for Brakemen.
10. The right to regular runs and to promotion will be governed by merit, ability and seniority. Everything being equal, the Conductor, Brakeman or Yardman longest in the service will have preference, the Superintendent to be the judge as to qualifications. Nothing in this rule shall be construed to mean that the Company will not employ men from other roads when, in the judgment of its officers, it is expedient to do so.
11. No employe will be suspended or discharged without just cause. In case of suspension or discharge of any employe, except for insubordination, or intoxication he may, if he desires, have a thorough investigation by the proper officers. Such desire shall be signified within five (5) days of the date of suspension or discharge, and the investigation shall be begun within ten (10) days from such notice, and proceed with as little interruption as may be until completed. The employe shall have full opportunity to present his case and to offer testimony. If the suspension or dismissal shall be found to have been without just cause, the employe shall be reinstated and paid full time for the period out of service.
12. When a Conductor is assigned to a regular passenger run he will not be used in freight or construction service unless in case of necessity.
13. When traffic becomes so light that reasonable monthly wages connot be made, the number of crews will be reduced. Other things being equal the youngest men will be laid off, the Superintendent to be judge as to qualifications. It is the intention to so apportion the crews that they may make approximately 2,600 miles per month.
14. When crews are required to do switching at terminal stations, they will be paid for such switching at the rate of 30 cents per hour for Conductors and 20 cents for Brakemen after the first thirty minutes, excepting when pay is arranged to include such switching.
15. Where callers are furnished by the Company, and men live within reasonable limits (to be fixed by the Trainmaster or Superintendent) crews will be called within a reasonable time of the departure of their trains, except in case of emergency. Such callers will be provided with a book in which shall be entered the leaving time of the trains. Men who are so called shall in each instance register their names with the time they are called. The above does not include men who are assigned to regular runs whose trains leave during the day-time.
16. If a trip report is incorrect, the trainmen will be notified in writing.
17. Trainmen attending court under instructions from the Company will be paid full rates for time lost, and living expenses if away from home; the Company to receive the witness fees.
18. In all the above rules where pay per hour or per day is mentioned; it refers to men of the first-class. A Conductor is of the first-class when he has served as such six months or over and a Brakeman is of the first-class when he has served as such three months or over. Men of the second-class to receive $2.70 and $1.80 per day, respectively, or 27 cents and 18 cents per hour, respectively.
19. Trainmen and Yardmen will not be required to pay fines on account of breakage.

RULES GOVERNING PAY OF TRAINMEN.

ART. 1. There will be two grades of freight Conductors established, and the compensation will be as follows: (a). For the first six months' service Conductors will be paid seventy dollars ($70.00) per month. (b). After six months' service as Conductor at seventy dollars ($70.00) per month Conductors will be paid seventy-eight dollars ($78.00) per month. (c). Pay for mixed train Conductors will be computed at freight rates.

ART. 2. (a). Should a freight Conductor, owing to light business, be reduced to a Brakeman, he will receive fifty-five dollars ($55.00) per month and excess mileage in proportion. (b). Passenger Conductors will be paid seventy-five dollars ($75.00) to one hundred and twenty-five dollars ($125.00) per month; the rates of pay to be governed by the run on which the service is rendered.

ART. 3. There will be two grades of freight Brakemen established, and the compensation will be as follows: (a). For the first three months' service Brakemen will be paid fifty dollars ($50.00) per month. (b). After three months' service as Brakeman at fifty dollars ($50.00) per month, Brakemen will be paid fifty-five dollars ($55.00) per month.

RULES FOR COMPUTATION.

ART. 4. (a). The monthly compensation for freight Conductors and Brakemen is to be based on a mileage of twenty-six hundred (2,600) miles per month; any excess over this mileage will be paid for proportionately. (b). Single or turn-around trips of fifty (50) miles or less, when not over six (6) hours is consumed in the trip, to be counted as fifty (50) miles, and the crew making such trip shall stand first out on arrival at terminal point. Single or turn-around trips of over fifty (50) miles, and less than one hundred (100) miles, to be counted as one hundred (100) miles, provided no more mileage is made in same day. In case other mileage is made same day, and the aggregate is over one hundred (100) miles, actual mileage to be allowed. A day is the twenty-four (24) hours from midnight to midnight. All trips to be credited to the day on which they begin. (c). Rule No. 4 of the General Rules Governing Train Service is inoperative on the Western Division because of the large through mileage made, except in extraordinary cases, when the Superintendent will use his discretion.

YARDMEN.

Yards to be first and second class. First-class yards to be paid for 12 hours: Day Foremen, $65.00; day Switchmen, $55.00; night Foremen. $70.00; night Switchmen, $60.00.

Second-class yards to be paid for 12 hours: Day Foremen, $60.00; day Switchmen, $50.00; night Foremen, $65.00; night Switchmen, $55.00.

List of first-class yards: Atchison, hired by the Hannibal; Kansas City rates 25 cents per hour. No change to be made. Denver, Switchmen, $67.50 for day men; $72.50 for night men. Lyons, Colorado, paid at Denver rates.

First-class yards to be paid as per Schedule: Omaha, Wymore, Red Cloud, Akron, Hastings, Newcastle, Nebraska City, Holdredge, McCook, South Omaha, Deadwood, Alliance, Oxford, Aurora, Lincoln, Ravenna.

Yards to be paid at second-class rates: Plattsmouth, Beatrice, Table Rock. A month to consist of twenty-six working days.

WAY FREIGHT AND BRANCH RUNS.

Kearney to Aurora and return—66 miles. On road 12 hours 35 minutes. Switch at Kearney and way; $85.00 rate. Conductor $111.82. Brakeman, $72.59.

Aurora to Arcadia—89 miles. 9 hours on road. Switches every other day at Arcadia. Allow 100 miles per day. Conductors $78.00. Brakeman $55.00.

Aurora to Burwell. 141 miles one day, 104 the next. Switches at Burwell every other day, at Ericson every other day. $85.00 and schedule; average time 12 hours. Conductors $103.09. Brakeman $67.09.

Arcadia to Burwell 123 miles; 11 hours. Switches at Palmer, Arcadia and Burwell. $80.00 rate and mileage. Conductor $98.40. Brakeman $67.64.

Ashland to Schuyler and return 98 miles; Switches Schuyler and Ashland. Allow 100 miles per day. Conductor $90.00. Brakemen $60.00. No allowance for switching.

Main line freights between Lincoln and Hastings—97 miles. Conductor $90.00. Brakeman $60.00, when run by two crews; when more crews are required they will be paid at the rate of $85.00 for Conductors and $55.00 for Brakemen, and be given other running at established rates.

Nebraska Railway, Aurora to Ravenna. Local run 100 miles round trip. $80.00 rate, with mileage. Conductor $97.00. Brakeman $55.00.

Orleans to St. Francis—134 miles. Conductor $104.52. Brakeman $73.69 at regular rates, and 9 to 10 hours on road. No allowance for switching at St. Francis or Orleans. Average 8½ hours on road.

Pool, two crews, Republican to Oberlin—78 miles. Conductor $78.00. Brakeman $55.00. 7 hours 15 minutes on road. Allow 100 miles per day. No allowance for switching.

McCook to Imperial, and switch at Imperial. 122 miles; 8½ hours; Conductor $95.16. Brakeman $67.08. No allowance for switching.

Lyons Branch. Pooled with Akron and Denver crews. Pay as per Schedule.

Wymore to Concordia. Pool with Wymore and Lincoln, and Wymore and Red Cloud; average 84 miles. Will pay regular rates and pay for switching at Concordia at rates as per rules.

Wymore to Edgar, Edgar to Lincoln, and Lincoln to Wymore. No extra mileage; 80 miles run each day; average 10 hours on road. Allow 100 miles per day, and switching at Edgar on train No. 100 in addition, about two hours.

Edgar to Holdrege. 81 miles; 6 hours 20 minutes schedule. Allow 100 miles per day and switching at Edgar in addition.
Chester to Fairmont and return. Distance 94 miles; consume about 10 hours per day. This is a light run. Allow 100 miles per day; no allowance for switching; crew are at home every night.
Edgar to Superior. Two round trips; total of 111 miles; one on freight, one on passenger; switches at Superior and Edgar. Will pay Schedule and allowance for switching; home every night.
Table Rock and Lincoln, mixed. 126 miles; home every day; night run; switches about 3 hours at Table Rock every night. Will pay Schedule; no allowance for switching.
Table Rock and Lincoln, way freight. Two assigned crews. Allow 100 miles per day, and allow for switching at Table Rock.
Deadwood and Edgemont. Distance 107 miles. Will pay at rate of 125 miles on account of mountain work.

NOTE—Where rates named in above special rules for way freight and branch runs are more than the $78.00 rate for Conductors, reference is made to full rate men.

T. E. CALVERT, General Superintendent.
Approved: G. W. HOLDREDGE, General Manager.

MISSOURI LINES.

HANNIBAL & ST. JOSEPH R. R., ST. LOUIS, KEOKUK & NORTHWESTERN R. R., KANSAS CITY, ST. JOSEPH & COUNCIL BLUFFS R. R., CHICAGO, BURLINGTON & KANSAS CITY R. R. GENERAL RULES GOVERNING TRAIN SERVICE.

1. Regular freight and passenger crews making extra trips will be paid on the basis of the rate fixed for the service performed. Crews running pay train, officers' specials or inspection trains, to be paid at the rate of 2¼ cents per mile for Conductor, and 1¼ cents per mile for Brakemen, with a minimum of $3.00 per day for Conductors, and $2.00 for Brakemen. If crews are laid up for a day they will be paid at the minimum rate given above. Living expenses of such crews will be borne by the Company, as heretofore.
2. Crews regularly assigned to construction trains, Conductors to receive $90.00 per month, Brakemen, $60.00; 12 hours or less to constitute a day's work; calendar working days to be considered a month. Where Conductor acts as Foreman $15 per month extra will be allowed. All time over 12 hours to be paid extra proportionately.
3. When other than construction trains are ordered to do construction train work, full time will be allowed at the rate of 30 cents per hour for Conductors, and 20 cents per hour for Brakemen.
4. Crews delayed one hour and thirty-five minutes in starting from or after arrival at terminals, will be paid at the rate of 30 cents per hour for Conductors, and 20 cents per hour for Brakemen, for the full delay, less one hour. In case crews have been called and afterward are notified they are not wanted, the same rule will apply with a minimum of two and a half hours' pay, and the crew shall stand first out. On all runs of less than 100 miles requiring more than 10 hours, overtime will be paid if the hours used on the trip exceed 11 hours, in which case all overtime exceeding 10 hours will be paid. On all runs exceeding 100 miles, trainmen will be paid overtime for all time used to complete the trip in excess of a rate of speed of 10 miles per hour when over one hour late.
5. Conductors will have the right to object to Brakemen for cause, and when objections are sustained by facts they will be furnished with other men.
6. It is the rule of the Company to run freight crews "first in, first out." This rule, however, cannot be rigidly carried out at all times, and the proper officers of the Company will vary from the rule as circumstances require.
7. Trainmen dead-heading over the road on Company business, on passenger trains, will be paid one-half rates. When dead-heading on freight trains, full rates will be allowed. When necessary to dead-head a crew, the first crew will be dead-headed and the second crew run the train. The crew dead-headed to stand ahead of the crew running the train on arrival at terminal point.
8. When light engines, or trains of other Companies are run on main line and principal branches, a Conductor will be sent in charge, when practicable, who will act as pilot.
9. Should a train be compelled to double a hill, crews will be paid for one hour's time at the rate of 30 cents for Conductors and 20 cents for Brakemen.
10. The right to regular runs and to promotion will be governed by merit, ability and seniority. Everything being equal, the Conductor, Brakeman or Yardman longest in the service will have preference, the Superintendent to be judge as to qualification.

Nothing in this rule shall be construed to mean that the Company will not employ men from other roads when, in the judgment of its officers, it is expedient to do so.

11. No employe will be suspended or discharged without just cause. In case of suspension or discharge of any employe, except for insubordination or intoxication, he may, if he desires, have a thorough investigation by the proper officers. Such desire shall be signified within five (5) days of the date of suspension or discharge, and the investigation shall be begun within ten (10) days from such notice, and proceed with as little interruption as may be until completed. The employe shall have full opportunity to present his case and to offer testimony. If the suspension or dismissal shall be found to have been without just cause, the employe shall be reinstated and paid full time for the period out of service.

12. When a Conductor is assigned to a regular passenger run he will not be used in freight or construction service unless in case of necessity.

13. When traffic becomes so light that reasonable monthly wages cannot be made, the number of crews will be reduced. Other things being equal the youngest men will be laid off, the Superintendent to be the judge as to qualifications. It is the intention to so apportion the crews that they may make approximately 2,600 miles per month.

14. When crews are required to do switching at terminal stations, they will be paid for such switching at the rate of 30 cents per hour for Conductors and 20 cents for Brakemen after the first thirty minutes, excepting when pay is arranged to include such switching.

15. Where Callers are furnished by the Company, and men live within reasonable limits (to be fixed by the Trainmaster or Superintendent) crews will be called within a reasonable time of the departure of their trains, except in case of emergency. Such Callers will be provided with a book in which shall be entered the leaving time of the trains. Men who are so called shall in each instance register their names with the time they are called. The above does not include men who are assigned to regular runs whose trains leave during the day time.

16. If a trip report is incorrect, the trainman will be notified in writing.

17. Trainmen attending court under instructions from the Company will be paid full rates for time lost, and living expenses if away from home; the Company to receive the witness fees.

18. In all the above rules where pay per hour or per day is mentioned, it refers to men of the first class. A Conductor is of the first class when he has served as such six months or over and a Brakeman is of the first class when he has served as such three months or over. Men of the second class to receive $2.70 and $1.80 per day, respectively, or 27 cents and 18 cents per hour, respectively.

19. Trainmen and Yardmen will not be required to pay fines on account of breakage.

MISSOURI LINES.—RATES OF PAY FOR PASSENGER SERVICE.

RUN.	ROAD.	MILES.	RATE.		
			Conduct'r	Brak'man	Bag'gemn
Quincy and Kansas City........	H. & St. J...............	6780	$125 00	$55 00	*$60 00
Brookfield and Quincy.........	H. & St. J...............	5408	115 00	50 00	Joint. 61 00
Brookfield and Kansas City....	H. & St. J...............	4792	115 00	50 00	Joint. 50 00
Cameron Junct. and Atchison..	H. & St. J...............	3360	90 00	50 00	Joint. 65 00
Hannibal and Palmyra Junct..	B. & St. J...............	1800	75 00	45 00	....
St. Louis and Kansas City......	H. & St.J.and St.L.K.& N.W.	73-0	125 00	55 00	Joint. *60 00
St. Louis and St. Joseph.......	H. & St.J.and St.L.K.& N.W.	6360	125 00	55 00	Joint. *60 00
Kansas City and Council Bluffs	K. C., St. J. & C. B........	4800	125 00	50 00	60 00
Kansas City and Omaha........	K. C., St. J. & C. B........	....	125 00	50 00	60 00
St. Joseph and Nebraska City..	K. C., St. J. & C. B........	4784	115 00	50 00	Joint. 60 00
Kansas City and St. Joseph....	K. C., St. J. & C. B........	3990	105 00	45 00	Joint. 60 00
St. Joseph and Creston.........	K. C., St. J. & C. B........	4160	100 00	50 00	60 00
Burlington and St. Louis.......	St. L., K. & N. W..........	6390	125 00	55 00	60 00
Burlington and Quincy.........	St. L., K. & N. W..........	4212	105 00	....	60 00
Kansas City and Lincoln.......	K. C., St. J. & C.B.and B.& M	5120	115 00	50 00	Joint.
Burlington and Carrollton.....	C. B. & K. C................	5790	115 00	....	60 00
Bigelow and Villisca...........	K.C.St.J.& C.B. and C B.& Q.	3588	90 00	45 00	Joint. 60 00
Corning and Clarinda	K.C.St.J.& C.B. and C.B. & Q	2392	75 00	45 00	Joint. 60 00

*Flagmen, $60.00.

MISSOURI LINES.—RATES OF PAY FOR FREIGHT SERVICE.

RUN.		ROAD.	MILES.	RATE. Conduct'r	Brak'man
rookfield and Kansas City	Way Freight.	H. & St. J..................	3172	$100 00	$67 50
ookfield and St. Joseph..	"	H. & St. J..................	2652	90 00	60 00
rookfield and Hannibal...	"	H. & St. J..................	2704	95 00	65 00
igelow and Villisca.......	"	K.C.,St.J.&C.B.and C.,B.&Q.	1790	75 00	50 00
reston and St. Joseph....	"	K.C.,St.J.&C.B.and C.,B.&Q.	2704	88 00	56 00
orning and Clarinda......	"	K.C.,St.J.&C.B.and C.,B.&Q.	....	75 00	50 00
annibal and St. Peters....	"	St. L., K. & N.-W............	2370	90 00	60 00
annibal and Burlington..	"	St. L., K. & N.-W............	3030	95 00	65 00
annibal and Quincy......	"	St. L., K. & N.-W............	2400	80 00	53 00
eokuk and Mt. Pleasant..	"	St. L., K. & N.-W............	3000	80 00	55 00
urlington and Moulton....	"	C. B. & K. C.................	2574	80 00	55 00
oulton and Laclede.......	"	C. B. & K. C.................	2132	80 00	55 00
aclede and Carrollton. ...	"	C. B. & K. C.................	2054	80 00	55 00

Through freight runs will be paid 3 cents per mile for Conductors, and 2 cents per
ile for Brakemen of the first class, and 2 7-10 cents per mile for Conductors, and
8-10 cents per mile for Brakemen of the second class.
  Single or turn-around trips of over fifty (50) miles and less than one hundred (100)
iles, to be counted as one hundred (100) miles, provided no more mileage is made the
ime day. In case other mileage is made same day, and the aggregate is over one
undred (100) miles, actual mileage to be allowed.
  No overtime to be allowed unless schedule time is exceeded one hour.
  On all lines except St. L., K. & N.-W. R. R. single or turn-around trips of fifty
0) miles or less, when not over six (6) hours is consumed in trip, to be counted as
fty (50) miles, and the crew making such trip shall stand first out on arrival at ter-
inal point.

MISSOURI LINES.—RATES OF PAY OF YARDMEN.

STATION.		ROAD.	RATE.
ansas City...............	Day Foreman..................	H.&St.J.and K.C.,St.J.&C.B.	$ 2 70 per day.
do	Day Switchmen............	"	2 50 per day.
do	Night Foreman.............	"	2 90 per day.
do	Night Switchmen..........	"	2 70 per day.
. Joseph.................	Day Foreman..................	"	2 70 per day.
do	Day Switchmen............	"	2 50 per day.
do	Night Forman..............	"	2 90 per day.
do	Night Switchmen..........	"	2 70 per day.
rookfield, Mo.............	Day Switchmen............	H. & St. J.	2 35 per day.
do	Night Switchmen..........	"	2 50 per day.
almyra Junction..........	Day Yardmaster.............	"	65 00 per month.
do	Night Yardmaster..........	"	60 00 per month.
imeron Junction..........	Day Yardmaster.............	"	65 00 per month.
do	Night Yardmaster..........	"	60 00 per month.
annibal, Mo...............	Day Foreman..................	S. L., K. & N.-W............	2 65 per day.
do	Day Switchman.............	"	2 40 per day.
do	Night Foreman.............	"	2 75 per day.
do	Night Switchman...........	"	2 50 per day.
eokuk.....................	Day Yardmaster.............	"	80 00 per month.
do	Night Yardmaster..........	"	70 00 per month.
do	Switchmen..................	"	55 00 per month.
ort Madison..............	Day Yardmaster.............	"	60 00 per month.
do	Switchmen..................	"	50 00 per month.
. Peters..................	Yardmaster...................	"	60 00 per month.
do	Switchmen..................	"	50 00 per month.
oulton, Mo...............	Yardmaster...................	C., B. & K. C.	55 00 per month.

  Monthly pay on basis of calendar month. Pay per day on basis of 12 hours. Pay per day on basis
 10 hours at Kansas City.
    Approved: S. E. CRANCE, General Superintendent.
       W. C. BROWN, General Manager.
    Accepted for the Order of Railway Conductors:
       E. O. WILLIAMS, Chairman General Grievance Committee, Chicago, Burling-
          ton & Quincy System.
    Accepted for the Brotherhood of Railroad Trainmen:
       W. A. WHEELING, Chairman General Grievance Committee, Chicago; Burling-
          ton & Quincy Rystem.
    August 1, 1892.

CHICAGO GREAT WESTERN RAILWAY COMPANY.

SCHEDULE OF WAGES PAID TO TRAINMEN.

Passenger Conductors, $100 per month; freight Conductors, 3 cents per mile; passenger Brakemen, $50 per month; freight Brakemen, 2 cents per mile; Baggagemen, $55 per month: Switchmen, $2.69 per day; Yard Foremen, $2.89 per day; Yardmasters, $100 to $125 per month. Twenty-six days constitute a month's work.

May 12, 1892.

JNO. M. EGAN, General Manager.

CHICAGO, MILWAUKEE & ST. PAUL RAILWAY.—PASSENGER TRAINMEN.

Conductors on Passenger Trains: Long runs, $125 for 26 days; $3.84 per day; overtime Short runs, $90 for 26 days; $3.20 per day; overtime.
Baggagemen: Long runs, $60 for 26 days; overtime at same rate. Short runs, $50 for 26 days; overtime at same rate.
Brakemen: Forty-five dollars for 26 days, all runs; overtime at same rate.

YARDMEN	Day Ydm'st r	Ass st'nt Day Ydm'st r	Night Ydm'st r	Assist'nt Night Ydm'st r	Day Foremn	Day Helpers	Night Foremn	Night Hlpers
POINTS PAYING CHICAGO SCALE								
Western Avenue	$125 00*	$115 00*	$125 00*	$115 00*	$70 00§	$65 00§	$75 00§	$70 00§
Savanna	115 00*	75 00§			70 00§	65 00§	75 00§	70 00§
Kansas City	125 00*				70 00§	65 00§	75 00§	70 00§
Milwaukee	{ 100 00* / 125 00*	100 00*	{ 110 00* / 100 00*	100 00*	70 00§	65 00§	75 00§	70 00§
North Milwaukee	100 00*				70 00§	65 00§	90 00*	70 00*
Minneapolis	125 00*	{ 100 00* / 95 00*	110 00*	95 00*	70 00§	65 00§	75 00§	70 00§
St. Paul	100 00*		95 00*		70 00§	65 00§	75 00§	70 00§
OTHER YARDS.								
Council Bluffs	100 00*		85 00*		65 00§	60 00§		65 00§
Sioux City	100 00*				65 00§	60 00§	70 00§	85 00§
Portage	100 00*		90 00*		65 00§	60 00§	70 00§	65 00§
LaCrosse	125 00*		100 00*		65 00§	60 00§	70 00§	65 00§
Madison	83 33*				65 00§	60 00§	70 00§	65 00§
Janesville	70 00*					60 00§	70 00§	65 00§
Green Bay	100 00*		75 00*		65 00§	60 00§	70 00§	65 00§
Iron Mountain	70 00§		65 00§		65 00§	55 00§		65 00§
Dubuque	85 00*				65 00§	60 00§	70 00§	65 0
Mason City	85 00*				65 00§	55 00§	70 00§	55 00§

*Per calendar month. §Per month of 26 days.

WORK AND FREIGHT TRAIN SERVICE.

ARTICLE 1. The wages of men employed on work trains will be $3.20 per day for Conductors, and $2.10 per day for Brakemen. Way freight Conductors and Brakemen will receive $3.00 and $2.00 per 100 miles, respectively. Through freight Conductors and Brakemen will receive $2.90 and $1.95 per 100 miles, respectively. Brakemen entering the service will receive $1.73 per day for the first three consecutive months' work, after which they shall receive full rate.

ART. 2. On work trains twelve hours or less shall constitute a day. If mileage exceeds 100 miles, actual mileage will be allowed at work train rates. Ten hours or less, when less time is required to make 100 miles, on freight trains, will constitute one day. On all runs ranging from 90 to 100 miles a full day will be allowed; on runs of less than 90 miles a full day will be allowed, provided no other mileage is made the same day; if other mileage is made, then actual mileage will be allowed. On the Chicago & Milwaukee division once over the road will constitute a day. One hundred and fifty miles will be allowed between La Crosse and Minneapolis. On branch lines where the regular run is less than 100 miles, overtime will be allowed when more than 10 hours are consumed in making the run and doing the necessary switching, at the rates in existence prior to December 28, 1890.

ART. 3. Overtime shall be computed on a basis of 10 miles per hour. In computing overtime, no fraction of an hour less than 30 minutes shall be counted; fractions of an hour over 30 minutes shall be counted one hour.

ART. 4. The time of extra trains shall be computed on the same basis as schedule trains. All allowances made to trainmen on through freight trains shall be made to trainmen on extra freight trains.

ART. 5. When men are held for snow plow service they shall be paid full time. In all cases where men are working in the snow and trying to open the road, they shall be paid hour for hour, so long as they are in that service, at through freight train rates. When men are away from home over one day at a time, owing to snow blockades, one-half time shall be allowed; men to remain subject to call. Time to begin after one day has expired.

ART. 6. Trainmen dead-heading over the road on Company's business on passenger trains, to be paid half mileage. When dead-heading on freight trains full mileage will be allowed. When attending law suits, full time will be allowed and expenses paid for every day off.

ART. 7. When trainmen are required to switch at terminal stations over one hour where switch engines are regularly employed, they shall receive compensation for such service at road rates, viz.: 10 miles per hour, no allowance to be made for less than one hour. At terminals where switch engines are not regularly employed, no time will be allowed for switching, unless the time consumed in doing the necessary switching and making a run of 100 miles, exceeds 10 hours. All time in excess of 10 hours, in such cases, will be paid for at road rates, viz.: 10 miles per hour.

ART. 8. At terminal or division stations where callers are employed, they shall call trainmen as near as practicable one hour before leaving time of trains, provided they live within one mile from the place where they take charge of trains. The caller's book shall state the leaving time of trains and the men who are called shall, in each instance, register their names together with the time at which they are called. In computing overtime, time of men shall begin at time specified in the caller's book for the train to leave.

ART. 9. In cases where trains are abandoned, trainmen having been called, they shall be paid for all time on duty until released, but in no case for less than 25 miles.

ART. 10. As a rule freight trainmen shall run on the freight division to which they are assigned. Crews not assigned to regular runs shall run first in, first out.

ART. 11. Freight train crews called to make a single run over their respective freight divisions with passenger trains or passenger equipment, shall receive full freight train rates therefor.

ART. 12. As near as practicable the number of crews in freight service, on all divisions, shall be kept down to correspond with the volume of business, so that they may make not less than 2,600 miles per month.

ART. 13. Promotions will be based upon the faithful discharge of duties, capacity for increased responsibility and fitness for the position, to be determined by the Superintendent. As a rule, promotions to freight Conductors are to be made from freight Brakemen and passenger Conductors from freight Conductors. The Company at all times reserves the right to hire experienced men outside of its own employes or to transfer men from one division to another whenever the business of the Company may require it. In case a trainman is transferred from one division to another, the same standing on the first division shall be maintained upon his return.

ART. 14. Actual mileage shall be allowed for doubling hills, provided trains are thereby delayed over 10 hours in making a run of 100 miles. No allowance will be made for doubling hills, as above, on runs of 90 miles or less.

ART. 15. Train crews shall not be required to repair disabled cars left at stations by other trains. When practicable to do so, without detriment to the Company's business, carsmiths shall be sent to make necessary repairs. Cars disabled in trains shall be repaired or chained up by the train crew and taken through to destination or division station, when possible and safe to do so, and it can be done without unreasonable delay to trains.

Passenger Train Service: ART. 16. No change shall be made in compensation of passenger train men. They shall be paid at the same rate and on the same basis as heretofore.

General Regulations: ART. 17. Conductors shall have full and entire control of Brakemen on their trains, and of the placing of them, and shall not be required to take out a Brakeman whom they know to be incompetent.

ART. 18. Trainmen shall rank from the day they are employed, and in the event of a surplus of men the oldest in the service on their respective divisions shall have the preference of employment; character, ability and merit being equal.

ART. 19. No trainman shall be suspended or discharged without just cause. In case of suspension or dismissal, if he thinks his sentence unjust, his case shall have a thorough investigation by the proper officers, at which he may be present if he so desires. Such investigation shall be made as soon as possible, and if found unjustly suspended or discharged he shall be reinstated and paid full time while so out of service.

ART. 20. When trainmen have been in continuous service so long as to require rest, they shall not be required to go out until sufficient time has been allowed them to recuperate; men to be the judges of their own physical condition.

ART. 21. When time is not allowed as per Conductor's daily time slip, it shall be returned at once with the reason for not allowing the time.

ART. 22. Any trainman suspended or dismissed shall have the privilege of appeal to the Superintendent. If he fails to adjust the case, appeal can then be made to the

Assistant General Superintendent, General Superintendent and General Manager, in regular order.

ART. 23. All subordinate officers and Conductors shall be provided with copies of the foregoing schedule, and copies shall be kept at all terminal and division stations, easily accessible to trainmen.

ART. 24. All schedules, rules and regulations in conflict with these, now adopted, are void.

W. G. COLLINS, General Superintendent.
May 9, 1892.   Approved: A. J. EARLING, General Manager.

CHICAGO, ROCK ISLAND & PACIFIC RAILWAY.

RULES RELATING TO CONDUCTORS.

ARTICLE 1. The occupation of a Conductor is one that requires a knowledge of the schedules of time governing the road on which he is employed, as well as those issued by connecting lines; a proper interpretation of the rules issued therewith, and under which trains, both passenger and freight, are operated. This, with proper experience, good judgment, considerable ability, and service previously rendered by the occupant of such a position (in the railway service), together with the required character and ability of the person himself, dignifies such occupation as a distinct profession.

ART. 2. Persons hereafter appointed Conductors should be men of undoubted reputation, good morals, temperate habits, and with an experience in train service on any line of road of not less than three years. It is believed that the Order of Railway Conductors is largely composed of men furnishing the necessary qualifications, and, so far as it can be done consistently, such persons should have preference in the filling of vacancies, when it can be done with proper regard for efficiency in the service, which necessitates at times promotions from the ranks.

ART. 3. Seniority in service as Conductor shall hereafter govern in all cases of promotion from freight to passenger runs, merit being equal, this to be determined by the Superintendent, subject to appeal to the General Superintendent, it being understood that the rule to be generally pursued does not permit of transferring an employe from one division to another, to the detriment of division employes. The future choice of runs shall be based upon this principle.

ART. 4. No Conductor shall be dismissed or suspended from the service of the Company without just cause. In case a Conductor believes his discharge or suspension to have been unjust, he shall make a written statement of the facts in the premises, and submit it to his Superintendent, and at the same time designate any other Conductor, who may be in the employ of the Company at the time on the same division, and the Superintendent, together with the Conductor last referred to, shall, in conjunction with the General Superintendent or some other superior officer agreed upon by them, investigate the case in question, and when at all practicable such investigation shall be made within five days from the date of the receipt of the communication from the Conductor, and in case the aforesaid discharge or suspension be decided to have been unjust, he shall be reinstated and paid half time for all time lost on said account.

ART. 5. When Conductors are laid off on account of dullness in business, it shall be done in the order of the dates of their employment as Conductor, beginning with the Conductor last employed.

ART. 6. Conductors having charge of trains will be held responsible for their safe management, and shall have a right to place their Brakemen as their best judgment may dictate, so long as it does not conflict with time-table rules.

ART. 7. Time of Conductors in freight and passenger service shall be computed on the basis of 100 miles or less for a day's work, and all time made by Conductors while on the road between terminal points in excess of 10 miles per hour, on freight, and eight hours per 100 miles, on passenger, will be considered overtime.

ART. 8. When Conductors are held in for snow plow service they will be allowed regular pay for each day of 24 hours that they are so held subject to orders, on the basis of 10 miles per hour.

ART. 9. When good cause can be shown for doubling hills, the pay shall be on the basis of the actual time lost, at 10 miles per hour, and all time spent in wrecking, repairing washouts or bucking snow, shall be paid for on same basis. Conductors deadheading on Company's business will be paid half mileage.

ART. 10. Delayed time at terminal stations, either before leaving or after arriving, will be paid for full delay, less one hour, if delayed one hour and 35 minutes. It is understood that fractions of an hour less than 35 minutes will not be counted. Thirty-five minutes or over will be counted a full hour. In freight service, 50 miles or less shall constitute 50 miles, or one-half day's pay. One hundred miles, or over 50 miles, shall constitute 100 miles, or one day's pay.

ART. 11. A caller shall be provided at the end of each main division, who shall have a register book' and have written therein the train the men are called for, the time of calling and their names. The pay of the Conductor shall begin from the time the train is ordered for, as shown on the order for calling, and shall continue to the time of arrival at the end of the run. When Conductors are required to switch at terminals 35 minutes or more, time shall be allowed.

ART. 12. Conductors called to make a trip shall be paid, provided the train is afterward annulled, for three hours time, on the basis of the of the pay they are receiving.

ART. 13. The following rates of pay will be allowed passenger and freight Conductors, both east and west of the Missouri river: Freight Conductors, local, 3 cents per mile, overtime, 30 cents per hour; through, 2.9 cents per mile, overtime, 29 cents per hour. Passsenger Conductors, through express runs, $125 per month, on a basis of from 4,000 to 6,510 miles per month; main line, local and dummy runs, $100 per month, on a basis of from 2,600 to 4,000 miles per month; short and branch trains, passenger or mixed, $75 per month, on a basis of 2,600 miles or less per month. Work train Conductors, 12 hours and over eight, one day; $90 per month; overtime, 30 cents per hour. Conductors of passenger trains must make during a month the minimum mileage established, else they will drop back to the pay established for Conductors making an equal mileage. Extra mileage over the maximums here established for passenger Conductors will be paid for at proportionate rates. When practicable there shall be no greater number of through freight crews employed on any division than can reasonably be expected to make 3,000 miles per month east of the Missouri river, or 2,600 miles, west of the Missouri river.

ART. 14. Promotions and preferment will be based upon merit and the general record of the men, and not entirely upon their ages or duration of service; economy in the running of his train, and care for the Company's property while under his control, will always be considered as meriting reward.

The articles enumerated above constitute, in their entirety, the agreement between this Company and its Conductors, and all rules previously in effect are by this agreement abolished.

The following constructions are agreed to:

ART. 3. Passenger Conductors should be promoted from freight Conductors, governed by seniority in Company's service, if they are in all ways qualified to handle and care for the traveling public. If not so qualified the reason shall be made known to them by their Superintendent.

ART. 4. It is not only expected, but desired on the part of the Company, that the Conductor who seeks a reinvestigation shall be present at such reinvestigation, together with his representative and Division Superintendent or other designated officer.

In cases where road engines and crews are sent from a division station to a given point on the road to do switching service for a quarter to one-half day or more, in place of the switch engine and crew, actual mileage should be allowed for as per Article 10, and switching time allowed for actual time consumed in switching on the basis of 10 miles per hour. However, where only the ordinary switching is done at any station by the road crew, the overtime rule on the basis of 10 miles per hour between termini should govern.

In the case of Conductor Donahue, train 99, Rock Island to West Liberty, Article 10 covers this point and allows but 100 miles, or 50 miles on the trip from Rock Island to West Liberty and 50 miles from West Liberty to Rock Island. However, in case overtime rule mentioned is accepted, overtime begins after having been out from Rock Island 10 hours, unless the crew is relieved at West Liberty by order of the Superintendent or Trainmaster.

ART. 11. A caller should be provided at Trenton and Brooklyn, with a register book showing the train men are called for, the time they are ordered to leave, and the time of calling, followed by Conductor's signature; and the pay of the Conductor so called should begin from the time the train is due to or ordered to leave. Local freight trains are such trains as handle merchandise peddling freight. Regular passenger Conductors called or required to do extra running, or sent in runs outside of their regular runs, should be allowed extra time at the regular rate as allowed the extra runs which they are required to make. Passenger Conductors laying off, not having made the required maximum mileage for the month, will lose such time.

On trains 7 and 8 between Washington and Chicago if over 4,000 miles are made in any month the extra time should be allowed at proportionate rates.

In the two cases cited by Mr Glaspell, first case leaving Trenton at 7:25 A. M., arriving at St. Joe at 12:45 P. M., leaving St. Joe at 6 P. M. to go to Horton, actual mileage, or 123 miles for that day should be allowed; on the other hand, in the second case leaving Trenton at 11 A. M., arriving at St. Joe at 5 P. M., leaving St. Joe at 2 A. M. for Horton. 100 miles should be allowed Trenton to St. Joe for first day's work, provided no other mileage is made, and 50 miles should be allowed for the second day's work, for the run from St. Joe to Horton, provided no other mileage is made on that day. In other words, the time is computed by the day or by trains starting from different termini during the hours between midnight and midnight.

In the case of Conductor Bledsoe, who claims to have been delayed two hours after time ordered to leave Brooklyn, one hour overtime should be allowed, although, in the case cited on June 10, when he claimed one hour overtime on account of being on the road 11 hours and 40 minutes, schedule has not provided for such overtime.

ART. 13. In the matter of branch runs, passenger or mixed, all mileage over 2,600 miles per month will be extra, and at proportionate rate of pay. Branch crews making extra trips on main line will be entitled to actual mileage so made at the rate governing such service. Extra trips made on the branch, as also switching necessary to be done at terminal yards, when performed within the schedule hours of the day's service, are not entitled to extra pay, but when performed outside of such schedule hours, are entitled to extra pay at proportionate rates, for branch service.

RULES RELATING TO BRAKEMEN.

The articles enumerated below constitute, in their entirety, the agreement between this Company and its freight and passenger Brakemen, and all rules previously in effect are by this agreement abolished.

ARTICLE 1. Seniority in service as Brakemen shall hereafter govern in all cases of promotion from Brakeman to Conductor, merit being equal. This to be determined by the Trainmaster, subject to an appeal to the Division Superintendent, it being understood that the rule to be generally pursued does not permit of transferring an employe from one division to another to the detriment of the division employe. The future choice of runs shall be based upon this principle.

ART. 2. No Brakeman shall be dismissed or suspended from the service of the Company without just cause. In case a Brakeman believes his discharge or suspension to have been unjust, he shall make written statement of the facts in the premises and submit it to the Trainmaster, and at the same time designate any other Brakeman who may be in the employ of the Company at the time on the same division, and the Trainmaster, together with the Brakeman last referred to shall, in conjunction with the Division Superintendent, or some other superior officer, investigate the case in question, and when at all practicable, such investigation shall be made within five days from the date of the receipt of the communication from the Brakeman, and in case the aforesaid discharge or suspension is decided to have been unjust, he shall be reinstated, and paid half time for all time lost on said account.

ART. 3. When necessary to lay off Brakemen on account of surplus of crews, it shall be done in the order of the dates of their employment as Brakemen, beginning with the Brakeman last employed.

ART. 4. When Brakemen are held in for snow-plow service, they will be allowed the regular rates they are receiving for each day of twenty-four hours that they are so held subject to orders, and on the basis of ten hours and ten miles per hour. When Brakemen are required by the Company to attend court, they shall be paid at the rate they are receiving, and on the basis of ten hours at ten miles per hour, and expenses, for each day of twenty-four hours during such attendance, and for actual time consumed in going to and coming from court.

ART. 5. When good cause can be shown for doubling hills, the pay shall be on the basis of actual time lost, at ten miles per hour, and all time spent in wrecking, repairing washouts or bucking snow, shall be paid for on same basis. Brakemen dead-heading on Company's business will be paid one-half mileage.

ART. 6. Delayed time at terminal stations, either before leaving or after arriving, will be paid for full delay less one hour if delayed one hour and thirty-five minutes: It is understood that fractions of an hour less than thirty-five minutes will not be counted. Thirty-five minutes or over will be counted a full hour. In freight service fifty miles or less shall constitute fifty miles or one-half day's pay. One hundred miles or over fifty miles, shall constitute one hundred miles or one day's pay.

ART. 7. A Caller shall be provided at the end of each main division, who shall have a registered book and have written therein the train the men are called for, the time of calling and their names. As near as practicable the men shall be called one hour before leaving time. The pay of the Brakemen shall begin from the time the train is ordered for, as shown on the order for calling, and shall continue to the time of arrival at the end of the run. When Brakemen are required to switch at terminals thirty-five minutes or more, time shall be allowed.

ART. 8. Brakemen called to make a trip shall be paid, provided the train is afterwards annulled, for three hours' time, on the basis of the pay they are receiving.

ART. 9. Fines shall not be assessed against Brakemen for injury to any of the train appliances furnished by the Company, when it can be shown that they were in no wise at fault in connection therewith.

ART. 10. The following rates of pay will be allowed passenger and freight Brakemen, both east and west of the Missouri river:

Freight Brakemen: Local, 2 cents per mile; overtime, 20 cents per hour. Through, 1.93 cents per mile; overtime, 19 cents per hour.

Passenger Brakemen: Through express runs, $55.00 per month, basis of 4,000 to 6,510 miles per month. Main line, local and dummy runs, $50.00 per month, basis of 2,600 to 4,000 miles per month. Short and branch trains, passenger or mixed, $40.00 per month, basis of 2,600 miles or less per month.

Work Train Brakemen: Twelve (12) hours and over eight (8), one day; $50.00 per month. Overtime at proportionate rates.

Brakemen of passenger trains must make during a month the minimum of mileage established, else they will drop back to the pay established for Brakemen making an equal mileage. Extra mileage over the maximums here established for passenger Brakemen will be paid for at proportionate rates.

RULES RELATING TO ENGINEERS.

ARTICLE 1. Engineers dead-heading on Company's business will be paid half mileage. When required by this Company to attend court, they shall be paid at the rate of $3.70 per day of twenty-four hours, and their expenses during attendance, and for all time lost while waiting the Company's orders, and for such time as they may lose while waiting to take their runs, and for all services not otherwise provided for in this schedule.

ART. 2. When Engineers are held in for snow plow service, they will be allowed regular pay for each day of 24 hours that they are so held subject to orders. In case a regular Engineer's engine is assigned, in reserve, to snow plow service, the Engineer shall be provided with another engine. When good cause can be shown for doubling hills, the pay shall be on the basis of the actual time lost. Freight Engineers doubleheading on passenger trains will receive passenger Engineers' pay for the same.

ART. 3. Engineers shall not be required to perform the duties of conductors, except in emergencies; and in case of running light engines, a Flagman shall, when practicable, be sent with them.

ART. 4. Engineers shall not be required to pack driving cellars, engine or tender trucks, valve-stems, or pistons, where facilities exist for such service by shop force.

ART. 5. No Engineer shall be required to continue on duty when he reasonably needs rest, but in extreme cases the Engineers on their part will tender every means in their power to assist the Company.

ART. 6. Seniority in the Company's service, as locomotive Engineers, shall govern in all cases, merit being equal; this to be determined by the Assistant Superintendent of Motive Power and Equipment or the Division Master Mechanic, subject to appeal to the Superintendent of Motive Power and Equipment, and the choice of runs and engines shall be based upon this principle, it being understood that the choice of engines shall not apply to engines of the same class. When a deficiency of Engineers in road service exists, Engineers in yard service will be considered in the line of promotion to road service Engineers. When an Engineer's engine assigned to regular runs is held in for repairs, the Engineer shall be permitted to keep up his mileage by taking his run in turn on the engines assigned to these runs. Engineers on runs that pay $105.00 or less per month shall be furnished with engines to keep up runs. In case of a surplus of Engineers, the younger in the service shall be taken off and shall do extra work, or firing. A surplus shall not be considered as existing while Freight Engineers are making 2,600 miles per month.

ART. 7. No Engineer shall be dismissed or suspended from the service of the Company without just cause, and should the Engineer be unable to plead his own case at the investigation (which shall be heard within five days from the date of such suspension or dismissal, if possible for the Superintendent to be present during that period, and if not, at such early date as he may decide upon, when all interested can be present, and which shall be held before the Superintendent or Assistant Superintendent and the Assistant Superintendent of Motive Power and Equipment, or the Division Master Mechanic, when both departments are interested), he shall be permitted to call upon some other Engineer in the service of the Company, and on the same division, who shall be permitted to plead his case for him; and in case an Engineer believes his discharge or suspension unjust, he shall make written statement of the facts in the premises, within ten days from the date of such suspension, or dismissal, and submit it to the Assistant Superintendent of Motive Power and Equipment or the Division Master Mechanic, and the Superintendent, in conjunction with the Assistant Superintendent of Motive Power and Equipment, or the Division Master Mechanic, together with the Engineer dismissed, or suspended, or his representative, shall investigate the case in question, and if their decision is not satisfactory, such Engineer shall have the right of further appeal to the next higher officer in rank, and from him in proper order to the General Manager; and when at all practicable such investigation shall be made within five days of the date of the receipt of the communication from the Engineer; and in case the aforesaid discharge or suspension is decided to have been unjust, he shall be reinstated and paid half time for all the time lost. Any grievance that may arise on the part of Engineers shall be presented in writing to the proper officer of the Company by the party aggrieved within sixty days of its occurrence. No attention shall be paid to grievances unless presented in writing within the time specified above.

ART. 8. Time of Engineers in freight and passenger service shall be computed on the basis of one hundred miles or less for a day's work; and all time made by Engineers while on the road between terminal points, in excess of ten miles per hour on freight, and eight hours per hundred miles on passenger, will be considered overtime.

ART. 9. Delayed time at terminal stations before leaving will be paid for full delay if delayed one hour; if delayed thirty minutes at terminal stations after arriving, one hour's time will be allowed. In computing delayed time before leaving, it is understood that one full hour must be consumed before time will be allowed. If one hour and thirty minutes, two hours' time will be allowed, and so on. After arriving at terminal station one hour will be allowed after thirty minutes' delay, two hours after one hour and thirty minutes' delay, and so on. All construction service performed by road Engineers not regularly assigned to construction, at terminal points, will be paid for at the regular rates. If more than five hours are consumed in this service, the Engineer will not be considered first out in any class of service except construction. Road Engineers required to do construction work between terminals will be paid actual mileage for miles run on freight or passenger, and construction pay for such construction service at the established rate for fractions of a day on construction.

ART. 10. A Caller shall be furnished at the end of each main division, who shall have a register book, and have written therein the train and time the men are called for, the time of calling, and their names, which shall be signed by the Engineer when called. Engineers called to make a trip shall be paid for three hours' time on the basis of the regular rates which they are receiving, provided the train is afterwards annulled and Engineer released, and shall occupy the same position they did before being ordered out. The time of the Engineer shall begin from the time the train is ordered for, as shown on the order for calling, and shall continue to the time he gives up his engine to the hostler at the end of the run. When road Engineers are required to switch at terminals thirty-five minutes or more, time shall be allowed.

ART. 11. When not otherwise required by the Company's necessities, all freight Engineers shall run first in and first out (except those assigned to regular runs) from all terminals and relay stations on their respective districts. All Engineers running on the extra list shall register on their arrival, in a book provided for that purpose, and be called in rotation when the services of an extra man may be required, and shall remain with engine called for until the regular Engineer returns.

ART. 12. Engineers will have rights on their respective divisions as they are now divided.

ART. 13. There shall be one Engineer hired for each Fireman promoted.

ART. 14 The following rates of pay will be allowed to Engineers for the service and class specified:

Freight and Construction Service: First class, 4 cents; second class, 3¼ cents; third class, 3 cents. The term of service between the classes to be nine months each.

Passenger Service: All runs, 3½ cents.

Switching Service: $2.70 per day.

In switching service ten working hours shall constitute a day's work. Five hours or less, half a day; over five hours, full day. In construction service twelve working hours or less shall constitute a day's work.

ART. 15. Overtime will be allowed on switching at the rate of 27 cents per hour, and in all other service at the rate of 37 cents per hour, irrespective of classification.

ART. 16. No fines shall be assessed against Engineers.

Promotions and preferments will be based upon merit and the general record of the men, and not entirely upon their ages or duration of service. Evidence of the willingness of an Engineer to serve the best interests of the Company at all times, in whatever capacity assigned, as well as economy in the running of his engine, and care for the Company's property while under his control, will always be considered as meriting reward. The articles enumerated above constitute, in their entirety, the agreement between this Company and its locomotive Engineers, and all rules previously in effect are by this agreement abolished.

RULES RELATING TO FIREMEN.

ART. 1. No Fireman shall be dismissed or suspended from the service of the Company without just cause. In case a Fireman believes his discharge or suspension to have been unjust, he shall make a written statement of the facts in the premises and submit it to his Master Mechanic; and at the same time designate any other Fireman who may be in the employ of the Company at the time on the same division, and the Master Mechanic, together with the Fireman last referred to, shall, in conjunction with the Superintendent or some other superior officer, investigate the case in question, and when at all practicable such investigation shall be made within five days from the date of the receipt of the communication from the Fireman, and in case the aforesaid discharge or suspension is decided to have been unjust, he shall be reinstated and paid half time for all the time lost on said account. The right of appeal in proper order from local to general officers is always conceded and to all organizations.

ART. 2. When not otherwise required by the Company's necessities, all freight Firemen shall run first in and first out (except those assigned to regular runs), from all terminals and relay stations on their respective districts. All Firemen running on the extra list shall register on their arrival, in a book provided for that purpose, and be called in rotation when the services of an extra man may be required, and shall remain with engine called for until the regular Fireman returns.

ART. 3. Firemen called to make a trip shall be paid, provided the train is afterwards annulled, for three hours' time, on the basis of the regular rates which they are receiving, and shall stand first out as per Article 2.

ART. 4. Firemen will have rights on their respective divisions as they are now divided.

ART. 5. Firemen shall not be required to clean fires, ash pans, or front ends of their engines at terminals of their respective runs, or at points where there is a round house, providing that the runs of the engine to be cleaned cover a mileage of not less than 150 miles.

ART. 6. No Fireman shall be required to continue on duty when he reasonably needs rest, but in extreme cases the Firemen on their part shall tender every means in their power to assist the Company.

ART. 7. Coal for engines on through express or fast passenger trains shall be broken suitable for furnace use, and for other passenger or freight trains shall be broken so that no lump shall exceed eight inches in length or thickness before delivery on engine tank.

ART. 8. The rights and preferences to runs, engines and promotions shall be governed by seniority, merit being equal; this to be determined by the Master Mechanic (subject to appeal to the General Master Mechanic), and the choice of runs and engines shall be based upon this principle, it being understood that the choice of engines shall not apply to engines of the same class. The same rule will apply to Firemen in yard service. When consistent to do so, and a deficiency of Firemen in road service exists, Firemen in yard service will be considered in the line of promotion to road service Firemen. When a Fireman's engine goes in the shop for general repairs, the Fireman will be considered an extra man, and assigned to such service as the Master Mechanic may determine. In case of a surplus of Firemen, the younger in the service shall be taken off and shall do extra work, or firing. A surplus shall not be considered as existing while Firemen are making 2,600 miles per month.

ART. 9. All charges or reports made against Firemen shall be made in writing, and such charges shall be subject to the inspection of the party against whom they are made.

ART. 10. Time of Firemen in freight and passenger service shall be computed on the basis of 100 miles or less for a day's work; and all time made by Firemen while on the road between terminal points, in excess of ten miles per hour on freight, and eight hours per 100 miles on passenger, will be considered overtime.

ART. 11. When Firemen are held in for snow plow service, they will be allowed regular pay for each day of twenty-four hours that they are so held subject to orders. When good cause can be shown for doubling hills, the pay shall be on the basis of the actual time lost. Freight Firemen, double-heading on passenger trains, will receive passenger Firemen's pay for the same.

ART. 12. Firemen dead-heading on Company's business will be paid half mileage, and when required by this Company to attend court, they shall be paid at the rate they are receiving and expenses, during attendance, and for actual time consumed in going to and coming from court.

ART. 13. Delayed time at terminal stations, either before leaving or after arriving, will be paid for full delay less one hour, if delayed one hour and thirty-five minutes. It is understood that fractions of an hour less than thirty-five minutes will not be counted. Thirty-five minutes or over will be counted a full hour. It is further understood that the Company will furnish blank forms for engineers to fill out for all delayed time between terminals and at terminals before departing and after arriving, which shall be verified by the train sheet and certified to by the Division Superintendent.

ART. 14. A Caller shall be provided at the end of each main division, who shall have a register book, and have written therein the train the men are called for, the time of calling, and their names. The pay of the Firemen shall begin from the time the train is ordered for, as shown on the order for calling, and shall continue to the time he gives up his engine to the hostler at the end of the run. When road engines are required to switch at terminals thirty-five minutes or more, time shall be allowed the Fireman.

ART. 15. Firemen on standard 8-wheel locomotives will receive two and twenty-five hundredths (2 25-100) cents per mile; on 6-wheel locomotives and local runs will receive two and forty hundredths (2 40-100) cents per mile. Firemen of construction trains shall receive 100 miles per day as per schedule, and Firemen of switch engines shall receive one dollar and seventy-five cents ($1.75) per day, it being understood that in switching service ten working hours shall constitute a day's work. Five hours or less, half day; over five hours, full day. In construction service twelve working hours or less shall constitute a day's work. Firemen on suburban trains between Chicago and Blue Island shall receive twenty (20) cents per hour while on duty.

ART. 16. Overtime will be allowed on switching at the rate of seventeen and one-half (17 50-100) cents per hour, and in all other service at the rate of twenty-two and one-half (22 50-100) cents per hour, irrespective of classification.

ART. 17. Evidence of the willingness of a Fireman to serve the best interests of the Company at all times, in whatever capacity assigned, as well as economy and cleanliness in the care of his engine, and the Company's property under his control, will always be considered as meriting reward. The articles enumerated above constitute, in their entirety, the agreement between this Company and its locomotive Firemen, and all rules previously in effect are by this agreement abolished.

For the Chicago, Rock Island & Pacific Railway,

H. F. ROYCE,   W. I. ALLEN.
Gen. Supt. Lines East of Mo. River.   Assistant General Manager.
C. DUNLAP,   GEO. F. WILSON,
Gen. Supt. Lines West of Mo. River.   General Master Mechanic.
May 11, 1892.   Approved: E. ST. JOHN, General Manager.

THE CHOCTAW COAL AND RAILWAY COMPANY.

Conductors receive $100 per month; Brakemen, $60 per month; Baggageman, $30 per month—I believe he receives the same amount from the Express Company. We do not employ any Switchmen or Yardmen as one of our train crews does all of our yard work.

GEO. E. STARR,
July 18, 1892.   Cashier and Paymaster.

CINCINNATI, NEW ORLEANS & TEXAS PACIFIC RAILWAY COMPANY; ALABAMA GREAT SOUTHERN RAILROAD COMPANY; NEW ORLEANS & NORTH EASTERN RAILROAD COMPANY; ALABAMA & VICKSBURG RAILWAY COMPANY; VICKSBURG, SHREVEPORT & PACIFIC RAILROAD COMPANY, AND EAST TENNESEE, VIRGINIA & GEORGIA RAILWAY COMPANY (LESSEE OF LOUISVILLE SOUTHERN RAILROAD).

1. Overtime will be allowed trainmen when the schedule time of the train has been exceeded two hours or more. When schedule time has been exceeded two hours or more, the first two hours will be included; after the schedule has been exceeded two hours or more, all fractional parts of an hour over thirty minutes will be counted a full hour; fractional parts of an hour less than thirty minutes will not be counted. Crews of work trains will be allowed overtime for all time on duty in excess of twelve hours per day. Fractional parts of an hour of more than thirty minutes will be counted as a full hour, fractional parts of less than thirty will not be counted. Time of extra trains will be computed from longest schedule time of trains of same class on current time table. On all trains delayed time will be paid for at the rate of 30 cents per hour for conductors, and 18 cents per hour for trainmen. Yard delayed time at terminals will be allowed after the train has been delayed in the yard thirty minutes or more, and when delayed immediately outside of the yard-limit board, at the rate of 30 cents per hour for conductors and 18 cents per hour for brakemen for each hour or fractional part of an hour in excess of thirty minutes.

2. In case a trainman believes his suspension or discharge to have been unjust, he shall, within thirty days after such suspension or discharge, make a written statement of the facts in the case and submit it through the Trainmaster to the Superintendent of the division on which he is employed and the latter will, as soon as practicable, make a thorough investigation of the matter; if such statement be not submitted within thirty days it will not be considered. If the suspension or discharge be found to have been unjust, the trainman will be reinstated and will be paid for time lost. Employes will have right of appeal to the General Manager.

3. Trainmen will be called not to exceed one hour before the leaving time of their trains. The time of trainmen will begin one hour after they have signed the Culler's book. The Caller will be furnished with a book showing the time the men are called and the time the train leaves, which book will be signed by the men. Failing to respond promptly, whether it be his turn out or not, the party at fault will be suspended or discharged at the discretion of the Trainmaster or Superintendent. When trainmen are called to go out and the train is afterward annulled, they shall be allowed three hours at the rate of 30 cents per hour for conductors, and 18 cents per hour for brakemen, provided that they are not notified that they will be required for another train within the three hours, in which event their time will begin one hour from the time they are first called. Trainmen thus called will be first out, provided it does not interfere with the men who have regular runs.

4. Crews assigned to regular runs will be paid extra for services rendered outside of their regular runs at regular rates for class of service performed.

5. For attending court or appearing before proper persons to give evidence, trainmen having regular runs will be paid the amount they would have made had they performed their regular duties. Other trainmen will be paid regular day's wages for the service to which they belong. They will also be furnished free transportation to and from court and their legitimate expenses. No time will be allowed in cases where the time so consumed does not interfere with the men making their regular trips and having eight hours' rest if they require it.

6. Trainmen dead-heading under orders will be allowed half pay for the service to which they belong. Crews running light with cabooses or engine without caboose will be allowed through freight pay.

7. When a man is traveling over the road for the purpose of relieving a man who has asked for leave of absence, he will not receive any compensation for the distance traveled.

8. Trainmen of wrecking trains will be paid 35 cents per hour or fraction thereof in excess of thirty minutes for Conductors, and 20 cents per hour or fraction thereof in excess of thirty minutes for Brakemen, time to be computed from time train starts or one hour after the men are called until they are relieved from wrecking duty. In case the train is laid up in order to give the men necessary time to rest and sleep, such portion of time will be deducted from the whole and only the actual time on duty will be paid for. A minimum of six hours will be allowed, but no mileage paid.

9. When time is not allowed as per time slip, trainmen will be advised of the amount allowed.

10. Trainmen on special train or pay train shall be paid the same wages as passenger trainmen.

11. After continuous service for sixteen hours, trainmen will be allowed eight hours rest before being called to go out, if they so desire and give notice thereof, except in case of wrecks, washouts and other emergencies.

12. When freight traffic is so light that all the freight crews in the service are not able to make reasonable wages, crews will be laid off, beginning with the youngest men in the service, until the crews that remain can make reasonable wages. Trainmen suspended from service under this rule will be given preference when the business of the road is better.

13. Crews will not be required to run off their respective divisions except when, in the opinion of the officers, the emergencies of the service require it.

In addition to the above I beg to advise:

1. The two back-up runs out of Oakdale will be allowed local pay for the division on which they are made. Any through freight crews required to do the work of these back-up trains will receive this local pay.

2. Three crews on the local runs between Chattanooga and Springville, Vicksburg and Meridian, and Hattiesburg and New Orleans. The rates of pay in connection with these three local runs will be $90 per month for Conductors, and $52 per month for Brakemen.

3. The day Yardmasters at Lexington, Somerset and Oakdale will be allowed $100 per month. The night Yardmasters at Lexington, Somerset, Oakdale and Chattanooga will be allowed $85 per month.

4. Conductors on trains 11 and 12, of the V. S. & P. R. R., will be allowed $3.25 per trip for either division. One white man, as Flagman, on those trains will be allowed $2

per trip; colored Brakeman, $1.50 per trip. On all other V. S. & P. freight trains, Conductors will receive $2.75 per trip; one white Flagman, $1.75 per trip, and colored Brakeman, $1.50 per trip.

5. Through freight Brakemen on the N. O. & N. E. will receive $2.50 per trip.

6. Yard Foremen at Lexington, Somerset, Oakdale Chattanooga, Meridian and New Orleans will receive $75 per month.

Following is the scale of wages in effect March 1st, 1892:

CINCINNATI, NEW ORLEANS & TEXAS PACIFIC RAILWAY.

CLASS OF TRAIN.	RANK.	BETWEEN.	RATE.	
			Trip.	Month.
Passenger	Conductors			$110 00
Passenger	Baggagemen			60 00
Passenger	Flagmen			60 00
Passenger	Brakemen			50 00
Passenger	Train Porters			40 00
Through Freight	Conductors	Ludlow and Lexington	$2 70	
Through Freight	Brakemen	Ludlow and Lexington	1 75	
Local Freight	Conductors	Ludlow and Lexington	3 25	
Local Freight	Brakemen	Ludlow and Lexington	2 10	
Through Freight	Conductors	Lexington and Somerset	2 70	
Through Freight	Brakemen	Lexington and Somerset	1 75	
Local Freight	Conductors	Lexington and Somerset	3 50	
Local Freight	Brakemen	Lexington and Somerset	2 25	
Through Freight	Conductors	Somerset and Oakdale	2 85	
Through Freight	Brakemen	Somerset and Oakdale	1 90	
Local Freight	Conductors	Somerset and Oakdale	3 50	
Local Freight	Brakemen	Somerset and Oakdale	2 25	
Through Freight	Conductors	Oakdale and Chattanooga	2 70	
Through Freight	Brakemen	Oakdale and Chattanooga	1 75	
Local Freight	Conductors	Oakdale and Chattanooga	3 50	
Local Freight	Brakemen	Oakdale and Chattanooga	2 25	

ALABAMA GREAT SOUTHERN RAILROAD.

CLASS OF TRAIN.	RANK.	BETWEEN.	RATE.	
			Trip.	Month.
Passenger	Conductors			$110 00
Passenger	Baggagemen			60 00
Passenger	Brakemen			50 00
Passenger	Train Porters			40 00
Through Freight	Conductors	Chattanooga and Birmingham	$3 82	
Through Freight	Brakemen	Chattanooga and Birmingham	2 25	
Through Freight	Conductors	Birmingham and Meridian	3 82	
Through Freight	Brakemen	Birmingham and Meridian	2 25	
Local Freight	Conductors	Chattanooga and Springville*		90 00
Local Freight	Brakemen	Chattanooga and Springville*		52 00
Local Freight	Conductors	Springville and Tuskaloosa	3 50	
Local Freight	Brakemen	Springville and Tuskaloosa	2 00	
Local Freight	Conductors	Tuskaloosa and Meridian	3 50	
Local Freight	Brakemen	Tuskaloosa and Meridian	2 00	

*Three crews.

NEW ORLEANS & NORTH EASTERN RAILROAD.

CLASS OF TRAIN.	RANK.	BETWEEN.	RATE.	
			Trip.	Month.
Passenger	Conductors			$110 00
Passenger	Baggagemen			60 00
Passenger	Brakemen			50 00
Passenger	Train Porters			40 00
Through Freight	Conductors	Meridian and New Orleans	$4 50	
Through Freigh't	Brakemen	Meridian and New Orleans	2 50	
Local Freight	Conductors	Meridian and Hattiesburg	3 25	
Local Freight	Brakemen	Meridian and Hattiesburg	2 00	
Local Freight	Conductors	Hattiesburg and New Orleans*		90 00
Local Freight	Brakemen	Hattiesburg and New Orleans*		52 00

*Three crews.

ALABAMA & VICKSBURG RAILWAY.

CLASS OF TRAIN.	RANK.	BETWEEN.	RATE.	
			Trip.	Month.
Passenger	Conductors			$110 00
Passenger	Baggagemen			60 00
Passenger	Brakemen			50 00
Passenger	Train Porter			40 00
Through Freight	Conductors	Meridian and Vicksburg	$3 78	
Through Freight	Brakemen	Meridian and Vicksburg	2 24	
Local Freight	Conductors	Meridian and Vicksburg*		90 00
Local Freight	Brakemen	Meridian and Vicksburg*		52 00

*Three crews.

VICKSBURG, SHREVEPORT & PACIFIC RAILROAD.

CLASS OF TRAIN.	RANK.	BETWEEN.	RATE.	
			Trip.	Month.
Passenger	Conductors			$110 00
Passenger	Baggagemen			60 00
Passenger	Brakemen			50 00
Passenger	Train Porters			40 00
Through Freight	Conductors	Delta and Monroe	$2 75	
Through Freight	Brakemen*	Delta and Monroe	1 75	
Through Freight	Brakemen†	Delta and Monroe	1 50	
Through Freight	Conductors	Monroe and Shreveport	2 75	
Through Freight	Brakemen*	Monroe and Shreveport	1 75	
Through Freight	Brakemen†	Monroe and Shreveport	1 50	
Local Freight	Conductors	Delta and Monroe	3 25	
Local Freight	Brakemen*	Delta and Monroe	2 00	
Local Freight	Brakemen†	Delta and Monroe	1 50	
Local Freight	Conductors	Monroe and Shreveport	3 25	
Local Freight	Brakemen*	Monroe and Shreveport	2 00	
Local Freight	Brakemen†	Monroe and Shreveport	1 55	

*White. †Colored.

LOUISVILLE SOUTHERN RAILROAD.

CLASS OF TRAIN.	RANK.	BETWEEN.	RATE.	
			Trip.	Month.
Passenger	Conductors			$85 00
Passenger	Baggagemen			50 00
Passenger	Brakemen			45 00
Through Freight	Conductors	Louisville and Burgin	$2 70	
Through Freight	Brakemen	Louisville and Burgin	1 75	
Through Freight	Conductors	Louisville and Lexington	2 70	
Through Freight	Brakemen	Louisville and Lexington	1 75	
Local Freight	Conductors	Louisville and Lexington	3 50	
Local Freight	Brakemen	Louisville and Lexington	2 25	

July 1, 1892.

R. CARROLL,
General Manager.

THE CLEVELAND, CINCINNATI, CHICAGO & ST. LOUIS RAILWAY COMPANY.

CONDUCTOR'S SCHEDULE.

1. Passenger Conductors running passenger trains, when their runs are seventy-five miles or more, will receive 25¼ mills per mile, except on Cairo and Peoria divisions.

2. Conductors running through freight trains will receive 29 mills per mile, and will be allowed the same number of miles that Enginemen and Firemen receive. They will be paid at the rate of 29 cents per hour for all detentions over two hours. When delayed over two hours, the first two hours will be included. Road overtime to be computed from the current time table of the respective divisions. The running time of extra trains to be computed in like manner. The longest run on current time card except local) on the division to govern.

3. Local freight Conductors on Chicago division will be paid $85 per month, or upon that basis for such portion of the month as they may work. Local freight Con-

ductors on Cairo division, that run daily, will be paid $95 per month. Should local freight Conductors on Cairo division run four days per week they will be paid $85 per month. Local freight Conductors on other divisions will receive an increase of $5 per month, or upon that basis for such portion of the month as they may work. They will be paid 29 cents per hour for all detentions over two hours. When delayed over two hours, the first two hours will be included. Road overtime to be computed from current time table of respective divisions.

4. Conductors running suburban trains between Cincinnati, Harrison and Aurora will receive $85 per month.

5. Branch Conductors running out of Greensburg to receive $70 per month. Conductors doubling between Seneca and Sheldon to receive $80 per month. Conductors doubling between Kankakee and Seneca to receive $75 per month. Conductors running connection trains between Lawrenceburg Junction and Aurora to receive $70 per month.

6. Conductors on work trains will be paid $2.75 per day, ten hours to constitute a day's work; less than five hours, a half day; over five hours, a full day; over ten hours, 25 cents per hour. Conductors on circus trains making stands on road will be allowed constructive mileage of 150 miles for each twenty-four hours in such service, at freight rates.

7. Conductors on wreck trains will be paid 25¼ mills per mile, to and from wreck, and 25¼ cents per hour while at wreck. Conductors on picnic trains will be paid 25¼ cents per hour, and are not to be released except when returned to starting point or assigned to other service. Freight Conductors handling picnic trains, if released not having made a full day, will be marked first out.

8. Conductors dead-heading over the road on company's business, other than specified, will be paid 2 cents per mile, the mileage allowed not to exceed 100 miles per day.

9. Conductors attending court as witnesses, by direction of an officer in authority, will be paid at the rate of $2 per day while off duty in such special service, and necessary expenses when away from home, except that no time will be allowed when the time consumed does not interfere with the men making their regular trips. If their crew is sent away during their absence at court, they will receive $2 per day until the crew returns or they are assigned to duty.

10. When a Conductor is called for a run and the train is annulled, he will receive the agreed rate per hour while on duty (see Articles 2 and 3) and will stand first out.

11. Crews that have been on duty for twenty consecutive hours should have eight hours rest before going on duty again, unless they go voluntarily.

12. When crews are marked for any run or are ordered by an officer in authority to be ready at a given time, and not released, if delayed over one hour they are to be paid at the agreed rate for their services (see Articles 2 and 3) from the time they were first marked or ordered to go out, except that no time will be allowed should train arrive at terminal having made schedule time; such schedule time to be computed from the time Conductor was ordered out.

13. If a Conductor is taken off his run, for any cause, he will be granted a full investigation, hearing and decision within five days. He may have another Conductor of his own selection appear and speak for him at the investigation, and will have the right to appeal from the decision of the local to the general officers of the road. If exonerated he will receive pay for lost time.

14. Freight Conductors will, whenever practicable, be assigned to divisions and run first in, first out, in the service to which they are assigned. The right to regular runs and promotions will be governed by merit, ability and seniority. Other things being equal, the Conductor who serves the longest on any division of the road will have the preference of runs on such division.

15. Conductors will not be expected to take charge of light engines in connection with their trains.

16. Callers will be furnished to call Conductors living within a radius of one mile and a half of the Yardmaster's office at all freight terminals.

17. This schedule is not to supersede or affect the present rate of pay on either the Sandusky or White Water divisions of the C., C., C. & St. L. Ry.

BRAKEMEN AND BAGGAGEMASTER'S SCHEDULE.

1. Freight Brakemen employed on the C., C., C. & St. L. Ry. will receive 2 cents per mile on through freight trains.

2. The pay of local freight Brakemen, on all divisions, will remain the same as at present. Local freight Foremen will be paid $5 per month in excess of Brakemen' rate.

3. Baggagemasters or Brakemen attending court by direction of an officer in authority will be paid at the rate of $1.50 per day while off duty in such special service and necessary expenses when away from home, except that no time will be allowed

when the time consumed does not interfere with the men making their regular trips. If their crew is sent away during their absence at court, Baggagemasters and Brakemen shall receive $1.50 per day until the crew returns or they are assigned to duty.

4. Baggagemasters or Brakemen dead-heading over the road on company's business, other than specified, will be paid 12 mills per mile, the mileage allowed not to exceed 100 miles per day.

5. Brakemen will be allowed overtime upon the same basis as Conductors, at 20 cents per hour.

6. Callers will be furnished to call Brakemen living within a radius of one mile of Yardmaster's office at all freight terminals.

7. Passenger Brakemen will receive 12 mills per mile and Baggagemasters 13 mills per mile on all through runs. On all commuter and passenger runs, including Aurora passenger run, Brakemen will receive $2 per day and Baggagemasters $2.15 per day, except on Cairo and Peoria divisions, where the pay will remain the same as at present.

8. In case a Brakeman is suspended he shall have a hearing within five days, and if the investigation exonerates him he will be reinstated and will receive pay for time lost.

9. Brakemen on work trains will be paid $1.75 per day; ten hours to constitute a day's work; less than five hours, a half day; over five hours, a full day; over ten hours, 17½ cents per hour. Brakemen on wreck trains will be paid 17½ mills per mile to and from wreck, and 17½ cents per hour while at wreck. Baggagemasters and Brakemen on picnic trains will be paid 15 cents per hour, the crew not to be released except when returned to starting point or assigned to other service. If a freight crew is released, not having made a full day, they will be marked first out. Brakemen on circus trains making stands on road will be allowed constructive mileage of 150 miles for each twenty-four hours in such service, at freight rates.

10. Whenever it becomes necessary to employ additional Conductors, the preference will be given to Brakemen according to their age and ability. This to be determined by the Superintendent, or his representative, when the applicant is examined.

11. Brakemen are not to be fined for any damage done to property, unless it can be shown that it was the result of their carelessness or negligence.

12. This schedule is not to supersede or affect the present rates on either the Sandusky or White Water divisions of the C. C. C. & St. L. Ry.

SANDUSKY DIVISION — CONDUCTOR'S SCHEDULE.

1. Passenger Conductors will receive $100 per month, except as per Article 15.

2. Conductors running through freight trains will receive 27½ mills per mile, and will be allowed same number of miles as Enginemen and Firemen receive. They will be paid at the rate of 27½ cents per hour for all detentions over two hours. When delayed over two hours, the first two hours will be included. Road overtime to be computed from the current time table of the respective divisions. The running time of extra trains to be computed in like manner. The longest run on current time card (except local) on the division to govern.

3. Local freight Conductors will receive 29 mills per mile. They will be paid at the rate of 29 cents per hour for all detentions over two hours. When delayed over two hours, the first two hours be included. Road overtime to be computed as per Article 2.

4. The following constructive mileage will be allowed: On local freights, 110 miles for round trip between Carey and Sandusky, and 110 miles for trip between Springfield and Carey. On through freights, 85 miles for round trip from Springfield to Bellefontaine, and 134 miles for round trip from Springfield to Grant's.

5. Conductors on work trains will be paid $2.60 per day; ten hours to constitute a day's work; less than five hours, a half day; over five hours, a full day; over ten hours, 26 cents per hour. Conductors on circus trains making stands on road will be allowed constructive mileage of 150 miles for each twenty-four hours in such service, at freight rates.

6. Conductors on wreck trains will be paid 25 mills per mile to and from wreck, and 25 cents per hour while at wreck. Conductors on picnic trains will be paid 25 cents per hour, and are not to be released except when returned to starting point or assigned to other service. Freight Conductors handling picnic trains, if released not having made a full day, will be marked first out.

7. Conductors dead-heading over the road on company's business, other than specified, will be paid 2 cents per mile, the mileage allowed not to exceed 100 miles per day.

8. Conductors attending court as witnesses, by direction of an officer in authority, will be paid at the rate of $2 per day while off duty in such special service, and necessary expenses when away from home, except that no time will be allowed when the time consumed does not interfere with the men making their regular trips. If their

crew is sent away during their absence at court, they will receive $2 per day until the crew returns or they are assigned to duty.

9. When a Conductor is called for a run and the train is annulled, he will receive the agreed rate per hour for his services while on duty (see Articles 2 and 3) and will stand first out.

10. Crews that have been on duty for twenty consecutive hours should have eight hours rest before going on duty again, unless they go voluntarily.

11. When crews are marked for any run or are ordered by an officer in authority to be ready at a given time, and not released, if delayed over one hour they are to be paid at the agreed rate for their services (see Articles 2 and 3) from the time they were first marked or ordered to go out, except that no time will be allowed should the train arrive at terminal having made schedule time, such schedule time to be computed from the time the Conductor was ordered out.

12. If a Conductor is taken off his run, for any cause, he will be granted a full investigation, hearing and decision within five days. He may have another Conductor of his own selection appear and speak for him at the investigation, and will have the right to appeal from the decision of the local to the general officers of the road. If exonerated he will receive pay for lost time.

13. Freight Conductors will, whenever practicable, be assigned to a division and run first in, first out, in the service to which they are assigned. The right to regular runs and promotion will be governed by merit, ability and seniority. Other things being equal, the Conductor who serves the longest will have the preference of runs.

14. Conductors will not be expected to take charge of light engines in connection with their trains.

15. Conductors on Findlay branch will receive $65 per month.

SANDUSKY DIVISION — BRAKEMEN AND BAGGAGEMASTER'S SCHEDULE.

1. Passenger Brakemen will receive $50 per month, except as per Article 12. Baggagemen will receive $55 per month, except as per Article 12.

2. Brakemen in through freight service will receive 17½ mills per mile.

3. Brakemen in local freight service will receive 19 mills per mile. Foremen on local freights will receive 20 mills per mile.

4. Constructive mileage will be allowed as follows: On local freight, 110 miles for trip Springfield to Carey, and 110 miles for round trip Carey to Sandusky. On through freights, 85 miles for round trip Springfield to Bellefontaine, and 134 miles for round trip Springfield to Grant's.

5. Baggagemasters or Brakemen attending court as witnesses, by direction of an officer in authority, shall be paid at the rate of $1.50 per day while off duty in such special service, and necessary expenses when away from home, except that no time will be allowed when the time consumed does not interfere with the men making their regular trips. If their crew is sent away during their absence at court, Baggagemasters or Brakemen shall receive $1.50 per day until the crew returns or they are assigned to duty.

6. Baggagemasters or Brakemen dead-heading over the road on company's business, other than specified, will be paid 12 mills per mile. Mileage not to exceed 100 miles per day.

7. Brakemen will be allowed overtime upon the same basis as Conductors, at the rate of 16 cents per hour.

8. In case a Brakeman is suspended he shall have a hearing within five days, and if the investigation exonerates him he will be reinstated and receive pay for time lost.

9. Brakemen on work trains will be paid $1.65 per day; ten hours to constitute a day's work; less than five hours, half a day; over five hours, a full day; over ten hours, 16¼ cents per hour. Brakemen on wreck trains will be paid 16¼ mills per mile to and from wreck, and 16¼ cents per hour while at wreck. Baggagemasters or Brakemen on picnic trains shall receive 15 cents per hour, the crew not to be released except when returned to starting point or assigned to other service. If a freight crew is released, not having made a full day, they shall be marked first out. Brakemen on circus train making stands on road will be allowed 150 miles for each twenty-four hours in such service, at freight rates.

10. Whenever it becomes necessary to employ additional Conductors the preference will be given to Brakemen according to age and ability. This to be determined by the Superintendent, or his representative, when the applicant is examined.

11. Brakemen are not to be fined for damage done to property, unless it can be shown that it was due to their carelessness or negligence.

12. Brakemen on Findlay branch will receive $45 per month. Baggagemaster on Findlay branch will receive $40 per month.

STATEMENT OF YARD RATES.

Cleveland Yard: Conductors, day, $2.60 per day; night, $2.70. Brakemen, day, $2.30 per day; night, $2.50.
Berea Yard: Conductors, 115 miles per day, 125 miles per night, $2.90 per 100 miles. Brakemen, 115 miles per day, 125 miles per night, $2 per 100 miles.
Galion Yard: Conductors, day or night, $2.40 per day. Brakemen, day or night, $1.90 per day.
Delaware Yard: Conductors, day or night, $2.40 per day. Brakemen, day or night, $1.90 per day.
Columbus Yard: Conductors, day, $2.58 per day; night, $2.70. Brakemen, day, $2.05 per day; night, $2.15.

CINCINNATI DIVISION.

Springfield Yard: Conductors, day, $2.40 per day; night, $2.50. Brakemen, day, $2.05 per day; night, $2.15.
Dayton Yard: Conductors, day, $2.40 per day; night, $2.50. Brakemen, day, $2.05 per day; night, $2.15.
Middletown Yard: Conductors, $2.90 per day. Brakemen, $2 per day.
Ivorydale Yard: Foremen, day, $2.75 per day; night, $2.90. Brakemen, day, $2.50 per day; night, $2.70.

INDIANAPOLIS DIVISION.

Union City Yard: One night Foreman, $80 per month. Six yard Brakemen, $1.90 per day.
Bellefontaine Yard: Brakemen, $50 per month.
Muncie Yard: Brakemen, $55 per month.

ST. LOUIS DIVISION.

Indianapolis Yard: Foremen, per month: One, $100; two, $90; seven, $85; two, $80. Conductors, day, $2.50 per day; night, $2.60. Brakemen, day, $2.30 per day; night, $2.40.
Terre Haute Yard: Brakemen, day, $2.20 per day; night, $2.30.
Mattoon Yard: Foreman, $70 per month. Conductors, day, $2.25 per day; night, $2 35. Brakemen, day, $2.05 per day; night, $2.15. (Ten hours per day.)
Litchfield Yard: Brakemen, $55 per month.
Wann Yard: Conductor, $65 per month. Brakemen, $55 per month.
East St. Louis Yard: Conductors, day, $70 per month; night, $75. Brakemen, day, $65 per month; night, $70. (For actual number of working days. Ten hours per day.)

CHICAGO DIVISION.

Cincinnati Yard: Conductors, day, $2.75 per day; night, $2.90; Passenger Pilot, $2.50. Brakemen, day, $2.50 per day; night, $2.70.
Greensburg Yard: Brakemen, day, $1.80 per day; night, $1.90.
Lafayette Yard: Conductors, day, $2.25 per day; night, $2.35. Brakemen, day, $2.05 per day; night, $2.15.
Kankakee Yard: Conductors, day, $2.25 per day; night, $2.35. Brakemen, day, $2.05 per day; night, $2.15.

CAIRO DIVISION.

Cairo Yard: Foremen, day, 28 cents per hour; night, 27 cents. Brakemen, day, 24 cents per hour; night, 23 cents.
Mount Carmel Yard: Brakemen, day or night, $61.25 per month.
Sandusky Yard: Foreman, $65 per month. Brakemen, $55 per month.

MICHIGAN DIVISION.

Benton Harbor Yard: Foreman, $50 per month. Helpers (Switchmen), $40 per month.
Elkhart Yard: Helpers (Switchmen), $45 per month.
Wabash Yard: Foreman, $50 per month. Helpers (Switchmen), $40 per month.
Marion Yard: Helpers (Switchmen), $40 per month.
Anderson Yard: Foremen, day or night, $60 per month. Foreman of engines, 24 cents per hour. Helpers (Switchmen), 19 cents per hour.

July 20, 1892.

J. RAMSEY, JR.,
General Manager.

CLEVELAND, LORAIN & WHEELING RAILWAY.*

Lorain: Foremen, $2.35 per day, 10 hours; Helpers, $2.00 per day, 10 hours.
Elyria: Foremen, $2.50 per day, 10 hours; Helpers, $1.80 per day, 10 hours.
Massillon: Foremen, $2.50 per day, 12 hours; Helpers, $1.80 per day, 12 hours.
Urichsville: Foremen, $2.50 per day, 12 hours; Helpers, $1.80 per day, 12 hours.
Hollaway: Foremen, $1.80 per day, 12 hours; Helpers, $1.80 per day, 12 hours.
Bridgeport: Foremen, $2.35 per day, 12 hours; Helpers, $1.95 per day, 12 hours.

* Not official.

Freight Conductors: First year, $2.77 per 100 miles; after first year, $2.87 per 100 miles. Local freight, 3 cents per mile. Twelve hours to constitute a day's work of 100 miles.

Freight Brakemen: First year, head Brakeman $1.65 per 100 miles; after first year, $1.75 per 100 miles. First year, rear Brakeman $1.75 per 100 miles; after first year, $1.85 per 100 miles. Local freight, 2 cents per mile. Twelve hours to constitute a day's work of 100 miles.

COLUMBUS, HOCKING VALLEY & TOLEDO RAILWAY COMPANY.

PASSENGER TRAIN SERVICE.

RUNS.	MILES.	ENGINEERS	FIREMEN.	CONDUCTORS.	BRAKEMEN	BAGGAGE MASTER.	REMARKS
Columbus and Toledo	124	$3 75	$1 87½	$3 00	$1 45	$1 65	
Columbus to Marion and return	91	3 37½	1 69	3 00	1 45	$20 per mo	
Columbus and Pomeroy	132	4 00	2 00	3 06	1 58	2 06	
Columbus to Athens and return	152	4 75	2 37½	3 12½	2 00	2 00	
Logan, Straitsville and Nelsonville	124	4 00	2 00	3 50	1 80	2 35	2r'd tr'ps
Logan and Athens, week days	104	3 30	1 65	}$90 per mo.	1 75	}$60 per mo.	2r'd tr'ps
Athens to Columbus & ret. Sunday	152	4 75	2 37½		1 75		

FREIGHT TRAIN SERVICE.

RUNS.	MILES.	ENGINEERS	FIREMEN.	CONDUCTORS.	BRAKEMEN.	OVERTIME.
Columbus and Toledo	124	$4 50	Mogul$2.37½ / $2 25	$3 25	$2 15	Begins after 13 hrs.
Columbus and Fostoria	88	3 37½	Mogul $1.78 / 1 69	2 37	1 60	" " 9 "
Columbus to Marion and return	91	4 50	Mogul $2.36 / 2 25	3 00	2 00	" " 13 "
Columbus and Fostoria,......Local	88	4 00	2 00	3 00	2 00	" " 12 "
Toledo to Fostoria and ret., Local	72	4 00	2 00	3 00	2 00	" " 12 "
Columbus to Logan, Straitsville and Nelsonville and return	124	4 50	2 25	3 25	2 15	" " 13 "
Logan to Pt. Pleasant and return	156	5 62	2 81	4 25	2 75	" " 16 "
Logan and Pomeroy	83	3 75	1 87½	2 75	1 80	" " 12 "
Logan and Pomeroy ......Local	83	3 87½	1 94	3 00	2 00	" " 12 "
Columbus and Athens ..... Local	76	3 87½	1 94	3 00	2 00	" " 12 "
(a) All Branches		3 60	1 80	2 90	2 00	" " 12 "
Work, Wreck and Circus Trains		3 50	1 75	3 00	2 00	" " 12 "
Rates of overtime per hour		36	18	25	17	

SWITCHING SERVICE.

YARDS.	HOURS.	ENGINEERS.	FIREMEN.	CONDUCTORS.	BRAKEMEN.	OVERTIME.
Columbus	12	$3 00	$1 65	{ $2 75 D'y. $2 10 / 2 87 Night. 2 22 }		Begins after 12 hrs.
Logan	12	3 00	1 50	2 45	1 95	" " 10 "
Nelsonville	10	2 50	1 50	2 45	1 95	" " 10 "
Pomeroy and Middleport	12	2 50	1 50	2 00	1 75	" " 12 "
(b) Marion	12	2 50	1 50	2 65	2 00	" " 12 "
Fostoria	10	1 50	1 50	2 50	1 85	" " 12 "
Rockwell	12	2 75	1 65	2 70 { Day 2 15 / Nig't 2 25 }		" " 12 "

(a) After January 1, 1893, Branch Conductors will receive $3.
(b) After January 1, 1893, Brakemen, Marion Yard, will receive $2.10.

The practice of imposing fines for damage to rolling stock or Company's property will be discontinued, and discipline will be administered by suspension and discharge. In computing overtime, no fraction of an hour less than thirty minutes will be counted; thirty minutes and over shall be counted as one hour; time to commence from the time set for trains to leave. Any Conductor or Brakeman causing delay to train, and overtime being made from said cause, the remainder of the crew to receive overtime and the person causing such delay to be discharged or suspended, as the case may warrant. Competent Callers will be appointed where necessary to call trainmen at least one hour before the leaving time of the trains, provided they live within the limits fixed for each yard, and have entered their address in a book to be kept for that purpose at the designated offices. Exceptions will be made to the rule in the cases of men assigned to regular runs, in such cases no call will be made. When trainmen are called for duty and their trains annulled, time will be allowed at overtime rates until relieved from duty (with a minimum of one hour). Such crews shall stand first out

Trainmen attending court at the request of an official of the Company shall be paid: $3 per day for Conductors and $2 per day for Brakemen, and their legitimate expenses. Trainmen dead-heading over the road, in their caboose or on passenger trains, will be allowed one-half their regular trip rates; when running light full time will be allowed. Employes held off pending investigation, shall be given a trial within a reasonable time, and if, on subsequent investigation, found not guilty, shall be paid the wages they would have earned during the time of suspension. All freight train crews, except local freight crews, shall be run first in, first out. Crews dead-heading shall stand first out with respect to the crew that they or their caboose dead-headed with. Crews shall be assigned to their respective divisions, and shall not be transferred to other divisions, except for temporary services. Freight crews running pay car or extra passenger, to be paid on the basis of freight pay. Work, wreck and circus trains to pay $3 and $2 per day for Conductors and Brakemen, respectively. Two Brakemen will be allowed on all through, and three on all local runs, except on the Hocking Valley division, where trains run double-header, when a third man will be allowed. This, on account of the fog to which the division is subject and local conditions existing. Promotion and reduction of force will be based on merit and ability. Where all things are equal, length of service will govern. When freight traffic is light, reductions in force will be so made that fair living wages may be earned by trainmen, this to be agreed upon between the officers and trainmen. Trainmen leaving the service of the Company will be given a letter stating time of service, capacity in which employed and reason for leaving. Trainmen will be notified when trip report is not allowed.

Accepted for the Order of Railway Conductors: A. E. ROBBINS,
   CHAS. H. WILKINS, Ass't G. C. C.   Supt. Toledo Division.
For the Brotherhood of Railroad Trainmen: M. S. CONNORS,
   P. H. MORRISSEY, First V. G. M.   Supt. H. V. and O. R. Divisions.
September 1, 1892.

COLUMBUS, SHAWNEE & HOCKING RAILWAY COMPANY.

1. The time on all regular trains will commence at schedule leaving time, and on all extra trains at the time listed, and end when relieved at terminal stations.
2. Callers will be provided at Columbus, Shawnee and Drakes to call men for trains leaving between 9 P. M. and 6 A. M. Men will be called as near one hour prior to leaving time as possible.
3. Hostlers will be furnished at all terminal stations to take charge of engines and put same in condition for return service.
4. When a crew has been called to go out, and the train for which they were called is annulled after they report for same, they will be allowed pay for one-half the time from leaving time to time train was annulled, one hour being a minimum.
5. Claims for extra or overtime will be sent directly to the Superintendent. When any overtime is rejected, it will be returned with full explanation.
6. Time as reported by Conductors and Enginemen will be checked with train list, train register and Yardmaster's report.
7. All train or enginemen after being on duty sixteen consecutive hours or more, unless in case of wreck or accident, will be allowed ten hours rest.
8. No fine shall be imposed for loss or damage to property or rolling stock, but if such do occur, and it be found upon trial that an employe has carelessly caused such loss or damage, he shall be suspended or discharged, as the case may justify. All employes will use great care and every effort in their power to avoid accident and damage to property.
9. All employes will be regarded as in the line of promotion, advancement depending upon the faithful discharge of duty and capacity for increased responsibility.
10. When an employe is relieved from duty for any cause he will be granted a trial immediately, and will be notified of the result within five days. In case he is found to be innocent, he will receive pay for the time lost, at his regular rate per day, for each calendar day.
11. For preparing shop engines for road service, Engineers shall receive $3 and Firemen $1.75 per day, ten hours.
12. Employes attending court or doing special service for the Company will be paid as per Article 10.
13. For dead-heading, on order of the Company, one-half of regular wages will be paid.
14. For special trains or pay trains, passenger rates apply. One hundred and ten miles, or eight hours, constitute a day.
15. Pay day will be on or before the 25th of each month.
16. The following scale of wages will be in force until modified by mutual agreement:

CORN. & LEB. R'Y.—DEL. & HUD. CANAL CO.—DEL., LACK. & WEST. R'Y.

TRAIN SERVICE.	Conductors	Baggagemen	Brakemen	Engineers	Firemen	Foremen	EXTRA, AT REGULAR RATE PER HOUR.
PASSENGER.							
Columbus and Zanesville....................	$3 25	$1 80	$1 60	$3 70	$1 85	......	None.
Shawnee and Zanesville..	3 25	1 80	1 80	4 00	2 10	..	None.
MIXED.							
Glouster and Malta.......	2 90	.....	1 85	3 50	1 90	......	None.
Cannelville and Redfield...................	2 50	.....	1 60	3 00	1 60	...	After 12 hours.
LOCAL FREIGHT.							
Columbus and Shawnee....................	3 00	.....	2 00	3 75	2 00	....	After 12 hours.
Zanesville and Redfield.................	2 80	.....	1 80	3 50	1 80	...	After 11 hours.
THROUGH FREIGHT.							
Columbus and Drakes.......................	2 50	.....	1 70	3 25	1 80	.....	After 11 hours.
Zanesville to Shawnee, Drakes, round trip..	2 50	.....	1 70	3 25	1 80	.....	After 11 hours.
Shawnee and Drakes to Fultonham, r'd trip..	1 87½	.....	1 27½	2 43¾	1 35	.....	After 8 hours.
Shawnee and Drakes, Thurston and return...	3 75	.....	2 55	4 87½	2 70	.....	After 16½ hours.
Columbus and Zanesville.....................	2 75	.....	1 75	3 50	1 90	.....	After 12 hours.
Short or irregular runs, per hour.............	25	.....	17	32½	18	.....	
Helpers.........	....	.....	1 75	3 50	1 90	.....	After 12 hours.
WORK TRAINS	2 75	.....	1 75	3 25	1 80	.....	After 12 hours.
YARDS.							
Columbus............... ..	....	.....	1 75	2 75	1 75	....	
Zanesville............................	....	.....	1 75	3 00	1 80	$2 00	After 12 hours.
Shawnee............	....	.....	1 90	3 00	1 80	2 25	After 12 hours.
Hill crews, day and night*......	....	.....	2 00	3 25	1 90	2 40	After 12 hours.

*No allowance for meals.

Agreeed to for the employes:
WM. M'CLURG, Chairman,
H. L. TIBBETTS, Secretary,
W. A. HAMER,
H. C. M'DANIEL,
THOS. PRICE,
A. B. ANDERSON,
J. J. SHAY,
   Committee.
May 7, 1892.

For the C. S. & H. Ry. Co.:
H. O. POND,
Superintendent.

CORNWALL & LEBANON RAILROAD.*

Passenger service: Conductors, $70 per month; Engineers, $3 per day; Firemen, $1.75 per day; Brakemen, $1.60 per day. Freight service: Engineers, $2.75 per day; Firemen, $1.90 per day; Conductors, $2.15 per day; Brakemen, $1.85 per day. Switching service: Engineers, $2.50 per day; Firemen, $1.75 per day; Conductors, $1.90 per day; Brakemen, $1.70 per day. Ten hours constitute a day; overtime paid after twelve hours.
June 11, 1892.

DELAWARE & HUDSON CANAL COMPANY.

Conductors: Passenger, main line, $95 per month; passenger, branch, $85 per month; freight, $65 per month for run of 100 miles per day. Baggagemen, $50 and $55 per month. Brakemen: Passenger, first six months, $45 per month, after six months, $50 per month; freight, first six months, $45 per month for run of 100 miles per day, after six months, $50 per month. Yardmen, $50 and $55 per month. Switchmen (throwing switches), $40 per month.
May 5, 1892.
H. G. YOUNG,
Second Vice President.

DELAWARE, LACKAWANNA & WESTERN RAILROAD COMPANY.

Schedule of wages paid by D., L. & W. R. R. Co. to trainmen (Conductors, Train Baggagemen, Brakemen, Switchmen and Yardmen), working-day month, beginning May 1, 1892. Rates vary according to the different runs and nature of work performed. Conductors: Passenger trains, $80 to $90 per month; freight and other trains, $65 to $80 per month. Train Baggagemen, $52 to $57 per month. Brakemen: Passenger trains, $1.75 to $1.90 per day; freight and coal trains, $1.80 to $2.10 per day; gravel and construction trains, Buffalo division, $2 per day, other divisions, $45 per month. Switchmen and Yardmen: Buffalo yards, day, $60 to $65 per month, night, $65 to $70 per month; other yards, $2 and $2.15 per day. W. F. HALSTEAD,
May 12, 1892. General Manager.

*Not official.

DENVER & RIO GRANDE RAILWAY COMPANY.

SECOND AND THIRD DIVISIONS — REGULATIONS.

1. Trainmen will be allowed one day's pay for short runs not scheduled; provided no other work is furnished on the same day. If other work is furnished, the short run will be figured pro rata of district rates and time.
2. Callers will be stationed at all freight terminals, who will call trainmen for service when needed. These Callers will be provided with a book giving the names of the crews and the number or kind of train for which they are wanted, in which book trainmen must sign their names and enter the time of the call. Time will be allowed crews from the time they are called to leave until arrival at end of run. District terminals are the only ones to be considered terminals.
3. In case trainmen are called and report for duty and their services are not required (for any cause not their own fault), they shall stand first out and shall be paid for one-half day's service.
4. Freight trainmen while on special or passenger service will be paid at the same rate as they would have made on their regular runs; provided time made on passenger or special train amounts to less than that of the regular freight run.
5. In case of the suspension or dismissal of any trainman or yardman, for any cause except drunkenness, he shall have the right to refer his case by written statement to the Division Superintendent within five days from the time he was taken off. The Superintendent shall give his case a thorough investigation, at which the aggrieved employe shall be present if he so desires, and also be represented by a disinterested employe in his class from his division, whom he may select. In case he shall not be satisfied with the result of the investigation, he shall have the right to appeal to the General Superintendent or General Manager. In case suspension or dismissal is found to be unjust, he shall be re-instated and paid for all time lost. In case of suspension, the time shall date from the time he was taken off for investigation.
6. Trainmen are to report time and overtime on the regular form, and in case time sent in is not allowed, slips will be returned for correction, stating the reason why over the Superintendent's signature.
7. Trainmen will not be required to go out when they claim to need rest, or are incapacitated by sickness, but are required to give timely notice to the proper official in order that their places may be filled. In cases of washouts, wrecks and other emergencies, it is not intended that this clause shall be used to avoid extra exertion.
8. In making promotions, Superintendents and others will consider seniority of service, and, everything else being equal, those longest in the service shall have the preference. When a reduction of force becomes necessary, those retained shall be of the longest in the service; i. e., as between those equally honest, sober and capable, but seniority is not to be made a covering for shortcomings of any kind, or to prevent the Company from securing the best possible service. In filling vacancies in the ranks of freight Conductors, for every three men promoted from the ranks, one Conductor may be hired as Conductor, or promoted from the ranks regardless of age in the service. The Conductor so employed to take his place at the foot of the list of extra Conductors, and may be temporarily used as extra Brakeman when not employed as Conductor. Nothing in this article shall be construed to refer to work-train Conductors.
9. When traffic becomes so light that train crews in service do not make full time, upon petition of a majority of the Conductors on that district, crews will be taken off, commencing with the youngest.
10. In case Conductors are needed for mixed runs by reason of regular Conductor laying off, the oldest freight Conductor available may take the run, and the oldest extra Conductor available may take the freight run.
11. Train crews dead-heading under orders will be paid full time. Individual trainmen dead-heading on passenger trains under orders will be paid one-half time.
12. Roadmen will retain no rights in yard service, and vice versa, except in case of Mr. Hawthorne, present Yardmaster at Salida.
13. No departure from the provisions of this agreement will be made by any party thereto, except after thirty days' notice of such desire, in writing, has been served upon the other party thereto.

SCHEDULE OF PAY FOR YARDMEN.

Salida: General Yardmaster, $145 per calendar month. Night Yardmaster, $130 per calendar month. Foremen, day, $2.69 per day, overtime at 27 cents per hour; night, $2.88, overtime at 29 cents per hour. Helpers, day, $2 50 per day, overtime at 25 cents per hour; night, $2.69, overtime at 27 cents per hour. For night and day Foremen and Helpers, ten hours shall constitute a day's work, overtime at rates stated. A reasonable time will be allowed for meals, and no deductions will be made for same.

Leadville: General Yardmaster, $140 per calendar month. Night Yardmaster, $120 per calendar month. Hill Conductors, $4 per day of ten hours, overtime at 40 cents per hour. Foremen, $3.50 per day of ten hours, overtime at 36 cents per hour. Helpers, $3 per day of ten hours, overtime at 30 cents per hour. No work will be done on the afternoons of Sundays or legal holidays, except what is absolutely necessary. On these days five hours will be considered a day's work.

SCHEDULE OF PAY FOR TRAINMEN—SECOND DIVISION.

Freight Service: Minturn to Tennessee Pass and return: Conductors, $3.35; Brakemen, $1.80. Overtime after five hours. If no more work is furnished Article 1 will apply.

Minturn to Malta or Leadville and return: Conductors, $4.25; Brakemen, $3.25. Overtime after eight hours.

Salida to Calumet and return—double: Conductors, $4; Brakemen, $3. Overtime after ten hours. For third double: Conductors, $1.25; Brakemen, $1 additional.

Leadville to Dillon and return: Conductors, $4; Brakemen, $3. Overtime after eight hours.

Salida to Minturn, via Malta and Leadville Junction: Conductors, $4.30; Brakemen, $3.30. Overtime after nine hours.

Salida to Minturn, via Leadville: Conductors, $4.50; Brakemen, $3.50. Overtime after nine hours.

Salida to Leadville or Malta: Conductors, $3.85; Brakemen, $2.90, for a single trip. Conductors, $5.77; Brakemen, $4.35, for round trip same date. Conductors, $9.62; Brakemen, $7.25, for three single trips on same day. Overtime on each trip after six hours.

Minturn to Glenwood Springs and return: Conductors, $4.50; Brakemen, $3.38. Overtime after ten hours.

Minturn to Aspen: Conductors, $4; Brakemen, $3. Overtime after nine hours.

Minturn to Grand Junction: Conductors, $5; Brakemen, $3.75. Overtime after eleven hours.

Glenwood to Aspen: Conductors, $2; Brakemen, $1.50. Overtime after four hours. If no other work is furnished, Article 1 will apply.

Work Train Service: Regular work train Conductors will receive $120 and Brakemen $80 per calendar month, twelve hours to constitute a day's work. If road crews are called for work train service, they shall be paid pro rata of district rates in running to and from their work, and overtime for actual time worked; except when the pay for running to and from the work amounts to one day's pay, the allowance for work shall not commence until the stated number of hours for a day's work on that district is exceeded.

Snow-Plow and Flanger Service: Crews assigned to snow-plow and flanger work to be paid as follows: Conductors, $4, and Brakemen, $3 per day of twelve hours, full time to be allowed during time assigned to this work. All other crews doing this work shall be paid at the regular trip rate for freight work in the district in which work is done.

Passenger Service: Special and extra passenger Conductors will receive $120 and Brakemen $80 per calendar month. Between Glenwood and Aspen, Conductors will receive $120 and Brakemen $80 per calendar month. Between Salida and Grand Junction, Conductors will receive $125 and Brakemen $80: six crews for the four runs either to Newcastle or Grand Junction; twenty single trips to constitute a month's work; overtime after train becomes thirty minutes late on schedule time. When crews are called to go out on lay-over day they shall be paid at the rate of $125 for Conductors and $80 for Brakemen.

Overtime: Overtime will be paid for at the rate of 40 cents per hour for Conductors and 30 cents per hour for Brakmen. Fractions less than thirty minutes will not be counted; thirty minutes or more will be counted as one hour.

SCHEDULE OF PAY FOR TRAINMEN—THIRD DIVISION.

Freight Service, First District: Gunnison to Salida: Conductors, $4; Brakemen, $3 per single trip. Overtime after ten hours.

Salida to Sargent and return: Conductors, $4.85; Brakemen, $3.65. Overtime after twelve hours.

Salida to Alamosa: Conductors, $4; Brakemen, $3. Overtime after nine hours. Swing Brakemen over Poncha Pass, $3 per round trip.

Salida to Moffat or Mirage and return: Conductors, $4; Brakemen, $3. Overtime after nine hours.

Salida to Villa Grove or Orient or Roundhill and return: Conductors, $4; Brakemen, $3. Overtime after nine hours.

Salida to Monarch and return: Conductors, $4; Brakemen, $3. Overtime after nine hours.

Freight Service, Second District: Between Cimarron and Montrose—assigned crews: Conductors, $120; Brakemen, $80, per calendar month.

Sapinero to Lake City and return: Conductors, $4; Brakemen, $3. Overtime to be paid after schedule time has been exceeded thirty minutes.

Montrose to Ouray and return: Conductors, $4; Brakemen, $3. Overtime after ten hours.
Gunnison to Grand Junction: Conductors, $5; Brakemen, $3.75. Overtime after twelve hours.
Gunnison to Ouray or Ridgway: Conductors, $4; Brakemen, $3. Overtime after ten hours.
Gunnison to Montrose and return: Conductors, $5; Brakemen, $3.75. Overtime after twelve hours.
Gunnison to Crested Butte: Conductor, $120, and Brakemen, $90, for thirty-nine round trips or less. Conductors, $2, and Brakemen, $1.50, for additional trips made during the month. Main line crews to be paid—Conductors, $2, and Brakemen, $1.50, per round trip, and stand first in, first out. If no other work is offered, Article 1 will apply.
Gunnison to Aberdeen and return: Conductors, $1.40; Brakemen, $1, per round trip, and stand first out.

Work Train Service, First and Second Districts: Regular work train Conductors will receive $120 and Brakemen $80, per calendar month, twelve hours to constitute a day's work. If road crews are called for work train service they shall be paid pro rata of district rates in running to and from their work, and overtime for actual time worked; except when the pay for running to and from their work amounts to one day's pay, the allowance for work shall not commence until the stated number of hours for a day's work on that district is exceeded.

Snow Plow and Flanger Service: Crews assigned to snow plow and flanger work to be paid as follows: Conductors, $4, and Brakemen, $3, per day of twelve hours, full time to be allowed during time assigned to this work. All other crews doing this work shall be paid at the regular trip rate for freight work in the district in which the work is done.

Passenger Service: Special and extra passenger Conductors will receive $120 and Brakemen $80, per calendar month. Conductors will receive $125 and Brakemen $80, per calendar month, between Salida and Grand Junction, three crews assigned. Between Montrose and Ouray: Conductors, $120, and Brakemen, $80, per calendar month, one crew assigned. Between Salida and Alamosa: Conductors, $120, and Brakemen, $80, per calendar month. When passenger crews are called to go out on lay-over day, to be paid at the rate of their regular monthly rate.

Overtime: Overtime will be paid for at the rate of 40 cents per hour for Conductors, and 30 cents per hour for Brakemen. Fractions less than thirty minutes will not be counted. Thirty minutes or more will be counted as one hour.

February 20, 1892.

N. W. SAMPLE,
General Superintendent.

DES MOINES, NORTHERN & WESTERN RAILWAY COMPANY.

RULES RELATING TO CONDUCTORS.

1. The occupation of a Conductor is one that requires a knowledge of the schedules of time governing the road on which he is employed, as well as those issued by connecting lines; a proper interpretation of the rules issued therewith and under which trains, both passenger and freight, are operated.

2. Persons hereafter appointed Conductors should be men of undoubted reputation, good morals, temperate habits, and with an experience in train service on any line of road of not less than three years.

3. Seniority in service as Conductor shall hereafter govern in all cases of promotion from freight to passenger runs, merit being equal, this to be determined by the Trainmaster; it being understood that the rule generally to be pursued does not permit of transferring an employe from one division to another, to the detriment of the division employes. The future choice of runs shall be based upon this principle.

4. No Conductor shall be dismissed nor suspended from the service of the Company without just cause. In case a Conductor believes his discharge or suspension to have been unjust, he shall make a written statement of the facts in the premises and submit it to the Trainmaster; and at the same time designate any other Conductor who may be in the employ of the Company at the same time on the same division; the Superintendent, together with the Conductor last referred to, shall investigate the case in question, and when at all practicable such investigation shall be made within five days from the date of the receipt of the communication from the Conductor. In case the aforesaid discharge or suspension be decided to have been unjust, he shall be reinstated and paid half time for all time lost on said account.

5. When Conductors are laid off, on account of dullness of business, it shall be

done in the order of the dates of their employment as Conductor, beginning with the Conductor last employed.

6. Conductors having charge of trains will be held responsible for their safe management, and shall have a right to place their Brakemen as their best judgment may dictate so long as it does not conflict with time-table rules.

7. Time of Conductors in freight and passenger service shall be computed on the basis of 100 miles or less for a day's work; and all time made by Conductors while on the road between terminal points, in excess of ten miles per hour on freight and eight hours per 100 miles on passenger will be considered overtime.

8. When Conductors are held in for snow plow service, they will be allowed regular pay for each day of twenty-four hours that they are so held subject to orders.

9. Conductors dead-heading on Company's business, will be paid half mileage; and when required by this Company to attend court they shall be paid at the rate of $3 per day of twenty-four hours, and their expenses during attendance. The time to be counted while awaiting the Company's orders until they have an opportunity to take a run.

10. Delayed time between terminal stations will be paid for full delay less one hour, if delayed one hour and thirty-five minutes. It is understood that fractions of an hour less than thirty-five minutes will not be counted. Thirty-five minutes or over will be counted a full hour. In freight service, fifty miles or less shall constitute fifty miles, or one-half day's pay; 100 miles or over fifty miles shall constitute 100 miles, or one day's pay.

11. The rules in regard to a Caller shall remain the same as heretofore. The pay of a Conductor shall begin from the time the train is ordered for, as shown on the order for calling, and shall continue to the time of arrival at the end of the run. When Conductors are required to switch at terminals, thirty-five minutes or more, time shall be allowed.

12. Conductors called to make a trip, provided the train is afterwards annulled, shall be paid for two and one-half hours' time, on the basis of the pay they are receiving.

13. The following rates of pay will be allowed passenger and freight Conductors: Freight Conductors, local, 3 cents per mile, overtime, 30 cents per hour; through, 2.9 cents per mile, overtime, 29 cents per hour. Passenger Conductors: Fonda division, $95 per month; Boone division, $75 per month. Work train Conductors: Twelve hours and over eight, one day, $70 per month, overtime, 25 cents per hour.

Promotions and preferments will be based upon merit and the general record of the men, and not entirely upon their age or duration of service; economy in the running of his train, and care for the Company's property while under his control, will always be considered as meriting reward.

The articles enumerated above constitute in their entirety the agreement between this Company and its Conductors, and all rules previously in effect are by this agreement abolished.

RULES RELATING TO BRAKEMEN.

1. Seniority in service as Brakeman shall hereafter govern in all cases of promotion from Brakeman to Conductor, merit being equal; this to be determined by the Trainmaster, subject to an appeal to the Superintendent. It being understood that the rule generally to be pursued does not permit of transferring an employe from one division to another, to the detriment of the division employes. The future choice of runs shall be based upon this principle.

2. No Brakeman shall be dismissed nor suspended from the service of the Company without just cause. In case a Brakeman believes his discharge or suspension to have been unjust, he shall make a written statement of the facts in the premises and submit it to the Trainmaster, and at the same time designate any other Brakeman who may be in the employ of the Company at the time, on the same division, and the Trainmaster, together with the Brakeman last referred to, shall, in conjunction with the Superintendent, investigate the case in question, and when at all practicable such investigation shall be made within five days from the date of the receipt of the communication from the Brakeman. In case the aforesaid discharge or suspension is decided to have been unjust, he shall be reinstated and paid half time for all time lost on said account.

3. When necessary to lay off Brakemen, on account of surplus of crews, it shall be done in the order of the dates of their employment as Brakemen, beginning with the Brakeman last employed.

4. Brakemen dead-heading on Company's business will be paid half mileage, and when required by this Company to attend court they shall be paid at the rate of $2 per day of twenty-four hours, and their expenses during attendance. The time to be counted while waiting the Company's orders until they have an opportunity to take a run.

5. When Brakemen are held in for snow plow service, they will be allowed the

regular rates they are receiving, for each day of twenty-four hours that they are so held subject to orders.

6. Delayed time between terminal stations will be paid for full delay, less one hour, if delayed one hour and thirty-five minutes. It is understood that fractions of an hour less than thirty-five minutes will not be counted. Thirty-five minutes or over will be counted a full hour. In freight service fifty miles or less shall constitute fifty miles, or one-half day's pay; 100 miles or over fifty miles shall constitute 100 miles, or one day's pay.

7. The rules in regard to a Caller shall remain the same as heretofore. The pay of the Brakeman shall begin from the time the train is ordered for, as shown on the order for calling, and shall continue to the time of arrival at the end of the run. When Brakemen are required to switch at terminals, thirty-five minutes or more, time shall be allowed.

8. Brakemen called to make a trip shall be paid, provided the train is afterwards annulled, for two and one-half hours' time on the basis of the pay they are receiving.

9. The following rates of pay will be allowed passenger and freight Brakemen: Freight Brakemen, local, 2 cents per mile, overtime, 20 cents per hour; through, 1.9 cents per mile, overtime, 19 cents per hour. Passenger Brakemen, $45 per month. Work train Brakemen, twelve hours and over eight, one day, $45 per month, overtime at proportionate rates.

December 31, 1891.

L. M. MARTIN,
General Manager.

DULUTH & IRON RANGE RAILROAD COMPANY.

We pay our freight and ore men: Conductors, 2¼ cents per mile; Brakemen, 2 cents per mile. Work train Conductors, 3¼ cents per mile; Brakemen, 2¼ cents per mile. Yard Foremen, $2.65 per day; Switchmen, $2.50 per day. Passenger Conductors, $100 per calendar month; Brakemen, $52 for twenty-six days.

May 31, 1892.

THOS. OWENS,
Superintendent.

DULUTH, SOUTH SHORE & ATLANTIC RAILWAY.

1. *Wages for Conductors:* The compensation shall be as follows: For the first year's services, $70; the second year, $75, and the third year, $78, for 2,600 miles or twenty-six days or less. The pay of mixed train Conductors to be computed at freight rates, the monthly compensation to be based on a mileage of 2,600 miles or twenty-six days per month, and any excess over 2,600 miles or twenty-six days, Conductors and Brakemen will be paid in the same proportion as the monthly compensation is to 2,600 miles. If the mileage of a freight Conductor or Brakeman falls below 2,600 miles in any one month, and he has been ready for service, losing no time on his own account, in such case full time for 2,600 miles shall be allowed, provided they report for work three times a day.

2. Should it become necessary to reduce the force on account of decreased business, the Conductor still remains in the employ of the Company as Brakeman, his promotion is to date from the time he made his first trip as Conductor; and he shall receive the highest rate paid Brakemen.

3. Conductors and Brakemen will be allowed ten miles per hour for dead-heading on passenger trains; all other dead-heading will be computed as actual miles run.

4. In case of dismissal or suspension of a Conductor or Brakeman by anyone below the Division Superintendent in rank, he shall have the right to appeal to the Division Superintendent for a full and impartial investigation; should the Division Superintendent fail to adjust the case, the Conductor or Brakeman may appeal to the General Manager.

5. No fault will be found with any Conductor or Brakeman who refuses to go out on account of needed rest, eight hours being considered sufficient.

6. When a freight Conductor or Brakeman is taken from his run for an alleged fault an investigation will be held within five days. If found innocent he shall receive pay for all time lost. No punishment will be fixed without a thorough investigation.

7. Conductors and Brakemen will be allowed to lay off on account of the sickness of themselves or their families, provided due notice is given to the proper officials so that their places may be filled by other men.

8. The rights of a Conductor commence on the day of his promotion, and he shall have the choice of runs to which his age and qualifications as Conductor entitle him.

9. Where passenger crews run over more than one freight division the oldest

freight Conductor on either division will be considered as entitled to passenger runs, merit and ability for increased responsibility to govern.

10. On other than assigned runs the crews will run, first in, first out.

11. Conductors and Brakemen will be paid for all delayed time at terminal stations, provided the delay exceeds thirty-five minutes, they will also be paid for all delayed time between terminal stations in cases of accidents, wash-outs and being snow-bound. No claim will be made unless there is thirty-five minutes delay. All delayed time will be paid at the rate of ten miles per hour, eleven hours to constitute a day's work.

12. The Switchmen's schedule to go into effect at the following yards, St. Ignace, Marquette, Negaunee, Ishpeming, Humboldt, Republic, Michigamme and Houghton, at the same time as trainmen's schedule.

13. The following rates of pay shall be paid yardmen: Day men in charge of engines shall be paid $65 for twenty-six days, ten hours to constitute a day's work, overtime to be paid at the same rate; day Helpers to be paid $60 for twenty-six days, ten hours to constitute a day's work, overtime to be paid at the same rate; night men in charge of engines to be paid $70 for twenty-six days, ten hours to constitute a day's work, overtime to be paid at the same rate; night Helpers to be paid $65 for twenty-six days, ten hours to constitute a day's work.

14. In the matter of overtime anything over twenty minutes shall go in as one hour.

15. The pay of mixed train Brakemen will be computed at freight train rates.

16. *Rules for Computation:* The monthly compensation is to be based on a mileage of 2,600 miles or twenty-six days per month, and any excess over the mileage made by freight Brakemen will be paid for on the same proportion as the monthly compensation is to 2,600 miles.

17. Brakemen who are laid off, owing to decreased business; will be reinstated and hold their rights, provided they report for work when wanted.

18. Freight Brakemen will be notified when time is not allowed, as per trip report, and reason given.

19. *Extra Mileage:* All runs of less than 100 miles will be computed as one day's work, provided the men do not go out again the same day, except in branch runs where the mileage is less than sixty miles per day, where the Company agrees to make special agreement with the Brakemen as to the compensation they will receive.

20. *Delayed Time:* Brakemen will be called as nearly as possible one hour before the leaving of their trains.

21. *Dead-head Time:* When freight crews and way cars are ordered dead-headed, the crews will accompany their way cars. In ordering crews the first crew will run the train, the next crew dead-heading, when such service is required, dead-head crews being ahead of said crew on reaching terminal run.

22. The rights of a Brakeman commence on the day of his first trip.

23. The employment of the Brakemen is placed in the hands of the Division Superintendents or their representatives, but Brakemen will in all cases be placed as the Conductor's best judgment may dictate. If a Brakeman transfers from either the freight or passenger departments to the other, he forfeits all rights in the department which he leaves, and will be classed as a new employe, except in the case of disability.

24. In examining men on the books of rules, for promotion, the oldest Brakeman must have the preference, merit and competency being equal.

25. Call boys will be provided with a book on which Brakemen will register their names and the time they are called.

26. All delayed time will be paid at the rate of ten miles per hour.

27. Extra men to be allowed duty time, same as men who are assigned to regular runs.

28. *Passenger Service:* Passenger train Baggagemen handling express to be paid $65 for present work and mileage.

29. Passenger train Brakemen to be paid at the rate of $50 per month for present work and mileage. Freight train Brakemen to receive $45 per month for first two months, and 2 cents per mile thereafter.

30. Where it becomes necessary to add to the force of Conductors, men shall be promoted from the ranks of Brakemen, merit and ability for increased responsibility to govern, but all old Brakemen to have a fair and impartial examination without prejudice.
W. F. FITCH,
For the Brotherhood of Railroad Trainmen: General Manager.
J. B. MASON, JAS. M'CURDY, CHAS. BEAUDRY, JAS. DORAN, HORACE FEE.
July 1, 1892.

EAST TENNESSEE, VIRGINIA & GEORGIA RAILWAY; KNOXVILLE & OHIO RAILROAD; MEMPHIS & CHARLESTON RAILROAD, AND MOBILE & BIRMINGHAM RAILWAY

1. All through passenger Conductors will be paid $110 per month.
2. All local freight Conductors will be paid $90 per month, and crews assigned as at present date.
3. Sunday or extra work, done by local crews, shall be paid extra at the regular rates for such service.
4. No more through freight Conductors than are necessary to conduct the business in a proper manner shall be employed. When Conductors are not making fair wages the Superintendent's attention shall be called to the matter and, if not corrected, the same shall be referred to the general officers. The younger Conductors shall be taken off first, and shall be allowed to drop back as oldest Brakeman.
5. All Conductors doing work, other than their regular runs, shall be paid extra for such service, at regular rates of pay. This does not apply to branch Conductors making extra trips on branches.
6. No Conductor shall be required, by the Railroad Company, to give bond for handling mail, baggage or express, unless he is paid extra for such work.
7. Delayed time will not be allowed until the schedule time of the train shall have been exceeded by two hours. When the schedule time has been exceeded by two hours, and less than two hours and thirty minutes, two hours will be allowed. If exceeded by two hours and thirty minutes, three hours will be allowed; all fractional parts in excess of thirty minutes shall be counted one hour.
8. Thirty cents per hour to be paid for all delayed time, as per Section 7.
9. In computing overtime for extra freight trains, the average time of the longest and shortest through freight schedule of the division on which the extra is run shall be taken.
10. If a Conductor is called and, for any reason other than his own action, does not go out, he will be paid 30 cents per hour for the time so held, and will retain his rights to first run out, except where crews are assigned to regular runs.
11. Conductors will be notified when time is not allowed, as per their time ticket.
12. Conductors reporting for duty, after being off, shall register on the train register, and take their turn out as they appear on said register; unless their crew has been run by an extra man, when they will take his turn out.
13. Conductors not assigned to regular runs shall run first in, first out, on their respective divisions.
14. The oldest Conductor in service shall be given choice of run, and stand in line of promotion, in accordance with time card rule No. 7, subject to decision of general officers in cases of differences of opinion.
15. Conductors shall not be required to wait over thirty minutes at terminal stations, where Conductors are required to check seals, for clerk to check and sign seal report; if so, delayed time shall be paid.
16. Conductors voluntarily transferring from one division to another shall stand as new men.
17. Conductors living within one mile of the yard office shall be called, as near as practicable, one hour before leaving time of their respective runs. The Caller shall be provided with a book, in which Conductors will sign their names and time called.
18. Conductors' time shall commence when they register for duty, in a book provided for that purpose.
19. Conductors attending court or legal investigations, as witnesses, shall be paid $3.50 per day and expenses; the Company being entitled to witness' certificates.
20. No Conductor shall be required to pay a fine for any accident, or for any short or damaged freight, unless he so desires.
21. No Conductor will be required to pay for lamps, equipment nor supplies of any kind. Conductors agree to take the best possible care of all equipment and supplies furnished them.
22. Conductors dead-heading with caboose shall be paid the regular rate of pay. If dead-heading to any point to take charge of a train, they shall be paid the regular rate of pay of the run taken charge of, and continue that rate until they are returned to their respective runs.
23. There shall be a Conductor with all light engines run over the road, except in cases of emergency. This does not apply to the pay-car engine.
24. Freight Conductors will not be required to wear caps nor uniforms, but will wear a badge furnished by the Company.
25. As far as practicable all short cars shall be switched in station order, and in front end of train; all open cars switched together, loads in front, and a sufficient

number of cars with good brakes to control the train, placed in the rear; such switching to be done by yard crews.

26. In case of accident, the Conductor shall only procure the signatures of his crew to accident report, except in cases of personal injury, such report to be left at proper office, for other signatures desired.

27. No Conductor relieved shall be suspended nor discharged until after a thorough investigation; all evidence shall be reduced to writing, and taken in the presence of a Conductor of his choice. If acquitted, he shall be paid all time lost; if discharged, he shall be paid for time in excess of five days required for the investigation.

28. The Division Superintendent shall preside over all investigating boards, when practicable, but no Conductor shall be discharged until the Superintendent has examined all the evidence in the case.

29. Any Conductor has the right to appeal from the decision of the division officer to the general officers, except dismissal for drunkenness.

30. It is further agreed, that, in case this agreement is violated by any party affected by it, instant notice shall be given to the Superintendent of the division within whose jurisdiction such violation occurred, such Superintendent shall immediately take all requisite proceedings, and make all necessary orders to correct the the violation, or failure of compliance, so as to enforce at all times strict performance of this agreement.

31. Complaints of violation of this agreement, not presented to Superintendent within thirty days of the occurrence, will not be considered.

SCHEDULE OF WAGES.

RANK.	RATE.
Passenger Conductors, through, per month.	$110 00
Passenger Conductors, local, per month.	90 00
Baggagemen, per month.	50 00
Passenger Brakemen, per month.	45 00
Freight Conductors, through, per 100 miles	2 80
Freight Conductors, local, per month.	90 00
Freight Brakemen, through, per 100 miles.	1 45
Freight Brakemen, local, per 100 miles.	1 80
General Yardmasters, per month.	110 00 / 125 00
Yardmasters, day, per month.	60 10 / 100 00
Yardmasters, night, per month.	70 00 / 90 00
Yard Conductors, per month.	40 00 / 75 00
Yard Couplers, per day.	1 25 / 2 00
Yard Switchmen, per day.	1 25 / 1 50

Approved: C. H. HUDSON, General Manager.
May 21, 1892.

W. A. VAUGHN,
General Superintendent.

ELGIN, JOLIET & EASTERN RAILWAY COMPANY.

Scale of wages, per month of twenty-six days: Conductors, freight and passenger, $90; Brakemen, $50; Yard Foremen, day, $65; Yard Helpers, day, $60; Yard Foremen, night, $75; Yard Helpers, night, $70.

May 10, 1892.

GEO. O. CLINTON,
Superintendent.

FALL BROOK COAL COMPANY.

Passenger Conductors receive $80 per month. Freight and coal train Conductors: First year, $2.25; second year, $2.40; third year and thereafter, $2.50, per day each year. From the commencement they are all entitled to $60 premium, provided their services have been ENTIRELY SATISFACTORY during the year. Train Baggagemen, from $50 to $70 per month, some of these are joint with the express company. Brakemen: First year, $1.62½; second year and thereafter, $1.75. Flagmen, $1.85. Switchmen: Day, $1.90; night, $2.15, for twelve hours' work. Our men run by the trip, and after a train is four hours late they get hour for hour until they reach terminal. As we pay our men overtime, for the year 1890 they averaged nine hours and fifty-three minutes for a day's work, and for the year 1891 they averaged nine hours and fifty-seven minutes.

May 17, 1892.

G. R. BROWN,
General Superintendent.

FERROCARRIL MEXICANO DEL NORTE.

Conductors, $150.00 per month; Baggagemen and Express Messengers, $80.00 per month, $45.00 by Express Company and $35.00 by Railroad; Brakemen, Mexican, $50.00 per month; Yardmasters, $135.00 per month; Switchmen, $60.00 per month.
May 11, 1892.   V. P. SAFFORD, Superintendent.

FERROCARRIL MEXICANO DEL SUR.

Engine-drivers, American, $150 per month; Engine-drivers, Mexican, $100 per month. Firemen, Mexican, $1.50 per day. Conductors, American, $125 per month. Baggagemasters (train), Mexican, $60 per month. Rear Brakemen, Mexican, $1.35 per day; ordinary Brakemen, Mexican, $1.25 per day. Yardmasters, American, $125 per month; Yardmasters, Mexican, $75 per month. Yardmen and Switchmen, Mexican, $1.50 per day. The foregoing wages are all payable in Mexican silver. No distinction is made at present between Engineers, Conductors, Firemen, etc., of passenger, freight or construction trains so far as their pay is concerned. No mileage basis is used, but trainmen of regular trains are allowed extra time when called upon to take out specials on their lay-over days. A fair monthly mileage average would be about 2,800 miles per month on mixed trains for each man, and more or less the same for freight and construction trains. We have no regular passenger trains at present.
May 15, 1892.   W. MORCON, Manager.

FLINT & PERE MARQUETTE RAILROAD.

Passenger: Conductors, $100 per month; Baggagemen, $2 per day; Brakemen, $1.90 per day. Local Freight: Conductors, 4 cents per mile; Brakemen, 2.8 cents per mile; overtime, at 27 and 18 cents per hour, to be allowed for over twelve hours from time of commencing work at one terminal until arrival at other terminal. Through Freight: Conductors, 3 cents per mile; Brakemen, 2 cents per mile; overtime after twelve hours on any division, at 27 cents per hour for Conductors and 18 cents per hour for Brakemen; time to commence from time marked or scheduled to leave one terminal until arrival at other terminal. Log: Conductors, 3 cents per mile; Brakemen, 2 cents per mile; overtime, at 27 and 18 cents per hour, after eight hours between main line points. Wood, Work, Tie and Gravel: Conductors, $3 per day; Brakemen, $2 per day; overtime after twelve hours, at 27 and 18 cents per hour. Snow Plow: Conductors, 3 cents per mile; Brakemen, 2 cents per mile; for actual mileage, but allowed ten miles per hour for actual time consumed. Yard Service: Night Foremen, $2.50 per day or 25 cents per hour; night Helpers, $2.10 per day or 21 cents per hour; overtime after ten hours, at 25 and 21 cents per hour; day Foremen, $2.35 per day or 23½ cents per hour; day Helpers, $2 per day or 20 cents per hour; overtime after ten hours, at 23½ and 20 cents per hour.
May 11, 1892.   W. F. POTTER, General Superintendent.

FORT WORTH & RIO GRANDE RAILWAY COMPANY.

Passenger Conductors, $100.00 per month. Freight Conductors, 3 cents per mile. Freight Brakemen, 2 cents per mile. Passenger Porters, $50.00 per month, no Brakemen. Passenger Engineers, 3½ cents per mile. Freight Engineers, 4 cents per mile. Freight Firemen, 2½ cents per mile. Passenger Firemen, 2 cents per mile. Overtime figured 10 miles per hour at same ratio.
May 28, 1892.   A. A. MILLER, Superintendent Transportation.

GREAT NORTHERN RAILWAY; WILLMAR & SIOUX FALLS RAILWAY, AND DULUTH, WATERTOWN & PACIFIC RAILWAY.

Passenger Conductors, $100.00 per month. Passenger Brakemen, $50.00 per month. Train Baggagemen, $55.00 per month. Freight Conductors, 3 cents per mile. Freight Brakeman, 2 cents per mile. Work train Conductors, $80.00 per month. Work train Brakemen, $60.00 per month. Yardmasters, $125.00 per month. Assistant Yardmasters, $105.00 per month. Night Yardmasters, $95.00 per month. Day Foremen, $2.69 per day. Night Foremen, $2.89 per day. Day Switchmen, $2.50 per day. Night

Switchmen, $2.69 per day. A standard day's work for freight trainmen is a run of 100 miles, to be made within a continuous period of ten hours or less, fractions of one-half hour or more, above 10 hours, to be computed as a full hour, and of less than one-half hour to be rejected, mileage being allowed for this overtime at the rate of ten miles per hour. For work train Conductors 12 hours constitute a day's work, and the work days in each calendar month constitute a month's work; all overtime to be paid pro rata. Snow plow men are paid on the same basis as freight trainmen. The salary of trainmen running mixed trains is fixed by Division Superintendent, with regard to the scale of wages established for other trainmen, on such basis as will offer a just compensation for the service rendered. Yardmen at points outside Minneapolis and St. Paul are paid in accordance with the amount of work they have to do, reference being had to the scale of wages paid in St. Paul and Minneapolis. C. W. CASE,
May 9, 1892. General Superintendent.

HOUSTON & TEXAS CENTRAL RAILWAY COMPANY.

Main line passenger Conductors, $120 per month; Brakemen, $55. Mixed train, Conductors, $100 per month. Freight Conductors, $90 per month, and 3 cents per mile for each mile over 3,000; Brakemen, $60 per month, and 2 cents per mile for each mile over 3,000. Train Baggagemen, $65 per month. Yard men, at Houston yard: General Yardmaster, $150 per month; night Yardmaster, $110 per month; day Foreman, 27 cents per hour; night Foremen, 29 cents per hour; day Switchmen, 25 cents per hour; night Switchmen, 27 cents per hour. At other points day Yardmasters are paid from $80 to $90 per month; night Yardmasters, $75 to $80 per month; Switchmen, $2.10 to $2.25 per day. G. A. QUINLAN,
May 13, 1892. Chief Engineer and General Superintendent.

ILLINOIS CENTRAL RAILROAD COMPANY.

1.   PASSENGER SERVICE.

RANK.	4,000 miles, or less on regular runs, per calendar month.	Over 4,000 miles to 6,000 per calendar month.	Over 6,000 miles per calendar month, extra per mile.
Conductors, through.	$100 00	$115 00	$0 02
Baggagemen, through.	55 10	60 00	0125
Brakemen and Flagmen, through.	50 00	55 00	01
Train Porters, through.	30 00	35 00	008
Conductors, local or branch.	90 00	105 00	0175
Baggagemen, local or branch.	50 00	55 00	01
Brakemen and Flagmen, local or branch.	45 00	50 00	009
Train Porters, local or branch.	30 00	35 00	006

2. Crews regularly assigned to fast mail runs between Chicago and Centralia will be allowed the maximum monthly rate established for through passenger service. This allowance to cover all mileage made on their assigned runs.
3. Passenger crews assigned to regular runs, failing to make a full month, will be paid pro rata for services performed.
4. Passenger crews on regular runs doubling to make up time lost by other men will be allowed the extra mileage so made at the regular rates for such runs in addition to their regular compensation.
5. When regularly assigned passenger men are called upon to run extra or special passenger trains, they will be paid the same mileage rate as they would receive on their regular runs for all mileage so made.
6. Freight crews temporarily on regular passenger runs will be paid at the regular rates for such runs. Freight crews assigned to special passenger trains will be paid at local passenger rates for mileage so made.
7. When through and local passenger runs are pooled, and passenger crews run around in turn, the classification of the pooled runs will be determined by the class of train which contributes the greatest portion of the mileage, and all crews will receive alike the rates of pay for that service.
8. Through passenger trains will comprise those runs which have a continuous schedule over more than one division, and change crews at division points. Trains scheduled on one division, and run through by the same crew, are local passenger trains.
9. Pay car and special runs will be classed as local.
10. When trainmen desire to lay off they shall do so at the point designated fo

the purpose by their Trainmaster, otherwise they will pay the mileage of men sent to take their places when they request to be relieved from duty.

11. It is the intention that no unreasonable service in making extra mileage shall be exacted under this schedule from passenger crews on regular, assigned runs.

12.   FREIGHT SERVICE.

RANK.	RATE.	OVERTIME.
Conductors, irregular freight runs..	$0 03 per mile.	10 miles per hour.
Brakemen, irregular freight runs..	02 per mile	10 miles per hour.
Conductors, local freight and mixed trains.................................	90 00 per month.	30 cents per hour.
Brakemen, local freight and mixed trains	60 00 per month.	20 cents per hour.
Conductors, work trains..	90 00 per month.	30 cents per hour.
Brakemen, work trains...	55 00 per month.	20 cents per hour.

Colored Brakemen on lines south of Ohio river will be paid 15 per cent. less than white Brakemen.

13. There shall be two grades of freight Conductors and Brakemen. For first year's service 10 per cent. less than the established rates will be paid. After one year's service full rates as provided in this schedule will be paid: 36,000 miles actual service to be considered the first year's service. To freight Conductors promoted between October 1, 1890, and November 1, 1891, a refund will be made of the 10 per cent. reduction from full rates on the last six months of the first year of actual service as Conductors; and to all freight Conductors promoted on or after November 1, 1891, a refund will be made of the full 10 per cent. reduction from full rates for the year. Refund will be made upon application at the expiration of the first year's service as above, provided they render faithful and efficient service, have clear record, and prove themselves reliable, competent men. Experienced Conductors and Brakemen employed from other roads will receive full rates of pay.

14. The actual number of days in any calendar month, of twelve hours per day, exclusive of Sundays, will constitute a month's work for that month in local or mixed freight or work train service, except on those local freight runs to which three crews are assigned. On local freight runs having three regular crews, four single trips per week over the district will constitute full time, thirteen hours being allowed for each trip. Crews assigned to regular freight runs will be paid additional, at established rates, for extra trips run outside of their regular work. No deduction will be made from the pay of work train crews by reason of their not working, when ready for duty and not assigned to other duty or relieved at district terminal.

15. Overtime will be allowed as follows: Crews in irregular freight service, on runs not otherwise specified, for time on duty in excess of one hour for each ten miles run. On local freight or mixed runs where single trip is made each working day, after twelve hours continuous service; and on such runs where four trips per week are made, after thirteen hours' continuous service. On local freight turn-around trips, where the time consumed on the road and in switching at turn-around points exceeds twelve hours. In work train service, after twelve hours on duty. In computing overtime any fraction of an hour, thirty minutes or less, will not be counted; over thirty minutes will be called an hour.

16. In local freight service there shall be three crews with three Brakemen on each crew assigned to each main line district between Chicago and New Orleans, Chicago and Sioux City, Centralia and Amboy; also between Springfield and Gilman. On the Water Valley district, during the months of light business, the number of crews may be reduced to two. On local freight runs not specified the Division Superintendent will arrange the assignment of men and crews as is consistent with the requirements of the service and business.

17. When a crew is called for a freight trip of 50 miles or less, 50 miles will be allowed; and where over six hours are consumed in a run, 100 miles will be allowed. When called for a freight trip of over 50 miles and less than 100 miles, 100 miles will be allowed; and when more than 100 miles, actual mileage will govern. Overtime on such trips will be allowed when the time consumed on the road and in switching at turn-around points is in excess of six hours on a run where 50 miles is allowed, and twelve hours on a run where 100 miles is allowed. Districts 90 miles or over, and less than 100 miles, will be allowed 100 miles for each single trip over the district. Districts less than 90 miles will be allowed 100 miles unless doubled on the same date, in which case actual mileage will be allowed. This rule not to interfere with the present allowance of mileage between Amboy and Freeport. Crews required to double between Mendota and Sublette will be allowed 20 miles extra for each double.

18. When a crew is called for work train service, one-half day will be allowed when on duty six hours or less; if over six hours, a full day will be allowed, with extra time for service over twelve hours.

19. Mileage will be allowed on the following runs, as specified below:

RUNS.	MILES.
Chicago to Kankakee or Otto and return	150
Champaign to Effingham and return	145
Centralia to DuQuoin and return	100
Centralia to Carbondale and return	130
Mounds to Carbondale and return	110
Mounds to DuQuoin and return	200
Clinton to Springfield and return	100
Clinton to Gilman and return	150
Clinton to Pana and return	135
Clinton to Vandalia and return	175
Mounds to Martin and return	200
Jackson, Tenn., to Grand Junction and return	100
Jackson, Tenn., to Holly Springs and return	200
Water Valley to Holly Springs and return	100
Water Valley to Durant and return	200
Canton to Durant and return	100
Canton to Grenada and return	200
McComb City to Jackson, Miss., and return	200

Overtime on the above turn-around trips will be allowed for all time used on the round trip in excess of ten miles per hour, less four hours at Kankakee, Otto, DuQuoin, Martin and Pana, and two hours at other turning points. Time to be reckoned from starting point to time of arrival back at starting point. An exception will be made in case of the turn-around trip from Centralia to DuQuoin and return, where only two hours will be deducted in computing time. When Chicago district crews are held over at Gilman to exceed fifteen hours, except Sunday, time in excess of fifteen hours will be paid for at the rate of ten miles per hour.

20. For light runs, engine and caboose, full mileage will be allowed.

21. Crews dead-heading under orders on passenger trains will be paid one-half their regular rates. On freight trains they will be paid full rates.

22. It is the intention to run crews not assigned to regular runs, first in, first out, but the right is reserved to depart from this rule when the interests of the Company require it.

23. On the main line and Memphis and Springfield divisions trainmen not on regularly assigned runs, and living within one mile of the yard, will be called as nearly as practicable one hour before the leaving time of their train. Men on regularly assigned runs will be called between the hours of 7 P. M. and 7 A. M. The working time of trainmen will begin at the time set for the departure of their train, except when crews assigned to regular runs are notified at least one hour before the leaving time of their train of the time at which they are required to report for duty.

24. Where time is not allowed as per Conductor's time slip it shall be returned to him at once, with reasons for not allowing same.

25. Conductors and Brakemen will not be dismissed nor suspended from the Company's service without just cause. In case of suspension or dismissal if the employe thinks his sentence unjust, he shall have the right within ten days to refer his case, by written statement, to the Division Superintendent. Within ten days from the receipt of this notice his case shall have a thorough investigation by the Division Superintendent, at which he shall be present. In case he shall not be satisfied with the result of said investigation, he shall have the right to appeal to the General Superintendent and to the General Manager. In case the suspension or dismissal is found to be unjust, he shall be reinstated and paid for time lost.

26. When freight crews are called and report for duty, and for any cause the train is abandoned, they shall be paid at overtime rates for each hour so held on duty and will stand first out.

27. Trainmen attending court at the request of the Company, if on assigned runs, shall be allowed full time, and when in irregular service, 100 miles per day, until ordered to resume work in the department in which they are employed, with the necessary expenses while away from home, same not to exceed $2 per day.

28. Trainmen will be allowed eight hours' rest after sixteen hours' continuous service, unless they go out voluntarily.

29. The right to regular runs and to promotion will be governed by merit, ability and seniority. Everything being equal, the men longest in continuous service will have preference, the Division Superintendent to be the judge as to qualifications. Nothing in this article shall be construed as preventing the Company from employing experienced men from other roads, when the good of the service requires it.

30. In event of there being a surplus of crews and it becomes necessary to reduce their number, the oldest men shall have preference in employment except where, in the judgment of the Division Superintendent, for good reasons which will be made

known upon application, younger men in the service are considered more reliable and efficient; it being the intention to retain the most capable men in the service. Conductors retired by reason of a reduction of crews shall have preference in employment as Brakemen.

31. So far as consistent with the interests of the Company the number of crews will be kept down to correspond with the business, so that crews in irregular freight service may make 3,000 miles per month.

32. It is hereby understood to be the duty of Conductors to promptly file charges, in writing, to their superior officer, against any unreliable or unsafe Brakeman who may have been assigned to them; and, in the interest of retaining in the service the best men, it shall be the duty of such superior officer to promptly investigate, and if the charges preferred are found correct, such Brakeman is not to be transferred to another crew, but promptly dismissed.

33. Any grievance which may exist and is not rectified shall be presented, in writing, to the Division Superintendent within thirty days of its occurrence, to the end that proper action toward its abatement may be taken without unnecessary delay.

34. All schedules, rules and regulations in conflict with these now adopted are void.

35. No portion of this agreement will be violated nor abrogated by any party thereto without written notice of such intention being served on all parties hereto, at least fifteen days before any action will be taken.   A. W. SULLIVAN,
For Passenger and Freight Trainmen :   General Superintendent.
W. J. MURPHY, Chairman of Committee.   Approved : J. T. HARAHAN,
December 1, 1891.   Second Vice President.

INDIANAPOLIS, DECATUR & WESTERN RAILWAY.

Passenger Conductors, 1¼ cents per mile. Passenger Brakemen, 8-10 cents per mile. Baggagemaster and Express Messenger (our proportion) 80 cents per trip. Baggagemaster and Express Messenger (Tuscola Accommodation), $20 per month. Local freight Conductors, 3 cents per mile. Through freight Conductors, 2¼ cents per mile. Local freight Brakemen, 2 cents per mile, three men to crew. Through freight Brakemen, 1¼ cents per mile. Passenger Engineers, 3 cents per mile. Local freight Engineers, 4 cents per mile. Through freight Engineers, 3¼ cents per mile. Firemen, 55 per cent. of Engineers' pay. Construction, gravel and wreck trains: Conductor, $2.50 per day of ten hours; 25 cents per hour overtime. Brakemen, $1.50 per day; 15 cents per hour overtime. Engineers, $3 per day; 30 cents per hour overtime. Indianapolis Yard: Yardmaster, day, $100 per month: night, $90 per month. Foreman, day, 25 cents per hour; night, 26 cents per hour. Brakeman, day, 23 cents per hour; night, 24 cents per hour. Yardmaster at Decatur, $65 per month. Brakemen, $45. Overtime for all time over one hour late on regular trains as follows: Conductors and Engineers, 30 cents per hour. Brakemen, 20 cents per hour. Firemen fifty-five per cent of Engineers.   L. A. BOYD,
May 12th, 1892.   Superintendent.

INTERCOLONIAL RAILWAY OF CANADA.

SERVICE.	CONDUCTORS, PER DAY.	BRAKEMEN† PER DAY.
First six months	$1 75	$1 20
Second six months	1 75	1 25
Second year	1 80	1 30
Third year	1 90	1 35
Fourth year	2 00	1 40
Fifth year	2 10	1 45
Sixth year*	2 20	1 50
Seventh year	2 30	
Eighth year	2 40	
Ninth year and afterwards	2 50	

* After the sixth year Brakemen and Switchmen receive $1.50 per day.
† Switchmen receive same pay as Brakemen.

Shunters in the yards 5 cents per day more than Brakemen, but not a higher rate than $1.50. Foreman Shunters, $1.60 per day. Yardmasters are paid $1.75 and $2 per day according to the importance of the station at which they are employed.
   D. POTTINGER,
May 19th, 1892.   Chief Superintendent.

INTERNATIONAL & GREAT NORTHERN RAILROAD.

SCHEDULE OF WAGES.

RANK.	RATE.
Conductors, passenger, per month.	$100 00
Brakemen, passenger, per month.	55 00
Train Porters, passenger, per month.	40 00
Baggagemasters, per month.	60 00
Conductors, freight, per mile.	03
Brakemen, freight, per mile.	02
Yardmasters, day, in large yards, per month.	125 00
Yardmasters, night, in large yards, per mont	100 00
Foremen, day, in large yards, per day of ten hours.	2 70
Foremen, night, in large yards, per day of ten hours.	2 90
Switchmen, day, in large yards, per day of ten hours.	2 50
Switchmen, night, in large yards, per day of ten hours.	2 70

May 9, 1892. T. G. GOLDEN,
General Superintendent.

INTEROCEANIC RAILWAY OF MEXICO, LIMITED.

Conductors, from $80 to $100 per month. Train Baggagemen, $70 per month. Brakemen, Switchmen and Yardmen, $1 per day.   CHARLES CLEGG,
May 20, 1892.   General Manager.

IOWA CENTRAL RAILWAY COMPANY.

Conductors: Passenger, $105 per month; through freight, $2.90 per 100 miles; local freight, $3 and $3.10 per trip, according to division. Brakemen: Passenger, $45 and $50 per month, according to run; through freight, $1.90 per 100 miles; local freight, $2 and $2.15 per trip. Yardmasters, $90 and $100 per month. Foremen, day, $2.25 per day; night, $2.40. Switchmen, day, $2 per day; night, $2.15, at all points except Bartlett, which is near Peoria, where we work days only, and pay: Foremen, 27 cents per hour; Switchmen, 25 cents per hour.   C. H. ACKERT,
May 16, 1892.   General Manager.

JACKSONVILLE SOUTHEASTERN LINE.

1. All Conductors and Brakemen in passenger service shall be paid as follows: Conductors on through runs between St. Louis and Eureka, $100 per month; Brakemen on through runs between St. Louis and Eureka, $50 per month; all other passenger Conductors, $90 per month; all other passenger Brakemen, $50 per month.

2. All Conductors and Brakemen in freight service shall be paid as follows: On all local freights, Conductors to be paid $3.45 per trip; on all local freights, Brakemen to be paid $2.30 per trip; 100 miles or less to constitute a day's work; twelve hours or less to constitute a day's work; no overtime to be allowed unless those hours are exceeded; for every hour or fractional part of an hour in excess of twelve hours shall be paid—Conductors, 30 cents per hour, and Brakemen, 20 cents per hour; more than thirty minutes counting one hour, less than thirty minutes counting nothing. Through freight crews to be run first in, first out of all terminals. Through freight Conductors to be paid 3 cents per mile; through freight Brakemen to be paid 2 cents per mile; 100 miles or less to constitute a day's work; ten hours or less to constitute a day's work; no overtime to be allowed unless those hours are exceeded; for every hour or fractional part of an hour in excess of ten hours Conductors shall be paid 30 cents per hour, Brakemen shall be paid 20 cents per hour; more than thirty minutes counting one hour, less than thirty minutes counting nothing. In computing delayed time for special or extra trains not run on schedule, the average train of the same class to be taken as their basis for schedule time. Exceptions: Through freight doubles between Jacksonville and Peoria, when made in eighteen hours or less, to be paid on mileage basis; if over eighteen hours, two days or 200 miles. Through freight doubles between Jacksonville and Litchfield, when made in sixteen hours or less, to be paid on mileage basis; if over sixteen hours, two days or 200 miles.

3. All work train Conductors shall be paid $3 per day; all work train Brakemen shall be paid $2 per day; twelve hours or less to constitute a day's work; 100 miles or less to constitute a day's work; no overtime to be allowed unless those hours are exceeded; for every hour or fractional part of an hour in excess of twelve hours Conductors shall be paid 30 cents per hour, Brakemen 20 cents per hour; more than thirty minutes counting one hour, less than thirty minutes counting nothing.

4. The time of all Conductors and Brakemen shall commence one hour after the Caller's book is signed, and to end when relieved from duty. Conductors and Brakemen shall not be called for duty until one hour before their train is ready to leave, unless otherwise arranged to get meals.

5. When Conductors and Brakemen are ordered out and are not used, on account of train being abandoned or from any other cause, Conductors shall receive 30 cents per hour and Brakemen 20 cents per hour for the time held, and stand first out.

6. Lights, viz., Conductor with light engine or with crew and caboose, whether running extra or as a section of a passenger train, the Conductor and Brakemen to be paid same as on through freight.

7. When Conductors or Brakemen are requested to dead-head over any portion of the road, per order of superior officer, on Company's business, Conductors shall be paid 1½ cents per mile and Brakemen 1 cent per mile. When Conductors are required to dead-head over any district of the road, in order to relieve a Conductor or Brakeman at his own request, said Conductor or Brakeman not being incapacitated from work through any illness of his own or member of his family, the said Conductor or Brakeman will pay the charge for dead-heading made by the man who relieves him; this charge to be deducted on the pay roll from the pay of the party relieved. Exceptions: No charge will be made by Conductors and Brakemen when it is necessary to send Conductors and Brakemen to relieve men on the locals between Pekin and Springfield, Litchfield and Mt. Vernon, Litchfield and Columbiana, Litchfield and Springfield, and Litchfield and St. Louis.

8. In case Conductors and Brakemen are required to attend court, on Company's business, Conductors to be paid $3 per day and necessary expenses, Brakemen $2 per day and necessary expenses.

9. When crews of freight trains are required to do switching at terminals or division stations, where yard crews are stationed, they will be paid extra for such service at the rate of 30 cents per hour for Conductors and 20 cents per hour for Brakemen; less than thirty minutes not to be counted, thirty minutes and over, and less than one hour, to be computed as one hour; except taking on or leaving cars at Havana.

10. Trainmen will be notified when time is not allowed as per trip report.
May 20, 1892.
D. W. RIDER,
General Superintendent.

KANSAS CITY BELT RAILWAY COMPANY.

We do not use any Conductors or other trainmen. Foremen, day, $70 per month; night, $75. Switchmen, day, $65 per month; night, $70. Flagmen, $50 per month.
May 19, 1892.
DAY K. SMITH,
Superintendent.

KANSAS CITY, FORT SCOTT & MEMPHIS RAILROAD COMPANY, AND ASSOCIATED COMPANIES.—WEST OF THE MISSISSIPPI RIVER.

PASSENGER SERVICE.

1. *Main Line:* Through runs and other runs of over 4,000 miles: Conductors, $125 per month; Baggagemen, $65; Brakemen, $60; Porters, $45. Short runs of less than 4,000 miles: Conductors, $100 per month; Brakemen, $50.

Branch Lines: Current River Railroad: Conductors, $100 per month; Brakemen, $50. Other runs: Conductors, $110 per month; Brakemen, $55; Brakemen on Joplin division, until the mileage now made by them is decreased, $60. Wages of men employed jointly as Baggagemen and Express Messengers to be fixed in each case by arrangement with express company.

2. Regular freight Conductors or Brakemen when running on regular passenger trains or on specials will be paid passenger train rates; but if for running specials or only one or two trips as extra passenger men their pay is not as much as they would have made in freight service, they are also to be paid the difference.

FREIGHT SERVICE.

3. *Through Freights:* Conductors, 3 cents per mile; Brakemen, 2 cents. One hundred miles will be allowed for runs of 100 miles or less. On runs of more than 100 miles actual mileage will be paid.

4. *Local Freights:* Kansas City division: Conductors, 3½ cents per mile; Brakemen, 2½ cents. Springfield division: Conductors, 3½ cents per mile; Brakemen, 2½ cents. Ozark division: Conductors, $5 per trip; Brakemen, $3.20; Nos. 57 and 58, mixed trains, Conductors, $95 per month; Brakemen, $60. Arkansas division, runs of 100 miles or less: Conductors, 3½ cents per mile; Brakemen, 2½ cents. Current River division: Conductors, 3½ cents per mile; Brakemen, 2½ cents. Clinton division, long run: Conductors, $5.40 per trip; Brakemen, $3.85. Clinton division, short run: Conductors, $3.60 per trip; Brakemen, $2.60. Joplin division, between Fort Scott and Webb City: Conductors, $5 per trip; Brakemen, $3.35; this rate to apply only so long as the schedule time makes it necessary for three crews, when two crews can run these trains rates to be: Conductors, 3½ cents per mile; Brakemen, 2½ cents. Cherryvale division, Cherokee to Cherryvale and return: Conductors, 3½ cents per mile; Brakemen, 2½ cents. Fort Scott to Cherokee and return over different divisions: Conductors, 3½ cents per mile; Brakemen, 2½ cents. On runs over 100 miles in length, of which a part is through freight and a part local, the part that is through shall be paid for at 3 cents and 2 cents per mile, and the part that is local at 3½ cents and 2½ cents per mile.

5. *Other Trains:* Mine runs: Conductors, 3½ cents per mile; Brakemen, 2½ cents. Rich Hill branch: Conductors, $100 per month; Brakemen, $60. Overtime not to apply on Rich Hill branch unless scheduled hours are exceeded.

6. *Work Train Service:* Conductors and Brakemen will be paid $3 and $2 per day, respectively, twelve hours or less to constitute a day. Two Brakemen to be allowed when working on main line.

7. *Overtime:* On all freight runs of 100 miles or less, overtime will be paid if the hours used on the trip exceed ten hours, in which case all overtime will be paid, 30 cents per hour for Conductors and 20 cents per hour for Brakemen. On all freight runs exceeding 100 miles, trainmen will be paid overtime for all time used to complete the trip in excess of an average speed of ten miles per hour, at the above rate.

8. In computing overtime no fraction of an hour less than thirty minutes will be counted. Any fraction of an hour over thirty minutes will be counted an hour. Time consumed for meals will not be computed as overtime.

GENERAL REGULATIONS.

9. On runs of ninety-eight miles or more when other than local trains are required to unload gravel or to do other construction work, if more than thirty minutes are consumed in such work, it shall be paid for at overtime rates. The amount so allowed to be deducted from any overtime made on the same run.

10. On runs of ninety-eight miles or more when compelled to double grades in consequence of heavy trains or bad rails, the additional miles made in doubling will be paid for at the established rate. Exceptions to this are Sac River and James River grades.

11. When trainmen are required to remain on duty at terminal stations where yard crews are on duty, they shall be paid at overtime rates.

12. Crews to be paid one-half rates when dead-heading on passenger trains, and full rates when dead-heading with their cabooses or running as first section of passenger trains. In cases of crews dead-heading with cabooses, the first crew out will run the train the next crew dead-heading, and the dead-head crew on reaching terminal station will stand ahead of crew with whom they dead-headed.

13. Trainmen living within three-fourths of a mile from calling office at Kansas City, Fort Scott, Springfield, Thayer and West Memphis will be called between hours of 7 P. M. and 7 A. M., and those not assigned to regular runs, between 7 A. M. and 7 P. M. (until such time as electric or other appliances may be adopted), as nearly as practicable one hour before leaving time, the times for and at which they are called to be shown in Caller's book, which is to be signed by the men when called. Time to begin at the time for which called.

14. When trainmen are called, and for any reason other than their own acts, do not go out, if held on duty less than six hours, shall be paid for the time so held at overtime rates, and stand first out. If held more than six hours they will be paid for one day and be last out.

15. On all main line local runs of over 100 miles a third Brakeman will be allowed. On all main line runs of over 100 miles, doing local work for a part of the distance, a third brakeman will be allowed for that portion on which local work is done. On all shorter main line local runs, and on all branch local runs, the question of allowing a third Brakeman for all or a part of the distance shall be left to the judgment of the Division Superintendent.

16. That after continuous service of sixteen hours, trainmen shall take eight

KENTUCKY & INDIANA BRIDGE CO.—KENTUCKY MIDLAND RAILWAY. 89

hours rest before being called to go out; except in cases of wrecks, washouts or similar emergencies.

17. When engines leave terminal stations without full supply of fuel, and in consequence Brakemen are obliged to shovel coal, they shall each be paid at the rate of 10 cents per ton.

18. When trainmen are required by their Division Superintendent to change their runs, and by so doing they are obliged to move their families and household goods, they shall be moved free of charge on application therefor. If they move at their own solicitation, one-half rates will be given. Men when first entering the service will receive no concession in rates.

19. When a trainman is suspended or discharged for an alleged fault he shall, within ten days after making written application to the Division Superintendent therefor, have a fair and impartial trial; and if found innocent shall be reinstated and paid for all time lost. Trainmen will be dismissed without hearing in cases of drinking on duty, intoxication, insubordination and collisions. Any trainman believing himself unjustly suspended or discharged shall have the right of appeal to the General Superintendent and General Manager. All men discharged or voluntarily quitting shall be given a card stating length and character of service and cause of leaving service.

20. Men requiring leave of absence shall give at least twenty-four hours notice; excepting in case of sickness, when as much time as practicable shall be given.

21. In the event of there being a surplus of crews and it becomes necessary to reduce their number, the oldest men shall have preference in employment; excepting where, in the judgment of the Division Superintendent, for good reasons which will be made known on application, younger men in the service are considered more reliable and efficient; it being the intention to retain the most capable men in the service. Conductors who are retired by reason of a reduction of crews shall have preference in employment as Brakemen. So far as consistent with the interests of the Company, the number of crews will be kept down to correspond with the business, so that crews in "chain-gangs" may make 3,000 miles per month.

22. In all cases when it becomes necessary to use an extra Conductor or Brakeman on any crew, the oldest extra Conductor or Brakeman shall have the preference when practicable; provided that no Conductor or Brakeman thus placed shall be relieved to make place for an older man until the regular man resumes work or the position is given permanently to the oldest extra Conductor or Brakeman.

23. It is hereby understood to be the duty of Conductors to promptly file charges, in writing, to their superior officer, against any unreliable or unsafe Brakeman who may have been assigned to them; and, in the interest of retaining in the service the best men, it shall be the duty of such superior officer to promptly investigate, and if the charges preferred are found correct, such Brakeman shall be assigned to other service or discharged, as the merits of the case may demand.

YARD SERVICE.

Kansas City Yard: Foremen, day, $70 per month; night, $75. Switchmen, day, $65 per month; night, $70. Counting working days only. Ten hours constitute a day's work. All overtime paid for at proportionate rates.

Memphis Yard: Foremen, day, $2.70 per day; night, $2.80. Switchmen, day, $2.35 per day; night, $2.50. Ten and one-half hours constitute a day's work. Overtime paid or at proportionate rates.

December 1, 1891.

W. W. FAGAN,
General Superintendent.

Approved: GEO. H. NETTLETON,
President and General Manager.

KENTUCKY & INDIANA BRIDGE COMPANY.

Passenger Conductors, $80 per month. Passenger Brakemen, $45 per month. Switchmen, $2.30 per day. Foreman switch engine, $2.70 per day. Yardmasters, $80 per month. Ten hours constitute a day's work.

May 18, 1892.

W. R. WOODARD,
General Manager.

KENTUCKY MIDLAND RAILWAY.

Passenger Conductors, $85 per month. Train Baggagemen, $50 per month. Passenger Brakemen, $45 per month. Mixed train Conductors, $75 per month. Freight Conductors, $2.50 per day (80 miles or ten hours). Mixed and freight train Brakemen, when two men on train, $2 per day. Mixed and freight train Brakemen, when three men on train, $1.85 per day.

May 16, 1892.

GEO. B. HARPER,
General Superintendent.

LAKE ERIE & WESTERN RAILROAD COMPANY.

RANK	RATE
Conductors, passenger, regular, except 5, 6, 9, 14, 16, and 17, per month	$100 00
Conductors, passenger, 5, 6, 9, 14, 16, and 17, and extra running, per month	90 00
Conductors, local freight, three crews to the district, per trip	4 90
Conductors, local freight two crews to the district, per trip	3 25
Conductors, through freight, per mile	03
Conductors, work or wreck trains, per day	3 00
Conductors, Minster branch, per month	65 00
Baggagemen, through runs, main line, per month	70 00
Baggagemen, I. & M. C. Division, except 9, 14, 16, and 17, per month	69 50
Baggagemen, trains 5, 6, 9, and 14, per month	57 50
Baggagemen and Brakemen, trains 7, 8, 16, and 17, per month	55 00
Brakemen, passenger, except 5, 6, 9, and 14, per month	47 50
Brakemen, passenger, 5, 6, 9, and 14, and extra running, per month	45 00
Brakemen, local freight, three crews to district per trip	3 15
Brakemen, local freight, two crews to district, per trip	2 10
Brakemen, through freight, per mile	02
Brakemen, work or wreck train, per day	2 00
Brakemen, Minster Branch, per month	40 00

Overtime. Local freight, where there are two crews to the district, will be paid overtime for all time over twelve hours; and where there are three crews to the district, for all time over sixteen hours, at the rate of 30 cents per hour for Conductors, and 20 cents per hour for Brakemen.

Through Freight or Extras. All time consumed in making the run in excess of that time necessary to complete the trip at an average rate of ten (10) miles per hour, will be paid for as overtime at the rate of 30 cents per hour for Conductors, and 20 cents per hour for Brakemen.

Work or Wreck. Will be paid overtime after twelve hours at the rate of 30 cents per hour for Conductors, and 20 cents per hour for Brakemen.

In computing delayed time no fraction of an hour less than thirty minutes shall be counted. Thirty minutes or over shall be counted an hour. Time to begin one hour after crew is called.

Lights will be paid, Conductors 2 cents, and Brakemen 1 4-10 cents per mile when running over an entire district, but when they turn and pick up train, or take freight over any portion of the run, full through rates will be paid.

Dead-heading on authority of proper officer, Conductors will be paid 1 5-10 cents, and Brakemen 1 cent per mile.

When attending court on Company's business Conductors shall receive $3.00, and Brakemen $2 00 per day; and in addition, when away from home station, $1.00 per day for expenses.

No Conductor or Brakeman shall be suspended or discharged upon any charge without having a fair and impartial hearing within five days of the time taken off; and at the hearing of the case shall have the right to have present any other Conductor or Brakeman he may select, with the Trainmaster, who shall hear the evidence of all witnesses. In case the decision rendered is not satisfactory an appeal may be taken from the Local to the General Officers. In case a final decision is not given within five days after the appeal is presented, the pay of the Conductor or Brakeman will be allowed thereafter at the rate he was receiving at the time of the offense.

Through freights between Peru and Indianapolis, or Peru and Michigan City, will be allowed ninety miles. Peoria and Paxton run will be allowed one hundred miles, except when train is run through to or from Lafayette; then actual mileage will be used, in either case, at through freight rates.

No extra will be allowed on account of train No. 15 handling freight.

Short turns, if made in six hours or less, and where the mileage is less than fifty miles, will be allowed fifty miles; or if more than fifty miles, actual mileage. Where over six hours is required, the mileage being less than one hundred miles, one hundred miles will be allowed. If over one hundred miles, actual mileage. When trainmen are called, and for any reason other than their own acts do not go out, if held for duty six hours they will receive fifty miles at through freight rates and stand first out. If held over six hours they will receive one hundred miles at same rate as above and fall behind other crews. For any time that is not covered properly by the above a fair allowance will be made by the trainmaster. When the switching at Bloomington makes it absolutely necessary for men to be on duty one hour or more longer than the time it would reasonably take to side-track ingoing trains, or couple up and get out of

g outgoing trains, the Conductor may be allowed 30 cents, and the Brakeman 20 nts overtime. This rule is only meant to cover extraordinary work at Bloomington, nd must not be taken advantage of.

Approved: GEO. L. BRADBURY,   O. W. BELL,
General Manager.   Master Transportation.
September 1, 1891.   D. S. HILL,
                                                General Superintendent.

LAKE SHORE & MICHIGAN SOUTHERN RAILWAY COMPANY.

Our main line passenger Conductors and Brakemen are paid $100 and $45, respectively, for as near 4,000 miles as the runs can be arranged. We have recently commenced to run passenger train crews through between Chicago and Toledo, and Toledo and Buffalo. These Conductors and Brakemen are paid $110 and $50 per month, respectively, for about 4,400 miles. On the branches passenger Conductors and Brakemen are paid $85 and $45, respectively; average mileage about 3,500 miles per month. Main line Baggagemen east of Toledo are paid $60 per month; west of Toledo, $55 per month. Average mileage about 5,000 miles. The difference in pay is on account of location and character of the work. Baggagemen on the branches are paid $50 per calendar month. When called upon to make extra trips they are paid at the same rate as above. Through freight Conductors and Brakemen are paid $70 and $50 per month, respectively, on a basis of 2,500 miles for a month's work; over 2,600 miles, pro rata. Way freight Conductors and Brakemen are paid $80 and $55 per month, respectively, month of 26 days. Overtime is paid to freight crews after twelve hours' service on the road; ten miles being allowed for each hour overtime. In our Chicago yards, yard Conductors and yard Brakemen are paid as below for ten hours per day or the number of working days in the month; over ten hours, pro rata: Day Conductors, $70 per month; night Conductors, $75 per month. Day Brakemen $65 per month; night Brakemen, $70 per month. At our other principal yards, such as Cleveland, Toledo, Buffalo and Detroit, we pay as follows on the same basis as at Chicago: Day Conductors, $67.60 per month; night Conductors, $70 per month. Day Brakemen, $60 per month; night Brakemen, $65 per month.

                                                  W. H. CANNIFF,
May 20, 1892.   General Superintendent.

LEHIGH & HUDSON RIVER RAILWAY COMPANY.

First-class Conductors, $2.75 per day; Baggagemen and Brakemen on express trains, $1.75 per day; Brakemen on local passenger trains, $1.60 per day; on way freight trains, $1.70 per day; on through freight trains, $1.60 per day. Freight and coal Conductors, $2.50 per day for first year; $2.75 thereafter if record is good. In the matter of freight Trainmen, we allow time in proportion when out over twelve hours, when delay is beyond their control.   N. L. FURMAN,
July 16, 1892.   Superintendent.

LOUISVILLE & NASHVILLE RAILROAD COMPANY.

1. There shall be established on each division a board of inquiry, to consist of the Superintendent or Assistant Superintendent (or both), the Master of Trains, and the Master Mechanic, or his representative (or both), whose duty it shall be to investigate accidents. In case employes are suspended to appear before this board, they will be given a hearing within five (5) days, and will receive prompt notice of the result of the investigation. All punishment shall consist of suspension or discharge. It shall not be necessary to convene the board except for the investigation of accidents. If the parties punished by the board, or otherwise, desire it, they may appeal, first, through the Master of Trains to the Superintendent, and then through the Superintendent of Transportation to the General Manager. All appeals must be presented to the Superintendent or Master of Trains within thirty (30) days after the decision of the board shall have been made known. Should the employes suspended be found innocent, they will be paid for the time the suspension was in effect—Conductors $2.85 per day, and Brakemen, Baggagemen and Yardmen $1.75 per day. To enable the division officers to make investigations, reports must be made to the proper officer at the end of each trip.

2. Road delay time will be allowed Conductors and Brakemen after the schedule of the train shall have been exceeded two hours, at the rate of thirty (30) and eighteen (18) cents, respectively, per hour, for every hour and fractional part thereof. When a train has been delayed to exceed two hours, the first two hours will be counted. In

case schedules are changed on the road, road delay time will be computed from schedule departed on. Wages shall be computed from one hour after the men are called, or the time that the train departs, if earlier. Road delay time for extra trains shall be arrived at by taking the average time of the schedule trains on the division, passenger or freight, as the case may be, except that on the Pensacola & Atlantic road the schedule of extra freight trains running between terminals shall be computed at the rate of twelve and one-half miles per hour.

3. Yard delay time at terminals shall be allowed at the rate of thirty (30) and eighteen (18) cents, respectively, per hour, for each hour or fractional part thereof after a train shall have been delayed within the yard limits beyond thirty minutes. Running time of the train within yard limits shall not be considered. When delayed immediately outside of the yard limit board, trainmen shall be allowed yard delay time at same rate, when delay exceeds thirty minutes. (Colored Brakemen will be paid for delay time ten per cent. less than white men.)

4. Trainmen will be called not to exceed one hour before leaving time of their trains, as at present. The Caller shall be furnished with a book, which must be signed by the men, showing the time that they are called, and the time the train is to depart. Failing to respond promptly, whether it is his turn out or not, the party at fault shall be suspended or discharged at the discretion of the Master of Trains. When trainmen come in on their runs, and are not able for duty, they must so notify the Master of Trains or his representative. If, afterward, on account of sickness, they can not go out, they must send a written notice to the Master of Trains or his representative, at least two hours before they are needed. They must not lay off, except by permission of an authorized officer, unless they, or a member of their immediate family, are suddenly taken sick, in which event they must give at least two hours' notice.

5. When trainmen are called to go out between the hours of 7 P. M. and 7 A. M., and the train is afterward annulled, they shall be allowed three hours at the rate of thirty (30) and eighteen (18) cents per hour, respectively; provided, they are not notified they will be required for another schedule train within one hour. When called to go out at other hours, in case train is annulled, they shall be paid at the same rate per hour; but time shall be computed from one hour after they are called until they are notified that train is annulled. Trainmen thus called will stand first out; provided it does not interfere with men who have regular runs.

6. For attending court or appearing before proper persons to give evidence, Conductors, Baggagemen and Brakemen, having regular crews, and yardmen having regular work, shall be paid the amount that they would have made had they performed their usual duties. This shall not prevent the Company from using these men on any run after they are through attending court, and before their regular crews are due to leave. Other Conductors and Brakemen shall be paid $3 and $2 per day, respectively, computed from the time they leave their homes, or the time they are marked to go out, until they return. They will be furnished with transportation to and from court. No pay shall be allowed in cases where the time so consumed does not interfere with the men making their regular trips and having eight (8) hours' rest, if they require it.

7. Conductors and Brakemen of wrecking trains shall be paid, respectively, thirty-five (35) and twenty (20) cents per hour or fractional part thereof, time to be computed from time train starts, or one hour after the men are called, until return to starting point. In case the train is laid up before returning, for the purpose of affording the men necessary time for rest and sleep, such proportion of the time shall be deducted from the whole, and only the actual time on duty will be paid for. A minimum of six hours will be allowed, but no mileage will be paid.

8. Conductors and Brakemen, when dead-heading on a freight train, will be allowed the rate of pay given the same class of men that are in charge of the train. When dead-heading on passenger train they will be paid one and one-quarter (1¼) and eight-tenths (8-10) of a cent, respectively, per mile for the distance traveled. When a man is traveling over the road for the purpose of relieving a man who has asked for leave of absence, he will not receive any compensation for the distance traveled.

9. After a continuous service of sixteen (16) hours, or more, Conductors and trainmen shall be entitled to and allowed eight (8) hours for rest at terminals, if they give proper notice of such desire, except in case of wrecks or similar emergencies.

10. Conductors will be notified when time is not allowed as per their trip reports.

11. Any trainman drinking intoxicants on duty, or being under their influence on or off duty, will be dismissed from the service of the Company.

12. All crews assigned to regular runs at a monthly rate, that are not provided for in the accompanying rate sheets, will be paid extra for all service performed in addition to their regular duties at established rates for class of service performed, except regular crews now performing extra duty without compensation.

13. Local grievances and differences of opinion as to construction of this agreement, shall be taken up with division officers; failing to be adjusted, they will be referred to the general officers, as per Article No. 1.

LOUISVILLE & NASHVILLE RAILWAY.

KENTUCKY CENTRAL DIVISION.

FROM.	TO.	CLASS OF TRAIN.	Length of run.	No. of trips per month.	Av. mileage per month.	CONDUCTORS.		BRAKEMEN AND FLAGMEN.		BAGGAGEMEN.	
						Trip.	Month	Trip.	Month	Trip.	Month
Cincinnati	Livingston	Passenger, 1 and 4	155	60							
Cincinnati	Lexington	Passenger, 5	99	30							
Cincinnati	Lexington	Passenger, 6	99	21							
Cincinnati	Cincinnati	Passenger, 2	99	4							
Lexington	Paris	Passenger, 13 and 16	19	52	4111	$45 00		$1 65		$1 70	
Lexington	Cincinnati and return	Passenger, 2 and 3	198	38							
Lexington	Paris, two round trips	Passenger	77	4							
Cincinnati	Falmouth and return	Passenger	80	36	5456		65 00		1 65		$22 50*
Lexington	Paris and return	Passenger			2080		70 00	$45 00		2 04	
Lexington	Paris and return	Passenger			4576		90 00		1 98		
Richmond	Maysville and return	Passenger	176	26	4576		75 00	45 00		1 70	60 00
Lexington	Milldale and return, five round trips	Passenger transfer	7				100 00		2 95		
Cincinnati	Livingston	Through freight	154			2 16	84 00		1 48		
Covington	Paris	Through freight	70			2 16	80 00		1 90		
Covington	Paris	Local freight	75			2 16	80 00		2 00		
Paris	Livingston	Through freight	75				80 00		1 86		
Paris	Livingston	Local freight	96			2 70	75 00		1 70		
Covington	Maysville and return	Local freight	98								
Richmond	Lexington	Mixed	96			4 05	75 00		2 75		
Covington	Rowland and return	Freight	150								
Paris	Rowland	Freight	57			2 70†			1 88†		
Paris	Ford and return	Freight	53								
Work train	Shearer and return	Freight						1 90‡			

* Express Company pays equal amount.   † Including switching.   ‡ Per day.   Parlor Car Porter, $1 per day.

LOUISVILLE, CINCINNATI & LEXINGTON DIVISION.

FROM.	TO.	CLASS OF TRAIN.	Length of run.	No. trips per month.	Av. mileage per month.	CONDUCTORS.		BRAKEMEN & FLAGMEN.		Baggagemen, per month.
						Trip.	Month	Trip.	Month	
Louisville......	Cincinnati....	Passenger.......	114	48.67	5548	......	$110 00	......	$45 00	$60 00
Louisville.......	Lexington....	Passenger.......	94	33		......	100 00	......	45 00	50 00
Louisville.......	Franktort....	Passenger.......	95	10.40	4065					
Louisville......	Lagrange....	Passenger.......	27	10.40						
Louisville......	Lagrange....	Passenger.......	27	52.17	1408	....	85 00	......	45 00	45 00
Louisville	Bloomfield ..	Passenger.......	57	60.83	3467	......	80 00	......	45 00	*55 00
Anchorage......	Bloomfield ..	Mixed.	45	52.17	2348	......	80 00	......	50 00	......
East Louisville..	Wilders.....	Through freight.	105			‡3 00		‡2 00		......
East Louisville..	Lexington...	Through freight.	92			2 75		1 85		......
East Louisville..	Lexington...	Local freight....	92				†85 00		†58 00	......
East Louisville..	Wilders.....	Local freight....	105				†85 00		†58 00	......
Lagrange........	Wilders.....	Freight.........	79			2 25		1 50		......
Work trains.....							‡85 00		‡58 00	......

*Joint pay with Express Company.   †Local crews work on an average 20.87 days per month
‡Extra pay for Sundays or when called at night for extra service.   Through passenger Flagme
Cincinnati division, $55 per month.

KNOXVILLE DIVISION.

The rates for turn-around freight runs between Rowland and Corbin shall be $4 fo
Conductors and $2.75 for Brakemen; overtime to commence at the expiration of six
teen hours.

All freight runs that are broken at Corbin will be run on same terms and unde
the same conditions as all single freight runs between Rowland and Corbin; viz., Con
ductors, $2, and Brakemen, $1.38 for a schedule trip.

The rates for turn around freight runs between Rowland and Pittsburg shall be $
for Conductors and $2 for Brakemen; overtime to commence at the expiration o
twelve hours.

The rates for single freight runs from Rowland to Pittsburg, or from Pittsburg t
Rowland, shall be $1.50 for Conductors and $1 for Brakemen; overtime to commenc
at expiration of seven hours.

Time is to be computed on these runs from the time the train departs, or one hou
after the crew is called, to the time the train is put away, or the crew relieved.

The rates for turn-around freight runs between Corbin and Livingston shall be $
for Conductors and $1.38 for Brakemen; one hour at Livingston for turning.

The rates for turn-around freight runs between Corbin and Jellico shall be $1.8
for Conductors and $1.20 for Brakemen; one hour at Jellico for turning.

LOUISVILLE DIVISION AND BRANCHES.

FROM.	TO.	CLASS OF TRAIN.	Length of run.	No of trips per month.	Mileage per month.	CONDUCTORS.		BRAKEMEN & FLAGMEN.		Baggagemen, per month.
						Trip.	Month	Trip.	Month	
Louisville.......	Nashville......	Passenger.......	186	30	5580	....	$110 00	*....	$45 00	$60 0
Louisville	Bowling Green..	Passenger.......	114	52	5928	......	85 00	......	45 00	50 0
Louisville.......	Jellico........	Passenger......	201	24	4824	......	110 00	......	45 00	50 0
Louisville	Springfield	Passenger.......	59	52	3068	......	100 00	......	45 00	30 0
Louisville.......	Springfield.....	Mixed.........	59	52	3068	......	80 00	......	50 00	......
Glasgow Junct...	Glasgow.......	Mixed.........	11	112	1232	......	55 00	......	37 50	......
Glasgow Junct...	Mammoth Cave†	Mixed.........	10½	120	1260	......	55 00			......
Lebanon.........	Greensburg.....	Mixed.........	31	52	1612	......	75 00	......	42 50	......
Louisville.......	Bowling Green..	Through freight.	114			‡3 25		‡2 10		......
Louisville.......	Bowling Green..	Local freight....	114				†85 00		†58 00	......
Louisville.......	Lebanon Junct..	Freight........	30			85		55		......
Louisville.......	Rowland.......	Freight........	105			3 10		2 05		......
Rowland........	Lebanon Junct..	Through freight.	75			2 27		1 56		......
Rowland........	Lebanon Junct..	Local freight....	75				85 00		58 00	......
Rowland........	Jellico.........	Through freight.	96			2 90		2 00		......
Rowland........	Jellico.........	Local freight....	96				85 00		58 00	......
Rowland........	Corbin.........	Freight........	66			2 00		1 38		......
Rowland........	London........	Freight........	52			1 57		1 08		......
Rowland........	Lebanon.......	Freight........	38			1 15		80		......
Rowland........	Greensburg....	Freight........	69			2 00		1 38		......
Lebanon........	Greensburg....	Freight........	31			90		63		......
Lebanon Junct ..	Corbin.........	Freight........	141			4 25		2 95		......
Work trains.....							85 00		58 00	......

*Parlor Car Porters, between Louisville and Nashville, $30 per month.   †Via Grand Avenu
Cave.   ‡Three crews average eighteen days per month.

LOUISVILLE & NASHVILLE RAILWAY. 95

CUMBERLAND VALLEY DIVISION.

FROM.	TO	CLASS OF TRAIN.	Length of run.	No. of trips per month.	Av. mileage per month.	Conduct'rs. per month.	Brakemen & Flagm'n. per month.	Baggagemen, per month.
Shawanee	Jellico and return	Passenger	159	30	4770	$90 00	$50 00	$30 00
Shawanee	Corbin and return	Passenger	100	30	3000	85 00	50 00	30 00
Shawanee	Norton and return	Passenger	136	30	4080	85 00	50 00	30 00
Shawanee	Middlesboro, 2 round trips	Passenger	25	30	750	30 00	50 00	
Corbin	Shawanee	Through and local	50			85 00	58 00	
Shawanee	Norton	Through and local	68			85 00	58 00	
Corbin	Norton	Through freight	117.9			*3 20	*2 10	

*Per trip. *Freight Crews:* Extra pay at same rates for Sunday work; 12 hours to constitute a day's work; additional hours to be paid for at the rate of 30 cents and 18 cents per hour, respectively.

MAIN STEM, SECOND DIVISION. NASHVILLE & DECATUR DIVISION. N. F. & S. R'Y.

FROM.	TO.	CLASS OF TRAIN.	Length of run.	No. of trips per month.	Av. mileage per month.	CONDUCTORS.		BRAKEMEN & FLAGMEN.		Baggagemen, per month.
						Trip	Month	Trip	Month	
Nashville	Pulaski	Passenger	79	52	4108		$80 00	*	$50 00	†25 00
Nashville	Montgomery	Passenger	304	20	6080		110 00		†50 00	60 00
Nashville	Decatur	Passenger	121	52	6292		95 00		55 00	†25 00
Nashville	Bowling Green	Mixed	72	52	3744		85 00	*	55 00	†20 00
Columbia	Sheffield	Passenger	85	52	4420		80 00	*	45 00	†25 00
Columbia	Iron City	Mixed	61	52	3172		75 00		50 00	
Bowling Green	East Nashville	Through freight	71			$2 25		$1 50		
Bowling Green	East Nashville	Local freight	71			3 00		2 00		
Bowling Green	White Stone Quarry ‖	Freight				1 25		75		
South Nashville	New Decatur	Through freight	121			3 10		2 05		
South Nashville	New Decatur	Local	121				85 00		58 00	
South Nashville	Columbia ‖	Through freight	90			3 10		2 05		
Columbia	Florence	Freight	80				75 00		50 00	
Iron City	Pinkney and Sharps ‖	Freight	25				45		20	
Napier Junction	Napier ‖	Freight	22				45		20	
Work trains							$85 00		$58 00	

*Porter, $15 per month. †Express Company pays equal amount. ‡Porter, $35 per month.
§And return. §Extra pay for Sundays, or when called at night for extra service.

SOUTH & NORTH ALABAMA R. R. BIRMINGHAM MINERAL R. R.

FROM.	TO.	CLASS OF TRAIN.	Length of run.	No. of trips per month.	Av. mileage per month.	Conduct'rs. per month.	BRAKEMEN AND FLAGMEN.		Baggagemen, per month.
							Trip.	Month.	
Nashville	Montgomery	Passenger	305	20.7	6314	$110 00	$1 80	$50 00	$40 00
Decatur	Birmingham*	Passenger	172	31	5332	85 00			†25 00
Birmingham	Montgomery	Mixed	96	62	5952	95 00	{1 40 / 1 60‡}		†25 00 / ‖1 80
Birmingham	Blockton*	Passenger	103	31	3193	90 00		50 00	†5 00
Birmingham	Champion*	Mixed	84	31	2604	85 00		50 00	†5 00
Decatur	Birmingham	Through freight	86			**2 75	{1 90 / 1 70‡}		
Decatur	Birmingham	Local freight	86	27	2322	85 00		58 00	
Birmingham	Blount Springs*	Freight	68	27	1836	85 00		{$57 00 / $51 00}	
Birmingham	Montgomery	Through freight	96			**2 75	{1 90 / 1 70‡}		
Birmingham	Montgomery	Local freight	96	18	1728	85 00		{58 00 / $53 00}	
Birmingham	Calera*	Freight	86	27	1782	85 00	*	{58 00 / $51 00}	
Work trains, S. & Fossil and Musco	N. and B. M. da Hills runs	Freight				85 00 90 00		{58 00 / ††60 00}	
All other freights on B. M. R. R.						85 00		{58 00 / $53 00}	

*And return. †Express Company pays equal amount. ‡Colored. ‖Per trip; does not act as Express Messenger. §Overtime after twelve hours, and extra pay for Sunday work at regular rates for class of service performed. **Per trip. ††Fossil Hill crew, extra pay for Sundays if train runs. Yardmaster at Warrior, $80 per month. Train Porters, $35 per month.

LOUISVILLE & NASHVILLE RAILWAY.

ALABAMA MINERAL RAILROAD.

FROM.	TO.	CLASS OF TRAIN.	Length of run.	No. of trips per month.	Av. mileage per month.	Conduct'rs, per trip.	Brakemen, per trip.	Flagmen, per trip.
Calera	Attalla	Passenger, 85-86*	119	60	4590	†$85 00	$1 00	$1 60
Attalla	Anniston	Mixed. 87-88	34	60	4590	‡2 50	1 00	1 60
Attalla	Anniston and return	Local freight	68	26	1768	3 25	1 25	1 60
Anniston	Calera and return	Through freight	170	26	4420	6 00	2 50	3 20
Anniston	Calera	Local freight	85	26	2210	3 25	1 25	1 60
Extra (twelve hours or less)						3 00	1 25	1 60

*Baggagemen, $26.25 per month, also acts as Express Messenger.   †Per month.   ‡Per day. Porters, $1 per day.

Conductors running regular freight trains when turned back from any point to do extra work, shall be paid at the rate of 30 cents per hour for the service performed in addition to their regular duties.

For turn-around trips on trains 95 and 96 Conductor will be entitled, according to rates of pay as per agreement, to $6 for round trip; delay time to be computed from arrival at Anniston; that is, if a man should arrive at Anniston to exceed two hours late he would be entitled to delay time as per Article 2.

Extra turn-around trips between Anniston and Calera, when in excess of twelve hours, shall be paid on the same basis as a schedule turn-around trip.

Two crews are to run Nos. 85 and 86 until a change of schedule is made that will permit of one crew running them; in that event, the rate of pay to be again adjusted.

MOBILE & MONTGOMERY DIVISION. PENSACOLA & SELMA, UPPER DIVISION.

FROM.	TO.	CLASS OF TRAIN.	Length of run.	No. of trips per month.	Av. mileage per month.	CONDUCTORS.		BRAKEMEN & FLAGMEN.		Bagg'emen, per month.
						Trip	Month	Trip	Month	
Montgomery	Mobile	Passenger	180	30	5400		$110 00		$50 00	$60 00
Montgomery	Mobile	Mixed	180	20	3600	$4 10		$2 80		
Pine Apple	Selma*	Mixed	94	26	2444		75 00		155 00	
Montgomery	Mobile	Freight	180			4 10		2 80		
Montgomery	Flomaton	Through freight	119			3 00		2 00		
Montgomery	Flomaton	Local freight	119				85 00		{ 58 00 / 50 00 }	
Mobile	Flomaton*	Through freight	121			3 10		2 10		
Mobile	Flomaton*	Local freight	121				85 00		{ 58 00 / 50 00 }	
Work trains							85 00		58 00	

*And return.   †White.   ‡Colored.   Train Porters, M. & M. division, $1.15 per day.

NEW ORLEANS & MOBILE DIVISION.

FROM.	TO.	CLASS OF TRAIN	Length of run.	No. of trips per month.	Av. mileage per month.	Conduct'rs, per month.	Brakemen & Flagm'n, per month.	Bagg'emen, per month.
New Orleans	Mobile	Passenger	141	36	5076	$110 00	$50 00	
New Orleans	Montgomery	Passenger	321	20	6420			$60 00
New Orleans	Ocean Springs	Passenger	84	52	4368	100 00	45 00	$30 00
New Orleans	Mobile	Mixed	141			80 00	55 00	
New Orleans	Mobile	Freight	141			80 00	55 00	

*Joint pay with Express Company.   Extra mileage on chartered, special and coast trains.

PENSACOLA, PENS. & ATL. AND PENSACOLA & SELMA (LOWER) DIVISIONS.

FROM.	TO.	CLASS OF TRAIN.	Length of run.	No. of trips per month.	Av. mileage per month.	Conduct'rs, per month.	BRAKEMEN. Per Trip.	
							White.	Col'ed.
Pensacola	Flomaton and return	Mixed	87	10 ‡	4090	$85 00	$1 60	$1 50
Pensacola	River Junction	Mixed	161	20 ‡				
Pensacola	Flomaton and River Junction	Passenger & mixed*	†165	30	4950	95 00	1 60	1 50
Pensacola	River Junction	Local freight	161			80 00	$2 45	$2 30
Pensacola	Caryville and return		199					
Pensacola	DeFuniak Springs and return		159			‡$2 50	‡$1 60	1 50
		Timber trains						
Pensacola	Repton	Mixed	73			**$3 50	1 60	1 50
Pensacola	Flomaton and return	All trains	87			‡2 50	1 60	1 50
Pensacola	Flomaton & ret. via Muscogee	All trains	97			‡2 50	1 60	1 50
Pensacola	Muscogee and return	All trains	40			‡2 50	1 60	1 50

*Baggagemen, $50 per month. †Average. ‡Per day. §With three crews on run. Conductors $80 per month, or for corresponding number of trips. Sunday work and extra trips paid extra, the same rate per trip between these points to apply. ‖Twelve hours or less constitute a day's work; additional hours paid for at 90 cents and 18 cents, respectively. **Per trip.

OWENSBORO & NASHVILLE RAILWAY.

FROM.	TO.	CLASS OF TRAIN.	Length of run.	No. of trips per month.	Av. mileage per month.	Conduct'rs, per month.	Brakemen & Flagm'n, per month.	Bagg'emen, per month.
Russellville	Owensboro and return	Passenger	144	30	4320	$85 00	$45 00	$40 00
Russellville	Owensboro	Mixed	72	30	2160	75 00	50 00	
Russellville	Adairville, two round trips	Mixed	52	30	1560	65 00	45 00	
Russellville	Owensboro	Freight	72			*70 00	*45 00	
Russellville	Central City and return	Freight	72			†70 00	†45 00	
Russellville	Mud River and return	Freight	52			†70 00	†45 00	

*One trip constitutes a day's work. †Round trip constitutes a day's work.

CLARKSVILLE & PRINCETON DIVISION.

FROM.	TO.	CLASS OF TRAIN.	Length of run.	No. of trips per month.	Av. mileage per month.	Conduct'rs, per month.	Brakemen, per month.	Bagg'men, per month.
Princeton	Clarksville and return	Passenger	110	30	3300	$60 00	*	$25 00
Princeton	Clarksville and return	Mixed	110	26	2860	50 00	$40 00	†

*Porter, $30 per month. †Flagman, $45 per month; acts as Baggagemen.

MEMPHIS LINE.

FROM.	TO.	CLASS OF TRAIN.	Length of run.	No. of trips per month.	Av. mileage per month.	CONDUCTORS.		BRAKEMEN & FLAGMEN.		Bagg'emen, per month.
						Trip	Month	Trip	Month	
Bowling Green	Memphis	Passenger	263	20	5260		$110 00		$50 00	$60 00
Memphis	Humboldt	Passenger	81	60	4860		*105 00			†80 00
Bowling Green	Paris	Freight	133			$3 70		$3 45		
Bowling Green	Clarksville‡	Freight	128			3 45		2 35		
Bowling Green	Guthrie‡	Freight	100			2 70		1 85		
Paris	Guthrie‡	Freight	165			4 35		3 05		
Paris	Erin‡	Local freight	83	26	2158		80 00		55 00	
Bowling Green	Erin	Local freight	91	26	2366		90 00		60 00	
Paris	Brownsville‡	Freight	147			3 75		2 50		
Paris	Memphis	Freight	130			3 65		2 40		
Memphis	Brownsville‡	Freight	112			3 00		1 95		
Paris	Humboldt‡	Freight	97			2 70		1 80		
Memphis	Paris	Local freight	130	17½	2253		85 00		58 00	
Memphis	Brownsville‡	Local freight	112	26	2912		85 00		58 00	
Paris	Brownsville‡	Local freight	73½	26	1911		$85 00		$58 00	
Work trains							85 00		58 00	

*$105 per month when running every day; $100 for week days only. †Express Company pays equal amount. ‡And return. On all freight runs for which round trip rates are given, two hours will be added to the schedule for work at turning point, after which the rule for delay time, in Section 2 will apply. §Includes switching at Brownsville. Porters, between Bowling Green and Memphis and Memphis and Humboldt, $30 per month.

LOUISVILLE, NEW ALBANY & CHICAGO RAILWAY.

HENDERSON AND ST. LOUIS DIVISIONS.

FROM.	TO.	CLASS OF TRAIN.	Length of run...	No. of trips per month.	Av. mileage per month.	CONDUCTORS.		BRAKEMEN & FLAGMEN.	
						Trip	Month	Trip	Month
St. Louis	Nashville	Passenger†	316	20	6320		$110 00	**	$50 00
St. Louis	Queens Lake*	Pass. Excurs'n	69			$3 00		$2 00	
Belleville	O'Fallon, 2 round trips	Mixed	26	26	676		80 00		†‡55 00
McLeansboro	Shawneetown*	Mixed	80	26	2080		75 00		50 00
Mt. Vernon	St. Louis	} Passenger‡	189	30	5670		100 00		45 00
St. Louis	Belleville								
Providence to and Evansville	Madisonville, Earlington and return to Earlington and Providence	Mixed‡	147	26	3822		85 00		58 00
Hopkinsville	Nashville*	Passenger‡	145	26	3770		90 00		50 00
Elkton	Guthrie, Clarksville*	Mixed	95	26	2470		75 00		25 00
Howell	East Nashville	Freight	154			3 60		2 45	
Howell	Earlington*	Through freight	104			2 80		1 85	
Howell	Earlington*	Local freight	104				85 00		58 00
Howell	East St. Louis	Through freight	159			3 60		2 45	
Howell	Mt. Vernon, Ind*	Through freight	36			$1 50		$1 00	
Howell	Carmi*	Through freight	73			$2 25		$1 50	
Howell	Mt. Vernon, Ill	Through freight	84			2 00		1 35	
Howell	McLeansboro*	Through freight	118			$3 60		$2 45	
Howell	Mt. Vernon, Ill	Local freight	84				85 00		58 00
Howell	Henderson*	Freight	20			1 00		75	
E. Nashville	Earlington	Freight	103			3 00		2 00	
E. Nashville	Guthrie*	Freight	94			|2 95		|2 00	
Earlington	Guthrie*	Freight	110			|3 10		|2 10	
Earlington	Providence*	Freight	41			1 75		1 15	
Hopkinsville	Earlington*	Local freight	62				85 00		58 00
Hopkinsville	East Nashville	Local freight	71				85 00		58 00
E. St. Louis	Belleville*	Freight	29			1 50		1 00	
E. St. Louis	Mt. Vernon, Ill	Through freight	76			2 00		1 35	
E. St. Louis	Mt. Vernon, Ill	Local freight	76				85 00		58 00
Work trains							85 00		58 00

*And return. On all freight runs for which round trip rates are given, two hours will be added to the schedule for work at turning point, after which the rule for delay time in Section 2 will apply. †Baggagemen, $60 per month. ‡Baggagemen, $25 per month. §Round trip, including making up train. ‖Round trip, including making up train at Guthrie. **Porters, $35 per month. ††Includes switching; twelve hours constitute a day's work. *Baker's Hill:* Conductors day and night, $65 per month; Brakemen on No. 76 going up hill and back with engine, helping No. 54, 20 cents per trip.

Approved: J. G. METCALFE,
               General Manager.
March 8, 1892.

G. E. EVANS,
Superintendent Transportation.

LOUISVILLE, NEW ALBANY & CHICAGO RAILWAY COMPANY.

1. Trainmen on through freight service will receive 3 and 2 cents per mile respectively for Conductors and Brakemen. Runs of less than 100 miles will be computed as 100 miles.

2. Turn-around runs between points other than division terminals will be computed as continuous trips and be paid for as per Articles 1 and 5.

3. Stone and local freight Conductors and Brakemen, running six days in a week, will be paid $3.45 and $2.30 per day, respectively. Overtime will be allowed after eleven hours per day. Local freight Conductors and Brakemen, on runs of but four days in a week, will be paid respectively $4.70 and $3.23 per day. Overtime on these runs will be allowed after thirteen hours per day. Main line local freight shall have three Brakemen.

4. Trainmen on work, circus, wreck or excursion trains will be paid $3.45 and $2.30 per day respectively for Conductors and Brakemen. Six hours or more and less than twelve hours shall constitute a day. Less than six hours shall constitute a half day; and the crew that makes but half a day shall stand first out. When a Conductor acts as Foreman of a construction or work train he will be paid $15 per month additional.

5. On all freight runs, unless otherwise provided for, of one hundred miles or less, overtime will be allowed for all time on duty in excess of ten hours. On runs of more than one hundred miles all the time consumed in making any one trip in excess of the time necessary to complete the trip on an average rate of ten miles per hour, will be paid for as overtime. In computing overtime no fraction of an hour less than thirty-five minutes will be counted. Thirty-five minutes or over and less than one hour will be counted as one hour. All overtime will be paid at the uniform rate of 30 cents per hour for Conductors and 20 cents per hour for Brakemen.

6. Trainmen compelled to double hills will be paid actual mileage made, provided no double will count less than ten miles. If overtime is made on account of doubling the amount paid for doubling will be deducted from overtime allowance.

7. Trainmen required to remain on duty over thirty minutes with their train after arrival at a terminal station, will be paid at the rate of ten miles per hour.

8. Trainmen called upon to attend court will be paid their regular rate of pay per day, and when called upon to leave home necessary expenses will be allowed.

9. The practice will be that no train or engine will be run on the road without a Conductor. Conductors of light engines, or Pilots of trains, will be paid 3 cents per mile.

10. In ordering crews for dead-heading the first crew out will run the train. The crew dead-heading will, upon arrival at a terminal station, come out ahead of the crew with which they dead-headed. Crews dead-heading under orders will be paid half their regular pay, except trainmen that dead-head over the road for the purpose of relieving a man who has asked for leave of absence, will not be paid for such dead-heading. Full time will be allowed for light trains. Conductors will be notified when time is not allowed as per time report, and reasons will be given for not allowing same.

11. Trainmen will be called within one mile at main line divisions or terminal stations, as nearly as practicable, one hour before the time set for departure of trains, by train caller, who will always be provided with a call book in which the Conductor and Brakeman will enter their names, together with the time they are called. The time of the trainmen will begin from the time set for the departure of train. Trainmen failing to respond, when properly called, will be subject to discipline.

12. When trainmen are called and report for duty, and for any reason not their own fault, do not go out, they will be paid as follows: If held on duty less than five hours they will be paid fifty miles and stand first out. If held five hours or more they will be paid one hundred miles and go out behind other crews at that point, it being understood that in case a crew goes out within five hours, time shall be reckoned from the time first called to go.

13. Conductors will be held responsible for the safe management of their trains, and will place their Brakemen as their best judgment shall dictate, so long as it does not conflict with time-card rules.

14. When Conductors make proper objections in writing to the Trainmaster or Division Superintendent against any Brakeman under their charge, such Brakeman shall be assigned to other duties or dismissed from the service, as circumstances may justify or warrant.

15. Trainmen will sign a receipt for switch keys and lanterns, agreeing that $1 may be deducted from their salaries for switch keys and 50 cents for lanterns, provided same are lost or not returned when trainmen leave the service, or a satisfactory excuse given for their non-return.

16. Trainmen reaching terminal stations after continuous service of sixteen hours or more, will be allowed eight hours for rest, provided they give notice by wire to the proper officer, before arrival, of their desire for rest.

17. When the freight traffic is light and the crews in service are not able to make reasonable time, crews will be taken off, beginning with the youngest, until the crews left in the service are enabled to make reasonable time. Conductors temporarily suspended under this rule will be given preference as Brakemen over younger men in the service, and will retain their rights as Conductors.

18. No fines will be imposed on trainmen for loss of tools or for damage to rolling stock, or for stock killed or injured. Trainmen on their part will use their best efforts to avoid accidents, damage or losses.

19. Trainmen will be allowed to lay off for good and sufficient reasons, of which the proper officers shall be the judge, provided due notice is given so that their places may be filled with other men.

20. All trainmen will be regarded in the line of promotion. The right to runs and to promotions will be governed by merit and ability, of which the Superintendent will be the judge. Everything being equal, the Conductors and Brakemen longest in the service will have preference. In filling vacancies in the ranks of freight Conductors, for every two Brakemen promoted from the ranks that are oldest in the service, one Conductor will be promoted, it being understood that two Brakemen will be promoted before any Conductor is appointed, and the Conductor so appointed will take his place at the foot of the list of extra train Conductors and may be temporarily used as extra Brakeman. Trainmen entitled to promotion and not receiving the same, will, upon application, be given reasons therefor in writing. Trainmen employed on the B. & B. division shall not be in line of promotion to main line positions, and the main-line trainmen shall not be in line of promotion to positions on the B. & B. division; but all the other Articles in this schedule shall govern the B. & B. employes.

21. No trainman will be suspended or discharged, except for good and sufficient reasons. If he thinks his sentence unjust, he shall within ten days file written request for an investigation. His case shall have a thorough investigation by proper officers

of the Company, at which he with his witnesses may be present. In the event of his being found guilty, he will, upon application, be allowed to see all evidence produced against him. In case he is found innocent, he shall be reinstated, and be allowed full pay for time lost, after three days off duty.

22. Unless leave of absence for a definite time is given in writing, trainmen leaving the service of the Company to engage in other business, or to work on other roads, or who are assigned to duties other than train service, and who are subsequently employed or return to train service of this Company, will rank as new men.

23. Pay for main-line passenger service will be as follows:

SINGLE TRIP	Conductor	Bag'e-man	Brakeman
Chicago and Louisville	$3 50	$2 20	$1 90
Chicago and Lafayette	2 40	1 50	1 30
Chicago and Monon	1 80	1 10	1.00
Indianapolis and Monon	1 90	1 25	1 15
Michigan City and Monon	1 50	1 00	85
Michigan City and Indianapolis	3 00	1 95	1 70
Lafayette and Louisville	3 75	2 25	2 00
Lafayette and Bedford	1 90	1 25	1 10
Louisville and Bloomington	1 85	1 15	1 00

24. Crews on B. & B. division will be paid as follows: Conductors $3 per day; Brakemen and Baggagemen $45 per month. If found necessary to run crews on turn around trips between Bloomington and Reed's Station, the trip will be considered as one turn-around.

25. Crews on French Lick branch will be paid as follows: Conductors 75 cents per single trip; Baggagemen 45 cents per single trip, and Brakemen $50 per month.

26. No change will be made in this agreement nor any departure from its provisions by any party thereto until thirty days' notice of such intentions have been filed in writing with all other parties interested.

Yard Service. Chicago, standard Chicago rates. Monon, day Yardmaster $2.90, night Yardmaster $2.70, day and night Switchmen $2. Lafayette, day Yardmaster $2.90, night Yardmaster $2.70, day and night Switchmen $2. Michigan City, Yardmaster $2.25, Switchmen $1.75. Bloomington, day Yardmaster $70 per month, night Yardmaster $65 per month, switchmen $2 per day. New Albany, day Yardmaster $110 per month, night Yardmaster $80 per month, day Switchmen $2.60 per day, night Switchmen $2.30 per day.

S. J. COLLINS,
General Superintendent.

Accepted by the Order of Railway Conductors:
   E. E. CLARK, G. C. C.; A. S. RAE, Chairman.
Accepted by the Brotherhood of Railroad Trainmen:
   S. E. WILKINSON, G. M.; JOS. CHENOWETH, Chairman.
July 1, 1892.

MICHIGAN CENTRAL RAILROAD COMPANY.

1. Commencing upon date of signature of both parties interested in this agreement, through freight Conductors and Brakemen will run the number of miles specified below for a month's work, for which regular Conductors will receive $75, and Brakemen $50 per month; apprentice Conductors to receive $70, and apprentice Brakemen $45 per month. Apprentice Conductors to receive full pay beginning one year from the date they are promoted; apprentice Brakemen, if men of experience from any other road, having evidence that they have worked one year and left the other road in good standing, shall receive full pay six months from the date they are hired. Brakemen, other than these, shall receive full pay one year from the date they are hired: Canada Division, Main Line, 2,900 miles; East Division, Main Line, 2,698 miles; Middle and Air Line, 3,000 miles; West and Joliet Divisions, 2,500 miles; Saginaw Division, 2,400 miles; Mackinaw Division, 2,100 miles; Grand Rapids Division, 2,200 miles; Toledo Division, 2,100 miles; Bay City Division, 2,698 miles.

2. Should they be called upon to make more than the above mileage, they will be paid same rate per mile as the rate per mile bears to the miles they are to make for a month's pay. Should they fail to make the stipulated mileage, but are on hand and ready for duty, they will receive: for regular Conductor, $75, apprentice Conductor, $70; regular Brakeman, $50, apprentice Brakeman, $45. This does not apply to extra men, waiting for employment. It is understood that men will be allowed to make as much excess mileage as they can, consistent with safety. Should it be deemed nece-

ary to reduce the force at any time during the month, the men dropped will receive the same proportion of monthly wages as the number of miles they have to run bears to the total mileage for the month. As no apprentice system has been in force in Canada, the Company agrees that any Brakeman now employed by this Company in Canada, if promoted in the future to Conductor, shall take rank at the time of his promotion as full Conductor and receive full Conductor's pay from the date he is promoted; but this shall not apply to Brakemen hereafter entering the Company's service.

3. Mackinaw division trainmen working on branches loading logs shall be allowed mileage at the rate of seven and one-half miles per hour; over thirty minutes to be counted as an hour; less than thirty minutes not to be counted.

4. Upon way freight runs where there are only two crews, the Conductor will be paid $90, and the Brakeman $62.50 per month; where there are three crews, Conductors $85, Brakemen $60 per month. Conductors running way freight on St. Clair division, $85, Brakemen $60 per month. On Pinconning division, Conductors $75, Brakemen $50 per month. Following divisions to have three crews upon way freight trains: Middle and Air Line; Saginaw; West divisions; South end of Mackinaw division; Canada, West division, and Grand Rapids division; Bay City division; east end of main line when considered by Division Superintendent necessary, and north end of Mackinaw division, same to be taken off when business warrants. Following to have three Brakemen: Middle and Air Line; west end of Canada division and Joliet division; Bay City division and West division, main line from May 1st to November 1st, to be taken off by Division Superintendent if not needed; Saginaw division, No. 83, third Brakeman from point where No. 72 meets No. 83; Saginaw division, No. 84, third Brakeman when business demands it; south end of Mackinaw division, to be taken off if found by Division Superintendent that falling off of business warrants it. When way freight trains are sent in upon the branches on Mackinaw division to do work, they shall be paid mileage extra for this work, it being understood that the word "branches" are such tracks as extend more than one mile from the main track upon which running order must be obtained.

5. Conductors on construction or road trains will receive $90, and Brakemen $60 per month, and extra time when called upon to work on Sundays; the road department to furnish men to handle cable when cable is used, if trainmen have to protect their train by flagging; that twelve hours shall constitute one day's work for all crews regularly employed in road train work for twenty-six consecutive days; all over twelve hours for such crews to be paid for at same rate, time to be computed from the time train is called to leave; that snow-plows and flangers shall be paid for the number of miles run, unless the number of miles run each day is less than a through crew should have made upon the division where their train is working, for a day's pay. If less than this amount, the men will be paid for one day's pay. This provision is made to cover work in yards and short runs. When sidetracks are plowed or flanged, the number of miles of sidetrack shall be added to the number of miles on main track in computing the number of miles that a plow or flanger is run. Wrecking trains shall receive mileage to and from the wreck, and one day for every twelve hours employed at the wreck, unless the whole time is less than twelve hours, then they shall receive one day. Way freight and work trains will be paid upon the basis of working days in the month; when called upon to work Sundays, they shall be paid extra, upon the same basis.

6. Crews not assigned to regular runs shall be run first in and first out. All freight and mixed trains, when detained more than one hour at starting terminal, and when detained more than thirty minutes at the terminal at the end of their runs, or end of their day's work, shall be paid overtime, computing as follows: Less than thirty minutes not to be counted; over thirty minutes to be counted one hour; one hour and thirty minutes, two hours, etc., it being understood that where any train lays up at night, in accordance with time card, or by orders, at any station, and is scheduled or ordered to leave at a certain hour in the morning, such stations shall be considered the terminal, the same as a division point, and overtime allowed accordingly. Pay for switching done by turn-around train on Saginaw, Mackinaw and Bay City divisions to be allowed at the discretion of the Division Superintendents. It is understood that in computing delays at starting point of any run, overtime shall be figured from the time train is marked or called for, or scheduled to leave. And for overtime at terminal yards the time of arrival of train at yard limits shall be taken. At Jackson Junction, yard limits for Air Line will be Ft. Wayne target; for main line, west, Jackson street bridge. Main line west-bound trains, if not stopped between Jackson Junction and Jackson, or at Jackson, shall not consider the time used from Jackson Junction to Jackson yard limits as detention time. If a through crew is sent out upon a regular way freight run in place of a way freight crew, they shall receive the pay of way freight crews. Where a crew is employed continually upon a train that does way freight work, and is not scheduled upon the card as a way freight train, but picks up, leaves and switches cars at stations, or sidetracks between stations, they shall receive

way freight crew's pay, but where a through crew, in its turn, occasionally takes a run not so scheduled, that does local work, and balance of time they are employed in through service, they shall receive mileage only for switching run.

7. When freight Conductors and Brakemen are held at terminals, or sent to any point to run specials, or taken off their car to run passenger trains, they shall receive the same rate of pay as passenger Conductors; provided, however, if the amount is less than they would have earned had they not been taken off their own car, then they shall receive the amount their way car earned.

8. As to all freight runs, not otherwise provided for, when a crew is called for a trip of 50 miles or less, one-half day's pay shall be allowed. If less than six hours is used, the crew stands first out: if over six hours is used, one day's pay shall be allowed, and crew stands last out.

9. In case of suspension or dismissal, the party shall be notified within ten days from the date of the occurrence by the Division Superintendent, as to his dismissal, or length of his suspension.

*10. When it becomes necessary to take Conductors and Brakemen from duty to investigate any accident or for any other cause, the investigation shall take place within ten days, and in case they are found to be entirely blameless, they shall be allowed the lost time on account of such investigation and at their regular daily pay. If any trainman thinks he has been unjustly dealt with, he may file his objection in writing, and he will be given a fair and impartial hearing, and if proven entirely innocent, he shall be reinstated in his former position and paid for the time lost. When trainmen are called and trains abandoned, and for any reason other than their own acts trainmen do not go out within four hours of the time called, they shall receive one-half day's pay.

11. The right to regular runs and promotion will be governed by merit, ability and seniority. Everything being equal the men longest in continual service will have preference.

12. Crews that have been on duty sixteen consecutive hours shall be entitled to eight hours rest before going out again, except in cases of washouts, wrecks or other similar emergencies. If any crew, at any time, becomes tired upon the road, or consider themselves unfit for their run, the despatcher, upon their application and statement of the above facts, will allow them to put their train upon a sidetrack and remain there until they are rested, or other provision has been made for taking care of their train.

13. Brakemen to receive ten cents per ton for shoveling coal, same to be determined by Engineers' tickets.

14. Brakemen, when sent upon trial trips for promotion to Conductors, to receive one-half Conductor's pay while upon trial trips.

15. The pay of main line passenger trainmen to remain as at present. The pay for passenger crews running upon branches, except South Haven and Battle Creek divisions, shall be for all crews making 4,000 miles or over, Conductors $90 per month, Baggagemen $55, and Brakemen $50 per month. For those making less than 4,000 miles the present rate of pay to remain in force. Any run upon the main line, not otherwise provided for, making equal mileage, shall come under the same rule. Any man performing the duties of Baggageman and Brakeman combined, to receive Baggageman's pay.

16. Two regular crews shall run trains 95 and 96; five regular crews on trains 203, 207, 202 and 208.

17. Saginaw division, two crews on trains 75, 76, 77 and 78. Mackinaw division, trains 87 and 88 to be run with one crew, and receive standard amount paid for over 4,000 miles. Crews on Nos. 75, 76, 77, 78, 202, 203, 206 and 207 to be paid according to standard allowed for less than 4,500 miles upon branches.

18. Two Brakemen to be run upon trains Nos. 101 and 108 regularly.

19. Crews to receive full mileage for dead-heading upon freight trains, and half mileage for dead-heading upon passenger trains.

20. Conductor on North Midland division shall receive $75 per month, and Baggagemen $50 per month.

21. When possible, time and detention sheets, when time is not allowed upon the same, shall be returned to the Conductor within five days.

22. The pay of transfer Conductors running between Montrose and Suspension Bridge shall be $75 per month. Any trip to and from Union Stock Yards by West division crews to be figured at fifty miles for the trip.

23. The basis of mileage in clause 1 is subject to revision if shown that improvements in double track or other facilities enable men to make excessive wages as compared with men on other divisions working an equal number of hours. The mileage on Saginaw division to be further reduced if, after a reasonable trial, the mileage is found to be too high to enable men on that division to earn a fair month's wages, as compared with other divisions.

24. One-fourth day will be allowed for freight crews running between Victoria and Black Rock, and one-half day from Victoria or Exchange street, Buffalo.
25. Mackinaw division crews not to be restricted to terminals when laying up for rest.
26. Any Brakeman selected by Division Superintendent for promotion to Conductor shall be examined by Division Superintendent, Chief Train Despatcher and Trainmaster, or their delegates. After such examination as to rules, etc., if he passes satisfactorily, he shall make one round trip upon his division with each of three Conductors; such Conductors will make a written report as to his competency to the Trainmaster, to be kept on file. If reported by the three Conductors as competent, he may be considered as a Brakeman who can be called upon at any time to run a train. If two of the Conductors report favorably, and one adversely, the Division Superintendent shall carefully examine into the reasons of the latter, and if satisfied that there is not sufficient ground for his rejection, he may pass the Brakeman for service as Conductor.

No part of the above agreement shall be abrogated by either party without notice, and then only after consultation between the two parties interested.

July 1, 1892

ROBERT MILLER,
General Superintendent.

MISSOURI, KANSAS & TEXAS RAILWAY COMPANY.

LEASED AND OPERATED LINES.

PASSENGER SERVICE.

1. Conductors will be paid $125 per month; Baggagemen, $65 per month; Brakemen, $55 per month, and Porters, $40 per month. The wages of Baggagemen who act as Express Messengers will be fixed by the Express Company.
2. Passenger Crews making extra trips, in addition to their regular assigned runs, will be allowed extra time upon the basis of pay allowed other crews in similar service.
3. Conductors will be paid 2¼ cents; Brakemen, 1¼ cents, and Porters, ¾ cents per mile for running special passenger trains, pay trains and excursion trains. One hundred and seventy-five miles or less to constitute a day.
4. The senior extra passenger Conductor at Sedalia and Parsons, the first and second extra passenger Conductors at Denison will be allowed $90 per month when they fail to earn the above amount, except when off duty at their own request, when the time lost will be deducted.

THROUGH FREIGHT SERVICE.—Except Trinity & Sabine Section.

5. Conductors and Brakemen will be paid 3 and 2 cents per mile respectively. On all runs of less than 100 miles requiring more than ten hours, overtime will be paid if the hours used on the trip exceed eleven, in which case all overtime exceeding ten hours will be paid. On all runs exceeding 100 miles, trainmen will be paid overtime for all time used to complete the trip in excess of a rate of speed of 10 miles per hour when over one hour late. One hundred miles will be allowed for runs of less than 100 miles when no other mileage is made on same date.

LOCAL FREIGHT AND MIXED TRAIN SERVICE.

RUNS.	NO OF CREWS.	WAGES.	
		Conductors.	Brakemen.
Hannibal and Moberly	2	$90 00	$60 00
Moberly and Sedalia	2	90 00	60 00
Sedalia and Nevada	2	90 00	60 00
Nevada and Parsons	2	90 00	60 00
Parsons and Junction City	3	90 00	60 00
Parsons and Paola	2	90 00	60 00
Parsons and Muskogee	2	95 00	65 00
Muskogee and Denison	2	95 00	65 00
Denison and Alvarado	3	90 00	60 00
Waco and Taylor	2	90 00	60 00
Taylor and Boggy Tank	2	90 00	60 00
Denison and Henrietta	2	95 00	60 00

6. Overtime to be allowed at rate of 30 cents per hour for Conductors, and 20 cents per hour for Brakemen for all time used on a trip in excess of a rate of speed of 10 miles per hour when more than one hour late. Crews on these runs will be paid extra for Sunday work on basis of service performed.

MISSOURI, KANSAS & TEXAS RAILWAY.

RATES OF PAY.

RUNS.	NO. OF CREWS.	WAGES.	
		Conductors.	Brakemen.
Denton and Dallas	1	$90 00	$60 00
San Marcos and Lockhart	1	80 00	55 00
Echo and Belton	1	100 00	55 00
McAlester and Krebs	1	90 00	60 00
Atoka and Lehigh	1	90 00	60 00

7. Ten hours to constitute a day. Overtime will be paid for at rate of 30 cents per hour for Conductors, and 20 cents per hour for Brakemen.

8. Denison and Greenville—One crew. Conductor, $90; Brakemen, $60 per month. Overtime to be allowed at rate of 30 cents per hour for Conductors and 20 cents per hour for Brakemen for all time in excess of ten hours when more than eleven hours are consumed in making the round trip, Denison to Greenville and return. Dead time at Greenville not to be included. Crew on this run will be paid extra for Sunday work on basis of service performed.

9. Greenville and Dallas—One crew. Conductor, $90; Brakemen, $60 per month. Overtime to be allowed at rate of 30 cents per hour for Conductors and 20 cents per hour for Brakemen for all time in excess of ten hours when more than eleven hours are consumed in making the round trip, Dallas to Greenville and return. Dead time at Greenville not to be included. Crew on this run will be paid extra for Sunday work on basis of service performed.

10. Greenville and Mineola—One crew. Conductor, $90; Brakemen, $60 per month. Overtime to be allowed at rate of 30 cents per hour for Conductor and 20 cents per hour for Brakemen for all time in excess of ten hours when more than eleven hours are consumed in making the round trip, Mineola to Greenville and return. Dead time at Greenville not to be included. Crew on this train will be paid extra for Sunday work on basis of service performed.

11. Alvarado and Waco—One crew. Conductor, $110; Brakemen, $75 per month. No overtime allowed on this run. Crew on this run will be paid extra for Sunday work on basis of service performed.

12. Dallas and Hillsboro—Two crews. Conductors, $90; Brakemen, $60 per month. Single trip to constitute a day, and mileage made in excess of one trip to be allowed at through freight rates; overtime to be allowed at rate of 30 cents per hour for Conductors, and 20 cents per hour for Brakemen for all time in excess of ten hours when more than eleven hours are consumed in making a single trip. Extra time will be allowed for Sunday work on basis of service performed.

13. Denison and Sherman—One crew. Conductor, $115; Brakemen, $65 per month. Conductors to run passenger and freight trains on alternate days. Freight crews to make as many trips as may be necessary and do necessary switching at Sherman; ten hours to constitute a day. All over ten hours to be paid for at rate of 30 cents per hour for Conductors, and 20 cents per hour for Brakemen.

WORK TRAIN SERVICE.

14. Conductors, $90; Brakemen, $60 per month. Twelve hours or less to constitute a day. Overtime will be paid for at rate of 30 cents per hour for Conductors, and 20 cents per hour for Brakemen. When more than 100 miles are run by work trains, Conductors will be paid 3 cents, and Brakemen 2 cents per mile for all mileage in excess of 100 miles. Extra time will be allowed for Sunday work at above rates.

YARD SERVICE.

YARDS.	YARDMASTERS.		FOREMEN.		SWITCHMEN.	
	DAY.	NIGHT.	DAY.	NIGHT.	DAY.	NIGHT.
Hannibal	$115 00 per mo.	$100 00 per mo.	$2 70 per day	$2 75 per day	$70 00 per mo.	$75 00 per mo.
Clinton	75 00 per mo.				60 00 per mo.	
Nevada	100 00 per mo.	90 00 per mo.	80 00 per mo	85 00 per mo.	70 00 per mo.	75 00 per mo.
Parsons	110 00 per mo.	100 00 per mo.	80 00 per mo.	85 00 per mo.	70 00 per mo.	75 00 per mo.
Junction City	60 00 per mo.					
Muskogee	90 00 per mo	85 00 per mo.			70 00 per mo.	75 00 per mo.
McAlester	90 00 per mo.				65 00 per mo.	
Denison	150 00 per mo.	125 00 per mo.	2 93 per day	$ 12½ per day	2 74 per day	2 93 per day
Alvarado	95 00 per mo.	85 00 per mo.			70 00 per mo	75 00 per mo.
Hillsboro	85 00 per mo.	80 00 per mo.			70 00 per mo	75 00 per mo.
Waco	90 00 per mo.				70 00 per mo.	75 00 per mo.
Dallas	115 00 per mo.	95 00 per mo.	2 93 per day	3 12½ per day	2 74 per day	2 93 per day
Greenville	110 00 per mo.	95 00 per mo.	2 93 per day	3 12½ per day	2 74 per day	2 93 per day
Henrietta	85 00 per mo.		70 00 per mo.		65 00 per mo.	65 00 per mo.

15. Twelve hours will constitute a day. Overtime will be allowed at above rates.

GENERAL REGULATIONS.

16. Trainmen required to remain on duty over 30 minutes with their trains after arriving at a terminal station will be paid at the rate of 10 miles per hour.

17. In computing overtime no fraction of an hour less than 30 minutes will be counted. Any fraction of an hour over 30 minutes will be counted an hour.

18. Trainmen ordered to dead-head on passenger trains will be allowed half pay; when dead-heading on caboose will be allowed full pay. The first crew out will run the train, and the second crew will dead-head. These crews on reaching terminal of run will come out in their turns.

19. Crews not assigned to regular runs will be run first in first out. Nothing in this article shall be construed as preventing the Company running crews out ahead of their turn for the purpose of getting them home, that may, from necessity, be run off their regular section.

20. Trainmen will not be required to go out when they claim to need rest; nor shall they be permitted to go out when it is the judgment of the Division Superintendent or Trainmaster that they require rest.

21. Trainmen living within one mile of terminal stations, shall be called, as early as practicable, one hour before leaving time by Caller, who will be provided with a book in which the men called will register their names and the time called, and the time of trainmen will begin at the time set for the departure of their train. If a train is held back they will be paid overtime for all hours delayed. Fractions of an hour shall not be counted.

22. Trainmen, when called, if for any cause or reason other than their own acts do not go out, if held on duty less than six hours, shall be paid one-half day, and stand first out. If held more than six hours they will be paid one day and go behind other crews at that point.

23. Train and Yardmen when ordered to attend court on business of this Company will be paid for time lost, and, if away from their home station, their necessary expenses; this Company being entitled to their witness fees.

24. Train or Yardmen will not be dismissed or suspended from the Company's service without just cause. In case of suspension or dismissal, if any employe thinks his sentence unjust, he shall have the right, within ten days, to refer his case by written statement to the Division Superintendent. Within five days (or as soon thereafter as practicable) of the receipt of this notice, his case shall have a thorough investigation, at which he may be present if he so desires, and also be represented by any disinterested employe. In case he shall not be satisfied with the result of said investigation, he shall have the right to appeal to the General Superintendent and to the General Manager. In case suspension or dismissal is found to be unjust, he shall be reinstated and paid for all time lost.

25. The right to regular runs and to promotion will be governed by merit, ability and seniority. Everything being equal, the Trainman or Yardman longest in service will have preference, the Division Superintendent or Trainmaster to be the judge as to qualifications. Nothing in this article shall be construed as preventing the Company from employing experienced men from other roads when the good of the service requires it.

26. In filling vacancies in the ranks of freight Conductors, all men in train service will be considered in the line of promotion according to their age in the service and their ability to assume the duties, except that for every two Brakemen promoted, one experienced Conductor may be appointed from the ranks or elsewhere at the option of the Company. A Conductor so appointed shall take his place at the foot of the list of extra Conductors, and may be temporarily used as extra Brakeman when not employed as Conductor.

27. When crews of local freight or mixed trains are required to do switching at terminal or division stations, they will be paid extra for such service at the rate of 30 cents per hour for Conductors and 20 cents per hour for Brakemen, less than thirty minutes not to be counted. Thirty minutes and over and less than one hour will be computed as one hour, excepting that on runs which occupy less than ten hours, no extra switching service will be allowed until the total time used in making the run exceeds eleven hours. The above not to apply to McAlester, Lehigh, Sherman, Belton and Lockhart branches.

28. Through freight crews delayed at any point more than one hour loading or unloading stock, loading or unloading material, or required to switch more than one hour shall be paid extra for such service at regular overtime rates.

29. The proper officers of the Company will listen to any reasonable complaints made by any individual, Trainman or Yardman, or by a committee of the same, provided that a proper notice is given in writing as to the subject of complaint, and special appointment is made as to the time and place to consider same.

30. Crews will not be run off their respective divisions except in cases of necessity.

31. It is the rule and intention of the Company to run through freight crews first in first out, but circumstances may arise where this should be changed, and the Company reserves the right to do so. For instance we may deem it advisable to run certain crews upon certain designated trains, and we must be at liberty to arrange such matters for the best interests of the Company.

32. Any employe included under the provision of these rules who is dissatisfied with the decision of any official of the Company shall have the right to appeal therefrom to the General Manager, after having first submitted his case to the decision of the General Superintendent.

33. When freight traffic is light so that the crews in service are not able to make reasonable time, crews will be taken off, beginning with the youngest, until the crews left in the service are enabled to make reasonable wages. Conductors temporarily suspended under this rule will be given preference as Brakemen over younger men in the service and will retain their rights as Conductors.

34. Trainmen and Yardmen leaving the service of the Company of their own accord, or if discharged from the service, shall forfeit all rights previously held, unless reinstated within ninety days.

35. Any Train or Yardman leaving the employ of the Company, will, at his request, be given a letter by his Division Superintendent, stating his term of service and the capacities in which he was employed, and whether he has been discharged or has left the service of his own accord, and if discharged, such letter shall state the reasons.

36. When necessary to send a pilot over the road, he shall be paid on same basis as a through freight Conductor.

37. Trainmen will be notified when time is not allowed as per trip report.

38. Perishable and local freight is to be unloaded by through freight crews when necessary, and overtime of one hour or more will be allowed at overtime rates in addition to time used in making the trip. When more than one car of local freight is put in through freight trains, three brakemen will be furnished when practicable.

39. For all freight trainmen employed by the month, the number of calendar working days shall be considered as a full month, and fractional time or parts of a month shall be paid for as so many fractional parts or days of such working-day month.

40. Brakemen to be paid 30 cents each for coaling up engines.

Schedule of pay of freight Trainmen on the Trinity and Sabine Section: Trinity to any point north of Willard and return, one-half day. Trinity to Willard and return, or to any point between Willard and Corrigan and return, one day. Trinity to Corrigan and return, one day. Trinity to any point between Fleming and Colmesneil, one day. Trinity to Colmesneil, one day. Work or wreck trains, for 12 hours, one day.

Overtime: When 9 or 12 hours are consumed in making run between Trinity and Willard, they will receive one day for same. Crews running between Trinity and Corrigan will receive overtime for every hour above 12 hours consumed in making run. The one day allowed for run between Trinity and Colmesneil to include switching at Colmesneil. When a crew runs beyond Corrigan and returns to Trinity in the same day, allow one day for the run up to Corrigan and return to Trinity and mileage beyond Corrigan; figuring the mileage at rate of 10 miles per hour.

All schedules, rules and regulations in conflict with the above are hereby made void.

Approved: H. C. CROSS,   J. J. FREY,
President and General Manager.   General Superintendent.
November 1st, 1891.

THE MISSOURI PACIFIC RAILWAY COMPANY; ST. LOUIS, IRON MOUNTAIN & SOUTHERN RAILWAY COMPANY, AND LEASED, OPERATED AND INDEPENDENT LINES.

1. Hereafter, in the employment of Conductors, Brakemen and Yardmen, in the service of the above Companies, Division Superintendents are hereby instructed to employ none but sober, reliable and competent men for this service, and all such employes will be directly responsible to and subject to the orders and control of the Division Trainmasters, Division and Terminal Superintendents and Yardmasters, at all times and in all matters pertaining to their duties. No other subordinate officer will be allowed to interfere in the discipline and control of these employes; but Brakemen will obey the instructions of their Conductors while on duty.

2. *Switchmen and Yardmen:* Wages and hours of Yardmen shall remain as at present at all points, with the following exceptions:

YARD.	H'rs per Day.	Day Helpers.	Night Helpers	Day Forem'n	Night Forem'n
Sedalia, per calendar month,...	12	$75 00	$80 00	$85 00	$90 00
Hiawatha, per calendar month,..	12	70 00	70 00	75 00	75 00
Weeping Water, per calendar month,....................................	12	65 00			
Greenleaf, per calendar month,..	12	65 00			
Fort Scott, per calendar month,...	12	65 00			
Wichita, per calendar month,..	12	65 00	65 00		
Eldorado, per Calendar month,...	12	65 00	65 00		
Winfield, per calendar month..	12	60 00			
Sawatomie, per day,...	12	2 50	2 50		
Fort Smith, per calendar month,...	12	65 00			
Van Buren, per calendar month,...	12		70 00		

3. *Wages of Trainmen, Passenger Service:* Trainmen will be paid the following schedule of rates: Conductors of passenger trains, $100 per month. Brakemen of passenger trains, $50, $55 and $60 per month, as at present. Conductors of pusher engines, $75 per month.

4. *Wages of Trainmen, Freight Service:* Conductors and Brakemen on through freight trains will be paid at the rate of three (3) and two (2) cents per mile respectively, for all runs of 100 miles or more; runs of less than 100 miles to be paid as 100 miles.

5. Crews of all local freight trains and mixed trains for regular runs of 100 miles or less, will be paid for full time of 26 or 27 days; Conductors $90 per month, Brakemen 80 per month. For fractional time they will be paid at the rate of $3.50 per day and 2.30 per day, excepting that on the several branch lines below specified they will be paid the following schedule rates:

ST. LOUIS, IRON MOUNTAIN AND SOUTHERN BRANCH LINES.

NAME OF BRANCH.	Rate per Month	Rate per Day.
Potosi..	$75 00	$2 90
Jackson..	85 00	3 25
Doniphan..	85 00	3 25
White River..	85 00	3 25
Camden..	85 00	3 25
Fort Smith..	85 00	3 25
Warren...	90 00	3 50

Brakemen's pay on the above lines will remain as at present.

Missouri Pacific Branch Lines: Monthly rates of trainmen will remain as at present on the Missouri Pacific branches named below: Carondelet branch; Lebanon branch; Jefferson City, Boonville and Lexington division; Boonville branch; Sedalia, Warsaw and Southern railway; St. Louis and Emporia division; Crete branch; Lincoln branch between Weeping Water and Lincoln; Central Branch division between Downs and Lenora; Republican Valley branch and Pacific Railway in Nebraska; Burr Oak branch; South Solomon branch and Rooks County Railroad; Kansas and Arizona division; Great Bend branch; Ft. Scott, Wichita and Western Railway between Wichita and Kiowa; Denver, Memphis and Atlantic (Eastern) division; McPherson branch; Grouse Creek Railway; Leroy and Caney Valley Air Line division; Kansas Southwestern Railway.

6. For running pay trains and special passenger and excursion trains, Conductors and Brakemen will be paid as follows: Conductors, for runs of 125 miles or less, $3.25 per day; for runs of more than 125 miles, 2½ cents per mile. Brakemen will be paid on same basis $2 per day, and 1½ cents per mile, except that regular freight crews required to run passenger trains will be paid freight mileage rates.

7. On all local freight and mixed trains, runs of over one hundred miles, Conductors and Brakemen will be paid, in addition to their regular daily rates, 3 and 2 cents per mile respectively for all mileage made in excess of one hundred miles, and overtime at 30 and 20 cents per hour, as per Article 12, excepting that Brakemen on local freights between Hiawatha and Omaha will be paid $3.25 per trip via Nebraska City and $3.15 per trip via Talmage, with overtime as above.

8. The monthly pay rates of local freight and mixed train crews will include the twenty-six or twenty-seven working days of each month. Road service rendered by local crews on Sundays, or other extra service, shall be paid for as extra work, at the regular rates for the class or service performed.

9. For all freight trainmen employed by the month, twenty-six or twenty-seven

days shall be rated as a full month, and fractional time or parts of a month shall be paid for as so many twenty-sixths of a month.

10. Crews of work trains will be paid, Conductors $85 per month, and Brakemen $60 per month, for the calendar working days in the month; service on Sundays will be paid extra, and overtime will be paid for all time used in excess of twelve hours a day.

11. *Overtime and Excess Mileage:* Overtime will be allowed and paid to all crews of local, through freight and mixed trains, as follows: On all freight train runs of less than one hundred miles, which runs may require more than ten hours' time, overtime will be paid for all time used in making any trip in excess of ten hours after deducting two hours for delayed time. When the delayed time on any trip amounts to more than two hours, all overtime will be allowed in excess of ten hours.

12. On all through freight runs of over one hundred miles, Conductors and Brakemen shall be paid 3 and 2 cents per mile, respectively, for all mileage made on each run; and in addition to actual mileage, overtime shall be paid them on the basis of ten miles per hour; for example, on a run of one hundred and fifty miles they shall be paid 3 and 2 cents per mile, for one hundred and fifty miles, and in addition thereto, for all overtime made in excess of fifteen hours.

13. Trainmen required to remain on duty with their trains after arrival at terminal stations thirty minutes or more shall be paid therefor as overtime.

14. Road crews delayed on the road more than one hour, loading or unloading material, or required to switch more than one hour at gravel pits, stone quarries, coal mines, or other similar places, will be paid extra for such time at overtime rates, after ten hours' service.

15. In computing overtime, no fraction of an hour less than thirty minutes shall be counted, but all overtime of thirty minutes or over, and less than one hour, shall be counted one hour.

16. All overtime made by train crews will be paid at the uniform rates of 30 cents per hour for Conductors, and 20 cents per hour for Brakemen.

17. No overtime will be paid to any passenger trainmen that are employed by the month in regular service. When they perform extra service they will be paid for actual service rendered at their regular rates of pay.

18. *Miscellaneous:* Trainmen or Yardmen required to dead-head shall receive half pay, and when attending court by request of an official, they shall be paid according to their regular daily pay, and one dollar per day for expenses.

19. When trainmen are called, and, for any reason other than their own acts, do not go out, they shall be paid for one-half day, if held on duty less than six hours, and stand first out. If held more than six hours, they shall be paid for one day and go behind all other crews at that point, at that time; it being understood that in case crews go out within six hours, they shall receive time from first call.

20. Trainmen living within one mile of main line, division, or terminal stations, shall be called as nearly as practicable, one hour before leaving time, by train Caller, who will be provided with a book in which the men called will enter their names, also the time called, and the time of trainmen will begin at the time set for the departure of their train.

21. When crews of through or local freight or mixed trains are required to do switching service at terminal or division stations, they will be paid extra for such service, at the rate of 30 and 20 cents per hour; less than thirty minutes not to be counted; thirty minutes and over and less than one hour will be computed as one hour excepting that on runs which occupy less than ten hours, no extra switching service will be allowed until the total time used in making the runs exceeds ten hours.

22. The actual time made by Conductors and Brakemen for switching service, as above specified, shall be kept by the Yardmaster, or where there is no Yardmaster by the Station Agent, in a book kept for that special purpose, and all such switching time shall be returned to the division office and made up in the pay rolls for the months in which this service is rendered.

23. The proper officers of the Railway Company will listen to any reasonable complaints made by either individual Conductors, Brakemen or Yardmen, or by committee of the same, provided proper notice is given, in writing, as to the subject of complaint, and special appointment is made as to the time and place to consider the same.

24. After continuous service of sixteen hours or more, trainmen shall be entitled to and allowed eight hours for rest before being called to go out, except in cases of wrecks, washouts, or similar emergencies.

25. Crews shall not be run off of their respective divisions, except in case of necessity or special emergency, when no crews of that division are there to take the trains.

26. Any Conductor, Trainman or Yardman, may be suspended from duty for a reasonable time or for investigation for any alleged misconduct, or for violation of rules or orders; and may be discharged from the service of the Company for good and sufficient causes. These causes shall include intemperance, incompetency, habitual neglect of duty, gross violation of rules or orders, dishonesty, or insubordination. For

ny of these causes, they may be suspended by the Division Trainmaster and discharged by the Division Superintendent.

27. When a Conductor, Trainman or Yardman is discharged or suspended for a efinite term, for an alleged fault, he shall have a fair and impartial trial within five ays after filing his request therefor with the Division Superintendent, and if suspended r investigation, such investigation shall be held within five days without such request. found innocent, he shall be paid at regular rates for time lost, and reinstated. If etained over five days, awaiting investigation, he shall be paid for extra time in ccess of five days, whether found guilty or not.

28. In filling vacancies in the ranks of freight Conductors, all Conductors, Brakeen and Baggagemen will be considered in the line of promotion, according to their ge in the service and their ability to assume the duties of Conductors, except that hree Brakemen shall be first promoted and then one experienced Conductor may be ired as a Conductor, at the option of the officer in charge. A Conductor so hired shall ake his place at the foot of the list of extra Conductors, and may be temporarily used s extra Brakeman, pending vacancy to be filled by him.

29. All employes in yard service shall be promoted according to age and ability, roviding the officers in charge of such men consider them competent for positions to hich they are entitled by seniority in service; and anyone feeling that he has not had fair and impartial examination, shall have a right to appeal to higher authority.

30. All Conductors will be considered in the line of promotion according to their erm of service, dependent upon their good conduct and ability. Whenever additional onductors are required in the passenger service, promotions will be made from the anks of freight Conductors, as above, giving each freight district representation in urn, except that the General Superintendent reserves the right to employ additional r new men for these positions when they consider the good of the service requires it.

31. Any employe included under the provisions of this agreement, who is dissatisfied with the decision of any official of the Company, shall have the right to appeal herefrom to the General Manager, after having first submitted his case to the decision of the General Superintendent.

32. The oldest Brakemen, when competent, will be given preference as passenger Brakemen, when they so desire.

33. On all main line local freight and mixed trains the train crews shall consist of a Conductor and three Brakemen; on branch roads, where the service is light, the crews shall consist of a Conductor and two Brakemen, excepting that on branches where the trains are heavy enough to require them, three Brakemen shall be employed at the discretion of the Division Superintendent.

34. When passenger or freight Conductors make reasonable objections to the Trainmaster or Division Superintendent against any Brakeman under their charge, such Brakeman shall be removed or assigned to other duty or dismissed from the service, according to the circumstances.

35. All instructions given to freight or passenger Conductors by Trainmasters or Train Dispatchers relative to movement of trains or disposition of cars, will be given in train orders, or in writing.

36. When a trainman is required by the Superintendent to change his run, and by so doing he would be obliged to move his family and household goods, they shall be moved free of charge on application therefor.

37. Passenger train Brakemen who have never worked on freight trains must work at least two years on a freight train before they shall be entitled to an examination for promotion to a freight Conductorship.

38. Freight cabooses and their crews shall not be laid over for the reason that their Conductor has laid off for any cause.

39. When the freight traffic on any portion of the road is so light that all the freight crews in service are not able to make reasonable wages, crews shall be laid off (beginning with the youngest men) until the crews in service are able to make reasonable wages. Any Conductors suspended from service under this rule will be given preference as Brakemen, and they will retain their rights as Conductors and will be replaced on their runs when the freight business requires an increase of crews.

40. If a Conductor, Brakeman or Yardman leaves the service of the Company of his own accord, or if he is discharged from the service, he shall forfeit all rights previously held unless he is reinstated within ninety days.

41. There shall be no discrimination against any employe of the Company on account of being a member of any of the railway organizations.

42. Any Conductor, Trainman or Yardman leaving the employ of the Company will, at his request, be given a letter by his Superintendent or Division Superintendent stating his term of service, capacities in which employed, and whether he has been discharged or has left the service of his own accord. If discharged, such letter shall state the reasons.

43. A copy of this letter of instructions will be furnished to all Division Superintendents, Trainmasters, and Yardmasters, and the same shall be accessible to any employe who may desire to see it.

Approved: S. H. H. CLARK,
First Vice President and General Manager.
May 1, 1891.

GEO. C. SMITH,
Assistant General Manager.
A. W. DICKINSON,
R. E. RICKER,
General Superintendents.

MOBILE & OHIO RAILROAD COMPANY.

1. This Company will employ or promote men to the position of Conductor, as in the judgment of the management may be required. None but sober, reliable, competent, able-bodied and experienced men will be employed. The right to promotion of regular runs will be governed by merit, ability and seniority. They will be directly responsible and subject to the orders and control of the Trainmaster and Division Superintendent at all times and in all matters pertaining to their duties. All employes will be dismissed without a hearing in cases of drinking on duty, intoxication on or off duty, insubordination, and no habitual frequenters of saloons will be retained in the service of the Company.

2. Passenger Conductors on trains 1, 2, 5, and 6, will be paid $100 per calendar month, Baggagemasters $57.50, and Brakemen $52.50 per calendar month. The Citronelle, Murphysboro and Branch service Conductors and Brakemen will remain the same as heretofore.

3. On the mixed trains Conductors will be paid $80 and Brakemen $55 per calendar month. Twelve hours to constitute a day's work.

4. There will be five local crews on Jackson and Mobile divisions, first in first out of Jackson and Meridian. Conductors will be paid $88.40 per month and Brakemen $60 per month, Sundays not included. Twelve hours to constitute a day's work. When a full month is not made pay shall be computed by days in current month.

5. Local freight Conductors will be paid $3.35 per trip between Murphysboro and East St. Louis, and $3.35 per trip from Murphysboro to Cairo and return. Local freight Brakemen will be paid $2.35 per trip between Murphysboro and East St. Louis, and $2.35 from Murphysboro to Cairo and return. Twelve hours to constitute a day's work.

6. Through freight Conductors will be paid as follows:

FROM	TO	Hrs. p'r day	Per Trip
East St. Louis	Cairo	12	$4 55
Murphysboro	Burkesville and return	12	3 35
East St. Louis	Murphysboro	12	2 75
Murphysboro	Cairo	10	2 50
Murphysboro	Gravel Pit and return	10	3 00
East Cairo	Jackson	12	3 45
Jackson	Okolona	12	3 45
Okolona	Meridian	12	3 50
Meridian	Mobile	12	3 50

Through freight Brakemen will be paid as follows:

FROM	TO	Hrs. p'r day	Per Trip
East St. Louis	Cairo	12	$3 05
Murphysboro	Burkesville and return	12	2 35
East St. Louis	Murphysboro	12	2 00
Murphysboro	Cairo	10	1 75
Murphysboro	Gravel Pit and return	10	2 00
East Cairo	Jackson	12	2 30
Jackson	Okolona	12	2 30
Okolona	Meridian	12	2 40
Meridian	Mobile	12	2 40

7. When freight crews are called to go out on picnic or excursion trains they will be paid, Conductors $3.33 per day, Brakemen $2 per day. Twelve hours to constitute a day's work. On work, wreck or circus trains, where freight crews are used, will be paid: Conductors $3 per day, Brakemen $2 per day. Twelve hours to constitute a day's work. On wrecking trains where less than six hours' service is required, the pay will be one-half work train rates as above. Where over six hours is required, they will be paid work train rates as above.

8. Conductors and Brakemen dead-heading on Company's business will be paid one-half rates, or running light engine and caboose through freight rates.

9. Conductors and Brakemen attending court at Company's request will be paid: Conductors $3 per day, Brakemen $2 per day of twenty-four hours and an allowance of $1 per day for expenses, when not at their homes. Where crews are called as witnesses in cases of investigation, they will be paid the rates that their cabooses make while held off for that purpose.

10. When Conductor or Brakeman is called and for any reason the train is abandoned, he will be paid at overtime rates per hour from the time called until relieved.

11. No more crews will be assigned to runs than in the judgment of the management is necessary to move the traffic of the road with promptness and regularity.

12. Crews will not be required to go out when they need rest, nor shall any crew be permitted to run on the road when their physical ability has been fairly taxed by previous service, before they have had the needed rest.

13. Conductors and Brakemen will not be suspended or discharged, except for just cause, and when suspended will be given a hearing in five days and will be notified of the result of the investigation. When a Conductor or Brakeman is suspended from duty and on investigation it is found they were not to blame for the act for which they were suspended, they will be paid: Conductors $3 per day, Brakemen $2 per day of twenty-four hours, for all the time they have lost by reason of suspension, but they shall have no claim to compensation for the time for which they were suspended if it is found they were to blame for the act for which they were suspended. When a Conductor or Brakeman, who is charged with wrong or fault, is called in for investigation if he sees proper to invite another Conductor or Brakeman to go in with him to hear the investigation, the management have no objection to his doing so.

14. The Caller will call all crews at the place they designate, within one mile of the yard office at Cairo, Murphysboro, East St. Louis, Jackson, Okolona, Meridian, and Mobile. No crews will be called in St. Louis. If he lives outside of the limit herein prescribed or is at any other point, he must make his own arrangements to ascertain whether he is wanted or not. When crews are called to go out, they must sign the Caller's book, giving the exact time at which they were called. Time will commence from one hour after they are called and will be ascertained from train reports and checked by Conductor's trip slips.

15. Overtime will be paid after twelve hours from time train is called to go out and will be paid: For Conductors 30 cents, and for Brakemen 20 cents per hour; thirty minutes counted as nothing and over thirty minutes as one hour.

16. On through freight runs, between St. Louis and Cairo, if crew is cut out by orders of the Trainmaster or Division Superintendent, or they are physically unable to complete the trip, the pay will be on the basis of Article 6. If not under these conditions, pay to be strictly on mileage basis.

17. If any employe is dissatisfied with the decision of the Division Officers, he has the right of appeal to the General Superintendent and General Manager.

ENGINEERS.

1. *Passenger Service:* Engineers of passenger trains will be paid 3¼ cents per mile, 100 miles or more. If delayed two hours beyond schedule time will be paid overtime, 35 cents per hour, counting thirty minutes as nothing, over thirty minutes one hour. Trip or round trips of sixty-five miles or less will be paid $2.50, provided the trip or trips are made within eight hours; will be paid 35 cents per hour thereafter. Sixty-five miles to 100 will be paid $3.25 trip or round trips, and overtime after eight hours. Excursion trains from Mobile to Citronelle and return, $3.50 per day; overtime after twelve hours.

2. *Freight Service:* Engineers on through freight will be paid 4 cents per mile, 100 miles or more. If more than twelve hours are consumed in making the run between relay points, 35 cents for each hour delayed thereafter, counting thirty minutes as nothing, over thirty minutes as one hour. Time to commence one hour after Engineer is called. Trip or round trips of sixty-five miles or less, $3.50, provided the run is made in ten hours. If over ten hours, 35 cents per hour for each hour thereafter, thirty minutes counting nothing, over thirty minutes one hour. Sixty-five miles to 100 miles will be paid $4 trip or round trips, and overtime after twelve hours. Engineers on local freight will be paid 4¼ cents per mile for 100 miles or more. If more than twelve hours are consumed in making the run between relay points, Engineer will be paid 35 cents per hour; thirty minutes counting nothing, over thirty minutes one hour. Time to commence one hour after being called. Trip or round trips of sixty-five miles or less, $3.50, provided the trip or round trips is made in ten hours, and will be paid 35 cents per hour thereafter. Trip or round trips of sixty-five miles to 100 miles, $4.25, and overtime over twelve hours.

3. Engineers running light engines and cabooses will be paid 3¼ cents per mile, 100 miles or more, and will be paid overtime over twelve hours, 30 cents per hour, counting

thirty minutes as nothing, over thirty minutes one hour. Sixty-five miles or less, trip or round trips, $2.50, and overtime after eight hours. Sixty-five miles to 100, trip or round trips, $3.25, and overtime after twelve hours.

4. Engineers pulling special, pay car, or excursion trains will be paid as per Article 1.

5. Engineers running the Murphysboro accommodation will be paid $3 each way and if delayed two hours beyond schedule time to be paid 35 cents per hour; thirty minutes as nothing, more than thirty minutes one hour.

6. Should an engine start out on a run and, from any cause, have to give up train and return, the distance being sixty-five miles or less, irrespective of service engaged in, the Engineer will be paid $2.50, and overtime over eight hours. Sixty-five miles to 100, $4, and overtime after twelve hours. If the run is over 100 miles, will be paid as per service engaged in.

7. Light engine mileage must be placed in column for that purpose on trip tickets, and must have spaces fully filled out, showing time of leaving and arriving for each trip or round trip, and must show time called and arriving.

8. Switch Engineers will be paid $2.75 per day at East St. Louis, Murphysboro Cairo, Jackson, Meridian, Mobile and Whistler. At Columbus, Miss., $2.50 per day Twelve hours to constitute a day's work, overtime at 25 cents per hour.

9. *Branch Runs:* On the Aberdeen branch, the Columbus and Starkville branches including all switching that may be necessary, and to run as many trips as may be required to do the business for passenger or mixed trains, the compensation of the Engineer shall be $3.50 per day. On the Millstadt branch, including all switching that may be necessary at any and all points, and as many trips per day as may be required to do the business of the Millstadt branch, the Engineer shall receive $85 per month Overtime on all branches will commence after twelve hours, and will be paid for such overtime at the rate of 30 cents per hour.

10. *Work Train Service:* On gravel, timber and all work trains, the Engineer running such trains will be paid $100 per month, and be required to remain with their trains unless relieved by the division officers. If they shall perform service every working day in such month they shall receive the same compensation as if they worked every day in the month. If they make any time less than the number of working days they will be paid at the rate of $100 per month for the actual number of days in the current month. Overtime on work trains will commence after twelve hours. The Engineer running pile driver trains, when required, shall run the pile driver engine, and shall receive, in addition to his regular pay, $10 per month for such service. Conductors, or men in charge of trains, shall certify to the Engineer's time tickets as being correct.

11. *Incline Service:* Engineers running incline engines will receive $100 per month provided they render service, when required, every day in the month. If any time less than a full month, they will be paid at the rate of $100 per month. Twelve hours is considered a day's work. Overtime in such service will begin after twelve hours, and will be paid for at the rate of 25 cents per hour. The Yardmaster shall certify to the Engineer's time ticket as being correct.

12. *Irregular Service:* When an Engineer is called to go out to perform two or three hours' work, and he returns in time to take out his regular train, he will be paid at overtime rates for the time he is out, and will not lose his run; but if he does not return in time to take his run, he will be paid $3.50, and will be considered the last man in. Extra Engineers called to perform irregular service, if they are out less than six hours, will be paid at overtime rates per hour. If over six hours, will be paid $3.50. On the St. Louis division on freight runs between St. Louis and Cairo, if engine is cut out by the orders of the Master Mechanic, or the Engineer is physically unable to complete the trip, the pay between St. Louis and Murphysboro shall be $4, and between Murphysboro and Cairo $3.50. If not under these conditions, pay to be strictly on mileage basis.

For the movement of wrecking car and material for wrecking at washout, or snow service: An Engineer called for this service shall receive as compensation $3.50 per day for all time over six hours, up to twelve hours, and thereafter overtime at the rate of 30 cents per hour. If under six hours, at the rate of 30 cents per hour. Any Engineer who is required to take an engine across the river at Cairo, shall be allowed 35 cents per hour for the time employed in such service; the Yardmasters at East Cairo and Cairo to certify to the time tickets.

13. *Overtime:* In order to have no misunderstanding as to what overtime means passenger and freight Engineers will be paid for overtime at the rate of thirty-five cents per hour: for work trains, thirty cents per hour; for all branch trains, thirty cents per hour; for switching service, twenty-five cents per hour; for incline service twenty-five cents per hour. Under thirty minutes, nothing; over thirty minutes, one hour.

14. Engineers of passenger and freight trains arriving at terminals, if they can

ot get their engines to the round house or are not relieved by a hostler, within thirty minutes, will be paid thirty-five cents per hour for each hour in excess of that time. Anything over thirty minutes, one hour, and less than thirty minutes nothing; except on passenger trains arriving at Mobile and East St. Louis, where overtime will not apply until one hour after arrival.

15. For watching engines in case trains are unable to reach terminals, one man only will be paid fifteen cents per hour. Engineers delayed beyond schedule time in arriving at terminals, caused by wrecks, washouts, or other causes which block the road, when Engineer is rendering service at such washouts, etc., he will be paid thirty-five cents per hour. When no service is performed, he will receive fifteen cents per hour for all delays over schedule time.

16. The rights of Engineers to regular runs will be determined by seniority and capacity; all Engineers to rank as to seniority from the date they are employed permanently as Engineers, and senior Engineers will have preference as to runs when merit and competency are equal.

17. No more Engineers will be assigned to runs than are necessary in the judgment of the management to move the traffic of the road with promptness and regularity.

18. The Company will exercise the right to run its engines in such manner and on such parts of its road as in the judgment of the management of the road is necessary to properly transact its business.

19. Engineers detailed to go over the road to attend to Company's business, such as attending court, or appearing before proper parties, will be allowed $5 per day of twenty-four hours, for all time lost and pay their own expenses, except for transportation, but the allowance for expenses does not apply at their homes on the division on which such Engineer is employed.

20. When Engineers are not regularly assigned to any engine, all work reported by them on arrival at the shops will be done at the shops, but they will be required to do all necessary work heretofore done by them, or work which is necessary to be done away from the shops, and Engineers running regular engines will do all work usually done by Engineers.

21. Engineers will not be held responsible for the loss of or damage to tools, or damage done to rolling stock, unless the same is caused by negligence on their part, and will not be suspended for killing or injuring live stock, unless it is shown that they have been negligent, or did not use proper and reasonable efforts to avoid the injury.

22. Engineers shall not be required to go out when they need rest, nor shall any Engineer be permitted to run on the road when his physical ability has been fairly taxed by previous service, before he has had the needed rest.

23. Engineers will be required to conform strictly to the schedule speed of trains they are running, except when they receive orders to exceed the speed provided for in the schedule. Engineers are expected to report to the Trainmaster or Superintendent when schedule speed is exceeded on down grades, by reason of Conductors and Brakemen failing to properly apply brakes when Engineers give the signal for that purpose. Good judgment is at all times expected from Engineers in passing over the summits, to have their trains well in hand and under control. When this is the case and prompt report is made of the failure of brakes being applied when called for, Engineers will not then be held responsible for excessive speed resulting from this cause.

24. Engineers will not be suspended or discharged except for just cause, and when suspended, will be given a hearing in five days and will be notified of the result of the investigation. When an Engineer is suspended from duty, and on investigation it is found that he was not to blame for the act for which he was suspended, he will be paid $ per day of twenty-four hours for all time he has lost by reason of such suspension, but he shall have no claim for compensation for time he was suspended if it is found he was to blame for the act for which he was suspended. When an Engineer is called for investigation, who is charged with wrong or fault, if he sees proper to invite any other Engineer to go in with him to hear the investigation, the management have no objection to his doing so.

25. Engineers when going over the road for an engine or returning after delivering one under orders, will be paid two cents per mile.

26. The Caller will call all Engineers at the place they designate, if within one mile of the round house. If he lives outside of the limits herein prescribed, he must make his own arrangements to ascertain whether he is wanted or not. When Engineer called to go out, he shall sign Caller's book giving the exact time at which he was called. Time will commence from one hour after the Engineer is called, and will be ascertained from train reports and checked by Engineer's trip reports. If the train is abandoned, they will be paid thirty-five cents per hour from the time they go on duty until they are relieved.

27. If any Engineer or other employe is dissatisfied with the decision of the division officers, he has the right of appeal to the General Superintendent or to the Super-

intendent of Machinery. If he is dissatisfied with their decision, he has the right o
appeal to the General Manager.

28. It is hereby agreed and understood that this agreement shall remain in ful
force and effect from the first day of January, 1891, to the first day of January, 1892
unless it is mutually agreed by both the contracting parties hereto to abandon thi
agreement, and that written notice of sixty days shall be given by either party afte
the first day of January, 1892, who desire to alter, amend, revise or abolish the same
All officers or the Mobile & Ohio Railroad Company will see that this agreement i
carried out in good faith on the part of the Company, and this committee acting fo
the Engineers on the Mobile & Ohio Railroad agree on their part to carry out thi
agreement in good faith for them. It is distinctly understood that when this agree
ment goes into effect that if a wrong or injury has been done to any one or more per
sons affected by this agreement, the management is ready at all times to take up an
consider in a spirit of fairness such grievance.

MOBILE & OHIO RAILROAD COMPANY,
Engineers Mobile & Ohio Railroad: By JAS C. CLARKE,
By J. B. COZART, General Chairman. President and General Manager
January 1, 1891.

YARD SERVICE.

East St. Louis, Ill: Yardmaster, day, $115 per month; night, $95. Foreman, day
29 cents per hour; night, 27 cents. Switchmen, day, 27 cents per hour; night 25 cents

Murphysboro, Ill: Yardmaster, day, $85 per month; night, $80. Switchmen, da
and night, $2 per day.

Cairo, Ill: Yardmaster, general, $100 per month. Foreman, day, 28 cents per hour
night, 27 cents. Switchmen, day, 24 cents per hour; night, 23½ cents.

East Cairo, Ky: Yardmaster, general, $100 per month. Foreman, day, $2.80 pe
day, 28 cents per hour overtime; Foreman, night, $3.24 per day, 27 cents per hour over
time. Switchmen, day, $2.40 per day, 24 cents per hour overtime; Switchmen, nigh
$2.82 per day, 23¼ cents per hour overtime.

Jackson, Tenn: Yardmaster, day, $100 per month; night, $75. Foreman, day, $6
per month; night, $65. Switchmen, day and night, $60 per month.

Okolona, Miss: Yardmaster, day, $100 per month; night, $75. Switchmen, day an
night, $60 per month.

Meridian, Miss: Yardmaster, day, $100 per month; night, $75. Foreman, day, $65
Switchmen, day and night, $60 per month.

Mobile, Ala: Yardmaster, day, $100 per month; night, $75. Foreman, day, $65 pe
month. Switchmen, day and night, $60 per month.   D. McLAREN,
For the Order of Railway Conductors: General Superintendent.
A. B. GARRETSON, G. S. C.
For the Brotherhood of Railroad Trainmen:
S. E. WILKINSON, G. M.

MONTANA UNION RAILWAY COMPANY.

1. Passenger Conductors, $120 per month; freight Conductors, $105 per month
Train Baggagemen, $85 and $90 per month. Passenger Brakemen, $80 per month
freight Brakemen, $75 per month. Foremen switching crews, $3.50 per day. Switc
men, $3 per day. Overtime after ten hours, excepting Train Baggagemen.

2. Ten hours or less to be considered a day's work for train or yard service.

3. For freight train crews a round trip between Anaconda and Butte, or Butt
and Anaconda, or Silver Bow and Anaconda and Garrison, or Garrison and Anacond
to be invariably considered a day's work. The pay and runs of passenger crews to r
main the same as in effect May 1, 1892, that is, on a basis of ten hours' work.

4. Trainmen to receive 35 cents and 25 cents per hour for switching at terminal
Anaconda, Butte and Garrison to be considered as terminals. All work not in exce
of thirty minutes to go to the Company, over thirty minutes to be counted an hou
Switching out bad orders or no bill cars, and doubling trains to or from different trac
not to be considered switching at terminals.

5. Train crews to make five doubles between Anaconda and Mill Creek, or An
conda and Stewart, or Butte and Silver Bow without additional compensation in ea
calendar month. Overtime after ten hours. Pay for all doubles after five doubles
35 cents per hour for Conductors, and 25 cents per hour for Brakemen.

6. Trainmen and yardmen will be allowed sixty days leave of absence, if leave
obtained in writing, and retain their rights.

7. Trainmen and yardmen on Company business will receive pay at their schedu
rates, and necessary expenses when away from home.

8. In case of breach of discipline, as a general rule, parties implicated will be)tified within five days after a decision is arrived at.
9. The rights to regular runs to be governed by seniority and ability.
10. Freight train crews to be called at a distance of one mile from station, and at ast one hour before leaving time, and to be entitled to eight hours' rest in every venty-four.
11. That $3.65 be paid to engine Foremen, and $3.15 to Helpers in all yards of the ontana Union Railway.
12. Any trainmen or yardmen who are suspended for any offense, if proven inno- ?nt, shall be paid full pay and be reinstated to all former rights.
13. One Foreman and three Helpers to be employed with engine 75, known as the uay engine, when employed in Butte yard.
14. If yardmen accept or are temporarily assigned to train service, they shall not irrender their rights in the yard nor obtain any in train service, and the same shall pply to trainmen assigned or accepting service in the yard, but must perform either rvice when called upon.
15. Time slips will be returned to Conductors and Foremen for correction when)t honored.
16. When helper switch engine, working between town track and Walkerville, is isigned to separate work at the Lexington, Anaconda supply and other tracks in that cinity, the pay of the helper, designated as Assistant Foreman, assigned to the work iall be $3.40 per day, and not more if engaged in bringing an ore train from the hill South Butte.
17. All switch tenders and engine herders working in any yard of the Montana nion Railway, shall be paid at the same rate as was in effect May 1, 1892, that is, no iange in pay or hours.
18. The oldest man employed in yard service will have the preference of what igine or job he is entitled to, if competent to perform the duty.
19. Men transferred from Butte or Anaconda to Silver Bow yard will hold their ghts in the yard transferred from.
20. Trainmen or yardmen leaving the service of the Company will be given letters ating length of service and cause of leaving.
21. Members of the O. R. C. and B. of R. T. will be furnished transportation upon ·esentation of traveling cards if engaged in train or yard service, or seeking employ- ent in such ; otherwise no transportation.
22. This schedule to supersede all other usages and rules heretofore in effect.

WM. H. BURNS,
)r the Order of Railway Conductors: General Manager.
JAS. STARK, J. K. MULLIN.
)r the Brotherhood of Railroad Trainmen:
C. J. KIRBY, JAS. S. STRAIN, M. J. ELLIOTT.
June 21, 1892.

ASHVILLE, CHATTANOOGA & ST. LOUIS RAILWAY, AND THE WESTERN & ATLANTIC RAILROAD.

TRAINMEN'S SCHEDULE.

1. There shall be established on each division a Board of Inquiry, to consist of the iperintendent or Assistant Superintendent (or both), and the Superintendent of otive Power or Master Mechanic (or both), whose duty it shall be to investigate acci- ?nts. In case employes are suspended to appear before this board, thay will be given hearing within five days, and will receive prompt notice of the result of the investi- ution. All punishments shall consist of suspension or discharge. It shall not be nec- ·sary to convene the board except for the investigation of accidents. If the parties inished by the board,· or otherwise, desire it, they may appeal, first, through the iperintendent to the Assistant General Manager and then to the General Manager. ll appeals must be made in writing and presented to the Superintendent within thirty ιys after the decision of the board shall have been made known. Should the employes ispended be found innocent, they will be paid for the time the suspension was in !ect—Conductors $2.85 per day, and Brakemen, Baggagemen and Yardmen $1.75 per .y. To enable the division officers to make investigations, reports must be made to e proper officer at the end of each trip.

2. Road delay time will be allowed Conductors and Brakemen after the schedule the train shall have been exceeded two hours, at the rate of thirty and twenty nts, respectively, per hour for every hour and fractional part thereof. When a ain has been delayed to exceed two hours, the first two hours will be counted. In .se schedules are changed on the road, road delay time will be computed from sched- e departed ·on. Wages shall be computed from one hour after the men are called,

or the time the train departs, if earlier. Road delay time for extra passenger trai[n] shall be arrived at by taking the average time of the schedule passenger trains on t[he] division. The schedule of extra freight trains running between terminals shall be computed at the rate of twelve and one-half miles per hour.

3. Yard delay time at terminals shall be allowed at the rate of thirty and twen[ty] cents, respectively, per hour, for each hour or fractional part thereof, after a tra[in] shall have been delayed within the yard limits beyond thirty minutes. Running ti[me] of the train within yard limits shall not be considered. When delayed immediate[ly] outside of the yard limit board, trainmen shall be allowed yard delay time at sa[me] rate, when delay exceeds thirty minutes.

4. At Nashville, Chattanooga, Atlanta and Union City, trainmen will be call[ed] not to exceed one hour before the leaving time of their trains, provided they li[ve] within one mile of the yard from which their trains start. The Caller shall be f[ur]nished with a book, which must be signed by the men, showing the time that they a[re] called, and the time the train is to depart. Failing to respond promptly, whether it [is] his turn out or not, the party at fault shall be suspended or discharged, at the disc[re]tion of the Superintendent. When trainmen come in on their runs, and are not ab[le] for duty, they must so notify the Superintendent or his assistant. If afterward, [on] account of sickness, they cannot go out, they must send a written notice to the Supe[r]intendent or his assistant at least two hours before they are needed. They must n[ot] lay off, except by permission of an authorized officer, unless they, or a member of the[ir] immediate family, are suddenly taken sick, in which event they must give at least t[wo] hours' notice.

5. When trainmen are called to go out between the hours of 7 P. M. and 7 A. [M.] and the train is afterward annulled, they shall be allowed three hours, at the rate [of] thirty and twenty cents per hour, respectively: provided, they are not notified th[ey] will be required for another schedule train within one hour. When called to go out [at] other hours, in case train is annulled, they shall be paid at the same rates per hou[r,] but time shall be computed from one hour after they are called until they are notifi[ed] that train is annulled. Trainmen thus called will stand first out; provided it does n[ot] interfere with men who have regular runs.

6. For attending court or appearing before proper persons to give evidence, Co[n]ductors, Baggagemen and Brakemen, having regular crews, and Yardmen having re[g]ular work, shall be paid the amount they would have made had they performed th[e] usual duties. This shall not prevent the Company from using these men on any r[un] after they are through attending court, and before their regular crews are due [to] leave. Other Conductors and Brakemen shall be paid $3 and $2 per day, respective[ly] computed from the time they leave their homes, or the time they are marked to [go] out, until they return. They will be furnished with transportation to and from cou[rt.] No pay shall be allowed in cases where the time so consumed does not interfere wi[th] the men making their regular trips and having eight hours rest, if they require it.

7. Conductors and Brakemen, when dead-heading on a freight train, will [be] allowed the rate of pay given the same class of men that are in charge of the tra[in.] When dead-heading on passenger train they will be paid one and one-quarter a[nd] eight-tenths of a cent, respectively, per mile for the distance traveled. When a m[an] is traveling over the road for the purpose of relieving a man who has asked for lea[ve] of absence, he will not receive any compensation for the distance traveled.

8. After a continuous service of sixteen hours, or more, Conductors and tra[in] men shall be entitled to and allowed eight hours for rest at terminals, if they gi[ve] proper notice of such desire, except in case of wrecks or similar emergencies.

9. Conductors will be notified in writing when time is not allowed as per their t[ime] reports.

10. Any trainman drinking intoxicants on duty, or being under their influence [of,] or off duty, will be dismissed from the service of the Company.

11. All crews assigned to regular runs at a monthly rate, that are not provid[ed] for in the accompanying rate sheets, will be paid extra for all service performed [in] addition to their regular duties at established rates for class of service performed.

12. All crews not assigned to regular runs will run first in first out.

13. All freight Conductors and Brakemen ordered out on short runs, less than 1[00] miles, shall be allowed 100 miles for the same. Overtime for all time used in excess [of] twelve hours.

SCALE OF WAGES OF TRAINMEN.

14. Main line passenger trains: Conductors, per mile run, 2 cents; Baggageme[n] per month, $52.50; Flagmen, per month, $47.50. Rome express, same rates as above.

15. Through freight trains: Conductors, 2 8-10 cents; Brakemen, 1 9-10 cents, p[er] mile run.

16. Local freight trains. Three crews to each division: Conductors, $90; Bra[ke]men, $60 per month.

17. Local Chattanooga to Bridgeport and Chattanooga to Shellmound. Two round ips daily: Conductors, $90; Brakemen, $60 per month. Chattanooga and Victoria in: Conductors, per day, *$2.80; Brakemen, *$1.90.

18. Cowan run: Mileage, and overtime, in case round trip is not made in twenty-ur hours, but it is understood this run will be discontinued and run made from Nashlle to Tracy City, 107 miles, on which rates will be: Conductors, $3; Brakemen, $2 r single trip.

19. Dalton and Marietta accommodations: Conductors and trainmen, same rates id service as at present.

20. Sequatchie Valley division: On passenger trains: Conductors, per day, *$2.80; aggagemasters, per month, †$25; Brakemen, per day, *$1.60. On freight trains: onductors, per day, *$2.80; Brakemen, *$1.90.

21. Huntsville, Fayetteville and Columbia division, and McMinnville branch: On issenger trains: Conductors, per day, *$2.65; Baggagemasters, per month, †$25; rakemen, per day, *$1.50. On freight and mixed trains: Conductors, per day, *$2.80; rakemen, *$1.60.

22. Centreville branch: Brakemen, $1.50 per day, and are to continue coaling and iping engines as at present.

23. Union City and Columbus run: Conductors, per day, *$2.80; Brakemen, *$1.90.

24. Construction or material trains: Conductors, $90 per month; twelve hours to nstitute a day's work; hours in excess of twelve to be paid as overtime.

25. Conductors and Brakemen of wood and wrecking trains shall be paid, respecvely, 35 and 20 cents per hour, or fractional part thereof; time to be computed from ie time train starts, or one hour after the men are called, until they return to startg point. In case the train is laid up before returning, for the purpose of affording ie men necessary time for rest and sleep, such proportion of the time shall be deicted from the whole, and only actual time on duty will be paid for. A minimum of x hours will be allowed, but no mileage will be paid.

26. Yardmasters at Marietta and Dalton will be paid $70 per month; Helpers, $2 r day for the days they work. One Helper with each engine.

27. When the business of the road is so light that the freight crews in service are iable to make 3,000 miles per month crews will be taken off, beginning with the oungest Conductors, until those that are left can make 3,000 miles per month. Conictors thus taken off shall have preference as Brakemen, and shall be restored to ieir positions as Conductors when the business of the road will justify the same.

28. The right to runs, both passenger and freight, shall be governed by seniority id ability on their respective divisions.

29. Local grievances and differences of opinion as to construction of this agreeent shall be taken up with division officers; failing to be adjusted they will be reirred to the general officers, as per Article 1.

ENGINEMEN'S SCHEDULE.

1. All through freight Engineers shall be paid 4½ cents per mile; 100 miles or less) constitute a day's work; all over 100 miles to be paid 4½ cents per mile. All through eight Firemen shall receive 53 per cent. of Engineers' pay.

2. All through passenger Engineers shall be paid 3½ cents per mile; 100 miles or ss to constitute a day's work; all over 100 miles to be paid 3½ cents per mile. Passener train Firemen to receive 53 per cent. of Engineers' pay.

3. All freight Engineers on short runs shall receive the following pay: From hattanooga to Stevenson and return, $4 per day; from Chattanooga to South Pittsirg and return, $3.75 per day, to be paid every day in the month; from Chattanooga) Shellmound and return, $4 per day, two round trips; from Cowan to South Pittsburg nd return, $3.75 per day, to be paid every day in the month, provided a trip is made in velve hours, if not made within twelve hours they shall receive 35 cents for each adtional hour or fractional part thereof. The Firemen shall receive 53 per cent. of the ngineers' pay.

4. Engineers on regular construction or work trains shall receive $4 per day; welve hours or less to constitute a day's work; all over twelve hours shall be paid 35 ents per hour, and shall be paid for every day in the month, except when men do not main on the engines on Sunday.

5. All switch Engineers shall receive $3 per day, twelve hours or less to constitute day's work; one hour to be allowed for dinner; all over twelve hours or fractional arts thereof to be paid 25 cents per hour. Engineers and Firemen to be paid every ay in the month. The Firemen shall receive 53 per cent. of Engineers' pay.

6. Hostlers shall receive $2.75 per day. Where Hostlers at Atlanta are required) do transfer work, they shall receive $3.25 per day; twelve hours or less to constitute day's work; all over twelve hours to be paid 25 cents per hour. The Firemen to reeive 53 per cent. of Engineers' pay.

*Paid for every day in month, and when necessary will work Sundays without extra compensaon. †Express Company pays $2 50 per month.

7. All Engineers pulling mixed trains to be paid freight train rates. The Firemen to receive 53 per cent. of Engineers' pay.

8. All Engineers running freight or passenger trains to be paid 35 cents per hour for all detentions over schedule time of trains they are running. Less than two hours nothing; over two hours shall include the first two hours, with each additional hour or fractional part thereof. The Firemen to receive 53 per cent. of Engineers' pay.

9. Engineers will not be held responsible for excess of speed in descending grades where they have no control over speed, provided they bring the train over the summit at the proper speed, using care and good judgment afterwards.

10. Hostlers will be kept at Nashville, Chattanooga and Atlanta for Nashville & Chattanooga and Western & Atlantic divisions, and at Union City and Hickman for Northwestern division. Where Engineers are required to hostler their own engines, at intermediate points, they shall receive one hour's compensation at 35 cents per hour. The Firemen shall receive 53 per cent. of Engineers' pay.

11. In case an Engineer or Fireman is held off to attend court on Company's business, he shall receive all time that his engine would have made had she made her regular trips; and shall be paid his board when away from home. The Company shall be entitled to certificates for witness fees.

12. Callers shall be kept at all terminals and relay points. The Caller will have a book, in which Engineers and Firemen shall register their names and time called. All Engineers and Firemen shall be called one hour before leaving time, provided they reside within one mile of round-house. Engineers' and Firemen's time shall commence one hour after signing Caller's book, and ends at the time designated on his trip ticket, it being understood that Engineers and Firemen shall be paid for all delays, before or after leaving or arriving at terminals.

13. The oldest Engineman and Fireman in road service shall have the preference of runs and promotion on their respective divisions, if competent and worthy, it being distinctly understood that merit and general fitness for the position are to be first considered; this to apply only after they shall have been in the service one year, except at the discretion of the Master Mechanic. Such time shall be counted in deciding rights for promotion. This rule to apply to Enginemen and Firemen of switch engines as between themselves. Engineers and Firemen having regular runs prior to March 1 shall not be affected by this Article.

14. In case an Engineer is required to go over the road with a light engine, he shall be furnished with a Conductor.

15. The Company will not retain any more extra Engineers or Firemen than are necessary to move the traffic of the road with promptness and dispatch.

16. Engineers and Firemen shall be allowed eight hours rest, when they have been on duty twelve hours, and will not be required to go out when they have been on duty twelve hours, unless they feel competent to make the trip. This Article to apply to terminal points only.

17. Should an Engineer or Fireman get into trouble, they shall have a fair and impartial trial within five days, and they shall be permitted to be present and hear all evidence against them. They shall have a right to appeal from the decision of sub ordinate officers to the General Manager, if they think their suspension or discharge is unjust. If exonerated they shall be paid for all time lost.

18. Enginemen and Firemen, when going for an engine or returning after delivering one, will be paid 1¼ and 8-10 of a cent, respectively, per mile for the distance traveled. When a man is traveling over the road for the purpose of relieving a man who has asked for a leave of absence, he will not receive any compensation for the distance traveled.

19. The Company will have all packing done, except on branch engines, and all brass on engines cleaned at their own expense, the same as the Louisville & Nashville Railroad Company, and supplies drawn and placed on engines at Nashville, Atlanta and Chattanooga. Firemen shall not be required to wipe engines. Where Firemen are required to wipe switch engines they shall receive $1.75 per day. Firemen shall not be required to fire up engines at terminal points.

20. Classification of Engineers' pay is abolished.

21. No Engineer or Fireman shall be discharged for serving on any committee.

22. No change shall be made in this contract or agreement by either party without giving thirty days' notice.

23. In the employment of Firemen by this Company, on and after March 1, 1891. the Master Mechanics are instructed to employ none but sober and reliable white men for this service; and all Firemen will be strictly subject to the orders of the Master Mechanic, at all times and in all matters pertaining to their duty.

24. All Engineers shall receive 35 cents per hour for all delay time, and Firemen shall receive 53 per cent. of Engineers' pay.

25. When Engineers are required to go to Cowan they shall receive $7.54 for the round trip; provided the trip is made within twenty-four hours. If not made within

twenty-four hours, they shall receive 35 cents for each additional hour. Firemen to receive 53 per cent. of Engineers' pay.

26. Engineer on passenger train on Jasper branch shall receive 3 cents per mile. The Fireman to receive 53 per cent. of Engineers' pay.

27. Engineers on passenger trains on Fayetteville and Huntsville branches shall receive 3 cents per mile, and mileage to be equalized so they shall receive the same mileage. The Firemen to receive 53 per cent. of Engineers' pay. Freight Engineers' pay to remain the same as now. Firemen to receive 53 per cent. of Engineers' pay.

28. Engineers of freight or mixed trains on the McMinnville branch shall receive 4 cents per mile. Firemen to receive 53 per cent. of Engineers' pay.

29. Freight Engineers on Tracy City branch shall receive $100 per month. Two Engineers to be retained in this service. Firemen to receive 53 per cent. of Engineers' pay. Engineers' and Firemen's pay on passenger train to remain the same as now.

30. Engineer on Shelbyville branch shall receive $3.25 per day; twelve hours or less to constitute a day's work; all over twelve hours shall receive 35 cents per hour. Fireman to receive 53 per cent. of Engineers' pay.

31. Engineers on pusher engines shall receive $4 per day. Firemen to receive 53 per cent. of Engineers's pay. All Engineers on branch roads, where required to help machinists or wash out engines, shall receive $3.50 per day. Firemen to receive 53 per cent. of Engineers' pay.

32. All Engineers on Centerville branch shall receive $90 per month. Firemen to receive 53 per cent. of Engineers' pay; except Barksdale, who is to receive $100 per month.

33. Engineers on Green Line, between Union City and Columbus and return, shall receive $4 per day; twelve hours or less to constitute a day's work. Firemen to receive 53 per cent. of Engineers' pay.

34. Engineers on the Marietta and Dalton accommodation to receive $4 per day. The Engineer of the Marietta accommodation to continue to do extra work at Atlanta the same as now. Firemen to receive 53 per cent. of Engineers' pay.

35. Any Engineer or Fireman drinking intoxicants on duty, or allowing it to be drank on his engine, or being under its influence on or off duty, will be dismissed from the service of the Company. J. W. THOMAS,
March 12, 1891. General Manager.

NEW YORK & NEW ENGLAND RAILROAD COMPANY.

Through passenger trainmen: Conductors, $3.50 per day; Baggagemen, $2.20; Brakemen, $2.10. Local passenger trainmen: Conductors, $3.10 per day; Baggagemen, $1.90; Brakemen, $1.80. Trainmen on the Rockville branch who perform both freight and passenger work, are paid as follows: Conductors, $3.25 per day; Baggagemen, $2.20; Brakemen, $2. Through freight trainmen: Conductors, $3 per day; Flagmen, $2.10; Brakemen, $2. Local freight trainmen: Conductors, $3.25 per day; Flagmen, $2.20; Brakemen, $2.10. Our yard Switchmen are paid at the rate of $2 per day, and in some cases are classified as Signalmen although doing Switchmen's work.
May 13, 1892. C. S. MELLEN, General Manager.

NEW YORK & NORTHERN RAILWAY COMPANY.

Conductors, $80 to $85. Train Baggagemen, $60. Brakemen: Passenger, $45; freight, $50 to $55. Yardmasters, $60 to $75. Switchmen, $60 to $75.
May 10, 1892. H. H. VREELAND, General Superintendent.

NEW YORK, CHICAGO & ST. LOUIS RAILROAD COMPANY.

PASSENGER TRAINS.

RUNS.	Miles	Conduct'rs, per trip.	Brakemen, per trip.	Baggagemen, per trip.
Buffalo to Bellevue, or reverse	248	$6 20	$3 15	*$2 70
Bellevue to Chicago, or reverse	275	6 40	3 25	3 60
Cleveland short runs		3 85	2 10	2 15
Cleveland to Bellevue and return	130	3 85	2 10	2 15
Bellevue to Fostoria and return	64	3 00	2 00	2 15
Cleveland to Chicago, or reverse	340			4 00

* Six trips per week.

NEW YORK, CHICAGO & ST. LOUIS RAILWAY.

THROUGH FREIGHT TRAINS.

Districts	RUNS.	Miles	Conduct'rs, per trip...	Brakemen, per trip...	OVERTIME.
1	Buffalo to Conneaut, or reverse....	114	$3 25	$2 15	After 12 hours.
2	Conneaut to Bellevue, or reverse...	132	3 60	2 40	After 12 hours.
3	Bellevue to West Fort Wayne, or reverse.	124	3 60	2 40	After 12 hours.
4	West Fort Wayne to South Island, or reverse...	140	3 75	2 55	After 12 hours.

Turn Arounds: Turn around trips will be computed as separate trips each way, and will be paid, for six hours or less, one-half district rates; over six hours and less than twelve hours, full district rates; leaving time on return trip to be computed from arriving time at turn around point, except that where round trip distance is less than sixty-five miles, half district rates will be paid for six hours or less; over six hours and under twelve hours, full district rates will be paid. For the short turn arounds referred to in the exception, for switching or waiting at turn around points, overtime rates will be paid; the overtime allowed not to be counted in the road time. Bellevue to Fostoria and return, or reverse, is to be included in the exception.

LOCAL FREIGHT TRAINS.

Districts	RUNS.	Miles	Conduct'rs, per trip...	Brakemen, per trip...	OVERTIME.
1	Buffalo to Conneaut, or reverse............	114	$3 50	$2 60	After 12 hours.
2	Cleveland to Conneaut, or reverse............	67	3 25	2 25	After 10 hours.
2	Cleveland to Bellevue, or reverse.	65	3 25	2 25	After 10 hours.
3	Bellevue to West Fort Wayne, or reverse.	124	5 00	3 25	After 13 hours.
4	Fort Wayne to South Island, or reverse............	141	5 00	3 25	After 13 hours.

Work Trains—all districts: Conductors, $3.50 per day; Brakemen. $2.50; overtime after twelve hours.

Overtime: Through freight Conductors, 30 cents per hour; Brakemen, 20 cents. Local freight Conductors, 35 cents per hour; Brakemen, 25 cents. Work train Conductors, 30 cents per hour; Brakemen, 20 cents.

RULES.

1. In computing overtime, no fractions of an hour under thirty minutes shall be counted. Any fraction of an hour over thirty minutes shall be counted one hour.

2. Freight or passenger crews making extra trips in addition to their regular assigned runs shall be allowed extra time upon the basis of pay allowed other crews in similar service.

3. Crews, or any part of a crew, dead-heading shall be allowed full time when dead-heading on freight, and one-half time when dead-heading on passenger, on the basis of freight pay, except that no overtime will be allowed.

4. When dead-heading is required, first crew out shall dead-head and shall stand first out on arrival at terminal station.

5. Crews required to run light with their caboose shall be allowed full through freight pay.

6. Crews not assigned to regular runs will run first in and first out in through freight service.

7. When trainmen are called, and for any reason other than their own acts do not go out, they shall, if held three hours or less, be allowed one-fourth district through freight rates. If held more then three hours and less than six hours, one-half rate. If more than six hours, full district rate and shall stand first out.

8. Crews shall be assigned to their respective districts, and shall not be transferred to any district on which they are not assigned, except the requirements of the service make it necessary.

9. Crews shall not be called over one hour and thirty minutes before leaving time, nor less than one hour before leaving time, except in case of emergency, when best interest of the Company is pending on it; the Caller to be provided with a book in which crews shall sign their names, together with the time they are called and time ordered for.

10. Conductors and Brakemen of regular crews shall not be called to go out with other crews, excepting when there are no extra men; all extra men to be called first

n first out. When extra men are called for a run, they are to remain on same until elieved by the regular man. This rule shall not apply to Conductors of through reight being called for local freight.

11. Trainmen will be notified when time is not allowed as per trip report.

12. Crews will be considered on duty from the time set for leaving until their trip s ended and train turned over to Yardmaster.

13. Trainmen attending court at the request of any official of the Company will e paid $3 per day for Conductors and $2 per day for Brakemen, and their legitimate xpenses.

14. At all coal docks, and at other stations where work trains are stationed, there hall be sufficient men to coal up train engines without the assistance of trainmen.

15. Conductors and Brakemen will not be dismissed nor suspended from the Company's service without just cause. In case of suspension or dismissal, if any employe hinks his sentence unjust, he shall have the right, within ten days, to refer his case, y written statement, to the Division Superintendent. Within ten days of the receipt f this notice, his case shall have a thorough investigation by the proper officers of the Railroad Company, at which he may be present if he so desires and also be represented y disinterested employes. In case he shall not be satisfied with the result of said investigation; he shall have the right to appeal to the General Superintendent. In case uspension or dismissal is found to be unjust, he shall be reinstated and paid for all ime lost.

16. Employes are regarded in the line of promotion dependent upon the faithful ischarge of duties, capacity for increased responsibility and length of time in service.

17. After continuous service of sixteen hours or more, trainmen shall be entitled o and be allowed eight hours for rest before being called to go out, except in case of vashouts, wrecks or other similar emergencies.

18. When freight traffic is light and it is necessary to reduce the number of teight crews, in order to allow the Conductors and Brakemen to make reasonable ages, the Conductors of crews thus taken off shall, as far as practicable, be given reference as Brakemen, until such time as the increase of business warrants them being reinstated as Conductors; the Conductors youngest in the service to be pulled off rst.

19. Every employe should understand that it is his privilege to make written appeals to his Division Superintendent whenever, by promotions, reductions or assignments, he deems an injustice has been done him.

YARD SERVICE.

General Yardmasters, from $100 to $125 per month. Assistant Yardmasters, day, $85 to $110 per month; night, $90 to $100. Conductors, day, $65 to $70 per month; night, $70 to $75. Brakemen, day, $60 to $65 per month; night, $65 to $70.

May 11, 1892.

LEWIS WILLIAMS,
General Superintendent.

NORTHERN PACIFIC RAILROAD COMPANY.

By advice with and consent of the General Manager the wages of trainmen on all divisions of the road will, from June 1, 1890, be established at rates in schedule below.

SCHEDULE.

RANK.	EAST OF MANDAN.			WEST OF MANDAN.		
	Rate	Overtime, per hour.	Per mile, over 100 miles.	Rate.	Overtime, per hour.	Per mile, over 100 miles.
*PASSENGER.						
Conductors						
Brakemen	$60 00			$65 00		
†THROUGH FREIGHT.						
Conductors	3 00	$0 30	$0 03	3 20	$0 32	$0 032
Brakemen	2 00	20	02	2 20	22	022
‡WORK TRAIN.						
Conductors	3 00	30		3 20	32	
Brakemen	2 00	20		2 20	22	
§SNOW PLOW.						
Conductors	3 50	35		3 50	35	
Brakemen	2 50	25		2 50	25	

*Per month. †Per day of ten hours or less, or 100 miles or less. ‡Per day of twelve hours or less. § Bucking snow, actual service, per day of ten hours or less.

RULES.

1. Overtime of trainmen on regular trains will begin when the schedule time of train is exceeded one hour. When schedule time of train is exceeded one hour or more, overtime will include the first hour's delay. When the schedule time of train averages more than ten hours for 100 miles or less, overtime will be paid according to this basis, ten hours. In computing overtime thirty minutes or over will be counted as one hour, after the first hour's delay.

2. Trainmen will be called as near as practicable one hour before the leaving time of trains. The Caller will have a book in which the trainmen will register the time they are called, signing their names.

3. Trainmen held waiting for trains beyond the time train was specified to leave, will be paid for each hour held at rate paid for overtime, provided train is held an hour or more.

4. When trains for which men have been called are abandoned, men will be paid for time held between time they were specified to leave and time train was abandoned, at schedule rate for overtime per hour, or fractional part over thirty minutes, but in no case trainmen will receive pay for less than one quarter of a day and stand first out.

5. The time of extra or wild trains will be computed on a basis of ten hours for 100 miles or less; all allowances made to regular trains will be made to extra or wild trains.

6. Sanding or cleaning stock cars, loading or unloading stock or waiting for the same, will be paid for in all cases on a basis of overtime at schedule rates, except when done by work train crews and train crews so employed will not be considered or paid for except as stock loading.

7. Trainmen on work trains will be paid one day for twelve consecutive hours or less: more than twelve hours will be paid for as overtime, at work train rates.

8. Conductors on work trains will be paid at the rate of $3 per day, east of Mandan, and $3.20 per day, west of Mandan, for twelve consecutive hours or less, including Sundays. Brakemen on work trains will be paid at the rate of $2 per day, east of Mandan, and $2.20 per day, west of Mandan, for twelve consecutive hours or less, including Sundays.

9. Trainmen assigned to snow plow service will be paid for one day, as per freight train schedule, for each twenty-four hours held in readiness to use. Where assigned to duty on the road, and run over district or division, they will be paid for mileage made, at schedule rates.

10. When snow plow crews are in actual service, bucking snow, they will be paid: Conductors $3.50, and Brakemen $2.50, per day of ten hours; over ten hours per day will be paid for at the same rate per hour, but Superintendent will select the men for this service without regard to turn. This applies to actual snow bucking and not to running over any district ahead of a train.

11. Freight trainmen dead-heading on their respective divisions will be paid full freight train rates for such service.

12. Trainmen or yardmen, when dead-heading on Company's business, will be paid at schedule rates, one day or 100 miles for each calendar day. In no case will less than one day be allowed, when no other services are performed. When held as witnesses for the Company, trainmen and yardmen will be paid at schedule rates, one day or 100 miles for each calendar day; necessary allowance for expenses will also be made when off their respective divisions. Time held attending court to be certified to by the Company's attorney.

13. Trainmen on runs of 100 miles or more, when required to do switching at terminals, will be paid for such service at schedule rates for overtime.

14. Dates will change at 12 o'clock, midnight, the same as calendar dates, and two runs on the road commencing on separate dates will be paid for at not less than one day for each run, provided no other run is made on that date.

15. Freight trainmen running over district, Livingston to Helena, Logan to Butte, Helena to Missoula, Missoula to Hope, and Ellensburg to Tacoma, will be allowed twelve miles constructive mileage for mountain service. Should the Company deem it advisable to put on regular mountain crews between Livingston and Bozeman, Whitehall and Butte, Helena and Elliston, Missoula to Arlee (or Jocko), and Easton to Weston, they will be paid as follows: One round trip or less, one day; three single trips or two round trips, two days.

16. The above allowances, as per Article 15, to apply only to mountain crews working between the points named as terminals; all miles run in either direction, outside of limits named, to be paid for per mile at schedule rate. Trips from Livingston to Timberline and return, Bozeman to Muir and return, Helena to Blossburg and return, and Missoula to Evaro and return, will be paid for same as round trip between the fixed mountain terminals, and single trips between the points mentioned same as single trips between the fixed mountain terminals. Trips from Livingston to Muir and

return, Bozeman to Timberline and return, Elliston to Blossburg and return, Arlee to Evaro and return, and Easton or Weston to Stampede or Martin and return, will be paid for as equal to a single trip between the fixed mountain terminals.

17. Conductors will be promoted from the ranks of Brakemen according to their age of continuous service, on their respective divisions, and their character and ability. Freight Conductors, when adapted to passenger service, will be promoted to passenger trains according to their ability and age of continuous service on their respective divisions. The question of ability and adaptation to be determined by the Superintendent.

18. Trainmen will rank from the date they are employed, and in the event of there being a surplus of men, the oldest in the service on their respective divisions shall have the preference of employment.

19. No more men will be employed in the service than are necessary to do the work and earn a reasonable monthly average compensation at the schedule established; and whenever in the judgment of the trainmen there are too many crews, a committee of trainmen in good standing, employed on the division, may call the attention of the Trainmaster or Superintendent to such surplus of men, when the matter will be fully investigated, and, if conditions are found to warrant it, will be remedied; it being always understood that men will be retained under seniority of rights.

20. No trainmen shall be suspended nor discharged without proper cause, and in case a trainman believes his suspension or discharge is unjust, he may make a written statement of the facts in his case and forward to Division Superintendent, designating a committee of not less than three trainmen in good standing, employed on the division, to meet in conjunction with the Superintendent of the division, and without unnecessary delay re-investigate the case, and prompt decision must be given in less than five days from the re-hearing of the case. If the trainman is decided blameless he shall be immediately reinstated, and paid at schedule rates for time lost on account of such suspension. Trainmen charged with offenses involving either suspension or discharge, except in cases involving fraud or dishonesty, will be advised of the offenses, in writing. All parties concerned will be present at the investigation.

21. Trainmen and yardmen will not be required to pay fines on account of breakage.

22. After continuous service of sixteen hours or more, trainmen will be entitled to and allowed eight hours rest before being called to go out, provided they so desire and give notice thereof; except in case of washouts, wrecks and other similar emergencies.

23. Freight trainmen not assigned to regular runs will run first in and first out on the division or district to which they are assigned.

24. Trainmen assigned to regular local freight trains on St. Paul division to be paid: Conductors $90 per month, and Brakemen $60 per month for regular local runs, and will be paid overtime for hill work at Little Falls and quarry work at Sauk Rapids, Conductors 30 cents and Brakemen 20 cents per hour. Trainmen assigned to regular local freight trains between Staples and Fargo to be paid: Conductors $90, and Brakemen $60 per month. If run with two crews, Conductors $95, Brakemen $65, or mileage and overtime.

25. Trainmen assigned to regular local freight between Fargo and Jamestown to be paid: Conductors $95, and Brakemen $65 per month, to run six days per week. Overtime after 12 hours. Trainmen assigned to regular local freight trains between Sprague and Hope: Conductors $4.50, and Brakemen $2.80 per single trip. Overtime to be paid at ten hour basis for all over 12½ hours making a single trip. That men on regular local crews between Weston and Tacoma to be paid, $95 for Conductors, and $65 per month for Brakemen. Overtime to be paid for after 12 hours at rate of ten hour basis. Trainmen assigned to regular local freight trains between Tacoma and Kalama, between Seattle and Tacoma, to be paid: Conductors $100, and Brakemen $75 per month. No overtime to be allowed. That freight train crews will be allowed full freight train rates of wages for handling passenger trains or passenger equipment.

26. When trainmen or yardmen leave the service of the Company, they shall be given letters stating time of service, in capacity or capacities employed, and cause of leaving the service. The said letters to be given them three days from application, provided they shall have worked on the division thirty days, to be signed by the Division Superintendent.

27. Transfer crews at Kalama to be paid as follows: Yardmaster $90 per month: Foreman $85 per month; night Helpers $2.50 per day; day Helpers $2.50 per day.

28. Trainmen who have been discharged and who upon further investigation are found to have been unjustly dealt with, will be reinstated, provided the matter is settled within three months from the time such trainmen were discharged; otherwise if re-employed shall rank as new men on the road.

29. Trainmen leaving the service will be paid at the earliest practicable moment in full, less usual deductions which may be found against their pay and that they have accepted up to date of ending service.

30. Yard Foremen and Switchmen west of Fargo in following yards shall be paid at the same rate of wages as are now being paid to Tacoma, viz.: Portland, Seattle, Tacoma, Livingston, Ellensburg, Pasco, Sprague, Mandan, Spokane Falls, Missoula, Helena, Jamestown.

31. The general board of adjustment do hereby agree for themselves and all trainmen, Yard Foremen and Switchmen to do their part towards the faithful observance of this schedule, and use every honorable means to avoid any cause for complaint.

32. Should any trainmen or yard crews violate any part of above contract, we would respectfully asked to be advised of the same, and will do all in our power to adjust the same.

ADDITIONAL RULES.

1. For the general good of the service and to promote a better understanding among men engaged in train work it is agreed that: When it is necessary for any Conductor to have seven different Brakemen within a period of three months, at request of either Conductor or Brakeman, or both, it will be considered that fault lies with the Conductor and will be sufficient cause for his dismissal at the discretion of the Superintendent. When objections have been made to any Brakeman by three different Conductors within a period of three months, or when a Brakeman has complained of three Conductors within the same period, it will be considered that the Brakeman is at fault, and will be sufficient cause for his dismissal, at the discretion of the Superintendent.

2. When a Brakeman is examined for promotion to Conductor and fails to pass such examination, and considers that he is unfairly dealt with, the subordinate officer making such examination shall report in writing to the Superintendent showing in detail the points wherein the candidate has failed. In such case the candidate shall be entitled to a second examination to be conducted by the Superintendent personally, and may select a Conductor or Engineer as witness to such examination.

3. Brakemen who are candidates for promotion to the position of Conductor shall be tested and examined in accordance with General Superintendent's Circular No. 248, dated November 11, 1891.

4. When Brakemen are required to shovel coal they shall be allowed one hour overtime for each engine coaled. Conductors not to be allowed overtime on this account.

5. When trainmen have been for six months on a run which is considered objectionable, or on a work train, they shall be entitled to a change of service, provided there are younger men in the service who are competent to perform the duties required.

6. Switchmen will stand in line of promotion from Helper to Foreman, and from Foreman to Assistant Yardmaster or night Yardmaster, according to their age in continuous service, character and ability. The question of ability and adaptation for the position of Yardmaster to be determined by the Superintendent. In the matter of promotion to the position of Yardmaster a division shall be considered as a whole and not each yard separately. NORTHERN PACIFIC R. R. CO.,
For Brotherhood of Railroad Trainmen: By M. C. KIMBERLY,
CHAS. ALEXANDER, General Superintendent.
Chairman General Grievance Committee.
November 12, 1891. Approved: W. S. MELLEN, General Manager.

OHIO & MISSISSIPPI RAILWAY COMPANY.

PASSENGER TRAINMEN.

Between Cincinnati and St. Louis: On trains No. 1, 2, 3, 4, 7 and 8, one Conductor, $120 per month; one Flagman, $65. To be run by nine crews, with an additional Brakeman on trains No. 1, 2, 3, and 4, at $55 per month; total of six additional men.

Between Cincinnati and Vincennes: On trains No. 6, 9 and 10, one Conductor, $100 per month; one Flagman, $60. To be run with two crews.

Between St. Louis and Vincennes: On trains No. 13 and 14, one Conductor, $90 per month; one Flagman, $50. To be run with two crews.

Between Cincinnati and Louisville: On trains No. 15, 16, 17 and 18, one Conductor, 1¼ cents per mile; one Flagman, $55 per month. To be run with two crews.

Between Cincinnati and Louisville: On trains No. 19 and 20, one Conductor, 1¼ cents per mile; one Flagman, $60 per month. To be run with one crew.

Between North Vernon and Louisville: On trains No. 105 and 106, one Conductor, $90 per month; one Flagman, $50. To be run with one crew.

Pay-car trip, first day, Cincinnati to Louisville, Jeffersonville and to Seymour: One Conductor, $3.30 per day; one Flagman, $2.20; Seymour to Shops, Shops to Flora, and Flora to Cone, through freight rate.

Officers' specials: One Conductor, $3 per day, twelve hours; one Flagman, $2. Extra sections of passenger trains on passenger train schedules, Cincinnati and Shops,

Shops and St. Louis, and Cincinnati and Louisville, one Conductor, $3 per trip; one Flagman $2. Trips run on a single freight division, one Conductor and one Flagman, through freight rates.

FREIGHT TRAINMEN.

Through Freight, Eastern Division: Storrs to Seymour, Conductor $2.90, Brakeman $1.93 per trip. Seymour and Shops, Conductor $2.70, Brakeman $1.80 per trip. Storrs and Louisville, Conductor $4.35, Brakeman $2.90 per trip. Seymour and Louisville, Conductor $2.40, Brakeman $1.60 per trip. Seymour to Cochran and return, Conductor $4.35, Brakeman $2.90 per round trip. Seymour to Milan and return, Conductor $2.90, Brakeman $1.93 per round trip. Vernon to Louisville and return, Conductor $3, Brakeman $2 per round trip. Freight trips not provided for as above to be paid 3 and 2 cents per mile (Conductors and Brakemen) with twenty miles additional for turn-around, a minimum of fifty miles being allowed (the turn-around to be added). Crews to consist of one Conductor and two Brakemen.

Local Freight, Eastern Division: Between Storrs and Seymour, Conductor $85 per month, Brakeman $60. Seymour and Shops, Conductor $85 per month, Brakeman $60. Louisville branch, round trip, Conductor, $85 per month, Brakeman $60. Crews to consist of one Conductor and two or three Brakemen, as business demands.

Through Freight, Western Division: Between Shops and Cone, Conductor $4.75 per trip, Brakeman $3.15. Shops and Flora, Conductor $2.25 per trip, Brakeman $1.50. Flora and Cone, Conductor $2.90 per trip, Brakeman $1.93. Shops to Vincennes and return, Conductor $2 per round trip, Brakeman $1.33. Cone to Breese, or intermediate station and return, Conductor $3 per round trip, Brakeman $2. Coal and construction trains, Conductor $85 per month, Brakeman $60. Freight trips not provided for as above to be paid 3 cents and 2 cents per mile, with allowance of twenty miles for turn-around, a minimum of fifty miles being allowed, turn-around to be added. Crews to consist of Conductor and two Brakemen, except coal train — three Brakemen when necessary.

Local Freight, Western Division: Between Shops and Flora, Conductor $85 per month, Brakeman $60. Flora and Cone, Conductor $85 per month, Brakeman $60. Crews to consist of one Conductor and two or three Brakemen, as business demands.

Construction Trains, Eastern and Western Divisions: Conductors, if paid by the month, $85, Brakemen $60; Conductors, if paid by the day, $3, Brakemen $2. Twelve hour s constituting a day's work, and Sundays included in Conductors' and Brakemen's rate when paid by the month.

Special Work, Picking up Wrecks, Etc.: Conductors to receive 35 cents per hour, Brakemen 25 cents, from time train leaves until time train arrives at point where sent from. Construction trains to be allowed this rate when working between 7 P. M. and 7 A. M.

YARD SWITCHMEN.

Cochran: Yard Foreman $70 per month, Yard Brakeman $50. North Vernon: Day Yardmaster $70 per month, night $65; Yard Brakemen $50. Seymour: Day Yard Foreman $2.35 per day, night $2.35; Yard Brakemen $2. Shops: Yardmaster $85 per month, Yard Foremen $2.35 per day, Yard Brakemen $2. Vincennes and Flora: Yardmaster $75 per month, day and night Foremen $2.25 per day; day and night Brakemen $1.90. Sundays will be divided between all crews at Shops.

EXTRAS.

1. For dead-heading on freight or passenger trains, Conductors and Brakemen (except men standing extra) to receive one-half pay, basis of pay being rate due to the service to or from which dead-head is made; except that Conductors dead-heading over the road to take the place of a Conductor getting a lay-off for his own convenience, either going to take a run or returning, shall receive no pay. When caboose is dead-headed over the road on freight train, one man to be sent with the caboose, and if practicable balance of crew to be provided transportation and sent on passenger train; otherwise all go on caboose. When an engine and caboose are run light on passenger train schedule, rate of pay to be two-thirds of freight trip rate. When run on freight schedule or extra, rate to be full freight trip rate. Men to be run on passenger schedule *only* when quick time is needed to get crews around, and when crews are not liable to be delayed at the turn-around.

2. All men paid by the month, when performing additional duties to those for which the monthly compensation they receive provides, shall be paid for such additional work at the agreed rates.

3. Employes attending court as witnesses for the Company to be allowed time lost for so doing, with reasonable expenses, it being understood that trainmen returning and having to wait for their caboose or crew can be used in extra service until their turn comes.

4. When a train is annulled after trainmen have reported for duty and their services are not otherwise required, each man shall receive twenty-five miles at agreed

rate and stand first out. In case of being notified of train annulled before they report for duty no time will be allowed.

5. When freight crews are delayed at terminals after they have been called, and such delay amounts to two hours or more from time train was marked up to leave, Conductors shall receive 30 cents per hour, and Brakemen 20 cents, for whole time delayed, less thirty minutes; but if delayed time is less than two hours no allowance to be made.

6. Extra mileage allowed for turn-arounds to apply only where turn-around is not at the end of a division.

7. *Promotions and Discipline:* Vacancies in ranks of passenger trainmen to be filled from ranks of freight trainmen when possible. Flagmen on passenger trains who have been promoted from freight service do not forfeit their rights to promotion to the position of freight Conductor. It is to be understood that with the taking effect of this agreement there shall be a grading made of passenger Brakemen, and seniority, record and ability shall govern.

8. Vacancies in the ranks of freight Conductors will be filled by promotion from the ranks of freight Brakemen according to ability and age in service, except that for every two Brakemen promoted one experienced Conductor may be hired as a Conductor or promoted from the ranks, regardless of age in service. Conductors hired under this rule may be temporarily employed as extra Brakeman, pending vacancy to be filled by him, and will not be considered an experienced Conductor unless he has had at least one year's experience as a Conductor.

9. Yard Brakemen to rank with extra road Brakemen and be eligible for road service when so desiring.

10. All promotions, either in service or runs, shall be by seniority in service of the O. & M. Company, other qualifications being satisfactory, except that intemperate habits or lack of education necessary to write up all reports required of Conductors and Yardmasters correctly, shall be considered a bar to promotion.

11. From time to time a list of trainmen eligible to promotion in any road service or run, will be posted and such employes will apply to the Trainmaster for examination. The applicant who passes the most satisfactory examination shall be considered the next in line for promotion; it being agreed that the applicant, if he so desires, can have present at the time of examination a brother employe, each applicant to be examined separately. In case of failure, the applicant shall be given an explanation, stating on what points he is deficient.

12. Passenger and freight crews to run first in first out, where practicable. Freight crews standing in order on list for regular schedules, their sections and extras.

13. Passenger Brakemen going into freight service to come in with extra or regular freight Brakemen according to seniority.

14. Conductors or Brakemen suspended or discharged summarily, to have, within ten days from the date of offense, an impartial hearing, and if found to be not guilty of offense, to be reinstated and allowed full time while laid off; except that any employe will be dismissed without a hearing in case of intoxication, insubordination or collisions.

15. Trainmen will be required to be on hand and ready for duty at least half an hour before their train is due to leave. A Caller will be provided at terminals for crews of through freight, their sections and extras (except crews of regular runs), and crews will be called as nearly as practicable one hour before train is due to leave. Trainmen must acknowledge time they were called by signing a book which the Caller will carry.

16. Trainmen not able to take their runs must give ample notice to avoid delay to trains; failure to do so, or delaying trains by reason of being late, will be considered cause for suspension.

17. Conductors are held responsible for the conduct of their Brakemen while on duty, but in case of complaint, must make same in writing and the case will be investigated, it being understood that should summary action be necessary the Conductor is authorized to take same and report to the division officer by telegraph, to be followed by written report to his superior officer.

18. It is agreed that any question arising among the employes governed by this agreement, regarding any article of the agreement, shall be submitted to the Company through the committee appointed by such employes. Said committee not to exceed five in number, and one of whom shall act as chairman. The Company's representative to whom question is referred being first the Trainmaster of the division where question is raised; if not settled by him, then to the Superintendent, and finally if necessary, to the General Manager.

19. In case of change of time card during the existence of this agreement, which affects the runs as herein provided, there shall be added as a supplement a written statement of the understanding between the parties of this agreement, relative to such change.

20. When through freight crews are to be reduced in number, after it becomes a

ettled fact that business is dull and likely to continue so for a season, reductions shall be made by taking the youngest Conductor in the service and giving him regular work braking until the remaining crews can make reasonable wages.

21. These articles of agreement being signed in good faith by the Trainmen, through their committee, and by the General Manager for the Railway Company, will continue in force not less than one year from the date they take effect, and cannot be changed in any way without thirty days' notice from the party desiring change. They are in force and effect March 1st, 1892.

BAGGAGEMEN'S SCHEDULE.

On all runs over 5,000 miles Baggagemen shall receive $70 per month. On all runs of over 3,000 miles and under 5,000 miles Baggagemen shall receive $60 per month. Crews on main line between Cincinnati and St. Louis to remain as at present. In case it becomes necessary for a Baggageman to make an extra trip, from any cause, he shall receive pro-rata payment for the same. In all future appointments, senior men in the service of the Ohio & Mississippi Railway Company to be given the preference in runs. Through main line Baggagemen shall do all extra running when practicable, and receive the same allowance for dead-heading as is given other parts of the train service. For dead-heading on passenger trains Baggagemen shall receive one-half pay, except that Baggagemen dead-heading over the road to take the place of Baggagemen getting lay-off for their own convenience, either going to take a run or returning, shall receive no pay. Baggagemen attending court as witnesses for the Company shall be allowed for time lost by so doing, with the necessary expenses for the period if required to remain away more than one day; it being understood that Baggagemen returning and having to wait for their regular runs may be used in extra service until their regular turns come. Baggagemen not able to take their runs must give ample notice, to avoid delay to trains; failure to do so, or delaying train by reason of being late, will be considered cause for suspension. Baggagemen suspended or discharged summarily shall have, within ten days from date of the offense, an impartial hearing, and, if found to be not guilty of the offense, shall be reinstated and allowed full time while laid off; except that Baggagemen shall be dismissed without a hearing in case of intoxication or insubordination. I. F. BARNARD,
For the Brotherhood of Railroad Trainmen: General Manager.
S. E. WILKINSON, Grand Master.
March 1st, 1892.

OHIO SOUTHERN RAILROAD COMPANY.

Passenger Conductors, $90 per month. Baggagemen and Passenger Brakemen, $60 per month. Local freight Conductors, $85 per month. Local freight Brakemen, $55 per month. Through freight Conductors, 2 9-10 cents per mile. Through freight Brakemen, 1 9-10 cents per mile. Local and through freight Conductors receive 26 cents per hour overtime, local freight Brakemen 17 cents per hour. Yard Conductors receive $2.35 and $2.40 per day; Switchmen, $1.90 and $2.04 per day.
W. H. VAN TASSELL,
May 14, 1892. Superintendent.

OMAHA & ST. LOUIS RAILWAY COMPANY.

We pay trainmen as follows: Passenger Conductors, $100 per month. Passenger Baggagemen, $55 per month. Passenger Brakemen, $50 per month. Passenger Porters, $40 per month. Freight Conductors, 3 cents per mile. Freight Brakemen, 2 cents per mile. Switchmen and Yardmen, $5 per month less than Chicago schedule.
F. M. GAULT,
May 12, 1892. General Manager.

PENNSYLVANIA LINES WEST OF PITTSBURGH.*
NORTHWEST SYSTEM.—P., Y. & A. DIVISION.

Through freight: Nine hours per day, 81 miles, Conductors, $2.75; Brakemen, $1.85; Flagmen, $1.95. Local freight: Nine hours per day, 81 miles, Conductors, $2.85; Brakemen, $1.90; Flagmen, $2. Passenger: 166 miles, Conductors, $3.30; Brakemen, $1.75; Flagmen, $1.75 per day. Short runs: Six hours per day, Conductors, $1.80; Brakemen, $1.25; Flagmen, $1.35. Work train: Conductors, $75 per month; Brakemen, $50 per month. Paid at standard rates, Conductors 3 cents per mile, and Brakemen 2 cents per mile. Yards: Day Foremen, 24 cents per hour: night Foremen, 25 cents per hour. Day Brakemen, 18 cents per hour; night Brakemen, 19 cents per hour.

* Not official.

PITTSBURGH, CINCINNATI, CHICAGO & ST. LOUIS RAILWAY COMPANY.*
SOUTHWEST SYSTEM.—LOGANSPORT DIVISION.

Hill engine, Conductors, 24 cents per hour; Brakemen, 16 cents per hour; day and night same. All other engines, Conductors, day, 22 cents per hour; night, 23 cents per hour. Brakemen, day, 17 cents per hour; night, 18 cents per hour. Twelve hours per day, calendar month. Richmond and Indianapolis yards same as Logansport. Chicago yard, days, 25 cents and 27 cents; nights, 27 cents and 29 cents. Sundays not included in schedule. Freight: Chicago to Logansport, 117 miles, per trip, Conductors, $3.10; Brakemen, $2. Overtime after 12 hours. Local, per trip, Conductors, $3.50; Brakemen, $2.35. Overtime after 13 hours. Logansport to Bradford, 114 miles, per trip, Conductors, $3: Brakemen, $1.90. Overtime after 12 hours. Local, per trip, Conductors, $3.50; Brakemen, $2.30. Overtime after 13 hours. Logansport to Effner, 61 miles, per trip, Conductors, $3; Brakemen, $1.90. Overtime after 8 hours. All trains on this division considered as locals. Passenger: Between Logansport and Chicago, and Logansport and Bradford, 40 days a month, per trip, Conductors, $3.05; Baggagemen, $1.70; Brakemen, $1.60. Between Logansport and Effner, same pay as above for round trip.

PEORIA & PEKIN UNION RAILWAY COMPANY.

We pay Conductors $85 per month, and Brakemen $50 each; no Baggageman on this train. Our rate for yardmen is as follows: Foremen, days, $2.70; nights, $2.90. Brakemen, days, $2.50; nights, $2.70. Switch tenders, $45 per month.
May 13, 1892. C. E. SCHAFF, General Superintendent.

PITTSBURGH & LAKE ERIE RAILROAD COMPANY.

1. All passenger Conductors to receive $3.40 per day, 136 miles or less, 10 hours or less to constitute a day's work. All over 10 hours to be paid 34 cents per hour. All over 136 miles, 2½ cents per mile.
2. All train Baggagemasters to receive $2.05 per day, 136 miles or less, 10 hours or less to constitute a day's work. All over 10 hours to be paid 20½ cents per hour. All over 136 miles, 1½ cents per mile.
3. All passenger Brakemen to receive $1.80 per day, 136 miles or less, 10 hours or less to constitute a day's work. All over 10 hours to be paid 18 cents per hour. All over 136 miles, 1.3 cents per mile.
4. All through freight Conductors to receive $2.60 per day, 10 hours or less, (64 miles or less) or the run between Chartiers and Youngstown, or between Chartiers and New Haven or Dickerson Run, or round trip between Chartiers and West Newton, or round trip between Chartiers and New Castle Junction, to constitute a day's work, if made within 10 hours. All over 10 hours to be paid 30 cents per hour.
5. All through freight Flagmen to receive $1.90 per day, 10 hours or less, (64 miles or less) or the run between Chartiers and Youngstown, or between Chartiers and New Haven or Dickerson Run, or round trip between Chartiers and West Newton, or round trip between Chartiers and New Castle Junction, to constitute a day's work, if made within 10 hours. All over 10 hours to be paid 20 cents per hour.
6. All through freight Brakemen to receive $1.80 per day, 10 hours or less, (64 miles or less) or the run between Chartiers and Youngstown, or between Chartiers and New Haven or Dickerson Run, or round trip between Chartiers and West Newton, or round trip between Chartiers and New Castle Junction, to constitute a day's work, if made within 10 hours. All over 10 hours to be paid 20 cents per hour.
7. All way freight Conductors to receive $3 per day, 12 hours or less to constitute a day's work. All over 12 hours to be paid 30 cents per hour.
8. All way freight Flagmen and way freight Brakemen to receive $2 per day, 12 hours or less to constitute a day's work. All over 12 hours to be paid 17 cents per hour.
9. All work train Conductors to receive $2.75 per day, 12 hours or less to constitute a day's work. All over 12 hours to be paid 23 cents per hour.
10. All work train Brakemen to receive $1.85 per day, 12 hours or less to constitute a day's work. All over 12 hours to be paid 16 cents per hour.
11. All wreck train Conductors to receive $2.75 per day, 12 hours or less to constitute a day's work. All over 12 hours to be paid 23 cents per hour.
12. All wreck train Flagmen and wreck train Brakemen to receive $1.85 per day, 12 hours or less to constitute a day's work. All over 12 hours to be paid 16 cents per hour.

* Not official.

13. In computing overtime, in all cases 30 minutes or less will not be counted; 35 minutes or more will be counted one hour.

14. Callers will be stationed at Dickerson Run, Chartiers and Youngstown. They will have register books and have written therein the train the men are called for, and the leaving time thereof, and the men shall register therein their names and the time they are called. Time of calling depends on the distance men are from the caboose rack. The pay of the crew will begin from the time the train is ordered for, as shown in the order for calling the men, and continue up to the time they give up their caboose at the track provided for that purpose at the end of the run. In case trainmen are called for any run and the train is abandoned, they shall receive overtime at regular rates per hour as stated in the foregoing articles, for the time on duty, and hall stand first out.

15. All Yardmen in all yards operated by this Company to be paid at the same rate as Pittsburgh Yardmen, *i. e.:* Conductors, day, 24 cents per hour; night, 25 cents per hour. Brakemen, day, 18 cents per hour; night, 19 cents per hour.

May 27, 1892. G. M. BEACH, General Superintendent.

PITTSBURG, SHENANGO & LAKE ERIE RAILROAD COMPANY.

SCHEDULE.

CLASS OF TRAIN.	MILES	RATE	
		Conductors.	Brakemen.
Market and freight, Shenango to Butler and return.............	112	$2 75	$1 75
Local freight between Butler and Wallace Junction............	107	3 40	1 90
Freight, Shenango to Branchton and return....................	70	2 75	1 75
Freight, Shenango to Coaltown and return.....................	76	2 75	1 75
Freight, Shenango to Wallace Junction and return.............	103	2 75	1 75
Mixed, between Branchton and Hilliard........................	50	2 75	1 75
Mixed, between Meadville and Linesville......................	84	2 90	1 90
Work train (same as freight).................................	......	2 75	1 75
Passenger..	180	3 85	1 90
Passenger..	162	3 85	1 90
Passenger..	242	4 81	2 38

Yardmaster at Shenango, $2.75; Brakemen, $1.90; Slip Carrier, $2.10. Baggage and Expressmen, 162 miles, $60 per month; 180 miles, $60; 242 miles, $75. Freight and yard crews receive overtime after 12 hours at same rate. J. T. BLAIR,
May 16, 1892. General Manager.

QUINCY, OMAHA & KANSAS CITY RAILWAY.

Conductors, passenger, $80 per month; freight, 02.95 per mile. Baggagemen, $50 per month. Brakemen, freight, 01.95 per mile. Yardmen, $55 per month. Runs of less than 100 miles will be allowed 100 miles. C. SOULE,
May 1, 1892. Superintendent of Transportation.

RICHMOND & DANVILLE RAILROAD COMPANY AND LEASED LINES.

CONDUCTOR'S SCHEDULE.

RICHMOND & DANVILLE RAILWAY.

CONDUCTORS' SCHEDULE — CONTINUED.

BETWEEN.

PASSENGER.
Charlotte, N. C., and Augusta, Ga.
Lancaster, S. C., and Lenoir, N. C.
Columbia, S. C., and Greenville, S. C.
Columbia, S. C., and Laurens, S. C.
Prosperity, S. C., and Anderson, S. C.
Walhalla, S. C., and Greenville, S. C.
Danville, Va., and Charlotte, N. C.
Danville, Va., and Charlotte N. C.*
Washington, D. C., and Charlotte, N. C., on Vestibule Limited
Charlotte, N. C., and Atlanta, Ga., on Vestibule Limited
Greensboro, N. C., and Goldsboro, N. C.
Raleigh, N. C., and Keysville, Va.; and Raleigh, N. C., and Goldsboro, N. C.
Richmond, Va., and West Point, Va.
Richmond, Va., and Amelia C. H., Va.
Greensboro, N. C. and Winston-Salem, N. C.
Atlanta, Ga., and Tallapoosa, Ga.
Birmingham, Ala., and Anniston, Ala.
Winona Miss., and Greenville, Miss.

LOCAL FREIGHT.
Alexandria, Va., and Orange, Va.
Orange, Va., and Lynchburg, Va.
Lynchburg, Va., and Danville, Va.
Alexandria, Va., and Strasburg, Va.
Alexandria, Va., and Round Hill, Va.
Richmond, Va., and West Point, Va.
Richmond, Va., and Clover, Va.
Clover, Va., and Greensboro, N. C.
Greensboro, N. C., and Charlotte, N. C.
Greensboro, N. C., and Raleigh, N. C.
On Oxford & Clarksville Railroad.
Charlotte, N. C., and Greers, S. C.
Greers, S. C., and Toccoa, Ga.
Tecooa, Ga., and Atlanta, Ga.
Lula, Ga., and Macon, Ga.
Salisbury, N. C., and Asheville, N. C.
Asheville, N. C., and Bryson City, N. C.
Spartanburg, S. C., and Paint Rock, N. C.
Asheville, N. C., and Paint Rock, N. C.
Charlotte, N. C., and Columbia, S. C.
Columbia, S. C., and Augusta, Ga.
Chester, S. C., and Lenoir, N. C.
Columbia, S. C., and Hodges, S. C.
Walhalla, S. C., and Greenville, S. C.
Alston, S. C., and Spartanburg, S. C.
Newberry, S. C., and Laurens, S. C.
Atlanta, Ga., and Heflin, Ala.
Heflin, Ala., and Birmingham, Ala.
Birmingham, Ala., and Columbus, Miss.
Columbus, Miss., and Winona, Miss.
Winona, Miss., and Greenville, Miss.
Birmingham, Ala., and Childersburg, Ala.*
Childersburg, Ala., and Columbus, Ga.

THROUGH FREIGHT.
Alexandria, Va., and Greenville, Miss
Manassas, Va., and Strasburg, Va.
Richmond, Va., and Danville, Va.
Birmingham, Ala., and Columbus, Ga.
Salisbury, N. C., and Paint Rock, N. C.
Richmond, Va., and West Point, Va.
Charlotte, N. C., and Augusta, Ga.
Columbia, S. C., and Belton, S. C.

MIXED.
Manassas, Va., and Strasburg, Va.
On Warrenton branch
On Franklin & Pittsylvania Railroad.
On Richmond, York River & Chesapeake Railroad
On High Point, Randleman, Ashboro & Southern Railroad
On State University Railroad.
On Milton & Sutherlin Narrow Gauge Railroad.
On Oxford & Henderson Railroad.
On Yadkin Railroad.
On North Carolina Midland Railroad
Greensboro, N. C., and Wilkesboro, N. C.
Greensboro, N. C., and Raleigh, N. C.
Asheville, N. C., and Murphy, N. C.
Charlotte, N. C., and Taylorsville, N. C.
Charlotte, N. C., and Statesville, N. C.
Hodges, S. C., and Abbeville, S. C.
Columbus, Ga., and Roanoke, Ala.

*Round trip.   †Per mile.

All runs of less than 100 miles, in passenger, freight or mixed service, to be counted as 100 miles; except when return or further trips are completed inside of twelve hours from the first start, in which case actual mileage will be counted, if over 100 miles. If such runs are not completed within twelve hours, overtime will be allowed at the rate of 25 cents per hour for all time over twelve hours. The pay for special runs, on special or extra trains, where rate is not provided for by this schedule of rates, is to be at the rate of $3.25 per day of twelve hours or less. All Conductors to be paid for overtime at the rate of 25 cents per hour, after the road delay shall have exceeded one and one-half hours, including the first one and one-half hours, or a fractional part thereof, less thirty minutes of the total delay. Conductors of trains leaving terminals, on the main line, will be called one hour before the leaving time of trains, provided they reside within one mile of starting point. Caller will have a book in which Conductors will register their names and record the time called. Conductors' time will commence one hour after they sign the Caller's book, and end at the time designated on mileage tickets, and verified by train sheets. If trains are abandoned after Conductors are called or notified to be in place, they will be paid for all time until relieved from duty, at the rate of 25 cents per hour, the time to be computed from one hour after they are called or notified, and shall stand first out; and Conductors arriving at terminals, on main line, if not relieved within thirty minutes will be paid 25 cents per hour for each hour, and the first thirty-five minutes shall count as one hour. Conductors dead-heading over the road, to or from their trains, to get them in place, will be paid half rate when dead-heading on passenger trains and full rate when dead-heading on freight trains. In case a Conductor is laid off to attend court, or on Company's business, he shall be paid $4 per day, and furnished transportation to and from his place of business, and an allowance of $1 per day for expenses, when called away from home to attend court. The pay of work train Conductors to be regulated by the division officers. Through freight Conductors will be run first in first out, so far as is practicable. The right of Conductors to regular runs to be determined by the division officers, due regard being had to capacity and seniority. No more Conductors will be employed than necessary to move the traffic of the road with promptness and regularity, division officers to decide. The rules and regulations of this Company will govern in the matter of discipline. Any Conductor suspended, for any cause, shall be granted investigation, hearing and decision, if possible, within five days. He shall be accorded the privileige of attending such investigation and hearing all the evidence, pro and con, touchng his responsibility, and shall have the right to appeal from the decision of the local officers to the general officers of the Company. If found blameless, after investigation, he will be paid for his lost time. If investigation cannot, for any cause, be held within five days, then when it is held, and the Conductor on trial be discharged, he will be paid for all time lost between five days after his suspension and the date of his discharge, provided he has made written application to the division officers, within ten days from the date of suspension, for investigation. No grievance will be entertained unless the same shall be presented in writing within thirty days after its occurrence.

November 1, 1891. W. H. GREEN, General Manager.

RICHMOND, FREDERICKSBURG & POTOMAC RAILROAD COMPANY.

Conductors average $3.16 per day. Baggagemasters $50 per month. Brakemen average $1.27 per day. Switchmen average $1 per day. Yardmaster $90 per month. Assistant Yardmaster $60 per month.   T. L. COURTNEY,
May 13, 1892.   Superintendent.

RIO GRANDE SOUTHERN RAILROAD COMPANY.

1. Telluride run, between Telluride and Vance Junction, to be paid for at the rate of $4 per day for Conductors, and $3 per day for Brakemen. Overtime after 10 hours.

2. Freight runs each way between Ridgway and Rico to be paid for at the rate of $20 per single trip for Conductors, and $3.15 per single trip for Brakemen. Overtime after 10 hours, including switching.

3. Snow plows, flangers, pile drivers, construction or other work trains to be paid or at the rate of $120 for Conductors, and $90 for Brakemen, per calendar month. Overtime after 12 hours.

4. Passenger runs to be paid for at the rate of $125 for Conductors, and $85 for Brakemen, per calendar month. No allowance made for extra runs.

5. Rate of overtime, 35 cents per hour for Conductors, and 25 cents per hour for Brakemen. Fractions less than 30 minutes not counted; 30 minutes or more to be counted one hour.   R. M. RIDGWAY,
   Superintendent.
Accepted for Conductors and Brakemen:
F. E. COWLES, W. T. SHIREY, Committee.
May 26, 1892.

RIO GRANDE WESTERN RAILWAY COMPANY.

SCHEDULE.

RUNS.	Conduct'rs, per month.	Brakemen, per month.
PASSENGER SERVICE.		
Through express runs, Ogden and Grand Junction, 7 crews	$125 00	$75 00
Salt Lake City and Ogden	115 00	75 00
Eureka and Salt Lake City	115 00	75 00
Salina and Thistles	115 00	75 00
Specials	115 00	75 00
MIXED TRAINS.		
Salt Lake City and Bingham, doubling and switching	115 00*	75 00
Scofield and P. V. Junction, doubling and switching	125 00	80 00
Bingham Junction and Wasatch, doubling and switching	100 00	75 00
FREIGHT SERVICE.		
Salt Lake City and Ogden, two round trips or less daily	110 00	80 00
Springville and Eureka, doubling and switching	110 00	80 00
Thistle and Salina, including switching	110 00	75 00
Castle Gate Swing, 12 hours or less per day, daily	115 00	80 00
Local, Salt Lake City and Clear Creek, except Sunday, 12 hours	110 00	80 00
Hill Brakemen, 12 hours or less from time of commencing work constitutes a day		75 00
Ogden and Helper, first in first out, double mil'ge bet. Clear Creek and Soldier Summit.*	42	3
Helper and Grand Junction, first in first out.*	35	25
PROVISIONS FOR SHORT RUNS.		
Clear Creek and P. V. Junction, actual 14 miles, allowed 25 miles.*	42	3
P. V. Junction and Scofield, actual 17 miles, allowed 20 miles *	42	3
WORK TRAINS.		
Conductors not acting as Foremen, per calendar month	110 00	
Brakemen, per calendar month		75 00
Brakeman and Operator, per calendar month		80 00

*Per mile.

Porters on all passenger trains, $50 per month. When it becomes necessary to dead-head a crew, the second crew out will dead-head, and will be allowed half time, and will stand out ahead of the crew they dead-headed with. Short runs, 50 miles or less, one-half day and stand first out; over 50 miles, mileage rate will be allowed, and stand out in turn. For turning around at intermediate stations, one hour will be allowed for putting away and picking up train; if over one hour, time will be allowed as follows: All time in excess of 10 hours per 100 miles, to be allowed as overtime; over 30 minutes one hour, and 30 minutes or less not computed. Overtime for Conductors, 35 cents, Brakemen, 25 cents per hour.

For Order Railway Conductors: RIO GRANDE WESTERN Ry. CO.,
S. P. PIERCE.   By A. E. WELBY,
For the Brotherhood of Railroad Trainmen: General Superintendent.
W. A. WHITE.
April 1st, 1892.

ST. JOSEPH & GRAND ISLAND RAILROAD COMPANY,
AND OPERATED LINES.

1. *Passenger Service:* Six crews will be assigned to the main line and will be paid $110 and $60 for Conductors and Brakemen, respectively. One crew will be assigned to the branch and will be paid $100 and $55 for Conductors and Brakemen, respectively. Trains Nos. 1 and 2 to be paid under this Article.

2. *Freight Service:* Conductors and Brakemen on through and mixed freight trains, other than Nos. 1 and 2, will be paid 3 and 2 cents per mile, respectively. Crews not assigned to regular service will run first in first out, and will be paid for on the mileage basis, with the following exceptions: The Alma branch run shall consist of the run between Fairfield and Alma, and one and one half hours switching in the Fairfield yard on alternate days, and 100 miles shall be allowed per trip on said run. The Fairbury branch run shall consist of the run between McCool Junction and Fairbury and return, the station switching at McCool Junction and the switching of their own train at Fairbury, for which 100 miles will be allowed. The Fairfield-Stromsburg run will consist of the run between Fairfield and Stromsburg and the making up of their own trains at Fairfield and Stromsburg, 130 miles to be allowed for the round trip, and 100 miles for the single trip. In consideration of the two short runs per week on the Fairbury branch and between Fairfield and Stromsburg, no overtime shall be allowed on these

runs, except in cases of unusual delays, such as washouts, wrecks and snow blockades.

3. *Local Freight:* Between St. Joseph and Grand Island crews on local freight trains shall receive 3 15-100 cents and 2 15-100 cents per mile for Conductors and Brakemen, respectively. Three Brakemen shall be assigned to each crew.

4. *Work Trains:* Work train Conductors and Brakemen shall be paid at the rate of $90 and $60 per month, respectively. The working days of a calendar month to constitute a month's work; twelve hours or less to constitute a day's work; overtime after twelve hours, at the same rate. Work train crews will consist of a Conductor and two Brakemen. The Company reserves the right to assign Conductor for this service.

5. Pilots will receive freight Conductors' pay and full mileage allowed.

6. Freight men handling special trains will be paid regular freight rates.

7. All freight Conductors and Brakemen not otherwise specified shall be paid on a mileage basis, 100 miles to be the minimum pay for any crew called and sent out.

8. On all freight runs of 100 miles or less, except those otherwise specified, requiring more than ten hours to make the run, overtime will be paid at the rate of ten miles per hour for Conductors and Brakemen. On all freight runs exceeding 100 miles, Conductors and Brakemen will be paid overtime for all the time used to complete the trip in excess of an average speed of ten miles an hour. In computing overtime, no fraction of an hour less than thirty minutes shall be counted; thirty minutes and over and less than one hour shall be computed as one hour.

9. When freight traffic is so light that the crews in unassigned service do not make about 3,000 miles per month, crews will be taken off, beginning with the youngest, until crews left in service are able to make the same. Conductors temporarily reduced under this rule will be given preference as Brakemen over younger men, and will retain their rights as Conductors; they will also again be placed on their runs when the traffic requires increasing of crews.

10. Trainmen attending court at the request of an officer of the Company will be allowed 100 miles per day for each day, and when away from their home station, in addition thereto, their legitimate expenses.

11. When a crew is compelled to double a hill they shall receive ten miles for the same, but one hour will be added to the time over the district, before overtime is allowed.

12. Full time will be allowed for all light runs, and where crews are dead-headed, in case crews are dead-headed, the freight crew dead-heading will be first out ahead of the crew dead-headed with.

13. All crews will be called at St. Joseph, Hanover and Grand Island; Train Caller will always be provided with a book in which the men called will enter their names together with the time they are called, and the time of trainmen will begin at the time set for the departure of their train when called, unless leaving earlier.

14. Conductors and Brakemen will not be suspended nor dismissed from the Company's service without just cause. In case of suspension or dismissal, if an employe thinks his sentence unjust he shall have the right within five days to refer his case by written statement to the Superintendent. Within five days of the receipt of this notice his case shall have a thorough investigation by the proper officer of the Railroad Company, at which he may be present if he so desires and also be represented by any disinterested employe of his choice. In case the suspension or dismissal is found to be unjust, he shall be reinstated and paid for all time lost. In case he shall not be satisfied with the result of the investigation he shall have the right to appeal to the General Manager.

15. When trainmen are called and for any reason other than their own act do not go out and are held on duty less than five hours they will be allowed fifty miles and stand first out, but if held more than five hours they will be paid one hundred miles and go behind crews at that point.

16. When a change of divisions or train runs require trainmen to change their place of residence they will be furnished with free transportation for their families and household effects to their new place of residence.

17. Freight or passenger crews making extra trips, in addition to their regular assigned runs, will be allowed extra time upon the basis of pay allowed other crews in similar service, except as provided in Article 6.

18. When crews of through or local freight or mixed trains are required to remain on duty with their trains, after arrival at end of run, or compelled to do switching service at terminal or division stations, they will be paid extra for such service at regular overtime rates.

19. Trainmen will not be required to pay fines on account of breakage.

20. After continuous service of sixteen hours trainmen will be entitled to and allowed eight hours' rest before being called to go out, except in cases of washouts, wrecks, or other similar emergencies. Following crews will have the right to run around any crew so lying over.

21. When proper notice is given, members of grievance committee shall be granted unlimited leave of absence.
22. When time is not allowed as per trip report, Conductors will be notified.
23. All freight Conductors and Brakemen on the St. Joseph & Grand Island and operated lines will be in line of promotion on all districts and divisions, according to length of service and ability to assume increased responsibility. The oldest freight Conductors to be in line of promotion in passenger service. When three Brakemen are promoted in the regular line of promotion, one experienced Conductor to be employed as Conductor; said Conductor to stand next in rank to the three Brakemen promoted.

The articles enumerated constitute, in their entirety, an agreement between the St. Joseph & Grand Island Railroad Company and its Conductors and Brakemen. No departure from the provisions of this agreement will be made by any party thereto, without reasonable notice of such a desire, in writing, has been served upon the other parties thereto. The rates of pay embodied in this schedule to remain in effect until January 1, 1894. All schedules, rules and regulations previously in effect are null and void.

BAGGAGEMEN AND YARD SERVICE.

Train Baggagemen are also Expressmen, and are paid $75 per month on main line and Stromsburg-Fairfield branch. On Alma branch and Fairbury branch the express and baggage work is performed by the Conductors of trains on those branches — no extra compensation. Hanover, Kansas, yard is the only place we have a switch crew. At this place we have a night switch crew only, consisting of Yardmaster at $75 per month, and two Switchmen at $60 per month each. Twelve hours constitute a day's work. Overtime paid after twelve hours at rate of 25 cents per hour for Yardmaster, and 20 cents per hour for Switchmen.

THE ST. JOSEPH & GRAND ISLAND RAILROAD CO.,
For the Order of Railway Conductors: W. P. ROBINSON, JR.,
A. B. GARRETSON, Grand Senior Conductor, O. R. C.   General Manager.
JOHN T. DAWSON, Chairman O. R. C.
For the Brotherhood of Railroad Trainmen:
S. E. WILKINSON, Grand Master B. of R. T.
CHAS. E. HEDRIX, Chairman B. of R. T.
November 1, 1892.

ST. LOUIS MERCHANTS BRIDGE TERMINAL RAILWAY.

Day Foremen, 27 cents per hour; Night Foremen, 29 cents per hour; Day Helpers, 25 cents per hour; Night Helpers, 27 cents per hour. Ten hours to constitute a day's work. Actual overtime allowed. This Company's service is wholly switching.
May 24, 1892.   H. W. GAYS, General Manager.

ST. LOUIS SOUTHWESTERN RAILWAY COMPANY.

This memorandum, made this 1st day of January, 1892, shall govern all Superintendents, Assistant Superintendents, Trainmasters and other officers in the service of the St. Louis Southwestern Railway Company, in the discipline and control of all Conductors and Trainmen in the service of said Company; shall regulate the pay rates of all such employes, and shall constitute a letter of instructions on all matters herein stated.

1. In the employment of Conductors and Trainmen in the service of the above-named Company Superintendents are hereby ordered to employ none but sober, reliable and competent men for this service; and all such employes will be directly responsible to and subject to the orders and control of the Assistant Superintendents and Trainmasters. No other subordinate officers will be allowed to interfere in the discipline and control of these employes, excepting that Brakemen will obey the instructions of their Conductors, so far as such instructions relate to their duty as such.

2. Train Conductors and Brakemen will be paid at the following schedule of rates: Conductors of passenger trains, $100 per month; Brakemen of passenger trains, $55 per month; Baggagemasters, $60 per month. All Conductors and Brakemen on through freight trains are to be paid not less than 3 and 2 cents per mile respectively; all runs of 100 miles or less to constitute a day's work.

3. The monthly pay of crews assigned to local freight or mixed runs shall be as follows: Conductors, $90 per month; Brakemen $60 per month of 26 or 27 working days, as the case may be; three crews will be assigned to runs of over 125 miles.

In the event that local trains are discontinued, the local crew that should have gone out on its run may be used in other service without extra compensation, so long as the extra mileage does not exceed the mileage the crew would have made on its regular run.

All Sunday runs, or extra service, in addition to the extra service hereinbefore specified, will be paid for as extra work of whatever class.

The provisions of this article are made subject to the following exceptions: New Madrid Branch: Conductor, $25 per month; Delta Section: Conductor, $100 per month; Brakemen, $72.50; Little Rock Section: Conductor, $90 per month; Brakemen, $65; Magnolia Section: Conductor, $75 per month; Porter, $35; Shreveport Branch: Conductor on freight, $100 per month; Brakeman on freight, $72.50; Conductor on passenger, $90; Porter, $35.

4. On all local and mixed trains, train crew shall consist of Conductor and three Brakemen, excepting on the following branches: New Madrid Branch, Magnolia Branch, Rob Roy Train.

Freight train crews on the Pine Bluff Section to consist of Conductor and three Brakemen, with the understanding that when power brakes are applied to freight trains, through freights that do no local work may be run with two Brakemen.

OVERTIME AND EXCESS MILEAGE.

5. Overtime will be allowed and paid to all Conductors and Brakemen of local and through freight trains and mixed trains, as follows:

On all freight runs of less than 100 miles, which runs may require more than ten hours time, the Conductors and Brakemen are to be paid overtime at the uniform rate of 30 and 20 cents per hour, deducting two hours for delayed time, when the delayed time on any trip amounts to more than two hours. All overtime in excess of ten hours will be paid for at above rates. When overtime is not allowed as per time slips, Conductors to be notified in writing by the Assistant Superintendent.

6. On all through freight runs of over 100 miles, Conductors and Brakemen shall be paid not less than 3 and 2 cents per mile respectively for all mileage made on each run; and in addition to actual mileage, overtime shall be paid them on a basis of ten miles per hour. For example: On a run of 150 miles they shall be paid 3 and 2 cents per mile for the 150 miles run, and in addition thereto, for all overtime made in excess of 15 hours, at the uniform rate of 30 and 20 cents per hour, less 2 hours allowed for delays.

7. In computing overtime, no fraction of an hour less than 30 minutes shall be counted, but all overtime of 30 minutes or over and less than one hour shall be counted as one hour. Trainmen will be paid overtime at the regular rate after arriving at terminals until relieved by Yardmaster.

8. Conductors and Brakemen on work trains shall be paid the following schedule: To receive not less than $90 and $60 per month respectively; ten hours to constitute a day's work; the working days of the month to constitute a month's work. All time over 12 hours to be paid for at the rate of 30 and 20 cents per hour. At non-coaling stations, where engines are to be coaled up, the watchman (if there be one) will be required to coal up engines, and be responsible for the safety of all switches used by him. If there be no Watchman and the Brakeman does the coaling, he will be paid at overtime rates.

Work train crew shall consist of a Conductor and two Brakemen on the main line, Cairo to Texarkana. On other portions of the road the number of Brakemen to be left to the discretion of the Superintendent.

9. Trainmen living within one mile of division and terminal stations, shall be called as nearly as practicable, one hour before the leaving time, by Train Caller, who will be provided with a book, in which the men called will enter their names; also the time called. The working time of all Trainmen shall commence at the time set for the departure of their trains.

10. When Trainmen are called, and for any reason other than their own acts do not go out, if held on duty less than six hours, they shall be paid for the time so held at overtime rates, and stand first out; if held more than six hours, they shall be paid for one day, and stand last out.

11. When the freight traffic on any portion of the road is so light that all the freight Conductors and Brakemen in the service are not able to make $90 and $60 per month respectively, a sufficient number of crews shall be laid off, beginning with the youngest men, until the Conductors and Brakemen in the service are able to make $90 and $60 per month respectively, as near as practicable. Any Conductor or Brakeman suspended from service under this rule will be given preference as Brakemen, and they will retain their rights as Conductors, and will be replaced on their runs when the freight business requires an increase of crews.

12. Whenever a change of divisions or train-runs requires a Conductor or brakeman to change his place of residence, he will be furnished free transportation for his family and household goods to his new place of residence, where such action by the Company is not in violation of state laws.

13. When passenger or freight Conductors make reasonable objections in writing to the Assistant Superintendent or Superintendent against any Brakeman under their

charge, such Brakeman shall be removed and assigned to other duty or dismissed from the service, according to the circumstances.

All instructions given to freight or passenger Conductors relative to the movement of trains or disposition of cars will be given in train orders or in writing, by the Assistant Superintendent.

14. Crews will be paid one-half rates when dead-heading on passenger trains, and full rates when dead-heading with their cabooses, or running as first section of passenger trains. In cases of crews dead-heading with cabooses, the first crew out will run the train, the next crew dead-heading; and the dead-head crew on reaching terminal station will stand ahead of crew with whom dead-headed.

15. When a Trainman is taken from his run for investigation of an alleged cause, he shall, if found innocent, receive pay for time lost while held off by the Company. No punishment shall be inflicted without a thorough investigation by the Assistant Superintendent, said investigation to be held within five days of the date of the removal from service.

Conductors and Brakemen shall not be discharged from the service of the Company, except for good and sufficient cause.

In case any Conductor or Trainman shall consider that he is unjustly discharged or suspended from the service of the Company, he may make a written statement of his case to the Superintendent, and within ten days after the receipt of such statement he shall be given a fair and impartial hearing by the Superintendent, in regard to the charges made against him. He shall have the right to appeal from the decision of the Superintendent to the General Manager.

16. When any Conductor or Trainman is detailed to attend court as a witness on the part of this or any other Railroad Companies, he shall be paid for such service the same rate of pay as now in force, viz: Conductors' and Brakemen's pay and expenses while away from home. The Railway Company to receive witness fees, if any are allowed by the court.

17. Conductors and Trainmen, after continued service of sixteen hours or more, shall be entitled to eight hours rest, if they so desire, before they are again called for service, excepting in cases of wash-outs, wrecks or other similar emergencies, provided they notify the Assistant Superintendent or Train Dispatcher on duty, in writing, on or before their arrival at terminal stations.

18. When crews of through or local freight, or mixed trains are required to do switching service at terminal or division stations, they will be paid extra for such service at the rate of 30 and 20 cents per hour; less than 30 minutes not to be counted; 30 minutes and over and less than one hour will be computed as one hour, excepting on such runs which occupy less than ten hours no extra switching service will be allowed until the total time used in making the runs exceeds ten hours.

The actual time made by Conductors and Brakemen for switching service, as above specified shall be returned by the Conductor on his trip slip, and in addition shall be kept by the Yardmaster, or where there is no Yardmaster by the Station Agent, in a book for that special purpose; and all such switching time shall be returned to the Assistant Superintendent's office, and made up in the pay rolls for the months in which the service is rendered.

19. The proper officers of the Railway Company will listen to any reasonable complaint, made either by individual Conductor or Brakeman, or by a committee of Conductors and Brakemen, provided proper notice is given in writing as to the subject of complaint, and a special appointment is made as to the time and place to consider the same.

20. Dates will change at 12 o'clock, midnight, the same as calendar dates, and two runs on the road commencing on separate dates will be paid for at not less than one day for each run, provided no other run is made on that date.

21. If a Conductor or Brakeman leaves the service of the Company of his own accord, or if he be discharged from the service, he shall forfeit all rights previously held, unless he be reinstated within ninety days. The oldest Brakeman, when competent, will be given preference as a passenger Brakeman, in the event of a vacancy, when they so desire.

22. Passenger train Brakemen, never having worked on freight train, must work at least two years in freight train service before they shall be promoted to Conductor.

Freight cabooses and their crews shall not be laid over for the reason that their Conductor has laid off, unless in case of emergency, and then not to exceed 24 hours.

23. Any Conductor or Trainman leaving the employ of the Company, will, at his request, be given a letter by his Superintendent, stating his term of service, and the capacity in which employed, and whether he has been discharged or has left the service of his own accord.

24. In filling vacancies in the ranks of freight Conductors, all Conductors, Brakemen and Baggagemen will be considered in line of promotion according to their age in the service and their ability to assume the duties of Conductor; except that two Brake-

hen shall be first promoted, and then one experienced Conductor may be employed as
Conductor, at the option of the officer in charge. A Conductor so employed shall take
his place at the foot of the list of extra Conductors, and may be temporarily used as
extra Brakeman, pending vacancy to be filled by him.

All Conductors will be considered in line of promotion according to their term of
service, dependent upon their good conduct and ability. Whenever additional Conductors are required in the passenger service, promotion will be made from the ranks
of freight Conductors, as above, giving each freight district representation, except
that the Superintendent reserves the right to employ new or additional men for these
positions when he considers that the good of the service requires it.

25. In cases where Trainmen, Conductors or Brakemen are used in temporary yard
service, they do not lose their rights as Trainmen.

YARDMEN'S SCHEDULE.

This memorandum, made this 1st day of January, 1892, shall govern all Superintendents, Assistant Superintendents, Trainmasters and other officers, in the service of the
St. Louis Southwestern Railway Company, in the discipline and control of yardmen in
the service of said Company; shall regulate the pay rates of all such employes; and
shall constitute a letter of instructions on all matters herein stated.

1. Hereafter, in the employment of yardmen in the service of the above Company,
assistant and terminal Superintendents are hereby instructed to employ none but
sober, reliable and competent men for this service, and all such employes will be directly responsible to and subject to the orders and control of assistant and terminal
Superintendents and Yardmasters, at all times and in all matters pertaining to their
duties. No other subordinate officer will be allowed to interfere in the discipline and
control of these men.

2. Wages and hours of yardmen shall remain as at present at all points.

3. Yard crews shall not be laid off after commencement of their days' work by
reason of disablement of their engines, or for any reason other than their own acts.

4. Crews working one-half day and one-half night, will be paid at night rates.
One hour shall be allowed yardmen for dinner between the hours of 11:30 and 1:30 night
and day. If held on duty until 1:30 oclock, they shall be allowed thirty minutes for
dinner and be paid for one extra hour.

5. In computing overtime, no fraction of an hour less than thirty minutes shall be
counted, but all overtime of thirty minutes or over, and less than one hour, shall be
counted one hour.

6. When attending court by request of an official, yardmen shall be paid according to their daily pay, and one dollar per day for expenses, if away from home.

7. The proper officers of the Railway Company will listen to any reasonable complaints made by either individual yardmen or by a committee of the same, provided
proper notice is given in writing as to the subject of complaint, and special appointment is made as to the time and place to consider the same.

8. Any yardman may be suspended from duty for a reasonable time, or for investigation for an alleged misconduct, or for violation of rules or orders; and may be discharged from the service of the Company for good and sufficient causes. These causes
shall include intemperance, incompetency, habitual neglect of duty, gross violation of
rules or orders, dishonesty or insubordination.

9. When a yardman is discharged or suspended for a definite term, for an alleged
fault, he shall have a fair and impartial trial within five days after filing his request
therefor with the assistant Superintendent; and if suspended for investigation, such
investigation shall be held within five days without such request. If found innocent,
he shall be paid at regular rates for time lost, and reinstated. If detained more than
five days awaiting investigation, he shall be paid for extra time in excess of five days,
whether found guilty or not.

10. All employes in yard service shall be promoted according to age and ability,
provided the officers in charge of such men shall consider them competent for positions
to which they are entitled by seniority in service; and anyone feeling that he has not
had a fair and impartial examination, shall have a right to appeal to higher authority.

11. In filling vacancies in the position of switch tenders, preference shall be given
to Switchmen crippled in the service of the Company, whenever their injuries are not
such as to unfit them for the duties of such positions.

All crippled Switchmen desiring to be considered in line for appointment to such
vacancies, will file their applications with the Superintendent of the lines upon which
their injuries are received.

12. Any employe included under the provisions of this agreement, who is dissatisfied with the decision of any official of the Company, shall have the right to appeal
therefrom to the General Manager, after having first submitted his case to the decision
of the Superintendent.

13. If a yardman leaves the service of the Company of his own accord, or if he is

discharged from the service, he shall forfeit all rights previously held, unless he is reinstated within ninety days.

14. There shall be no discrimination against any employe of the Company on account of being a member of any of the railway organizations.

15. Any yardman leaving the employ of the Company will, at his request, be given a letter by his Superintendent or Assistant Superintendent, stating his term of service, capacities in which employed, and whether he has been discharged or has left the service of his own accord.

16. It is agreed that an engine's crew shall consist of foreman and three men or engine or engines working in down town yard at Pine Bluff, during the busy season.

17. Whenever a change of stations requires a yardman to change his place of residence, he will be furnished free transportation for his family and household goods to his new place of residence, where such action by the Railway Company is not in violation of state laws.

A copy of this letter of instructions will be furnished to all Assistant Superintendents, Trainmasters and Yardmasters, and the same shall be accessible to any employe who may desire to see it. W. B. DODDRIDGE,
January 1, 1892. General Manager.

ST. LOUIS SOUTHWESTERN RAILWAY COMPANY OF TEXAS AND TYLER SOUTHEASTERN RAILWAY COMPANY.

This memorandum, made this first day of January, 1892, shall govern all Superintendents, Assistant Superintendents, Trainmasters and other officers in the service of the St. Louis Southwestern Railway Company of Texas and the Tyler Southeastern Railway Company, in the discipline and control of all Conductors and trainmen in the service of said Companies; shall regulate the pay rates of all such employes, and shall constitute a letter of instructions on all matters herein stated.

1. In the employment of Conductors and trainmen in the service of the above named Companies, Superintendents are hereby ordered to employ none but sober, reliable and competent men for this service; and all such employes will be directly responsible to and subject to the orders and control of the Assistant Superintendents and Trainmasters. No other subordinate officers will be allowed to interfere in the discipline and control of these employes—excepting that Brakemen will obey the instructions of their Conductors, so far as such instructions relate to their duties as such.

2. Train Conductors and Brakemen will be paid at the following schedule of rates: Conductors of passenger trains, $100 per month; Brakemen of passenger trains, $55 per month; Baggagemasters, $60 per month.

All Conductors and Brakemen on through freight trains are to be paid not less than 3 and 2 cents per mile respectively; all runs of 100 miles or less to constitute a day's work.

3. The monthly pay of crews assigned to local freight or mixed runs shall be as follows: Conductors, $90 per month; Brakemen, $60 per month of 26 or 27 working days, as the case may be; three crews will be assigned to runs of over 125 miles.

In the event that local trains are discontinued, the local crew that should have gone out on its run may be used in other service without extra compensation, so long as the extra mileage does not exceed the mileage the crew would have made on its regular run.

All Sunday runs, or extra service, in addition to the extra service hereinbefore specified, will be paid for as extra work of whatever class.

4. On all local and mixed trains: Train crews shall consist of Conductor and three Brakemen, excepting on the following sections: Waco section; Hillsboro section; Sherman section; Tyler Southeastern Railway; with the understanding that two Brakemen may be run on local trains on the Tyler section and the Fort Worth section when in the discretion of the Superintendent that number of Brakemen are sufficient to properly handle the business.

OVERTIME AND EXCESS MILEAGE.

5. Overtime will be allowed and paid to all Conductors and Brakemen of local and through freight trains and mixed trains, as follows:

On all freight runs of less than 100 miles, which runs may require more than ten hours time, the Conductors and Brakemen are to be paid overtime at the uniform rate of 30 and 20 cents per hour, deducting two hours for delayed time, when the delayed time on any trip amounts to more than two hours. All overtime in excess of ten hours will be paid for at above rates. When overtime is not allowed as per time slips, Conductors to be notified in writing by the Assistant Superintendent.

6. On all through freight runs of over 100 miles, Conductors and Brakemen shall be paid not less than 3 and 2 cents per mile respectively for all mileage made on each

run; and in addition to actual mileage, overtime shall be paid them on a basis of ten miles per hour. For example: On a run of 150 miles, they shall be paid 3 and 2 cents per mile for 150 miles run, and in addition thereto, for all overtime made in excess of 5 hours, at the uniform rate of 30 and 20 cents per hour, less two hours allowed for delays.

7. In computing overtime, no fraction of an hour less than 30 minutes shall be counted, but all overtime of 30 minutes or over and less than one hour shall be counted as one hour. Trainmen will be paid overtime at the regular rate after arriving at terminals until relieved by the Yardmaster.

8. Conductors and Brakemen on work trains shall be paid the following schedule: To receive not less than $90 and $60 per month respectively; ten hours to constitute a day's work; the working days of the month to constitute a month's work. All time over 12 hours to be paid at the rate of 30 and 20 cents per hour. At non-coaling stations, where work engines are to be coaled up, watchman (if there be one) will be required to coal up engines, and be responsible for the safety of all switches used by him. If there be no watchman and the Brakeman does the coaling, he will be paid at overtime rates.

Work train crew shall consist of a Conductor and two Brakemen on the main line, Texarkana to Tyler. On other portions of the road the number of Brakemen to be left to the discretion of the Superintendent.

9. Trainmen living within one mile of division and terminal stations shall be called as nearly as practicable one hour before the leaving time, by train Caller, who will be provided with a book, in which the men called will enter their names; also the time called. The working time of all trainmen shall commence at the time set for the departure of their trains.

10. When trainmen are called, and for any reason other than their own act do not go out, if held on duty less than six hours, they shall be paid for the time so held at overtime rates, and stand first out; if held more than six hours, they shall be paid for one day, and stand last out.

11. When the freight traffic on any portion of the road is so light that all the freight Conductors and Brakemen in the service are not able to make $90 and $60 per month respectively, a sufficient number of crews shall be laid off (beginning with the youngest men), until the Conductors and Brakemen in the service are able to make $90 and $60 per month respectively, as near as practicable. Any Conductor or Brakeman suspended from service under this rule will be given preference as Brakemen, and they will retain their rights as Conductors, and will be replaced on their runs when the freight business requires an increase of crews.

12. Whenever a change of divisions or train runs requires a Conductor or Brakeman to change his place of residence, he will be furnished free transportation for his family and household goods to his new place of residence, where such action by the Company is not in violation of state laws.

13. When a passenger or freight Conductor makes reasonable objections in writing to the Assistant Superintendent or Superintendent against any Brakeman under his charge, such Brakeman shall be removed and assigned to other duty or dismissed from the service, according to the circumstances.

All instructions given to freight or passenger Conductors relative to the movement of trains or disposition of cars, will be given in train orders or in writing, by the Assistant Superintendent.

14. Crews will be paid one-half rates when dead-heading on passenger trains, and full rates when dead-heading with their cabooses, or running as first section of passenger trains. In cases of crews dead-heading with cabooses, the first crew out will run the train, the next crew dead-heading; and the dead-head crew on reaching terminal station will stand ahead of crew with whom dead-headed.

15. When a trainman is taken from his run for investigation of an alleged cause, he shall, if found innocent, receive pay for time lost while held off by the Company. No punishment shall be inflicted without a thorough investigation by the Assistant Superintendent, said investigation to be held within five days of the date of the removal from service.

Conductors and Brakemen shall not be discharged from the service of the Company except for good and sufficient cause.

In case any Conductor or Brakeman shall consider that he is unjustly discharged or suspended from the service of the Company, he may make a written statement of his case to the Superintendent, and within ten days after the receipt of such statement he shall be given a fair and impartial hearing by the Superintendent, in regard to the charges made against him. He shall have the right to appeal from the decision of the Superintendent to the President.

16. When any Conductor or trainman is detailed to attend court as a witness on the part of this or other railroad companies, he shall be paid for such service the same rate of pay as now in force, viz: Conductors' and Brakemen's pay and expenses, while

away from home. The Railway Company to receive witness fees, if any are allowed by the court.

17. Conductors and trainmen, after continued service of sixteen hours or more shall be entitled to eight hours rest, if they so desire, before they are again called for service, excepting in cases of wash-outs, wrecks or other similar emergencies, provided they notify the Assistant Superintendent or Train Dispatcher on duty, in writing, on or before their arrival at terminal stations.

18. When crews of through or local freight, or mixed trains, are required to do switching service at terminal or division stations, they will be paid extra for such service, at the rate of 30 and 20 cents per hour; less than 30 minutes not to be counted; 30 minutes and over and less than one hour, will be computed as one hour, excepting that on such runs which occupy less than ten hours no extra switching service will be allowed until the total time used in making the runs exceeds ten hours.

The actual time made by Conductors and Brakemen for switching service, as above specified, shall be returned by the Conductor on his trip slip, and in addition shall be kept by the Yardmaster, or where there is no Yardmaster, by the Station Agent, in a book for that special purpose; and all such switching time shall be returned to the Assistant Superintendent's office, and made up in the pay rolls for the months in which the service is rendered.

19. The proper officers of the Railway Company will listen to any reasonable complaint, made by either individual Conductor or Brakeman, or by a committee of Conductors and Brakemen, provided proper notice is given in writing as to the subject of complaint, and a special appointment is made as to the time and place to consider the same.

20. Dates will change at 12 o'clock, midnight, the same as calendar dates, and two runs on the road commencing on separate dates will be paid for at not less than one day for each run, provided no other run is made on that date.

21. If a Conductor or Brakeman leave the service of the Company of his own accord, or if he be discharged from the service, he shall forfeit all rights previously held, unless he be reinstated within 90 days. The oldest Brakemen, when competent, will be given preference as passenger Brakemen, in the event of a vacancy, when they so desire.

22. Passenger train Brakemen, never having worked on freight train, must work at least two years in freight train service before they shall be promoted to Conductor.

Freight cabooses and their crews shall not be laid over for the reason that their Conductor has laid off, unless in cases of emergency—and then not to exceed 24 hours.

23. Any Conductor or trainman leaving the employ of the Company, will, at his request, be given a letter by his Superintendent, stating his term of service and the capacity in which employed, and whether he has been discharged or left the service of his own accord

24. In filling vacancies in the rank of freight Conductors, all Conductors, Brakemen and Baggagemen will be considered in line of promotion according to their age in the service and their ability to assume the duties of Conductor; except that two Brakemen shall be first promoted, and then one experienced Conductor may be employed as Conductor, at the option of the officer in charge. A Conductor so employed shall take his place at the foot of the list of extra Conductors, and may be temporarily used as extra Brakeman, pending vacancy to be filled by him.

All Conductors will be considered in line of promotion according to their term of service, dependent upon their good conduct and ability. Whenever additional Conductors are required in the passenger service, promotions will be made from the ranks of freight Conductors, as above, giving each freight district representation, except that the Superintendent reserves the right to employ new or additional men for these positions when he considers that the good of the service requires it.

25. In cases where trainmen, Conductors or Brakemen are used in temporary yard service, they do not lose their rights as trainmen.

YARDMEN'S SCHEDULE.

This memorandum, made this 1st day of January, 1892, shall govern all Superintendents, Assistant Superintendents, Trainmasters, and other officers, in the service of the St. Louis Southwestern Railway Company of Texas and the Tyler Southeastern Railway Company, in the discipline and control of Yardmen in the service of said Company; shall regulate the pay rates of all such employes; and shall constitute a letter of instructions on all matters herein stated.

1. Hereafter, in the employment of Yardmen in the service of the above Companies, assistant and terminal Superintendents are hereby instructed to employ none but sober, reliable and competent men for this service, and all such employes will be directly responsible to and subject to the orders and control of assistant and terminal Superintendents and Yardmasters, at all times and in all matters pertaining to their duties.

o other subordinate officer will be allowed to interfere in the discipline and control of these men.

2. Wages and hours of Yardmen shall remain as at present at all points.

3. Yard crews shall not be laid off after commencement of their day's work by reason of disablement of their engines, or for any reason other than their own acts.

4. Crews working one-half day and one-half night will be paid at night rates. One hour shall be allowed Yardmen for dinner between the hours of 11:30 and 1:30 night and day. If held on duty until 1:30 o'clock, they shall be allowed thirty minutes for dinner and be paid for one extra hour.

5. In computing overtime, no fraction of an hour less than thirty minutes shall be counted, but all overtime of thirty minutes or over, and less than one hour, shall be counted one hour.

6. When attending court by request of an official, Yardmen shall be paid according to their daily pay and one dollar per day for expenses if away from home.

7. The proper officers of the Railway Company will listen to any reasonable complaints made by either individual Yardmen or by a committee of the same, provided proper notice is given in writing as to the subject of complaint, and special appointment is made as to the time and place to consider the same.

8. Any Yardman may be suspended from duty for a reasonable time, or for investigation for any alleged misconduct, or for violation of rules or orders; and may be discharged from the service of the Company for good and sufficient causes. These causes shall include intemperance, incompetency, habitual neglect of duty, gross violation of rules or orders, dishonesty or insubordination.

9. When a Yardman is discharged or suspended for a definite term, for an alleged fault, he shall have a fair and impartial trial within five days after filing his request therefor with the Assistant Superintendent; and if suspended for investigation, such investigation shall be held within five days without such request. If found innocent, he shall be paid at regular rates for time lost, and reinstated. If detained more than five days awaiting investigation, he shall be paid for extra time in excess of five days, whether found guilty or not.

10. All employes in yard service shall be promoted according to age and ability, provided the officers in charge of such men shall consider them competent for positions to which they are entitled by seniority in service; and anyone feeling that he has not had a fair and impartial examination, shall have a right to appeal to higher authority.

11. In filling vacancies in the position of switch tenders, preference shall be given to Switchmen crippled in the service of the Company, whenever their injuries are not such as to unfit them for the duties of such positions.

All crippled Switchmen desiring to be considered in line for appointment to such vacancies, will file their applications with the Superintendent of the lines upon which their injuries were received.

12. Any employe included under the provisions of this agreement, who is dissatisfied with the decision of any official of the Company, shall have the right to appeal therefrom to the President, after having first submitted his case to the decision of the Superintendent.

13. If a Yardman leaves the service of the Company of his own accord, or if he is discharged from the service, he shall forfeit all rights previously held, unless he is reinstated within ninety days.

14. There shall be no discrimination against any employe of the Company on account of being a member of any of the railway organizations.

15. Any Yardman leaving the employ of the Company will, at his request, be given a letter by his Superintendent or Assistant Superintendent, stating his term of service, capacities in which employed, and whether he has been discharged or has left the service of his own accord.

16. It is agreed that an engine's crew shall consist of Foreman and three men on engine or engines working in down-town yard at Tyler, during the busy season.

17. Whenever a change of stations requires a Yardman to change his place of residence, he will be furnished free transportation for his family and household goods to his new place of residence, where such action by the Railway Company is not in violation of state laws.

A copy of this letter of instructions will be furnished to all Assistant Superintendents, Trainmasters and Yardmasters, and the same shall be accessible to any employe who may desire to see it.
S. W. FORDYCE,
President St. L., S. W. R'y Co. of Texas.
WILLARD FISHER,
January 1, 1892.
President Tyler Southeastern R'y Co.

SAINT PAUL & DULUTH RAILROAD.

Passenger Conductor, $100 per month; passenger Baggageman, $45 per month; passenger Brakemen, $45 per month; freight Conductors, $90 per month; freight Brakemen, $60 per month; day yard Foremen, $2.69 per day; day yard Switchmen, $2.50 per day; night yard Foreman, $2.89 per day; night yard Switchmen, $2.69 per day. Freight Conductors are allowed overtime at the rate of 3 cents per mile. Freight Brakemen are allowed overtime at the rate of 2 cents per mile. Work train Conductors, $85 per month; work train Brakemen, $55 per month.   A. B. PLOUGH,
May 18, 1892.   Vice President and General Manager.

SAN ANTONIO & ARANSAS PASS RAILWAY.

Passenger Conductors, main line, $125 per month; branch service, $100 per month. Train Porters, $50 per month. Freight Conductors, local, $90 per month of twenty-six calendar days, ten hours per day constituting a day's work, overtime at the rate of 30 cents per hour. Freight Conductors other than local, 3 cents per mile, one hundred miles or less to constitute a day's work at $3 per day, all over one hundred miles 3 cents per mile; 30 cents per hour overtime. Work train Conductors, $90 per month; twenty-six calendar days constitute a month's work, ten hours or less constitute a day's work. Brakemen, two-thirds of Conductors' pay.

Yard Service: At Alice, $85 per month for Yardmaster; Corpus Christi Yardmaster, $90; Yoakum, Waco, Houston and San Antonio Yardmasters, $110. The above is for day service. Night Yardmaster at Waco and Yoakum, $100. Switchmen — Day Foreman. 27 cents, and Night Foreman 29 cents per hour; Day Switchmen 25 cents, and Night Switchmen 27 cents per hour. At present we are not working any Yardmasters at Waco and Houston, but work Foreman with engine, allowing him Yardmaster's rate. At San Antonio we are not at present keeping any night Yardmaster, but allow day Yardmaster $125 per month, be attending to both night and day service.

Our baggage service is joint with Express Company. They employ the men, and we pay them an agreed price monthly for the entire line.
                                         GEO. L. SANDS,
May 24, 1892.   General Superintendent.

SAVANNAH, AMERICUS & MONTGOMERY RAILWAY.

Conductors, passenger, $90 per month; local freight, $80 per month; through freight, $70 per month; service train, $60 per month. Baggagemasters, $45 per month. Flagmen, all classes of service, $45 per month. Brakemen, front, local freight train, $35 per month; all others, $30 per month. We at present have no Yard Conductors. We have been paying them $60 per month. The average pay of our Switchmen is $32.50 per month.   W. E. HAWKINS,
May 16, 1892.   Second Vice President.

SEATTLE, LAKE SHORE & EASTERN RAILWAY COMPANY.

Passenger: Conductors, $115 per month; Brakemen, $65. Local freight: Between Seattle and Woolley — Conductors, $95 per month; Brakemen, $75; double between Seattle and Gilman — Conductors, $95 per month; Brakemen, $75; six days per week; no overtime. Double between Seattle and North Bend: Conductors, $100 per month; Brakemen, $75; six days per week; no overtime. Double between Seattle and Sallal: Conductors, $100 per month; Brakemen, $75; six days per week; overtime for doubling hills — one hour for Preston hill and one hour for Keith hill. Extra trains: Conductors, per day, 100 miles or less, $3.20; Brakemen, $2.20. Work trains: Conductors, $90 per month; Brakemen, $70; seven days per week; overtime after twelve hours. Crews on regular runs which exceed 100 miles per day will be paid overtime for work on the Seattle Belt Line Railroad or "3 S" Railway. All overtime will be computed same as extra trains: Conductors, per hour, ten miles, 32 cents; Brakemen, 22 cents. Brakemen on passenger runs which are required to do freight work will be paid $70 per month. Crews dead-heading on Company's business will be paid the same as extra trains. In addition to this we pay yardmen as follows: Yardmaster, $100 per month; Foremen, $2.60 per day, ten hours: Switchmen, $2.25 per day, ten hours.
Approved: I. A. NADEAU, Superintendent.   M. K. JONES,
May 18, 1892.   Trainmaster.

SOUTH CAROLINA RAILWAY.
LEASED AND OPERATED LINES AND BRANCHES.

1. *Passenger Service:* On main line and Columbia divisions, in regular service, Conductors, $90 per month; Baggagemasters, $45 per month, and Brakemen, $1.25 per day. Six crews to run two trains each way per day, between Charleston and Columbia and between Charleston and Augusta. If regular trains between Charleston and Augusta or Charleston and Columbia are cut off at Branchville, corresponding short runs between Branchville and Columbia or Branchville and Augusta will be run by these crews without additional compensation. Regular passenger men making trips other than their regular runs, and extra passenger men, will be paid: Conductors, 1 65-100 cents; Baggagemasters, 83-100 cent, and Brakemen, 70-100 cent per mile. No allowance for short runs to be less than for eighty-eight miles; runs of more than eighty-eight miles will be paid actual mileage. Summerville, Lambs, C. C. G. & C , and Columbia and Blocksburg runs: Conductors $75 and Baggagemasters $45 per month, and Brakemen $1.25 per day.

2. *Through Freight Service:* On through freight runs Conductors and trainmen will be paid 2 60-100 cents and 1 70-100 cents per mile, respectively. Short runs of less than fifty miles will be allowed fifty miles. Crews coming in from short runs, having made but fifty miles allowance, will stand first out; if they have made more than fifty miles allowance, they will go behind other crews at that point.

3. *Local Freight Service:* On local freight runs between Charleston and Columbia Conductors will be paid $80 per month, and Brakemen $45; between Branchville and Augusta, Conductors $75 per month and Brakemen $45; and between Camden and Kingville, Conductors $65 per month and Brakemen $45. Except on the Camden and Kingville run local crews will be paid extra for all service performed outside of their assigned runs.

4. *Phosphate and Material Service:* Conductors and trainmen in phosphate service will be paid $65 and $42 per month, respectively. Conductors and trainmen, not in charge of the road department, temporarily in material train service, for short runs and loading or unloading trains, will be paid fifty miles for six hours or less, and 100 miles for more than six and less than twelve hours; hours in excess of twelve will be paid extra at same rate.

5. *Dead-head Service:* Conductors and trainmen required to dead-head, will be paid one-half passenger mileage for dead-heading on passenger trains and one-half freight mileage for dead-heading on freight trains, with or without caboose. When it is necessary to dead-head a crew, the first crew out will run the train, and the dead-head crew will, at other end of run, start out ahead of the crew with whom they dead-head.

6. *Light Runs:* Crews running light with engine, or with engine and caboose, will be paid passenger mileage. No allowance of less than fifty miles.

7. *Attending Court:* Conductors and trainmen attending court on behalf of the Company will be paid the amount they would have made on their regular run.

8. *Calling:* Conductors and trainmen arriving at terminals before 9 A. M. will examine book on arrival, and if listed at that time to go out that afternoon are expected to be on hand without being called. Men having regular assigned runs will not be called. In other cases men will be called within one-half mile of Dispatcher's office. At Charleston, Caller will have a book in which are entered the train called for and the time expected to leave. The men called will sign this book, entering the time at which they are called.

9. *Rest:* Conductors or trainmen after twelve consecutive hours of service will be allowed seven hours for rest, provided they give proper notice of such desire and take the rest at a terminal station.

10. *Overtime:* Conductors of passenger, freight or mixed trains will be paid overtime at the rate of 20 cents per hour, and trainmen at the rate of 10 cents per hour. Overtime will be paid for all time over twelve hours consecutive duty, except on schedules when the time on duty is in excess of twelve hours. On these trains (scheduled at more than twelve hours) overtime will be computed from the arriving time of the train at destination; no overtime will be allowed for the first two hours' delay, but if the delay exceeds two hours the first two hours will be included. This rule to be inoperative until July 1, 1893.

11. *Investigation:* A Conductor or trainman taken from his run for an alleged fault will be given a hearing within five days, if practicable, and will have the right to have another employe of his class and choice to represent him. The accused will be promptly notified of the result of the investigation, and if found blameless will be paid for time lost.

12. *Reduction in Forces:* During dull seasons, so far as is consistent, the number of crews in service will be arranged so they will be able to make 2,400 miles per month.

13. *Hiring Conductors, and Promotions:* Promotions and preferment will be based

upon merit and the general record of the men, and not entirely upon their age in the service. In filling vacancies in the ranks of Conductors all trainmen will be considered in the line of promotion, according to their age in the service and their ability. An experienced Conductor may be hired as a Conductor, at the option of the officer in charge.

14. *Life of Agreement:* This agreement shall remain in force until December 31, 1893, and will continue after that date until either party gives sixty days' notice, in writing, to other parties thereto of desire for change.

For the Order Railway Conductors: SOUTH CAROLINA RAILWAY,
E. E. CLARK, G. C. C., J. F. KIRKLAND, Chairman.   C. M. WARD,
For Brotherhood of Railroad Trainmen: General Manager.
S. E. WILKINSON. G. M., W. A. STALEY, Chairman.   I. M. TURNER,
November 1, 1892.   Superintendent.

SOUTHERN PACIFIC COMPANY—ATLANTIC SYSTEM; LOUISIANA WESTERN EXTENSION RAILROAD COMPANY; TEXAS & NEW ORLEANS RAILROAD COMPANY; SABINE & EAST TEXAS RAILWAY COMPANY; GALVESTON, HARRISBURG & SAN ANTONIO RAILWAY COMPANY; NEW YORK, TEXAS & MEXICAN RAILWAY COMPANY; GULF, WESTERN TEXAS & PACIFIC RAILWAY COMPANY.

ATLANTIC SYSTEM.

1.   PASSENGER SERVICE, MAIN LINE.

DIVISIONS.	MONTH'S WORK.	CONDUCTORS.	BRAKEMEN.
El Paso	6,400 miles or less	$120 00	$70 00
San Antonio	4,450 miles or less	120 00	65 00
Houston	5,000 miles or less	120 00	60 00
Louisiana	5,305 miles or less	120 00	60 00
Morgan	3,600 miles or less	120 00	60 00
Victoria	3,700 miles or less	110 00	55 00
Sabine & East Texas Railway Company	4,500 miles or less	110 00	

Excess mileage, pro rata.

2.   BRANCH SERVICE, PASSENGER AND MIXED.

DIVISIONS.	MONTH'S WORK.	CONDUCTORS.	BRAKEMEN.
Eagle Pass branch	4,350 miles or less	$100 00	$60 00
Gonzales branch	Calendar month	65 00	55 00
LaGrange branch	26 or 27 days or less	90 00	60 00
Port Lavaca branch	Present rate for present work		
Beeville branch	Present rate for present work		
Harrisburg and Clinton	Calendar month	80 00	60 00
Sabine Pass branch	Calendar month	90 00	
Alexandria branch	3,000 miles or less	90 00	60 00
St. Martinsville branch	Calendar month	83 33	54 00
Cypremort branch	Calendar month	83 33	54 00
Thibodeaux branch	Calendar month	83 33	54 00
Salt Mine branch	Calendar month	83 33	54 00
Houma branch	Calendar month	83 33	54 00

3.   THROUGH FREIGHT SERVICE.

DIVISIONS.	MONTH'S WORK.	CONDUCTORS.	BRAKEMEN.
El Paso	3,000 miles or less	$90 00	$72 50
San Antonio	Conductors, 3,000 miles or less / Brakemen, 3,180 miles or less	90 00	67 50
Houston	3,000 miles or less	90 00	60 00
Louisiana	3,000 miles or less	90 00	60 00

Excess mileage, pro rata. The Company will not assign any more crews to each division than are necessary to move traffic with promptness and certainty.

SOUTHERN PACIFIC RAILWAY. 145

4. LOCAL FREIGHT SERVICE.

DIVISIONS.	MONTH'S WORK.	CONDUCT-ORS.	BRAKE-MEN.
Del Rio and San Antonio	3,400 miles or less	$102 00	$70 00
San Antonio and Glidden	Twenty trips or less	90 00	60 00
Glidden and Houston	Twenty-six days or less	90 00	60 00
Houston and Beaumont	3,000 miles or less	90 00	60 00
Beaumont and Lafayette	Twenty trips or less	90 00	60 00
Lafayette and Algiers	2,800 miles or less	90 00	60 00
Eagle Pass branch	3,000 miles or less	90 00	70 00
LaGrange branch	1 900 miles or less	80 00	60 00
Victoria Branch	26 or 27 days or less	90 00	60 00
Sabine & East Texas Railway Company	26 or 27 days or less	90 00	

Excess mileage, pro rata. Ten hours to be the schedule for all runs on Morgan division; except locals between Lafayette and Morgan City, which will be taken from time card.

5. Rates of pay, work or construction, on all divisions, for month of twenty-six days of twelve hours or less, will be as follows: Conductors, $90; Brakemen, $60. Overtime: Conductors, 30 cents per hour; Brakemen, 20 cents. Youngest men will be assigned to duty on work or construction trains. Temporary service is defined to be any length of time less than ten days.

6. YARD SERVICE.

YARD.	DAY'S OR MONTH'S WORK.	Yardmas-ter, day.	Yardmas-ter, night.	Foremen, day.	Foremen, night.	Helpers, day.	Helpers, night.
El Paso	10 hours	$110 00	$90 00	*$0 27	*$0 29	*$0 25	*$0 27
Valentine	Calendar month	90 00	90 00				
Sanderson	Calendar month	90 00	90 00				
Del Rio	12 hours, calendar month	90 00	80 00			† 2 10	† 2 10
Eagle Pass	12 hours, calendar month	90 00				† 2 10	
Glidden	12 hours, calendar month	80 00	85 00			† 2 10	† 2 10
Lafayette	12 hours, calendar month	90 00	90 00			63 00	63 00
Morgan City	12 hours, calendar month	88 50				60 00	
New Orleans	10 hours, calendar month			75 00	75 00	63 00	63 00
New Orleans, overtime				* 25	* 25	* 20	* 20

*Per hour.   †Per month.   Overtime: Foremen and Helpers, pro rata.

YARD SCHEDULES NOT INCLUDED IN THE ABOVE.

YARD.	DAY'S OR MONTH'S WORK.	Foremen, day.	Foremen, night.	Helpers, day.	Helpers, night.
San Antonio	10 hours	*$0 27	*$0 29	*$0 25	*$0 27
Houston	10 hours	* 27	* 29	* 25	* 27
Beaumont	12 hours, calendar month	70 00	75 00	† 2 15	† 2 25
Algiers	10 hours, calendar month	75 00	75 00	63 00	63 00
Algiers, overtime		* 25	* 25	* 20	* 20

*Per hour.   †Per day.   Overtime: Foremen and Helpers, pro rata.

7. Freight trainmen will be called at division or terminal stations one hour and thirty minutes before time set for departure of train they are to go on, by a train Caller, who will be provided with a book in which the men called shall enter their names, together with the time they are called. The time of trainmen will begin with the time set for the departure of trains. Trainmen will be called within a radius of three-fourths of one mile of Dispatcher's or telegraph office. This radius shall not apply to trainmen at Algiers and New Orleans.

8. *Delayed Time:* (a.) All delays of two hours or over will be paid for at the rate of 30 cents per hour for Conductors and 20 cents per hour for Brakemen. When delays exceed two hours, the first two hours to be included.

(b.) In computing delayed time under this article, the time of regular trains is to be taken from current time tables. The time of irregular trains is to be computed on a basis of 12 miles per hour.

(c.) When trainmen are held waiting for stock cars to be cleaned, bedded, loaded or unloaded, they shall receive pay for delayed time at the rate of 30 cents and 20 cents per hour, respectively, for Conductors and Brakemen; provided, however, that they arrive at terminals two hours or more late; running time to be determined as above.

(c. 2.) When trainmen are held to load or unload material they shall receive pay at the rate of 30 cents and 20 cents per hour, respectively, for Conductors and Brakemen, for all time consumed over one hour, it being understood that this service is not to be paid for twice.

(d.) When trainmen are required to remain on duty over thirty minutes with their trains on arrival at main line terminals, overtime will be allowed in full as per above, if all delays, both on run and at terminals, exceed two hours. If two hours is not exceeded, allowance for the terminal delay may be made in such special cases as in the judgment of the Division Superintendent may seem proper.

(e.) Turn around trips will be paid mileage to and from turn around point, and extra at overtime rates for all hours on duty at turn around point. When mileage is less than 100 miles, 100 miles will be allowed, and overtime for all hours used in making turn around trip in excess of eight and one-half hours.

9. All freight crews on their respective divisions, not assigned to regular runs, shall run first in and first out, as they are headed, as at present, except the Louisiana and Morgan division, which are to remain as at present. Freight crews will not be required to make more than two turns before being allowed to return to division headquarters; provided, there are other crews at terminals that have not made two turns. Freight crews will be given lay-overs at division headquarters as far as the exigencies of traffic will permit.

10. Train crews will be relieved from duty at main line terminals when road engines are detached from train, as at present, except at Valentine and Sanderson, where crews will be relieved upon arrival of the trains.

11. When trains for which men have been called are annulled and men relieved from duty, they will be paid for time held, between the time specified for train to leave and the time same was annulled, at schedule rates for overtime per hour or fractional part over thirty minutes, but in all such cases trainmen shall receive pay for not less than three hours, and will stand first out.

12. Freight train crews will be allowed regular freight train rates for handling passenger trains or passenger equipment, and regular or extra freight Conductors, who are not extra passenger Conductors, shall receive for passenger service not less than they would have earned had they remained in freight service.

13. All runs of 100 miles or less will be considered 100 miles; all runs over 100 miles will be paid for actual mileage made.

14. All trainmen will be paid full time for dead-heading.

15. Trainmen and Yardmen when held as witnesses for the Company will be paid for actual time lost and all necessary expenses. Time held attending court will be certified by Company's attorney.

16. When time is not allowed as per time slip, same will be returned, stating amount allowed. Overtime to be turned in on a separate slip.

17. Trainmen and Yardmen shall not be required to pay for supplies used in the discharge of their respective duties, or be liable for any other charge, excepting for switch keys and one white and one red hand-lantern, and charges for them shall be limited to one dollar each, such amount to be refunded at the termination of service, upon the return to the Company of the property charged for.

18. In the event of there being a surplus of men, the oldest in the service on their respective divisions shall have the preference of employment. In case of reduction of crews, Brakemen shall be entitled to their guarantee, according to their age of continuous service.

19. It is the policy of the Company to promote freight Conductors from freight Brakemen and passenger Conductors from freight Conductors. In making promotions Division Superintendents will consider seniority of service; in other words, those longest in service, other things being equal, shall have the preference. When a reduction in forces becomes necessary the Company will retain those who have been longest in the service; that is to say, as between those equally honest, sober and capable. But "seniority" is not to be made a cover for shortcomings of any kind, nor shall this rule be construed so as to prevent the Company securing the most efficient service that may be obtainable. Each Division Superintendent is held responsible for the proper performance of all duties devolving upon the men working under his supervision, and,

as he is in the best position to look after the welfare of the Company, he shall be the judge regarding the respective merits and qualifications of those working under his directions. If any employe feels that an injustice has been done him under this rule, he has the right of appeal to the General Superintendent or the General Manager.

20. No trainman will be held responsible for cut journals or flat wheels where it can be shown that proper attention had been given by the crew.

21. At all terminals where trains are made up, the car inspector will test all airbrake cars and see that they are in good order, and the Yardmaster will place all airbrake cars ahead as far as practicable.

22. When Yardmasters have a train made up and ready to go they will notify the Conductor, and will not place any more cars on that train unless the Conductor has been first notified.

23. Trainmen running into main line terminals where there are no yard crews, and required to do switching, will be paid for such service at the schedule rate of overtime. Any freight, local or extra, crew required to do switching at Victoria, will be paid for such service at schedule rates for overtime, any fractional part of first hour to be considered one hour. Switching in schedule time will be considered in computing overtime. Switching at Alexandria will be paid for at overtime rates, provided more than one hour be consumed.

24. Freight crews, after making two division trips without rest will be entitled to eight hours' rest if they require it and give due notice thereof, except in cases of wrecks and washouts.

25. Oldest extra Conductors and Brakemen shall do all extra running on their respective divisions, but in no case shall an extra Conductor receive less than a Brakeman's guarantee.

26. Passenger Brakemen and Yardmen can claim no seniority or rights in train service. Freight Brakemen or Conductors assigned temporarily to passenger or branch service, shall not lose their main line rights.

27. Trainmen can claim no seniority or rights in yards.

28. When trainmen leave the service of the Company they shall be given letters showing time of service, in capacity or capacities employed, and cause of leaving service; provided they have worked on division sixty days or more; said letters to be given them within two days of personal application, and to bear office stamp and Division Superintendent's signature.

29. No trainman or yardman will be discharged nor suspended without proper cause. In case a yardman or trainman believes his discharge or suspension unjust, he may make a written statement of his case and forward to Division Superintendent. In case satisfaction cannot be had from Division Superintendent, a committee of three trainmen or yardmen in good standing, and in Company service, shall be designated to meet in conjunction with Division Superintendent and place the matter before the General Superintendent or proper officers, and without unnecessary delay the case shall be reinvestigated and a decision given in less than ten days from the rehearing. If the trainmen or yardmen are decided blameless, they shall be immediately reinstated and paid for the time lost on account of said suspension at schedule rates. Trainmen or yardmen charged with offenses involving either suspension or discharge will be advised of the offense, in writing, and all parties concerned will be present at the investigation if desired.

30. Conductors will be held responsible for position of switches, as per Rule No. 117, which will be interpreted to mean that when a Conductor does not throw a switch himself he must know that it has been properly set.

31. Yard crews will not do any unnecessary switching with cabooses on any part of the Atlantic System.

32. When crews turn at Orange to pick up a train, yard crew will make up the train.

33. Distance between Lafayette and Algiers will be considered 150 miles in freight service.

34. When Conductors and Brakemen are allowed twenty-four hours at Algiers and New Orleans, and are due to leave between the hours of 7 A. M. and 12 midnight, they will be governed by bulletin board in Dispatcher's office.

35. All crews on the M. L. & T. division sent out on short rest will be called, and all crews due to leave between the hours of 12 midnight and 7 A. M., whether sent out on short rest or not, will be called. Conductors and Brakemen who reside within one-half mile of New Orleans ferry landing will be called.

36. No Conductor or Brakemen will be run out of Algiers with less than twelve hours' rest.

37. Statements showing expenditures of hospital fund will be posted on bulletin boards at division headquarters monthly. A committee composed of a representative from each class of employes in the service, in company with the Medical Director, will make annual examination of hospital accounts.

38. Conductors will not be required to take out inexperienced men when acceptable experienced men can be secured. Conductors will have the right to object to Brakemen for cause, and when objections are sustained by facts they will be furnished with other men.

39. The use of intoxicating liquors, or insubordination, while on duty will be sufficient cause for dismissal from the Company's service. Trainmen will have the right to refuse to work with or for any man under the influence of liquor.

For the Order of Railway Conductors:
    E. E. CLARK, G. C. C., W. QUINN, Chairman.
For the Brotherhood of Railroad Trainmen:
    S. E. WILKINSON, G. M., E. W. WALES, Chairman.
December 1, 1891.

J. KRUTTSCHNITT,
General Manager.

SOUTHERN PACIFIC COMPANY.
PACIFIC SYSTEM AND LINES IN OREGON.

WESTERN DIVISION.

RUNS.	Conductors	Brakemen	Mil'ge for month's work	Number of crews	REMARKS.
PASSENGER.					
Oakland Pier, Sacramento	$120 00	$70 00			Via Benicia.
Oakland Pier, Sacramento	120 00	70 00			Via Niles.
Oakland Pier, Lathrop and Stockton	120 00	70 00			Baggageman on Stockton swing, $85.
Oakland Pier, San Jose	110 00	70 00			
Oakland Pier, San Jose and Livermore	115 00	70 00		2	
San Jose, Martinez	115 00	70 00			
South Vallejo, Calistoga	115 00	70 00			
South Vallejo, Santa Rosa	110 00	70 00			
Sacramento, Tracy and Lathrop	110 00	70 00			
Extra	110 00	70 00			
MIXED.					
Niles, San Jose	100 00	75 00			
Martinez, San Ramon	100 00				
Galt, Ione	100 00	75 00			
South Vallejo, Suisun and Davis	100 00	75 00			
Elmira, Rumsey and Vacaville	100 00	75 00			
FREIGHT.					
West Oakland, Sacramento	95 00	75 00	2740		90 miles per trip.
West Oakland, Lathrop	95 00	75 00	2740		90 miles per trip.
West Oakland, Lathrop	95 00	75 00	2740		Via Niles; 90 miles per trip.
West Oakland, San Jose	100 00	80 00	2740		95 miles per round trip.
West Oakland, Calistoga	95 00	75 00	2740	3	146 miles per trip.
West Oakland, Tracy	95 00	75 00	2740		Actual mileage.
Sacramento, Lathrop and Tracy	95 00	75 00	2740	3	79 miles to Tracy, 68 miles to Lathrop.
Tracy, Mendota	95 00	75 00	2740		92 miles per trip.
Suisun, Santa Rosa	95 00	75 00			
Oakland, Mendota	95 00	75 00	2740		130 miles per trip.

Extra passenger Conductors or freight Conductors will be allowed compensation at rate of $110 per month for extra passenger service. On arriving at turn around points, if crews are notified that they will not be required within five hours, time so held will not be figured as part of trip. On Lodi branch Conductors and Brakemen will be paid $90 and $70 per month, respectively.

SACRAMENTO DIVISION.

RUNS.	CLASS OF TRAIN	Conductors	Brakemen	Number of crews	Mil'ge for month's work
Sacramento, Truckee	Passenger	$125 00	$75 00		
Sacramento, Colfax	Passenger	115 00	70 00		
Sacramento, Truckee	Freight	105 00	82 50		2400
Rocklin, Truckee	Freight	105 00	82 50		2400

SOUTHERN PACIFIC RAILWAY.

SHASTA DIVISION.

RUNS.	CLASS OF TRAIN.	Conductors...	Brakemen...	Number of crews.	Mil'ge for month's work.
Red Bluff, Ashland.................	Passenger........................	$125 00	$75 00	.....	.....
Red Bluff, Dunsmuir...............	Freight...........................	95 00	75 00	.....	2900
Dunsmuir, Ashland.................	Freight...........................	100 00	80 00	.....	2150

For switching at Dunsmuir regular rates for overtime will be paid. All switching over one hour before leaving time, at Ashland, will be paid for at regular rates of overtime.

OREGON AND PLACERVILLE DIVISIONS.

RUNS.	CLASS OF TRAIN.	Conductors...	Brakemen...	Number of crews.	Mil'ge for month's work.
Sacramento, Red Bluff.............	Through passenger...............	$120 00	$70 00	.....	.....
Sacramento, Red Bluff.............	Local passenger..................	110 00	70 00	.....	.....
Sacramento, Redding...............	Local passenger..................	110 00	70 00	.....	.....
Sacramento, Oroville...............	Mixed...........................	110 00	70 00	.....	.....
Sacramento, Red Bluff*............	Freight..........................	95 00	75 00	.....	*2700
Marysville, Oroville................	Mixed...........................	85 00	70 00	.....	.....
Sacramento, Placerville............	Passenger.......................	100 00	70 00	.....	.....
Sacramento, Placerville............	Mixed...........................	100 00	70 00	.....	.....

*Via Marysville or Willows. On Oroville run we will pay Conductors and Brakemen, respectively, $95 and $75 per month after July 1, or before, if run is made through from Oroville to Roseville Junction.

TRUCKEE DIVISION.

RUNS.	CLASS OF TRAIN.	Conductors...	Brakemen...	Number of crews.	Mil'ge for month's work.
Truckee, Carlin....................	Passenger.......................	$125 00	$75 00	.....	.....
Truckee, Wadsworth...............	Freight..........................	100 00	80 00	.....	2950
Wadsworth, Carlin.................	Freight..........................	100 00	80 00	.....	3700
Truckee, Reno and return.........	Freight..........................	105 00	85 00	*1	.....

*No overtime.

SALT LAKE DIVISION.

RUNS.	CLASS OF TRAIN.	Conductors...	Brakemen...	Number of crews.	Mil'ge for month's work.
Ogden, Carlin......................	Passenger.......................	$125 00	$75 00	6	.....
Ogden, Terrace....................	Freight..........................	100 00	80 00	.....	3470
Terrace, Carlin....................	Freight..........................	100 00	80 00	.....	3470

SAN JOAQUIN DIVISION.

RUNS.	CLASS OF TRAIN.	Conductors...	Brakemen...	Mil'ge for month's work.	REMARKS.
Lathrop, Bakersfield*..............	Passenger.......................	$125 00	$75 00	5500	.....
Stockton, Merced..................	Mixed...........................	110 00	75 00	.....	.....
Berenda, Raymond................	Mixed...........................	90 00	70 00	.....	.....
Goshen, Alcalde...................	Mixed...........................	110 00	75 00	.....	.....
Fresno, Porterville.................	Mixed...........................	110 00	75 00	.....	Via Porterville.
Fresno, Bakersfield................	Mixed...........................	100 00	75 00	2600	30-day month.
Lathrop, Bakersfield...............	Freight..........................	95 00	75 00	2700	31-day month.
Bakersfield, Mendota..............	Freight..........................	95 00	75 00	3550	.....

*Crews to make one extra trip, 220 miles (included in the 5,500 above), without additional compensation; if they return with train, to be paid extra; if dead-head, nothing. Three Brakemen on local between Mendota and Bakersfield. Brakeman on Yosemite division to act as Baggageman.

LOS ANGELES AND VENTURA DIVISIONS.

RUNS.	CLASS OF TRAIN.	Conductors.	Brakemen.	Number of crews.	Mil'ge for mo'th's work.
Bakersfield, Los Angeles	Passenger	$125 00	$75 00		
Los Angeles, Santa Barbara	Passenger	110 00	70 00		
Saugus, Santa Barbara	Passenger	110 00	70 00		
Bakersfield, Los Angeles	Freight	100 00	80 00		2600
Los Angeles, Santa Barbara	Freight	100 00	80 00		2750

For turn around, Bakersfield to Mojave, crews will be allowed 100 miles. The third crew was put on the Ventura division with the understanding that the men should do special work for the Los Angeles division, handling pay car, officers' specials, etc., on their lay over days. This arrangement will be continued. As extra men for the Los Angeles division are all held at Mojave, employes must report to the Superintendent's office at division headquarters when they wish to lay off, unless it may be arranged between the trainmen so that the dead-head trip to Los Angeles and return, to relieve trainmen at Los Angeles, shall be made without expense to the Company. Present arrangement for switching at Santa Barbara will be continued.

YUMA DIVISION.

RUNS.	CLASS OF TRAIN.	Conductors.	Brakemen.	Mil'ge for month's work.	REMARKS.
Los Angeles, Yuma	Passenger	$125 00	$75 00		
Los Angeles, Redlands	Passenger	110 00	70 00		
Los Angeles, Chino	Passenger	110 00	70 00		To do extra running as at present.
Los Angeles, Santa Monica	Passenger	110 00	70 00		
Los Angeles, San Pedro	Passenger	110 00	70 00		
Los Angeles, Santa Ana	Passenger	110 00	70 00		
Los Angeles, Whittier and Tustin	Passenger	110 00	70 00		
Los Angeles, Long Beach	Passenger	100 00	65 00		W. F. & Co. pay a part of Brakeman's salary.
Los Angeles, Yuma	Through freight	100 00	80 00	3300	
Los Angeles, Colton	Local freight	105 00	85 00	3192*	No overtime.
Los Angeles, San Pedro	Local freight	95 00	75 00		
Santa Monica, Santa Ana	Local freight	100 00	80 00		No overtime.
Banning, Colton†	Mixed	105 00	85 00		

*For twenty-seven days. †This crew to run to Redlands with freight and switch at Colton. When they get Sundays off, they are to get $100 and $80 again. When crews are held at Colton with stock, crews shall have 100 miles for unloading and loading stock and for bringing train from Colton to Los Angeles.

TUCSON AND GILA DIVISIONS.

RUNS.	CLASS OF TRAIN.	Conductors.	Brakemen.	Number of crews.	Mil'ge for month's work.
Yuma, El Paso	Passenger	$125 00	$75 00		
Tucson, El paso	Freight	100 00	80 00		3350
Tucson, Yuma	Freight	100 00	80 00		3550

When crews are called upon to take trains over lines of other roads, this Company will pay them for such service.

LINES IN OREGON.

RUNS.	CLASS OF TRAIN.	Conductors.	Brakemen.	Number of crews.	REMARKS.
EAST SIDE DIVISION.					
Portland, Roseburg	Passenger	$120 00	$70 00	3	15 and 16.
Roseburg, Ashland	Passenger	120 00	75 00		15 and 16.
Portland, Roseburg	Passenger	110 00	70 00	3	17 and 18.
Portland, Albany	Passenger	110 00	70 00		19 and 20.
Portland, Junction	*Freight	95 00	75 00		31 and 32.
Junction, Roseburg	Freight	95 00	75 00		31 and 32.
Roseburg, Grant's Pass	Freight	95 00	75 00		31 and 32.
Grant's Pass, Ashland	Freight	95 00	75 00		31 & 32 (Swing).
WOODBURN SPRINGFIELD BRANCH.					
Natron, Woodburn and return to Silverton	Mixed	95 00	70 00		11, 12, 13 and 14.

SOUTHERN PACIFIC RAILWAY. 151

LINES IN OREGON – CONTINUED.

RUNS.	CLASS OF TRAIN.	Conductors	Brakemen	Number of crews	REMARKS.
WEST SIDE DIVISION.					
Portland, Corvallis and return	Passenger	120 00	70 00		3 and 4.
McMinnville, Portland and return	Passenger	100 00	70 00		1 and 2.
Portland, Corvallis	Freight	95 00	75 00		5 and 6.
P. & W. V. AND OREGONIAN N. G. DIVISIONS.					
Portland, Airlie	Mixed	95 00	70 00		25 and 26.
Portland, Sheridan	Passenger	100 00	70 00		27 and 28.
Portland, Oswego	Passenger	100 00	70 00		Suburban.
Regular and extra	Freight	95 00	70 00		
LEBANON BRANCH.					
Albany, Lebanon and yard work at Albany	Mixed	95 00	75 00		7, 8, 9 and 10.

Extra freight: Portland to Roseburg—Conductors $5 per trip, Brakemen $4; Roseburg to Ashland —Conductors $3 60 per trip, Brakemen $2.85; overtime after twelve hours. Engines to be wooded up at Junction, Roseburg, Grant's Pass and Ashland; trainmen to wood engines as at present at Irving for trains 17 and 31, and at all other points. While only one crew is run on the suburban trains between Portland and Oswego, one-fourth day will be paid Conductor and Brakeman for Saturday nights. Should it be necessary to use the lay-over crew of 17 and 18 for a special passenger, they will not receive any extra compensation.

SANTA CRUZ DIVISION.

RUNS.	Conductors	Brakemen	REMARKS.
PASSENGER.			
Alameda Mole, Santa Cruz	$115 00	$70 00	Conductor to be allowed one day off each week, for which
Alameda Mole, Los Gatos	100 00	70 00	he will be paid if he works.
MIXED.			
Almaden branch	90 00	75 00	This train to run to Felton in summer and do work in San
Boulder Creek branch	90 00	75 00	Jose yard; also help to Glenwood in winter.
FREIGHT.			
Alameda Point, Santa Cruz*	95 00	75 00	Freight crew to run 5 and 6 when run as excursion, and
Boulder Creek branch	90 00	70 00	to be paid extra for all Sunday work.
Alameda Point, San Jose	95 00	75 00	To run train 5 and 6 when run as "Hunters'" train.

*Three Brakemen to be on this run from April 1 until December 1 of each year. All switching at San Jose and Santa Cruz by regular freight crews to be paid at regular rates for overtime.

COAST DIVISION.

RUNS.	CLASS OF TRAIN.	Conductors	Brakemen	Baggagemen	MONTH'S WORK.
MONTEREY LINE.					
San Francisco, Pacific Grove	Passenger	$125 00	$70 00	$80 00	
San Francisco, San Jose	Passenger	110 00	70 00	75 00	
San Francisco, Menlo Park	Passenger	110 00	70 00		
San Francisco, Pacific Grove	Freight	100 00	75 00		8½ round trips.
San Francisco, Aptos	Freight	100 00	75 00		8½ round trips.
San Francisco, San Jose	Freight	100 00	75 00		13½ round trips.
TRES PINOS LINE					
Gilroy, Tres Pinos	Mixed	115 00	75 00		
SANTA CRUZ LINE.					
Pajaro, Santa Cruz	Passenger	115 00	70 00	75 00	
Pajaro, Santa Cruz	Freight	100 00	75 00		
SANTA MARGARITA LINE.					
Castroville, Santa Margarita*	Passenger	115 00	70 00	80 00	
Castroville, Salinas	Passenger	85 00			
Castroville, Santa Margarita	Freight	100 00	75 00		8½ round trips.

*For short turn around, made within one and one-half hours, by Santa Margarita passenger crews, no extra compensation. Whenever it may be necessary, trainmen on San Francisco and San Jose freight will be called on to make two special round trips San Jose to Gilroy, without extra compensation. If made Sunday, extra compensation. Trainmen of Menlo Park and San Jose passenger runs will be called on for special services, as heretofore, without extra compensation. No extra compensation for switching at terminals other than San Jose and San Francisco. Where mileage is not given, same work to be performed as under schedule of 1890. * On Monte Vista and Aptos specials, Conductors will receive $125 per month when logging, and $100 at other times; Brakemen, $75 per month.

SOUTHERN PACIFIC RAILWAY.

YARD SCHEDULE.

YARDS.	Yard-mast'r	Night Yard-mast'r	Fore-men.	Yard-men.
San Francisco	$95 00	$100 00	$80 00	$75 00
West Oakland	95 00	100 00	80 00	75 00
Port Costa	95 00	100 00	80 00	75 00
Tracy	95 00	100 00	80 00	75 00
Lathrop	95 00	100 00	80 00	75 00
Stockton	95 00			75 00
Sacramento			80 00	75 00
Rocklin		90 00	85 00	75 00
Truckee		100 00	100 00	80 00
Red Bluff	95 00			75 00
Wadsworth	100 00			80 00
Winnemucca and Carlin		90 00		80 00
Reno	90 00			75 00
Terrace	100 00	90 00		80 00
Fresno	95 00	90 00		75 00
Bakersfield	95 00	100 00		80 00
Mojave	100 00	100 00		80 00
Los Angeles			85 00	75 00
Yuma		90 00		80 00
Tucson	105 00	95 00		80 00
East Portland	95 00			75 00
Salem*	90 00			· 75 00
San Jose (C. D.)	90 00			75 00
Alameda Point	95 00	†80 00		‡75 00
San Jose§	90 00			‡75 00

*Only switchman with this engine. †Assistant Yardmaster. ‡Brakemen. §This crew makes run to Glenwood, and helps other trains up the hill when necessary. Day yardmen in Sacramento will be allowed every second Sunday, and night yardmen will have every third Sunday night, off duty without deduction of wages. If yardmen are called on, unexpectedly, on the days they are laying off, they are expected to respond, and will be paid for that day's work over and above what constitutes a month's work. San Francisco, West Oakland, Port Costa, Tracy, Lathrop, Sacramento and Los Angeles yards, ten hours will constitute a day's work; any excess to be paid pro rata.

GENERAL RULES.

1. Main line Baggagemen to be paid $80 per month. Local Baggagemen, $75 per month; over 5,500 miles, $80.

2. Where mileage is not given in schedules it is understood that trainmen will do the same work as heretofore for the wages given; where mileage is stated, all excess mileage to be paid pro rata.

3. Where a Brakeman acts in the capacity of both Brakeman and Baggagemaster, and receives compensation from Wells, Fargo & Co., this is a privilege we accord him, as it does not in any way interfere with the duties devolving upon him in the train service. We will make arrangements of this kind as they may arise, from time to time, on the various divisions.

4. Division Superintendents will make such regulations in relation to yard service as they may deem necessary, in defining the work to be performed, as between trainmen and yardmen.

5. Trainmen will be called for duty at division terminals, where Callers are maintained, within the limits prescribed by the Division Superintendent, by the regular Caller, one hour, as nearly as practicable, before time of starting trains. The Caller will be provided with a book, giving names of crews and numbers of trains for which crews are wanted, in which trainmen must sign their names and enter the time of call. The working time of all trains will be computed from the time crews are ordered out.

6. As far as practicable trains scheduled over the different divisions during daylight will do the way work on their respective divisions. The Division Superintendent is expected to use his best judgment in these cases.

7. Trainmen running snow plows, flangers, pile drivers, construction trains and all other work trains, six hours or less will constitute half a day's work; over six hours and under twelve hours a day's work, at regular rates of pay. Any excess over twelve hours to be paid pro rata. In computing overtime, fractions less than half an hour will not be counted; thirty minutes or more will be counted as one hour.

8. All freight train crews detained on the road, or at terminals, on scheduled trains, will be paid overtime as follows: For any delay less than two hours (late of carded time), nothing; for two hours or more, payment according to the rate of 30 cents and 20 cents per hour, for Conductors and Brakemen, respectively. Overtime for regular freight trains to be calculated on the basis of the card time of the train; for extra freights, the longest schedule in the direction going shall be the basis for calculating overtime under this rule.

9. When trainmen are required to remain on duty over thirty minutes with their trains, after arrival at main line terminals, overtime will be paid at the rate of 30 cents and 20 cents per hour for Conductors and Brakemen, respectively.

10. Freight train crews will be allowed regular freight train rates for handling passenger trains or passenger equipment, and regular freight Conductors, or extra Conductors who are not extra passenger Conductors, shall receive for passenger service not less than they would have earned had they remained in freight service.

11. When freight train crews are held waiting for stock cars to be cleaned, loaded or unloaded, they shall receive overtime at the rate of 30 cents and 20 cents per hour for Conductors and Brakemen, respectively, provided that crews so held arrive at terminals two hours or more late of card time; east of Los Angeles, regardless of card time.

12. When a train is abandoned for which a crew has been called, the crew shall be paid 30 cents for Conductors and 20 cents for Brakemen, per hour, for all time over one hour that the crew may be held between the time of calling and notice of abandonment of such train.

13. For turn arounds, made in six hours or less, crews will be allowed half day; for over six and less than twelve hours, full day; for all time over twelve hours, Conductors 30 cents and Brakemen 20 cents per hour. For a turn around in less than six hours crews shall not lose their turn out.

14. Crews working fractional parts of a month will receive pro rata of the guarantee, if they fail to make stipulated number of miles. Individuals working fractions of a month will be paid for the actual mileage made.

15. Trainmen dead-heading over the road on passenger or freight will be allowed two-thirds mileage. When going over the road with caboose and an engine, full time.

16. When trainmen are held waiting for their own crews, after having been taken off regular runs and sent out on special or other runs, they will be paid full compensation for such time as they are so held.

17. Trainmen will be notified, and the reasons given, when time is not allowed as per trip report.

18. Trainmen will not be required to coal engines at terminal points, excepting on short branch lines or runs where the mileage is not excessive and the work is light. In cases of emergency trainmen will coal engines between terminal points and at regular intermediate coaling stations.

19. When a trainman has served sixteen consecutive hours on duty, at his request he may have at least eight hours rest; excepting in cases of emergency, such as wrecks, washouts, etc.

20. Crews unassigned to regular runs shall run first in first out.

21. In ordering freight crews for dead-heading on any freight train, the first crew will run the train, the next crew will dead-head and will be the first out, ahead of accompanying crew, at other terminal.

22. When a trainman is detailed to attend court as a witness in behalf of the Company he will be paid for such service at the same rate of pay, for actual time absent from duty, as he would have received if regularly employed; he will also be allowed his actual living expenses while away from home.

23. All trainmen will be regarded as in the line of promotion, advancement depending upon the faithful performance of duty and capacity for increased responsibility. The question of promotion shall be understood to apply to employes working in the same department and same branch of service.

24. When a trainman believes he has been unjustly treated, he shall have the right to present his case personally to the Division Superintendent, with such evidence in his favor as he may have to offer. It will be the duty of the Superintendent to investigate the matter thoroughly without unnecessary delay, and his decision will be given to the trainman. Should the latter wish to appeal to higher authority, the Superintendent will give such trainman his decision in writing (excepting in cases involving drunkenness, or fraudulent or dishonest action), which the trainman may present, with his own written statement of his case, to the General or the Assistant General Superintendent.

25. Where a trainman is taken from his run for an investigation for an alleged offense, he shall, if found innocent, be paid for time lost, no punishment to be fixed without a thorough investigation; ordinarily said investigation to be held within five days from the date of removal from service.

26. Clearance cards will be given to all deserving employes leaving the services of the Company.

27. The Company will continue the practice of blacklisting on its own lines, when employes have been discharged for good and sufficient cause, such as dishonesty, criminal carelessness, insubordination, drunkenness, violation of rules whereby the Company's property is endangered or destroyed, and offenses of like character. This blacklist is distributed only over our own lines, purely as a matter of protection to the interests of

154 TAMPICO ROUTE.—TERM. R. R. ASS'N OF ST. L.—T. C. R'Y.—T.; A. A. & N. M. R'Y.

this Company, which practice we believe inures to the advantage of all deserving trainmen. It is not our purpose to blacklist a trainman dismissed for a minor offense, nor because of incompetency for the particular work in which he may be engaged, as he may be very useful in some other capacity.

28. Trainmen will be disciplined by suspension or discharge, as each case may seem to justify.

29. Trainmen leaving the service will be paid at the earliest practicable moment.

30. Letters of recommendation will be filed with personal records of trainmen, and will be returned upon application when they leave the service.

31. When trainmen are transferred from one point to another for convenience of the service, their families and household effects will be transported free.

32. If, in the judgment of a Division Superintendent, a Conductor can show good cause (in writing) for the removal of a Brakeman working with him, it will be done.
Accepted for Order Railway Conductors: J. A. FILLMORE,
  E. E. CLARK, G. C. C.   General Superintendent.
Accepted for Brotherhood of Railroad Trainmen:
  S. E. WILKINSON, G. M.   Approved: A. N. TOWNE,
  June 1, 1892.   Second Vice President and General Manager.

TAMPICO ROUTE.—COMPANYIA DEL FERROCARRIL DE MONTEREY AL GOLFO MEXICANO.

Passenger service, independent of mileage: Conductors, $130 per month; Brakemen, $50. Freight service, 160 kilometers, equal to 100 miles run, is considered a day's work: Conductors, $130 per month; Brakemen, $70. Yard service, graded according to importance of the yard: Yardmasters, $95 to $125 per month; Switchmen, $70, $75 and $80. Twelve hours are considered a day's work on work trains, and sixteen kilometers, or ten miles run, equals an additional hour's service.   C. A. MERRIAM,
  May 14, 1892.   General Superintendent.

TERMINAL RAILROAD ASSOCIATION OF ST. LOUIS.

Yard Conductors, day, $70; night, $75; Helpers, day, $65; night, $70 per month, for the actual number of working days. Extra for Sundays, at a proportionate rate.
  May 13, 1892.   J. Q. VAN WINKLE,
                                                  General Superintendent.

TEXAS CENTRAL RAILWAY.

Passenger: Conductors, $100 per month; Brakemen, $60; Baggagemen, $65; Porters, $35. Local freight: Conductors, $100 per month and 3 cents per mile for all over 3,000 miles; Brakemen, $65 and 2 cents per mile. Through freight: Conductors, $90 per month and 3 cents per mile for all over 3,000 miles; Brakemen, $60 and 2 cents per mile. Work train: Conductors, $90 per month and 3 cents per mile for all over 3,000 miles; Brakemen, $60 and 2 cents per mile. Yardmaster, $90 per month and 27 cents per hour for overtime; yard Brakemen, $60 and 20 cents per hour.
  May 13, 1892.   CHARLES HAMILTON,
                                                            General Manager.

TOLEDO, ANN ARBOR & NORTH MICHIGAN RAILWAY COMPANY.

SCHEDULE.

CLASS OF SERVICE.	Engineers.	Firemen.	Conductors.	Brakemen
Passenger, per mile*	$0 023	$0 012	$0 017	$45 00
Freight, per mile	036	019	028	01
Work train, per day	3 00	1 75	65 00†	45 (0
Switching, per day (all points except Manhattan and Ann Arbor)	2 50	1 50	2 25	1 75
Switching, per day (Manhattan)	2 50	1 50	2 60	2 15
Switching, per day (Ann Arbor)	2 50	1 50	2 00	1 85
Wreck train, per day	3 00	1 75	2 25	1 85
Snow plow, per day	4 00	2 25	2 75	2 00

*Passenger Engineers, southern division, 2.6 cents per mile; Firemen, 1.3 cents.   †Per month.

Overtime will be allowed for all time on the road after fourteen hours at the following rates: Engineers, 30 cents per hour; Firemen, 15 cents; Conductors, 25 cents; Brakemen, 15 cents; no fraction of one-half hour will be counted. Half pay will be allowed employes attending law suits, or Company's interests, which take them from regular work. One-half pay will be allowed for dead-heading on order of the heads of the mechanical or transportation departments. Local freight trains on first division, when run by two crews, will be paid for 111 miles per day and overtime after fourteen hours. When three crews, Conductors will be paid $75 per month; Brakemen, $50; no overtime, each trip being credited at one and one-half days. Mileage basis: Toledo to Owosso, 111 miles; Owosso to Clare, 105 miles, and Clare to Copemish, 105 miles.
March 1, 1892.
H. W. ASHLEY,
General Manager.

TOLEDO & OHIO CENTRAL RAILROAD COMPANY.

PASSENGER SERVICE.

RUNS.	Miles	Enginemen, per trip	Firemen, per trip	Conduct'rs, per month	Brakemen, per month	Bagg'men, per month
Toledo and Columbus	176	$5 00	$2 75	$100 00	$50 00	$60 00
Toledo and Corning	184	5 25	2 89			
Bucyrus to Toledo and return	138	3 75	2 06			
Bucyrus and Corning	115	3 50	1 92			
Bucyrus and Columbus	107	3 50	1 92			
Bucyrus and Athens	137	3 75	2 06			
Corning to Columbus and return	130	3 75	2 06			
Columbus to Athens and return	174	5 00	2 75			

No extra pay allowed for mixed trains.

FREIGHT SERVICE.

RUNS.	Miles	Enginemen	Firemen	Conductors	Brakemen	Time for run, h'rs
Bucyrus and Toledo, through	69	$3 25	$1 79	$2 25	$1 50	
Bucyrus and Toledo, local	69	4 00	2 20	3 33½	2 00	
Bucyrus and Corning, through	115	4 00	2 20	3 25	2 10	
Bucyrus and Corning, local	115	5 00	2 75	3 33½	2 00	
Bucyrus and Thurston, local	78	4 00	2 20	3 33½	2 00	
Corning and Columbus, through	65	3 25	1 79	2 25	1 50	6½
Corning and Columbus, local	65	4 00	2 20	3 33½	2 00	
Corning and Alum Creek, through	60	3 00	1 65	2 05	1 35	6
Corning to Alum Creek and return, through	120	6 00	3 30	4 10	2 70	12
Bucyrus to Fostoria and return, through	70	3 25	1 79	2 25	1 50	8
Corning to Thurston and return, through	156	6 50	3 58	4 50	3 00	
Corning to New Lexington and return, with helper	74	3 25	1 79	2 25	1 50	8
South of Corning, Buckingham and short run				1 50	1 00	
South of Corning, local freight		3 05	2 00	2 00	2 00	12
Construction, gravel, work or wreck train, without Cond'r				80 00*		12
Construction, gravel, work or wreck train, with Conductor		4 50	2 47			12
Helping engine, Johnstown hill		3 50	1 92	3 25	2 10	12
Switching engine, all yards		3 00	1 65			12
Helping engine, Corning, 1 trip, if not more than 4 hours		3 00	1 65			12
Helping engine, Corning, 3 trips, inside of 12 hours		1 16	64			
Foremen on local		3 50	1 92			
Rates of overtime, per hour		35	19¼	28	2 20	
					18	

*Per month.

Enginemen: Enginemen running light over road with light engines or with cabooses to be paid same as through freight. Crews or any part of crews dead-heading with caboose, on freight or passenger trains, will be allowed half time of through freight. Enginemen dead-heading over road on Company's business shall receive one-half pay of through freight. Enginemen suspended shall have time of suspension stated, and if on subsequent investigation found not guilty, shall be paid one-half wages they would have earned during time of suspension. The right is granted to select other Enginemen to assist in defense when suspensions or dismissals are made. No time to be allowed when men are taken off for investigation, but investigations to be made without unnecessary delay. Through freight crews will not be run south of Corning, except in cases of emergency. South end crews will not be run to Thurston, except in cases of emergency. The train first in shall be first out. All trainmen will be paid full time when absent from their duties attending court, when summoned by Company, and expenses when absent from home. Overtime to be allowed when trains are more than one hour later than schedule time, or number of hours fixed for trip, on all through freight trains: over one hour and not more than one and one-half late, overtime to be allowed one hour; more than one and one-half hours late and not more than two and one-half hours late, overtime to be allowed two hours, and so on. Overtime to be allowed on local freight trains when more than three hours late on same basis as through freight trains, except that when three crews are running between Bucyrus and Corning, no overtime will be allowed. The time on extras to be taken from first through freight schedule running ahead of the extra. Time to be computed from the time men are called to leave, until relieved at the end of trip or engine delivered on track designated. No time to be deducted from overtime actually made. Overtime to be paid monthly, same as schedule pay. Overtime blanks will be furnished all departments. Employes shall be regarded in the line of promotion, dependent upon the faithful discharge of duties, capacity for increased responsibility and length of service. When an Engineman is called for an extra or regular train, at time as notified, and train is annulled, he will be allowed $1. When the presence of an Engineman in the freight service is required at a telegraph office or a register station, the Fireman (if he has fired one year) be allowed to move the engine, and be held responsible for such movement as is required to save delays, but no switching to be done by Firemen. On Bucyrus and Thurston turn through freight, two hours will be allowed for switching at Thurston, disposing of any making up their train, on overtime basis. No further switching to be required, except in cases of emergency. Wreck trains to have a Conductor if one can be reached without delay; if not, will be run with orders to Engineman. On Alum Creek and Columbus run, if crew makes more than one trip on Sunday or goes east of Alum Creek, one day will be allowed in addition to monthly pay; if only one trip to Alum Creek, no extra time allowed. On local south of Corning, one round trip, one-half day, time six hours; two round trips, one day. On Buckingham run, same as local south of Corning. On short runs south of Corning, one round trip allowed one-half day. On short runs south of Corning, two round trips allowed one day (if only two trips). On short runs south of Corning, three round trips allowed one day (full day, twelve hours). Time allowed for Sunday work for all trains south of Corning, same basis as above. Local freight, Thurston to Bucyrus, time to be computed from time work begins making up train until relieved at end of trip.

Firemen: Wages of Firemen to be 55 per cent. of Enginemen's scale of wages. Overtime to be allowed on same basis as Enginemen. No succeeding time table to exceed the average time of Schedule No. 36.

Conductors and Brakemen: Through freight crews will not be run south of Corning, except in cases of emergency. South end crews will not be run to Thurston, except in cases of emergency. The first train in shall be first out. Employes shall be regarded in the line of promotion, dependent upon the faithful discharge of duties, capacity for increased responsibility and length of service. Trainmen suspended shall have time of suspension stated, and if, on subsequent investigation, found not guilty, shall be paid one-half wages they would have earned during time of suspension. The right is granted to select other trainmen to assist in defense, when suspensions or dismissals are made, No time to be allowed when men are taken off for investigation, but investigations to be made without unnecessary delay. Crews or any part of crews deadheading with caboose, on freight or passenger trains, will be allowed half time of through freight. When dead-heading on freight, will stand first out ahead of crew dead-headed with. Through freight pay will be allowed for running with engine and caboose. All trainmen will be paid full time when absent from their duties attending court, when summoned by Company, and expenses when absent from home. Overtime blanks will be furnished all departments. Overtime to be paid monthly, same as schedule pay. When crews are taken off on account of light business, Conductors best qualified under our rules shall be given preference in places to be filled, and the oldest Brakemen the next places to be filled in line of promotion, same as Conductor. Wreck trains to have a Conductor, if one can be reached without delay, if not, will be run with orders to Enginemen. No time to be deducted from overtime actually made. On Bucyrus and Thurston turn through freight, two hours will be allowed for switching at Thurston, disposing of any making up their train, on overtime basis. No further switching to be required, except in cases of emergency. The time on extras to be taken from first through freight schedule running ahead of the extra. On Alum Creek and Columbus run, if crew makes more than one trip on Sunday or goes east of Alum Creek, one day will be allowed in addition to monthly pay; if only one trip to Alum Creek, no extra time allowed. On local south of Corning, one round trip, one-half day, time six hours; two round trips, one day. On Buckingham run, same as local south of

Corning: On short runs south of Corning, one round trip allowed one-half day. On short runs south of Corning, two round trips allowed one day (if only two trips). On short runs south of Corning, three round trips allowed one day (full day, twelve hours). Time allowed for Sunday work for all trains south of Corning, same basis as above. On local freight, four Brakemen; other freight trains, three Brakemen. Overtime to be allowed when trains are more than one hour later than schedule time or number of hours fixed for trip, on all through freight trains. Over one hour and not more than one and one-half hours late, overtime to be allowed one hour. More than one and one-half hours late and not more than two and one-half hours late, overtime to be allowed two hours, and so on. When three crews are runing on local freight between Bucyrus and Corning, six trips will be allowed for four trips. Overtime to be allowed on local freight trains when more than three hours late on same basis as through freight trains, except when three crews are running between Bucyrus and Corning no overtime will be allowed. Time to be computed from the time men are called to leave until relieved at the end of trip. Local freight, Thurston to Bucyrus, time to be computed from time work begins making up train until relieved at end of trip. When Conductors and Brakemen, called for extra or regular train at time as notified, and train is annulled, Conductors will be allowed 75 cents and Brakemen 50 cents. No succeeding time table to exceed the average time of Schedule No. 36. T. M. PEELAR,
For Order of Railway Conductors: General Superintendent.
W. B. BAYLOR, W. C. BOYLE. L. E. WHARTON, JAMES SLATTERY.
For Brotherhood of Locomotive Firemen:
W. C. BRUCE. CHARLES COLLINS, J. H. BAUR, ED. M'GUIRE, JOE VETTA, T. QUILTER, JAMES KINNEY.
For Brotherhood of Railroad Trainmen:
JAMES CONNEL. J. W. MONTGOMERY, G. H. CARSEY, W. B. RUSSELL, M. H. SULLIVAN.
November 1, 1891.

TOLEDO, PEORIA & WESTERN RAILWAY.

Passenger: Conductors, $100 per month; Brakemen, $45; Baggagemen, $50; average monthly mileage, Conductors and Brakemen, 4,866 miles, Baggagemen, 6,271 miles. Mixed: Conductors, $90 per month; Brakemen, $55; Baggagemen, $55; average monthly mileage, 3,954 miles. Through freight: Conductors, 3 cents per mile; Brakemen, 2 cents; average monthly mileage, 2,975 miles. Local freight, east end: Conductors, $4.85 per single trip; Brakemen, $3.50; average four single trips per week. Local freight, west end: Couductors, $4.35 per single trip; Brakemen, $2.90; average four single trips per week. No Switchmen or yardmen.
May 12, 1892. E. N. ARMSTRONG,
General Superintendent.

TOLEDO, ST. LOUIS & KANSAS CITY RAILROAD COMPANY.

TRAINMEN AND YARDMEN.

1. Through passenger train Conductors shall receive $100 per month of twenty-six working days. Local passenger train Conductors shall receive $90 per month of twenty-six working days. Through passenger train Brakemen shall receive $50 per month of twenty-six working days. Local passenger train Brakemen shall receive $47.50 per month of twenty-six working days. Conductors and Brakemen in passenger train service shall be permitted to purchase their uniforms where they can be obtained the cheapest, and comply with the regulation of the Company. Summer suits shall be ready by the first day of May, winter suits the fifteenth day of October. Caps, summer and winter, to correspond with the suits.
2. Through freight train Conductors shall receive 3 cents per mile; Brakemen, 2 cents. Local freight train Conductors shall receive $90 per month; Brakemen, $62.50. Local freight Conductors and Brakemen shall receive full pay for all legal holidays, and shall be paid for doubling hills on same basis as through freight trains.
3. Conductors on work, wreck or circus trains shall receive $3 per day; Brakemen, $2; twelve hours or less shall constitute one day. Through freight crews hauling material for construction or maintenance of way shall receive through freight mileage for actual miles made, and shall receive actual hours at overtime rates while loading or unloading. Crews doing such work shall receive not less than one day.
4. Yardmen at Delphos, Frankfort and Charleston shall be paid as follows: Yardmasters, day, $75 per month; night, $70. Foremen, day or night, $2.10 per day. Helpers, day or night, $2 per day. Yard crews not to work short handed; they shall be

allowed one hour each day for meals, and one Sunday off duty e
hours to constitute one day's work. Yard crews at Charleston sha
master, Foreman and two Helpers. Yard crews at Frankfort and l
Yardmaster, Foreman and one Helper. Day Yardmaster shall be
ter, and yard employes shall be subject to his orders.

5. *Overtime:* Conductors and Brakemen running and braking
and passenger trains will receive 30 and 20 cents per hour, resp
layed time, as follows: After train is one hour and thirty-five n
current time tables eighteen and nineteen—and less than two h
minutes late, one hour shall be allowed; when two hours and thir
and less than three hours and thirty-five minutes late, two hours sl
so on. Between Toledo and Delphos the running time must be te
time will be paid. On local freight train runs of less than 100 mi:
paid for all time used in making trip in excess of twelve hours. O
runs of over 100 miles overtime will be paid for all time used in
excess of that time necessary to complete the trip at an average
per hour; except that between Frankfort and Marion thirteen he
and that between Frankfort and Charleston thirteen hours and th
allowed. Fractions of an hour of less than thirty minutes will n
tions of an hour over thirty minutes will be counted a full hour. W
allowed as per time slip, Conductors shall be notified in writing.
crews on local freight trains between Toledo and Delphos, two cre
and Marion, one crew between Marion and Frankfort, three crew
and Charleston, two crews between Charleston and New Douglass a:
New Douglass and East St. Louis. There shall be three Brakemer
trains. Time of turn around locals to be computed from leavin,
and East St. Louis.

6. All crews running light shall receive through freight rate
extra, or special passenger train shall be sent over the road with
Engineer. A Pilot shall be paid same as freight Conductor.

7. Conductors and Brakemen dead-heading on passenger tra
business, shall receive one-half through freight rates for actual mi
dead-heading is required, the first crew shall dead-head and shall s
of the crew with which they dead-head, on arrival at terminal.

8. When attending court on Company's business Conductors
day and Brakemen $2, and both Conductor and Brakeman shall rec
expenses, the Company to provide transportation.

9. Crews doubling Cayuga hill shall receive twenty miles; all
mileage, provided no double shall count less than ten miles.

10. When Conductors are needed, one experienced Conductor
one may be promoted from the Brakemen, alternately, when prac
the foregoing shall be construed so as to prevent the hiring of an
turn, that may be at the time employed as Brakeman. The rights
commence on the day of their promotion and they shall have t
which their age as Conductors entitle them, provided they ar
morally fitted for it. The rights of a Brakeman shall commence
gaged, and his line of promotion shall be considered so far as his a

11. The Toledo division shall be divided into two districts
trains, Toledo to Delphos to constitute one district, and crews
miles for each trip over same. Delphos to Frankfort to constit
which through freight train crews shall be allowed actual mileage

12. All mileage made, less than 100 miles, shall be consider
miles, or more, actual mileage will be paid.

13. For a train from Delphos to Continental and return crew
miles, and actual time, at overtime rates, shall be paid for a
switching at Continental. Local crews between Charleston and N
paid two hours each day, at overtime rates, for time consumed
Douglass, one hour for each crew per day.

14. The number of through freight crews shall be kept down s
make less than 3,000 miles per month.

15. If for any cause a Conductor is unable to take crew. an e:
be furnished, so that Brakemen shall lose no time. When Condu
pilot freight engines, the last freight Conductor in shall be cal
extra Conductor available.

16. When Conductors and Brakemen are called and report i
cause the train is annulled, they shall be paid at overtime rates f
on duty, and shall stand first out. Conductors and Brakemen sh:
respective divisions and districts.

17. At all terminal stations yardmen shall take charge of trains immediately on rrival, and no switching shall be done by train crews where switch engines are kept. .ll trains shall be made up in station order, and cars equipped with air shall be witched next to engine by yardmen. A caboose track shall be provided at terminal oints, and no switching shall be done with cabooses.

18. No Conductor or Brakeman shall be called more than one hour and fifteen ιinutes nor less than fifty minutes before leaving time of train they are called for. 'he Company shall provide a Caller who shall have a book in which the Conductors nd Brakemen must register; time to begin when called to leave the yard, and the asis for authority for computing overtime shall be the Caller's book and the register t the other end of the division or district, and there shall be a register at East t. Louis.

19. There shall be a Gâteman at railroad crossing at Marion. Employes who are ιaimed while in the Company's service shall have preference for positions of gate ttendants.

20. Cars disabled in trains shall be repaired or chained up by the train crew and aken through to destination or division stations, when possible and safe to do so and : can be done without unreasonable delay. It shall be the duty of Car Inspectors to ze that the air brakes on passenger trains are in good working order and that all air ose is coupled. Cabooses on local freight trains shall be cleaned at Charleston, 'rankfort, Delphos and East St. Louis.

21. In case any difference of opinion as to the construction of this agreement hall arise between the Conductors, Brakemen, Switchmen and Yardmasters and the ivision officers, a written statement of the question at issue must be submitted by the onductors, Brakemen, Switchmen and Yardmasters to the President or General Man- ger, through the Superintendent, for his consideration and adjustment.

22. No Conductor or Brakeman shall be discharged nor suspended upon any charge hatever, without first having a fair and impartial hearing within five days of time aken off, at which time he shall have the right to have present any other Conductor r Brakeman of his choice, with the Trainmaster, who shall hear the evidence of all he witnesses. question and cross-question them upon any and all points he may desire ι connection with the case; the witnesses called by the defendant to be subject also o cross-examination. In case the decision rendered by the examining board is not ound to be satisfactory, an appeal may be taken from the local to the general officers. ι case a final decision is not given within five days after presenting such an appeal, ιay of Conductor or Brakeman shall begin and continue, until a decision is made, for lass of train on which he was running or braking at the time of offense.

23. This agreement to supersede all previous schedules or arrangements. No part f this agreement shall be repealed or annulled without the mutual consent of all par- es herein named.

24. No Conductor, Brakeman, Switchman or Yardmaster shall be censured or dis- ιarged for acting on this or any other committee.

ENGINEERS AND FIREMEN.

1. All passenger Engineers, 3 3-10 cents per mile; all passenger Firemen 55 per ent of Engineers' pay; 100 miles or less to constitute 100 miles; over 100 miles, same te per mile.

2. All Engineers running through freight, 4 cents per mile; all Firemen firing rough freight engines, 2 2-10 cents per mile; 100 miles or less to constitute 100 miles; l over 100 miles, same rate per mile.

3. Engineers running way freight engines, 4¾ cents per mile; Firemen firing way eight engines, 2 7-10 cents per mile; 100 miles or less to constitute 100 miles; all over 0 miles, same rate per mile.

4. All work train Engineers, $3.50 per day; all work train Firemen, $2 per day; velve hours or less to constitute a day's work; all over twelve hours; 30 cents per ur for Engineers and 18 cents per hour for Firemen.

5. Switch Engineers, $2.50 per day; switch engine Firemen, $1.60 per day, for velve hours or less, one hour to be allowed for dinner; over twelve hours, Engineers cents per hour, Firemen 15 cents per hour. Switch Engineers at East St. Louis to be lowed $2.90 per day, Firemen $1.80 per day.

6. When Engineers and Firemen are required to dead-head over any division of e road by order of their superior officer, on Company business, Engineers shall receive cents per mile and Firemen 1½ cents per mile; except when attending court Engin- rs shall receive $3.50 per day and $1 per day for board, Firemen $2 per day and $1 per y for board.

7. Engineers of helping engines, $3.50 per day; Firemen of helping engines, $2 per y; twelve hours or less to constitute one day; all over twelve hours, Engineers 30

cents per hour, Firemen 18 cents per hour. Crews doubling Cayuga hill shall receive twenty miles, all other places actual mileage; provided no double shall count less than ten miles.

8. Engineers and Firemen to be assigned regular divisions and so remain and run first in and first out upon all trains, except local trains and passenger trains.

9. The right to regular engine runs and promotions will be governed by merit, ability and seniority, considered by examining board; everything being equal, Engineers and Firemen serving the longest in road service on his division will have the preference.

10. In case an Engineer or Fireman has been on the road fifteen hours he will not be required to go out without eight hours' rest, unless he considers himself competent to do so; the arriving time to be taken from the round house register, instead of Conductors' register or train sheet.

11. Engineers and Firemen not to be called for duty until an hour before their train is ready to leave, the Caller to have a book to register their names and time when called. Pay of Engineers and Firemen to begin one hour after they have signed the Caller's book, unless they go on duty sooner, and continue up to time on Engineers register at end of run. In case Engineers and Firemen are called for a train and the train afterward annulled, Engineers to receive 30 cents per hour and Firemen 20 cents per hour for time on duty, and stand first out. Engineers and Firemen shall be called for all trains.

12. Hostlers to be promoted from the rank of Firemen who have been longest in road service, and to receive $2.12½ per day; twelve hours or less, one day or night.

13. Engineers and Firemen running and firing through freight and passenger engines will receive 35 and 20 cents per hour, respectively, for delayed time as follows: After train is one hour and thirty-five minutes late, as per current time tables 18 and 19, and less than two hours and thirty-five minutes late, one hour shall be allowed. When two hours and thirty-five minutes late and less than three hours and thirty-five minutes late, two hours shall be allowed, and so on. Between Toledo and Delphos the running time must be ten hours before overtime will be paid. On local freight train runs of less than 100 miles, overtime will be paid for all time used in making trip in excess of twelve hours. On local freight train runs of over 100 miles, overtime will be allowed for all time used in making any trip in excess of that time necessary to complete the trip at an average speed of nine miles per hour; except that between Frankfort and Marion thirteen hours will be allowed, and that between Frankfort and Charleston thirteen hours and thirty minutes will be allowed. Fractions of an hour less than thirty minutes will not be counted; fractions of an hour over thirty minutes will be counted a full hour.

14. Engineers and Firemen shall receive the same that other roads pay their Engineers and Firemen for running over St. Louis bridge.

15. Engineers and Firemen on gravel trains to receive: Engineers 4 cents, Firemen 2 2-10 cents per mile, while running, and Engineers 30 cents, and Firemen 18 cents per hour while loading and unloading.

16. Engineers and Firemen pulling local and through freight will not be required to do switching where switch engines are employed.

17. That all freight engines will be rated as to number of cars they are able to haul, tonnage considered.

18. That when an Engineer or Fireman is wanted on passenger the oldest freight Engineer or Fireman available to be taken, and first extra man on road to have regular freight engine.

19. Fifty per cent. of Engineers to be hired and 50 per cent. of Firemen to be promoted, hiring and promoting alternately, when practicable.

20. There shall be a man at all terminal stations to inspect engines and tighten up loose bolts and nuts, and report other work that is necessary; the Fireman will not be required to clean fires, paint fire boxes, bore out flues, clean out arches, clean brass in or out of cab, paint or black front of engines, or clean engines below running board.

21. No more extra Engineers and Firemen will be assigned than are necessary to move traffic with promptness and dispatch.

22. No Engineer or Fireman running or firing a regular engine, either on passenger or freight, will be allowed to exchange the old engine for a new one, but the old extra man will have the new engine, except when the new engine goes on passenger or local freight regularly, then the Master Mechanic will use his own discretion.

23. When a freight engine is required to haul passenger or local freight for a few trips, freight Engineers or Firemen running said engines will run his own instead of being taken off and passenger or local Engineers and Firemen put on said engine.

24. All coal shall be cracked before being put on engine tenders at all coaling stations, and Company to furnish cushions for all engines.

25. When disputes arise between Engineers and Firemen they are both to have a fair and impartial trial, as per Article 31, and the one at fault shall suffer the consequences. Switch engine Firemen will have no rights over road Firemen, and when leaving switch engine to go on road he shall go on extra list as a new man.

26. Firemen that have been promoted to the position of Engineer shall at all times have the preference of regular engines over Engineers that have been hired since their promotion. In case it is necessary for Firemen to watch engines, they shall receive $1.60 for twelve hours or less.

27. All errors made in computing time of Engineers and Firemen shall be properly corrected and any amount of pay omitted in any one month shall be paid them on the following month of such omission.

28. All officers and employes shall observe strict courtesy of manner of intercourse with each other. That on the adoption of this schedule it shall be printed, that each employe interested may have a copy of the same. All previous schedules shall be considered void.

29. No Engineer or Fireman shall be discharged or suspended upon any charge whatever without first having a fair and impartial hearing within five days from the time taken off at which they shall have the right to have present any other Engineer or Fireman of his choice with the Master Mechanic and the Train Master, who shall hear all the evidence, all the witnesses, question and cross question them upon any and all points he may desire in connection with the case, the witnesses called by the defendant to be subject also to cross examination. In case the decision rendered by the examining board is not found to be satisfactory an appeal may be taken from the local to the general officers. In case a final decision is not given within five days after presenting such an appeal, the pay of Engineers and Firemen shall begin and continue until a decision is made per class of train running or firing at time of offense.

30. For Continental turn-round fifty miles will be allowed and overtime switching.

31. That Hostlers be placed at Marion and New Douglass who are capable to turn engines and do switching.

32. Local freight between Toledo and Delphos to pay the same rate as west of Delphos.

33. That one hundred and fifty miles will be allowed for a round trip on passenger between Toledo and Delphos.

34. It is further agreed that any Engineer or Fireman who shall serve on this or any other committee shall not in any manner prejudice his standing with the officials of this Company.

DISPATCHERS AND OPERATORS.

1. No Train Dispatcher, Agent and Operator, or Operator shall be suspended or dismissed from the Company's service without just cause. Intoxication or like misdemeanors shall be considered just causes for suspension or dismissal. In case of suspension or dismissal other than for causes above stated, if any employe herein named thinks his sentence unjust he shall have the right within five days to refer his case by written statement to the proper local officer. Within five days of the receipt of his statement his case shall have a thorough investigation by the proper officer. If the decision rendered by local officers is not satisfactory, an appeal can be made to the Superintendent. In case any suspension or dismissal is found to be unjust, Train Dispatcher, Agent and Operator, or Operator shall be reinstated and paid for all time lost at a rate of pay received previous to such suspension or dismissal. All cases appealed from local to general officers must be first submitted in writing within thirty days from the date of such decision, stating why the decision as rendered is in error. No case will be considered after thirty days have elapsed. No Train Despatcher, Agent and Operator or Operator shall be censured or dismissed for acting on this or any other committee.

2. Dispatchers, Agents and Operators or Operators will be promoted according to seniority, other considerations being satisfactory, and they shall have choice of positions accordingly. Agents and Operators, or Operators desiring promotion and being in line of promotion by right of seniority, can request and will be allowed an examination by Superintendent, Chief Dispatcher, Train Dispatcher or Train Master. Line of promotion will be from night Operator to day Operator, day Operator, or Agent and

Operator to Agent and Operator and third trick Dispatcher, third trick Dispatcher t second trick Dispatcher, second trick Dispatcher to first trick Dispatcher. On Agent and Operator, or day Operator, shall be promoted to Dispatcher alternatel with the hiring of one Dispatcher, provided nothing in this article is construed a abridging the right of the Company to hire any number of Dispatchers necessary fo the good of the service, should no Agent and Operator or day Operator be able to pas proper examination for promotion to third trick Dispatcher. Any Dispatcher, Agen and Operator, or Operator accepting any situation other than stated herein shall for feit his rights for time off telegraph service.

3. The compensation of the train Dispatcher, Agents and Operators or Operator shall be as follows: Dispatchers shall receive $100 per calendar month, eight hour and time to complete transfer to constitute a day's work. Agents and Operators, o Operators shall receive an advance of $7.50 per calendar month over salary receive for December, 1892, provided that no Agent and Operator or Operator shall receiv less than $40 per calendar month. The salary of Agents at stations where day Opera tors are employed shall exceed that of such day Operator by not less than $5. Twelv hours shall constitute one day's work, which shall include one hour a day for meal Agents and Operators and day Operators shall be relieved of Sunday work as far a possible. Present rates of pay are based upon the total amounts Agents and Operator receive from stated salary and commission. The Company reserves the right to abol ish the payment of commissions at any time. If done it will make the sum of the tota salary equal to that paid under this schedule.

4. Despatchers, Agents and Operators and Operators shall receive pay for over time as follows: Despatchers, 40 cents an hour. Agents and Operators and Operator 15 cents per hour. Twenty-nine minutes will not be counted. Thirty minutes and les than sixty minutes will be counted an hour. Agents and Operators, or day Operator called once during the night shall receive one-half day's pay therefor, provided h does not remain on duty to exceed three hours. All time in excess of three hours to b paid for at regular overtime rates. If any Agent and Operator, or day Operator, l called but twice during one night he shall receive pay for second call at regular over time rates. Any Agent and Operator, or day Operator, called three times during on night shall receive one day's pay therefor. Offices where there are day and nigh Operators they must relieve each other. At other offices Agent and Operator, or da Operator will be considered relieved at the expiration of twelve hours service, unles required to remain on duty, when he will be paid overtime as herein before provided Time shall count from seven o'clock a. m to seven o'clock p. m., except in cases when it may be mutually agreeable to arrange other hours of service. The Company reserv ing the right to arrange the hours so that early and late trains will receive attention Any Agent and Operator being required to attend any passenger train outside of hi regularly arranged twelve hour service shall receive one hour overtime for each trai so attended, unless two or more passenger trains should be attended within the on hour when he shall receive one hour's overtime. Delayed passenger and local freigh trains not to be considered in this connection.

5. Charges made against any Dispatcher, Agent and Operator or Operator, or b them against other employes, must be made in writing. No verbal complaint shall b considered.

6. Any Dispatcher, Agent and Operator or Operator having been on duty seven teen consecutive hours, shall be entitled to eight hours rest, and shall be allowed sam except in cases of wrecks. The above shall in no way relieve Agents and Operators o proper performance of their agency duties during their regular hours of duty.

7. Dispatchers, Agents and Operators and Operators attending law suits of th Company shall receive same compensation as if on duty, and necessary expenses, th Company being entitled to any witness fees that may accrue.

8. The Company on its part, and the Dispatchers, Agents and Operators, an Operators on their part, agree that they will perform the several duties and stipula tions provided for in this agreement until thirty days' notice has been given by eithe party to the other, requesting change in same.

9. In case any differences of opinion as to the construction of this agreement shal arise between the Train Dispatchers and Telegraph Operators and the division officers a written statement of the question must be submitted by the Train Dispatchers o the Telegraph Operators to the President or General Manager, through the Superin tendent, for his consideration and adjustment.

10. It is understood that the term "Agent and Operator," as used in the foregoing designates those Operators who handle Agencies in addition to their duties as Operators.

TOLEDO, ST. LOUIS & KANSAS CITY RAILROAD.

By S. R. CALLAWAY, President.
C. N. PRATT, Superintendent.

Committee for Trainmen and Yardmen:
J. W. DAILY,
JAMES PATTERSON,
C. F. LOSSING,
J. D. FORTUNE,
W. HARPER,
J. HARRIS,
S. L. HAMILTON,
F. TAYLOR.

Committee for Engineers and Firemen:
CHAS. H. BISSELL,
J. A. HARLEY,
J. C. BARNES,
L. E. ACKERLY,
G. S. CABLE,
PERRY ROBERTS,
W. B. BROWN.

Committee for Dispatchers and Operators:
W. H. SMITH,
E. M. KELLER,
JOHN W. REDENBAUGH,
S. D. YARNELL.

August 1, 1892.

UNION PACIFIC SYSTEM.

NEBRASKA DIVISION.

DISTRICT.	BETWEEN.	CLASS.	Mil'ge, time card.	Mileage, allowed.	No. crews assigned.	Conduct'rs, per month or mile.	Brakemen, per month or mile.
Main line	Council Bluffs, Cheyenne	Fast mail	519.1		4	$125 00	*$90 00
1st and 2d	Council Bluffs, North Platte	Passenger	293.7		9	120 00	70 00
3d and 4th	North Platte, Cheyenne	Passenger	225.4		5	115 00	70 00
3d Julesburg	North Platte, Denver	Passenger	278.3		3	110 00	70 00
1st O. & R. V.	Council Bluffs { Beatrice / Blue Springs	Passenger / Passenger	134.4 / 148.6		3	100 00	65 00
O & R. V.	Lincoln, Manhattan (double)	Passenger	132.2		1	120 00	75 00
O. & R. V.	Lincoln, Stromsburg (double)	Passenger	72.7		1	100 00	65 00
O & R. V.	Lincoln, Sioux City	Passenger	186.6		2	100 00	65 00
O & R. V.	Grand Island, Ord (double)	Passenger	63.1		1	100 00	65 00
Julesburg	Julesburg, Denver	Mixed	197.3		2	110 00	70 00
O. & R. V.	Columbus, Sioux City	Mixed	125.9		1	95 00	70 00
O. & R. V.	Columbus, Albion	Mixed	43.2		1	95 00	70 00
O. & R. V.	Genoa, Cedar Rapids	Mixed	30.3		1	95 00	70 00
O. & R. V.	Grand Island, { Ord / Loupe City	Mixed			1	95 00	70 00
O. & R. V.	Grand Island, { Loupe City / Pleasanton	Mixed			1	95 00	70 00
1st	Council Bluffs, Grand Island	Freight	156.2	160		03	02
1st	Omaha, Grand Island	Freight	153.4	153		03	02
1st	Omaha, Columbus	Local	91.3	91	3	95 00	70 00
1st	Columbus, Grand Island	Local	69.1	62	1	95 00	70 00
2d	Grand Island, North Platte	Freight	137.5	138		03	02
2d	Grand Island, North Platte	Local	137.5	138	3	95 00	70 00
3d	North Platte, Sidney	Freight	123.9	123		03	02
4th	Sidney, Cheyenne	Freight	102.2	102		03	02
Julesburg	Julesburg, Sterling	Freight	138.6	139		03	02
Julesburg	Sterling, { Denver / Jersey	Freight	137.5	139		03	02
1st O. & R. V.	Omaha, Beatrice	Local	131.6	132	5	95 00	70 00
O. & R. V.	Beatrice, Manhattan	Local	92.5	93	2	95 00	70 00
O. & R. V.	Valparaiso, Stromsburg	Local	52.9	53	2	95 00	70 00

*Brakemen also act as Baggagemen. Daily rates: Passenger Conductors, $3.50; freight Conductors, $3.25; Baggagemen, $3.25; Brakemen, $2.17. Rates of overtime: Conductors, 30 cents per hour; Brakemen, 20 cents. Dead-heading: Full time will be allowed for dead-heading, except when necessary to equalize crews and power, in which case only half time will be allowed.

WYOMING DIVISION.

DISTRICT.	BETWEEN.	CLASS.	Mil'ge, time card.	Mileage, allowed.	No. crews assigned.	Conduct'rs, per month or mile.	Brakemen, per month or mile.
5th, 6th, 7th ..	Cheyenne, Green River...............	Fast mail.....	328.6	......	3	$125 00	$$85 00
5th, 6th, 7th ..	Cheyenne, Green River...............	Passenger....	328 6	......	7	125 00	75 00
8th, 9th........	Green River, Ogden.................	Passenger....	186.1	......	4	125 00	75 00
9th, E. & P.C..	Ogden, Park City (double)...........	Passenger....	135.8	......	1	110 00	75 00
5th	Cheyenne, Laramie..................	Freight......	56.5	85	......	03	02
5th	Cheyenne, Sherman (double)........	Freight......	65.4	85	......	03	02
5th	Sherman, Laramie (double).........	Freight......	47.6	85	......	03	02
6th	Laramie, Rawlins...................	Freight......	136.4	137	......	03	02
6th	Laramie, Medicine Bow (double).....	Freight......	144.6	150	......	03	02
6th	Laramie. Hanna (double).............	Freight......	185.2	200	......	03	02
6th	Laramie, Carbon (double)............	Freight......	166.4	200	......	03	02
7th	Rawlins, Green River................	Freight......	135.7	136	......	03	02
7th	Rawlins, Wamsutter (double)........	Freight¹.....	85	100	......	03	02
8th	Green River, Evanston	Freignt......	110.3	111	......	03	02
8th	Green River, Granger (double)......	Freight......	61	100	......	03	02
9th	Evanston, Ogden	Freight......	75.8	100	......	03	02
C. & N	Cheyenne, Orin Junction............	Freight ...	153.9	154	......	03	02
6th	Hanna coal run*....................	....	......	......	......	100 00	75 00
6th	Carbon coal run*...................	....	......	......	......	100 00	75 00
7th	Rock Springs coal run (double)†.....	Freight......	15.1	......	1	1(0 00	75 00
E. & P. C......	Echo, Park City (double)............	Mixed........	56	......	1‡	100 00	75 00
C. & N........	Cheyenne, Orin Junction............	Mixed........	153 9	......	2	110 00	80 00

*Overtime after twelve hours; when business is light, one crew to do the work at both places. †Overtime after twelve hours. ‡Does switching at Echo and Park City. §Brakemen also act as Baggagemen. Daily rates: Passenger Conductors, $3 25; freight Conductors, $3 25; Baggagemen, $2 83½; Brakemen, $2.25. Rates of overtime: Conductors, 30 cents per hour; Brakemen, 20 cents. Deadheading: Full time will be allowed for dead-heading, except when necessary to equalize crews and power, in which case only half time will be allowed. Utah Eastern Switchmen will be paid $90 per month to do switching and work at Home Coal Company's mine and to make trip as Brakemen on E. & P. C. freight, Coalville to Park City and return; overtime after twelve hours. "Swing" trains to put up coal in chutes at Medicine Bow and Wamsutter.

KANSAS DIVISION.

DISTRICT.	BETWEEN.	CLASS.	Mil'ge, time card.	Mileage allowed.	No. crews assigned.	Conduct'rs, per month or mile.	Brakemen, per month or mile.
1st, 2d........	Kansas City, Ellis...................	Passenger....	302 5	......	......	$115 00	†$55 00
1st............	Kansas City, Junction City (double)..	Passenger....	138.7	......	......	115 00	†55 00
3d, 4th........	Ellis, Denver	Passenger....	336 6	......	......	115 00	†55 00
L. & L	Lawrence, Leavenworth (double)....	Passenger...	34	......	......	100 00	†55 00
J. C. & F. K ..	Junction City, Belleville (double)*...	Passenger....	94.4	......	......	110 00	†55 00
Sol............	Solomon, Beloit (double)	Passenger....	57.3	......	......	1(0 00	†50 00
1st............	Kansas City, Junction City..........	Freight......	138.7	139	......	03	02
1st............	Kansas City, Junction City..........	Local........	138 7	......	3	95 00	70 00
2d	Junction City, Ellis	Freight......	163.8	164	......	03	02
2d	Junction City, Salina (double).......	Local........	46.9	......	1	95 00	70 00
3d	Ellis, Cheyenne Wells...............	Freight ...	159 4	159½	......	03	02
4th	Cheyenne Wells, { Denver / Jersey }	Freight......	175	175	......	03	02
L. & L........	Lawrence, Leavenworth (double)....	Mixed........	34	......	......	95 00	70 00
L. T. & S W..	Leavenworth, Meriden Jc. (double)..	Mixed........	46.6	......	......	95 00	65 00
K. C..........	Leavenworth, Garrison Cg...........	Mixed........	117.6	......	2	95 00	70 00
K. C..........	Garrison Cg., Miltonvale (double)....	Mixed........	48.3	......	......	95 00	70 00
J. C. & F. K ..	Junction City, Belleville*............	Mixed........	94.4	......	2	95 00	70 00
Sol............	Solomon, Beloit (double)	Mixed........	57.3	......	......	95 00	70 00
S. & S. W	Salina, McPherson (double)	Mixed........	35.5	......	1	95 00	70 00
U. P. L. & C...	Salina, Oakley......................	Mixed........	225.3	225	......	03	02

*Via Concordia. †Porters. Daily rates: Passenger Conductors, $3.50; freight Conductors, $3.25; Baggagemen, $2.25; Brakemen, $2.17. Rates of overtime: Conductors, 30 cents per hour; Brakemen, 20 cents. Dead-heading: Full time will be allowed for dead-heading, except when necessary to equalize crews and power, in which case only half time will be allowed.

UNION PACIFIC RAILWAY.   165

COLORADO DIVISION.

DISTRICT.	BETWEEN.	CLASS.	Mil'ge, time card	Mileage, allowed	No. crews assigned	Conduct'rs, per m'nth, m'le or tr'p	Brakemen, per m'nth, m'le or tr'p
Denver Pac..	Denver, Cheyenne*	Passenger	106.7		{4	$110 00	$70 00
Fort Collins..	Denver, Greeley (double)*	Passenger	98.6			110 00	70 00
D. P. & Ft. C..	Denver, Fort Collins (double)†	Passenger	76.2		1	110 00	70 00
Fort Collins..	Denver, Fort Collins (double)‡	Passenger	74.1		1	110 00	70 00
Fort Collins..	Marshall Jc., Lafayette (3 double)§	Passenger	6.1		1	95 00	70 00
Graymont....	Denver, Graymont (double)	Passenger	58.1		1	110 00	70 00
Graymont....	Denver, Silver Plume (double)‖	Passenger	54		1	95 00	70 00
Graymont....	Forks Creek, Central City (2 d'ble)¶	Passenger	11.1		1	95 00	70 00
South Park..	Denver, Leadville	Passenger	151.1		3	110 00	70 00
Denver Pac..	Denver } Cheyenne	Freight	104 5	117		03	02
	Jersey }						
Fort Collins..	LaSalle, Stout (double)	Freight	43 9		1	95 00	70 00
Fort Collins..	Denver, Fort Collins**	Freight	97		2	95 00	70 00
Fort Collins..	Denver, Boulder (double)††	Freight	37.1		1	95 00	70 00
Graymont....	Denver, Georgetown (double)‡‡	Freight	49.9		1	95 00	70 00
Graymont	Golden, Black Hawk (2 double)‡‡	Freight	20 7		1	95 00	70 00
D. L. & G....	Denver, Leadville	Freight	151.1		3	110 00	80 00
D. L. & G....	Denver, Como	Freight	88.2			3 55	2 61
D. L. & G....	Como, Leadville	Freight	62.9			3 65	2 61
Sunset.......	Boulder, Sunset (2 double)	Mixed	13.1		1	95 00	70 00
Graymont....	Denver, Golden (2 double)	Mixed	15.2		1	100 00	70 00
D. L. & G....	Denver, Morrison (3 double)	Mixed	17.2		1	100 00	70 00
D. L. & G....	Keystone, Breckenridge (2 d'ble)§§	Mixed	13 3		1	95 00	70 00
D. L. & G....	Como, Romley (double)‖‖	Mixed	77.1		1	110 00	70 00
D. L. & G....	Como, London (double)	Mixed	31.8			95 00	2 61
D. L. & G....	Baldwin, Pitkin (double)	Mixed	44.6		1	95 00	2 61
D. L. & G....	Como, King ¶¶	Mixed	3.8			80 00	(a)2 50

*Via Fort Collins. †Via Greeley. ‡Via Boulder. §Includes switching. ‖Includes switching at Georgetown and Silver Plume; when run Sunday, Conductor shall be paid at rate of $110 per month, Brakeman's pay to remain the same. ¶Includes switching at Black Hawk and Central City, and double Black Hawk and Central City. **Via Brighton and Arkins. ††Via Marshall Junction and Louisville. ‡‡Overtime after eleven hours. §§Includes double via Breckenridge and Boreas. ‖‖Via Buena Vista. ¶¶Work done by yard crew. (a) Per day. Daily rates: Freight Conductors, $3 50; Brakemen, $2.50. Special passenger Conductors, $110 per calendar month; Brakemen, $70. Rate of overtime: Conductors, 35 cents per hour; Brakemen, 25 cents. Dead-heading: When dead-heading on other trains, with or without caboose, one-half the regular rate will be allowed; dead-head crews to take turn out ahead of crew in charge of train, provided both crews are assigned to the same runs or are employed on unassigned runs.

NEW MEXICO DIVISION.

DISTRICT.	BETWEEN.	CLASS.	Mil'ge, time card	Mileage, allowed	No. crews assigned	Conduct'rs, per m'nth, m'le or tr'p	Brakemen, per m'nth, m'le or tr'p
1st, 2d.....	Denver, Trinidad	Passenger	216 4		3	$110 00	$70 00
1st.........	Jersey, Pueblo	Freight	126.7	127		03½	02¼
1st..........	Franceville, McFerran*	Freight			1	100 00	72 00
2d	Pueblo, Trinidad and El Moro	Freight	91 9			3 35	2 35
2d	Trinidad, {Berwind / Hastings / Forbes} †	Freight				110 00	75 00
3d...........	Trinidad, Texline	Freight	136 2	137		03	02
Maxwell.....	Trinidad, Soprist	Freight				110 00	75 00
Maxwell.....	Trinidad, Vasques } (double)‡	Mixed	43 2			110 00	75 00
Maxwell.....	Catskill, Endoftrack }						
Manitou.....	Manitou Jc., Colorado Sp'gs (4 d'ble)§	Mixed	9		1	100 00	72 00

*Includes switching and helping; overtime after twelve hours. †For twenty-six days; overtime after twelve hours. ‡Includes one double, Catskill to top of hill; for twenty-six days; overtime after twelve hours. §Includes switching; overtime after twelve hours. Daily rates: Freight Conductors, $3.50; Brakemen, $2 50. Special passenger Conductors, $110 per month; Brakemen, $70. Rates of overtime: Conductors, 35 cents per hour; Brakemen, 25 cents. Dead-heading: When dead-heading on other trains, with or without caboose, one-half the regular rate to be allowed; dead-head crew to take turn out ahead of crew in charge of train, provided both crews are assigned to same runs or are employed on unassigned runs.

UNION PACIFIC RAILWAY.

FORT WORTH AND DENVER CITY DIVISION.

DISTRICT.	BETWEEN.	CLASS.	Mil'ge, time card...	Mileage, allowed...	No. crews assigned...	Conduct'rs, per month or mile...	Brakemen, per month or mile...
4th	Trinidad, Clarendon	Passenger	310.9		3	$120 00	$60 00
5th, 6th	Clarendon, Fort Worth*	Passenger	277.1		4	120 00	60 00
4th	Texline, Clarendon	Freight	174.7	175		03	02
5th	Clarendon, Wichita Falls	Freight	163	163		03	02
5th	Clarendon, Wichita Falls	Local	163		3	100 00	65 00
6th	Wichita Falls, Fort Worth	Freight	113 7	114		03	02
6th	Wichita Falls, Fort Worth	Local	113.7		3	90 00	60 00
Pan Handle	Amorilla, Pan Handle City (d'ble)†	Mixed	32		1	90 00	60 00

*Includes Wichita Falls local. †Includes switching. Daily rates: Freight Conductors, $3; Brakemen, $2. Special passenger Conductors, $100 per month; Brakemen, $60. Rates of overtime: Conductors, 30 cents per hour; Brakemen, 20 cents. Dead-heading: When dead-heading on other trains, with or without caboose, one-half the regular rate will be allowed; dead-head crews to take turn out ahead of crew in charge of train, provided both crews are assigned to same runs or are employed on unassigned runs.

UTAH DIVISION.

DISTRICT	BETWEEN.	CLASS.	Mil'ge, time card...	Mileage, allowed...	No. crews assigned...	Conduct'rs, per month or mile...	Brakemen, per month or mile...
Main line	Ogden, Juab*	Passenger	138.9		5	$110 00	$70 00
S. L. & W	Lehi Junction, Eureka	Passenger	58.3		1	100 00	65 00
U. & N	Salt Lake, Garfield†	Passenger	18.2			100 00	65 00
1st	Ogden, Salt Lake	Freight	36.5	50		90 00	65 00
1st	Ogden, Salt Lake (double)‡	Freight	73	100	4	90 00	65 00
1st	Ogden, Salt Lake (via Syracuse)	Freight	48.1	62		90 00	65 00
1st	Syracuse Junction, Syracuse (d'ble)§	Freight	11.6	12		90 00	65 00
2d	Salt Lake, Juab	Freight	109.4	103		90 00	65 00
2d	Salt Lake, Provo	Freight	47 5	50		90 00	65 00
2d	Salt Lake, Provo (double)	Freight	95	100		90 00	65 00
2d	Salt Lake, Lehi Junction‖	Freight	29	50		90 00	65 00
2d	Salt Lake, Lehi Junction (d'ble) ‖	Freight	58	100		90 00	65 00
2d	Lehi Junction, Point Mtn. (d'ble)	Freight	9	10		90 00	65 00
2d	Salt Lake, Sandy (double)¶	Freight	26	100	1	90 00	60 00
3d	Juab, Frisco**	Freight	136		3	90 00	65 00
3d	Juab, Milford	Freight	119			90 00	65 00
3d	Milford, Frisco (double)††	Freight	33.8			90 00	65 00
3d	Milford, Frisco (2 double)††	Freight	67 6			90 00	65 00
S. L. & W	Lehi Junction, Ironton‡‡	Freight	49 8	50	1	90 00	60 00
S. L. & W	Lehi Junction, Ironton (double	Freight	99.6	100		90 00	60 00
U. & N	Salt Lake, Terminus (double)§§	Freight				85 00	60 00
S. L. & W	Ironton, Eureka‖‖	Freight	74		1	90 00	60 00

*Five crews to do all the passenger work. †Bathing trains; no overtime. ‡Conductors $100, Brakemen $60, for 2,600 miles; over 2,600 miles at 3 cents and 2 cents per mile, respectively. § Time allowed while lying at Syracuse, in addition to mileage made. Overtime after schedule time of train between Salt Lake and Ogden, less the time used going from Syracuse Junction to Syracuse and return. ‖ Includes switching and other necessary work at Lehi Junction, and where double and single trips are made same day only one day to be allowed; overtime after ten hours, in case of double. ¶ Working days only; overtime after ten hours; does all work between Salt Lake and Sandy, switch their own trains at both terminals, and where two doubles are made in same day or crew goes to Lehi Junction only one day to be allowed. ** Working days only; one crew to work between Milford and Frisco, if desired, and the other two between Milford and Juab. †† Do all switching at Milford and Frisco and such other work as may be necessary. ‡‡Working days only; time allowed for making up train at Lehi Junction; overtime after ten hours. §§ Working days only. ‖‖ Working days only; overtime after ten hours; crew to do all the work west of Ironton, make up east bound trains, and help to Doremus when necessary. Rates of overtime: Conductors, 30 cents per hour; Brakemen, 20 cents. Work trains: Conductors, $90 per calendar month; Brakemen, $65; overtime after twelve hours. Dead-heading: Conductors $3 and Brakemen $2, twenty-four hours or less; in no case more than would be allowed in regular service over same district.

UNION PACIFIC RAILWAY. 167

IDAHO DIVISION.

DISTRICT	BETWEEN.	CLASS.	Mil'ge, time card.	Mileage, allowed.	No. crews assigned.	Conduct'rs, per month or mile.	Brakemen, per month or mile.
it and 2d	Green River, Pocatello	Passenger	244.9		3	$125 00	$75 00
1 and 4th	Pocatello, Huntington	Passenger	326 9		7	125 00	75 00
h	Ogden, Pocatello	Passenger	134 2		2	125 00	75 00
h	Ogden, Preston (double)	Passenger	91		1	125 00	75 00
h and 8th	Pocatello, Butte	Passenger	262 2		6	125 00	75 00
it	Green River, Montpelier	Freight	145 6	145		03	02
1	Granger, Montpelier	Freight	115.1	115		03	02
1	Montpelier, Pocatello	Freight	99.3	108		03	02
1	Pocatello, Glenn's Ferry	Freight	159 9	160		03	02
1	Pocatello, Shoshone	Freight	107.7	108		03	02
h	Glenn's Ferry, Huntington	Freight	107	167		03	02
h	Ogden, Pocatello	Freight	134.2	134		03	02
h	Pocatello, Lima	Freight	145.1	1¤3		03	02
h	Lima, Butte	Freight	117 1	141		03	02
h	Lima, Silver Bow	Freight	110 3	132		03	02
h	Shoshone, Ketchum (double)	Mixed	69 4	139	1	100 00	75 00
oise	Nampa, Boise (3 double)	Mixed	19		1	100 00	75 00
h	Cache Junction, Preston (2 d'ble)	Mixed	42 2		1	110 00	75 00

Daily rates: Passenger Conductors, $4; freight Conductors, $3.25; Baggagemen, $3.25; Brakemen, l.17. Rates of overtime: Conductors, 30 cents per hour; Brakemen, 20 cents. Dead-heading: Full me will be allowed for dead-heading, except when necessary to equalize crews and power, in which ase only half time will be allowed. Trip to Hams Fork mines: One hour allowed, unless an unusual elay occurs, when one hour and overtime is allowed.

PACIFIC DIVISION.

DISTRICT.	BETWEEN.	CLASS.	Mil'ge, time card.	Mileage, allowed.	No. crews assigned.	Conduct'rs, per month or mile.	Brakemen, per month or mile.
it and 2d	Huntington, Pendleton	Passenger	173 5		4	$125 00	$75 00
1, 3d and 4th	Pendleton, Portland	Passenger	230.9		5	125 00	75 00
h and 6th	Pendleton, Spokane	Passenger	251.4		3	125 00	75 00
lullan	Tekoa, Mullan	Passenger	86.7		1	100 00	70 00
it	Huntington, LaGrande	Freight	99 1	125		03	02½
1	LaGrande, Umatilla	Freight	118.4	150		03	02½
1	LaGrande, Pendleton	Freight	74.4	100		03	02½
1	Umatilla, Dalles	Freight	98 6	100		03	02½
h	Dalles, Albina	Freight	88.3	100		03	02½
h	Pendleton, Starbuck	Freight	94 8	125		03	02½
h	Walla Walla, Starbuck (double)	Freight	47 4		1	90 00	67 50
h	Starbuck, Spokane (via Colfax)	Freight	156 6	170		03	02½
h	Starbuck, Tekoa (via Colfax)	Freight	107 4	190		03	02½
h	Starbuck, Tekoa (via P. V. district)	Freight	96.8			90 00	65 00
h	Tekoa, Spokane	Freight	49 2	50		03	02½
lullan	Tekoa, Mullan		86.7		2	90 00	65 00
lgin	LaGrande, Elgin (2 double)	Mixed	20 9		1	90 00	67 50
eppner	Arlington, Heppner (double)	Mixed	55.7		1	90 00	67 50
'allula	Walla Walla, Umatilla (double)	Mixed	58 3		1	100 00	70 00
ayton	Bolles Junction, Dayton (3 d'ble)	Mixed	12 6		1	90 00	67 50
omeroy	Starbuck, Pomeroy	Mixed	29 9		1	90 00	67 50
onnell	LaCrosse, Connell (double)	Mixed	53			90 00	67 50
loscow	Colfax, Moscow (2 double)	Mixed	27.9			100 00	75 00
urke and Mullan	Wallace, Burke } (double) Wallace, Mullan }	Mixed	6 7		1	125 00	75 00

Daily rates: Passenger Conductors, $3 50; freight Conductors, $3; Brakemen, $2 33 Rates of vertime: Conductors 30 cents per hour; Brakemen, 1st and 2d districts 23½ cents. all other districts 1½ cents. Work train: Conductors, $90 per month; Brakemen, $70. Dead-heading: Crews when ead-headed with cabooses will be allowed half time.

RULES.

1. *General:* All runs and compensation allowed for same shall be designated in chedules prepared on a fair and equitable basis, consistent with the general plan erein given.

2. *Mileage Rates:* Unassigned freight runs, first in first out, based on mileage: !onductors 3 cents per mile, Brakemen 2 cents per mile, except as hereinafter provided.

3. *Monthly Rates:* Assigned regular runs on monthly pay as per schedule.

4. *Short Runs:* (a.) All runs not otherwise provided for, of 50 miles or less, not on uty over five hours, single trip or doubled, 50 miles, overtime after five hours; 100 niles, if only one trip and not called on duty again until after ten hours from starting

time of run. Two trips not on duty over ten hours, 100 miles; overtime after ten hours as per rule.

(b.) Short runs over 50 miles and less than 75 miles, not on duty over seven and one-half hours, single trip, 100 miles; overtime after seven and one-half hours. Doubled, not on duty over average freight time of that district, 150 miles; overtime after average time.

(c.) Short runs over 75 miles and less than 100 miles, single trip, not on duty over ten hours, 100 miles; overtime after ten hours. Doubled, mileage and overtime.

5. *Short Irregular Runs:* Short irregular runs not otherwise provided for, to be based on day's work, as per schedule.

6. *Work Train:* Conductors, $90 per calendar month; Brakemen, $65 per calendar month. Twelve hours or less to constitute a day's work; overtime after twelve hours, as per schedule; except that runs before and after regular working hours shall be computed on mileage basis.

7. *Snow Plow Service:* Trainmen held for snow plow service will be paid daily rates for every twenty-four hours so held. When in service will be paid daily rates; overtime arter twelve hours. When running over district with flanger or plow, ahead of trains, district rates will be paid.

8. *Light Runs:* Light runs with engine and caboose will be paid for at regular rates for freight train service.

9. *Dead-heading:* Dead-heading will be paid for as per schedule.

10. *Attending Court:* When attending court, or employed in other than train service, trainmen will be paid daily rates, and allowed legitimate expenses, when away from home station.

11. *Pilots:* Light engines when run over district will be accompanied by pilot, who shall be a Conductor, or Brakeman who has passed examination for Conductor, and shall receive Conductor's pay.

12. *Extra Service:* Crews assigned to regular runs at monthly pay will receive extra compensation at regular rates for service performed, when used on lay-over days.

13. *Freight Crews Handling Passenger Trains:* Freight train crews handling passenger trains will be allowed freight train rates of pay.

14. *Computing Overtime:* (a.) All delayed time in excess of schedule time of regular freight trains shall be paid for. Where the schedule time of a train averages less than ten miles per hour, overtime will be paid for on this basis.

(b.) Delayed time on passenger trains will be paid for, less two hours.

(c.) Delayed time on extra or irregular trains in excess of average time of all regular sreight trains on each district will be paid for without reduction from average time.

(d.) In computing overtime or delayed time, any fraction of an hour less than thirty minutes will not be counted; thirty minutes or over will be counted one hour.

15. *Detention at Terminals:* Trainmen required to do switching, load stock, etc., at main line district terminals before starting on run, or when held on duty with their trains after arrival at main line district terminals, will be allowed overtime, as per schedule rates, in addition to time on road.

16. *Doubling Hills:* When trains are made up with the intention of having them double hills, trainmen will be allowed ten miles for each double, unless the mileage is more than ten miles, in which case actual mileage will be allowed. If any overtime is gained by such double the amount allowed for doubling will be deducted from the amount paid for overtime.

17. *Yard Service:* If trainmen accept permanent yard service voluntarily, they forfeit all road rights.

18. *Reducing Crews:* (a.) When freight traffic becomes so light that reasonable wages cannot be made, the number of crews will be reduced, (beginning with the youngest), until those left in service can make reasonable wages.

(b.) Conductors temporarily suspended under this rule will be given preference as Brakemen and will retain their rights as Conductors.

19. *Conductors' Rights:* Conductors' rights will date from the time they are given their own regular crews.

20. *Tie-up:* Trainmen will be considered on duty until they reach the end of a run or return to starting point. The idea being not to tie crews up between ends of runs so as to avoid paying the overtime they would otherwisr make.

21. *Calling:* (a.) Trainmen will be called within a reasonable distance at main line, district or terminal stations, by the train Caller, who will always be provided with a book in which their names will be registered, together with the time they are called. Time will begin at the time set for the departure of trains.

(*b.*) When trainmen are called, and for any reason their train does not go out, and they are held on duty less than five hours, they will be paid for one-half day and stand first out; if held more than five hours, they will be paid one day and stand last out, it being understood that if crews go out within five hours, the time on duty will be computed from the time first called.

22. *Rest:* After continuous service of sixteen hours or more, trainmen will be entitled to and allowed eight hours for rest before being called to go out, provided they so desire, except in cases of washouts, wrecks or other emergencies.

23. *Time not Allowed:* Conductors will be notified when time is not allowed as per trip report.

24. *Suspension:* When a trainman is taken from his run for the investigation of an alleged fault, he will, if found innocent, receive pay for time lost. No punishment to be fixed without a thorough investigation; ordinarily such investigation to be held within five days from date of removal from service.

25. *Service Letter:* When trainmen leave the service they will be given a letter stating time and character of service and reasons for leaving.

March 1, 1892.
E. DICKINSON,
Assistant General Manager.

VALLEY RAILWAY COMPANY.

PASSENGER SERVICE.

Passenger Conductors, Cleveland to Valley Junction and return, shall receive $3.75 per day. Cleveland to Canton and return, $3 per day.

Baggagemasters, Cleveland to Valley Junction and return, shall receive $65 per month. Cleveland to Canton and return, $60 per month.

Brakemen, Cleveland to Valley Junction and return, shall receive $1.92 per day. Cleveland to Canton and return, $1.80 per day.

FREIGHT SERVICE.

Conductors in through freight service shall be paid at the rate of $2.87 per day. Through freight Brakemen shall be paid at the rate of $1.90 per day. Ten hours or less to constitute a day's work.

LOCAL FREIGHT.

Cleveland to P. & W. Junction and return, Conductors shall receive $3 per day; Brakemen $2 per day.

Canton to P. & W. Junction, thence to Valley Junction and return to Canton, Conductors shall receive $3 per day; Brakemen, $2 per day.

Ten and one-half hours or less to constitute a day's work. Overtime, Conductors, 30 cents per hour; Brakemen, 20 cents per hour.

THROUGH FREIGHT—SPECIFIED RUNS.

Cleveland to Akron, P. & W. Junction, East Akron, Cottage Grove, Myersville, Krumroy and Greentown, Conductors shall be paid $2.87 per day; Brakemen, $1.90 per day. Overtime after ten hours.

Cleveland to Canton and return, Conductors shall receive $3.44 per day; Brakemen, $2.28 per day. Overtime after twelve hours.

Cleveland to Sandyville and return, Conductors shall receive $4.01 per day; Brakemen $2.66 per day. Overtime after fourteen hours.

Cleveland to Valley Junction and return, Conductors shall receive $4.30 per day; Brakemen $2.85 per day. Overtime after fifteen hours.

Canton to Valley Junction and return; Conductors shall receive $2.87 per day; Brakemen $1.90 per day. Overtime after ten hours.

Newburgh run, Conductors shall be paid $2.87 per day; Brakemen $2.30 per day. Eleven hours or less to constitute a day's work.

Thornburg Ore run, Conductors shall receive $3 per day; Brakeman $2.30 per day. Conductors and Brakemen to assist in dumping ore. Ten hours or less to constitute a day's work.

WORK TRAIN SERVICE.

Conductors shall receive $2.87 per day; Brakemen, $1.90 per day. Eleven hours or less to constitute a day's work.

RULES.

1. Ten hours or less for runs of 100 miles or less shall constitute a day's work for Conductors and Brakemen in freight service.

2. On all freight runs exceeding 100 miles trainmen will be paid overtime for all time used to complete the trip in excess of an average speed of ten miles per hour at the above rates. Through freight overtime to be paid, Conductors, 28.7 cents per hour; Brakemen, 19 cents per hour.

3. No fraction of an hour less than 35 minutes to be counted, 35 minutes and less than one hour to be paid as one hour.

4. If crews on excursion trains are required to do extra work, such as pulling over the hill, working the mines, or construction work, they shall be paid for such service at the same rate of pay allowed per hour for that class of service.

5. Any trainman sent over the road or held at any point on any Company business shall be paid for time lost at rate of pay allowed for their class of service.

6. Any Conductor or Brakeman called, and if for any cause or reason other than his own he does not go out, if held two and one-half hours or less he shall be paid for one-fourth day and stand first out; and if held longer shall be paid for time so held at regular overtime rates.

7. As near as practicable the board at yardmaster's office at Cleveland shall be made up at 4 p. m. for the succeeding 24 hours. Conductors and Brakemen shall be called within certain limits prescribed by the Superintendent—about one hour before time set to leave—for all runs leaving between 9 o'clock p. m. and 6 o'clock a. m.; and at any other time if the board has been changed. The Caller shall be provided with a book in which the men called shall register their names and time called.

8. Any crew that has been sixteen hours or more on continuous duty shall be entitled to eight hours rest at terminals before being called to go out, provided they so desire; except in cases of washouts or similar emergencies. Notice by telegraph to Trainmaster being required. Following crews shall have right to run around crew laying over for rest under these provisions.

9. No trainman shall be suspended or discharged without just cause; in case of suspension or dismissal if he thinks his sentence unjust, his case shall have a thorough investigation by the proper officers within five days from the time he makes application, at which he may be present if he so desires. If found unjustly suspended or discharged he shall be reinstated and paid full time while so out of service.

10. No fines shall be imposed for any cause whatever.

11. No departure from the propositions of this agreement will be made by any party thereto without thirty days' notice of such desire in writing has been served upon the other parties thereto. The articles enumerated constitute in their entirety an agreement between the Valley Railway Company and its Conductors and Brakemen.

YARDMEN'S SCHEDULE—AKRON YARD.

Day Conductor shall receive $2.60 per day; day Brakemen, $2.10 per day; night Conductor, $2.65 per day; night Brakeman, $2.25 per day.

CANTON YARD.

Day Conductor shall receive $2.50 per day; day Brakemen, $2.04 per day; night Conductor, $2.60 per day; night Brakeman, $2.16 per day.

RULES.

1. Ten hours or less shall constitute a day's work.

2. All time in excess of ten hours shall be paid for at the same rate. No fraction of an hour less than thirty-five minutes shall be counted; thirty-five minutes and less than one hour shall be paid for as one hour.

3. Promotions in yard service shall be made according to age and ability to assume the increased responsibility. The oldest night Brakeman shall be entitled to position as day Brakeman, should any vacancy occur. The oldest day Brakeman shall be entitled to the position of night Conductor, should a vacancy occur. Vacancies in day Conductors shall be filled from the oldest night Conductor.

4. No Yardman shall be suspended or discharged without just cause; in case of suspension or dismissal, if he thinks his sentence unjust, his case shall have a thorough investigation by the proper officers within five days from the time he makes application, at which he may be present, if he so desires. If found unjustly suspended or discharged, he shall be reinstated and paid full time while so out of service.

The articles here enumerated constitute an agreement between the Valley Railway Company and its Yardmen specified. No departure shall be made by either party thereto without thirty days' notice in writing on the other party.

All schedules, rules and regulations conflicting with this agreement previously in effect are null and void.

For the Order of Railway Conductors:
A. B. GARRETSON, Grand Senior Conductor.

For the Brotherhood of Railroad Trainmen:
P. H. MORRISSEY, Acting Grand Master.

May 24, 1892.

J. T. JOHNSON,
General Superintendent.

VANDALIA LINE.

SCHEDULE.

RUNS.	Miles	Conductors	Brakemen	Baggagemen	REMARKS.
PASSENGER SERVICE.					
Indianapolis to St. Louis, per trip	240	$5 10	$2 45	$2 85	Average 23½ trips per
Trains Nos. 20 and 21, per trip	......	4 60	2 00	2 35	Daily. [month.
Indianapolis to Terre Haute, per round trip	73	4 00	1 85	2 00	Daily except Sunday.
Terre Haute to Effingham, per month	68	100 00	....	2 00†	Daily except Sunday.
Effingham to St. Louis, per round trip	100	4 16	2 00	2 50	Daily.
Terre Haute to St. Joseph, per trip*	223	5 00	2 25	2 75	Daily except Sunday.
Terre Haute to South Bend, per trip	182	4 10	1 95	2 25	Daily except Sunday.
FREIGHT SERVICE					
Indianapolis to Terre Haute, through, per trip	73	2 25	1 70	....	
Indianapolis to Terre Haute, local, per month	73	85 00	57 00	....	Daily except Sunday.
Terre Haute to Effingham, through, per trip	68	2 00	1 50	....	
Terre Haute to Effingham, local, per month	68	80 00	55 00	....	Daily except Sunday.
Effingham to East St. Louis through, per trip	98	3 00	2 00	....	
Effingham to East St. Louis, local, per month	98	85 00	57 00	....	Two r'd trips per week.
Terre Haute to Logansport, through, per trip	116	3 50	2 32	....	
Terre Haute to Logansport, local, per month	116	90 00	60 00	....	Two r'd trips per week.
Logansport to South Bend, per month	66	85 00	57 00	....	Four r'd trips per week.
South Bend to St. Joseph, per month	40	85 00	57 00	....	R'd t'p daily ex. Sund'y.
Coal trains, 32 to 80 mile runs, per month	......	85 00	57 00	....	Daily except Sunday.
Work and wrecking trains, per day	......	3 00	2 00	....	Twelve hours.

*Five crews for four trains.   †Per round trip.

RULES.

Main line passenger crews to run first in first out, except on trains Nos. 20 and 21. Dead-heading and lights, when ordered by the Company, at the same rate as if in charge of a train. When attending court on the Company's business, pay to be whatever the crew would have made. In all investigations the accused to be represented by a member of committee. Promotions will be governed by merit and ability. When trains arrive at terminal stations late, Conductors shall be paid at the rate of 30 cents per hour and Brakemen 20 cents per hour, when more than one hour late, first hour included; time of specials to be computed from longest through freight run on time cards, No. 86 on main line, and No. 25, on T. H. & L. division.

August 24, 1892.

N. K. ELLIOTT,
Superintendent Transportation.

THE WABASH RAILROAD COMPANY.

PASSENGER SERVICE.

Through Passenger Runs: Conductors shall receive $100 per month for runs of 5,500 miles or less, and 2 cents per mile for all mileage over 5,500 miles. On runs where Flagmen are required they shall receive $55 per month for runs of 5,500 miles or less, and 1¼ cents per mile for all mileage over 5,500 miles, and to be experienced trainmen. Baggagemen, other than joint men, shall receive $55 per month for runs of 5,500 miles or less, and 1¼ cents per mile for all mileage over 5,500 miles. Where Baggagemen are joint men between the Railroad and Express Companies the Railroad Company shall pay a proportion of any excess mileage made according to the proportion of the salary paid by the Railroad Company. Brakemen shall receive $50 per month for runs of 5,500 miles or less, and 1 cent per mile for all mileage over 5,500 miles. On Chicago and Detroit runs 6,500 miles per month will be computed the same as 5,500 miles on other runs. Crews assigned to regular runs will be paid extra for any service performed outside of their regular runs, at regular rates for class of service performed. The run between Chicago and Forrest, Decatur and St. Louis, Decatur and Bluffs, Hannibal and Bluffs, and Lafayette and Fort Wayne, shall be paid upon the same basis as through passenger runs.

SHORT PASSENGER RUNS.

RUNS.	PER MONTH.		
	Conductors.	Bag'gemen.	Brakemen.
Pattonsburg Branch	$ 90 00		$60 00
Glasgow Branch	65 00		40 00
Columbia Branch	80 00		50 00
Montgomery Accommodation	100 00		50 00
St Charles Accommodation	90 00		55 00
Ferguson Accommodation	95 00		50 00
Worth Accommodation	90 00		50 00
Streator Accommodation	90 00		
Pittsfield Branch	75 00		50 00
Clayton and Keokuk	80 00	$55 00	
Danville and Champaign	75 00	50 00	
Effingham and Decatur	90 00		
Edwardsville Branch	90 00		60 00
Covington Branch	75 00		50 00
Peru and Logansport	65 00		
Defiance Accommodation	90 00	45 00	60 00

FREIGHT SERVICE, LOCAL FREIGHT RUNS.

RUNS.	Mileage Allowed.	PER MONTH OR TRIP.	
		Conductors.	Brakemen.
Detroit and Butler		$100 00	$66 00
Butler and Peru		3 75	2 50
Toledo and Fort Wayne		3 75	2 50
Fort Wayne and Andrews		90 00	60 00
Andrews and Lafayette		3 75	2 50
Lafayette and Tilton		3 75	2 50
Tilton and Decatur		90 00	60 00
Decatur and Springfield		90 00	60 00
Springfield and Clayton		90 00	60 00
Hannibal and Bluffs		90 00	60 00
Clayton and Keokuk		90 00	60 00
Chicago and Forrest		90 00	60 00
Streator Branch		3 00	2 00
Forrest and Bement		90 00	60 00
Bement and Effingham		90 00	60 00
Decatur and Litchfield, including Litchfield switching		95 00	65 00
Litchfield and East St. Louis		3 60	2 40
St. Louis and Moberly	177	03*	02*
Moberly and Randolph	152	03*	02*
Moberly and Ottumwa	164	03*	02*
Moberly and Pattonsburg	140	03*	02*
Ottumwa and Des Moines	100	03*	02*

* Per mile.

Road service rendered by local train crews on Sundays or other extra service shall be paid for as extra work at regular rates for the class of service performed. On coal runs between East St. Louis and Litchfield or intermediate stations, Conductor will be paid $90 per month and Brakemen $60 per month. Extra crews will receive fifty miles each way between East St. Louis and Staunton, and sixty miles each way between East St. Louis and Litchfield. The regular run between Forrest and Bement will be paid 3 and 2 cents per mile, respectively, for Conductor and Brakemen, who will be allowed sixty miles each way.

Through Freight Runs: On all through freight runs of 100 miles or more, Conductors shall receive 3 cents and Brakemen 2 cents per mile for the entire distance run. On all turn-arounds between Peru and Laketon Junction, and between Peru and Chili, fifty miles will b eallowed if the round trip is made in six hours. If round trip is not completed in six hours, overtime will be allowed for all hours in excess of six. On all turn-arounds between Decatur and Mt. Olive or Staunton, Tilton and Decatur, Forrest and Chicago, Forrest and Decatur, Andrews and Lafayette, Defiance or Jewell, actual mileage will be allowed for the round trip, provided it is completed within that time necessary to complete the round trip at an average speed of ten miles per hour. If not completed within that time, 100 miles will be allowed each way. On all turn-arounds between Moberly and Excello, and between Ottumwa and C., B. & K. C. Junction, fifty miles will be allowed if the round trip is made in five hours or less. If round trip is not completed in five hours 100 miles will be allowed, and time used in excess of twelve hours shall be paid for as overtime. On all trips from Union Depot to Luther, or vice versa, fifty miles will be allowed for each trip. On all turn-arounds between Ottumwa and Moulton 100 miles will be allowed. On all turn-arounds and divisions not specified, where mileage, is less than fifty miles, fifty miles will be allowed if round trip is completed in five hours or less. If not completed in five hours, or if mileage is more than fifty miles and less than 100 miles, 100 miles will be allowed, and time used in excess of twelve hours shall be paid for as overtime. If turn-around mileage exceeds 100 miles actual mileage will govern. On turn-around trips crews will be considered on duty from time of starting until turn-around is completed. Crews used on short turn-arounds and making only fifty miles allowance, will stand first out, and those making 100 miles or more will stand behind all other crews at that point. Conductor on Ferguson run shall receive $90 and Brakemen $60 per calendar month. Crews on wrecking trains shall receive mileage for all mileage made running to and from wreck, and in addition overtime rates for all hours used at wreck. If mileage and hours aggregate less than fifty miles, fifty miles will be allowed. If mileage and hours aggregate more than fifty miles and less than 100 miles allowance, 100 miles will be allowed. Crews on circus or snow-plow trains will be allowed 100 miles for six hours or less service, and 150 miles for over six hours. Crews running light, or freight trains running as a section of a passenger train, shall receive through freight pay. All Pilots shall receive Conductor's pay for class of service performed. Work train Conductors shall receive $90 and Brakemen $60 per calendar month, twelve hours or less to constitute a day's work. Crews required to help trains over Baylis Hill will be allowed actual mileage both ways. If overtime is gained by reason of helping trains over this hill, no overtime will be allowed for the time detained by doubling. In other words, this service is not to be paid for twice.

Overtime: On all through and local freight train runs of less than 100 miles overtime will be paid for all time used on any trip in excess of twelve hours. On all through freight train runs of more than 100 miles overtime will be paid for all time used in making any trip in excess of that time necessary to complete the trip at an average speed of ten miles per hour, except that on runs between Butler and Chicago, overtime will be paid after sixteen hours. On all local freight train runs of over 100 miles, overtime will be paid for all time used in making any trip in excess of that time necessary to complete the trip at an average speed of nine miles per hour. Fractions of an hour less than thirty minutes will not be counted. Fractions of an hour over thirty minutes will be counted a full hour. All overtime will be paid for at the rate of 30 cents per hour for Conductors and 20 cents per hour for Brakemen. Passenger or freight crews, or individuals, required to make dead-head trips, shall receive one-half regular rates for the class of service which requires such dead-head trips. When dead-head service is required, the first crew out will run the train and the crew dead-heading will stand ahead of the crew with whom they dead-head on reaching terminal. Trainmen attending court on Company's business will be paid their regular rate per day and necessary expenses. Trainmen, after a continuous service of sixteen hours or more, shall take eight hours' rest before they are again called for service, except in case of wrecks or similar emergencies. Trainmen will be called for duty as nearly as practicable one hour before the time they are expected to leave. The Caller will have a book in which trainmen shall register their names and the time called. The pay of trainmen will begin one hour after they sign the Caller's book, unless they go on duty sooner. When trainmen are called for a train and the train is abandoned, the Conductor shall receive 30 cents and the Brakemen 20 cents per hour for the time held, and will stand first out. Trainmen will be notified when time is not allowed as per time slips, and reason given why it was not allowed. If a trainman is taken off his run for any cause he shall be granted a full investigation, hearing and decision within five days, at which time he shall have the right to be present, and to have another trainman, of his own selection, to appear and speak for him, and shall have the right to appeal from the decision of the local to the general officers of the road. Should no decision be rendered at the expiration of five days, he shall receive his regular pay until such decision is rendered. The convicted party shall, if he so desires, be allowed to see all evidence produced against him. The use of intoxicating liquors, or visiting saloons, while on duty, will be met with dismissal. Any employe will be dismissed without a hearing in case of intoxication, insubordination or collisions. Trainmen will be in the line of promotion according to their term of service, dependent upon their general good conduct, faithful discharge of their duties and ability to assume increased responsibilities. The Superintendent to be the judge of qualifications. Promotions in train service will be confined to the ranks of train employes as above. When the freight traffic on any portion of the road is so light that all the crews in service are not able to make 2,600 miles per month each, a sufficient number of crews shall be laid off, beginning with the youngest men, until the crews in service are able to make reasonable wages. Any Conductor suspended under this rule shall be given preference as Brakeman.

Approved: CHAS. M. HAYS, General Manager. H. L. MAGEE,
February 1, 1891. General Superintendent.

WEST VIRGINIA CENTRAL AND PITTSBURG RAILROAD.*

Passenger Conductors, $75 per month. Baggagemen, $30 per month from Railroad Company and $30 per month from Express Company. Passenger Brakemen, $1.60 per day. Freight Conductors, $2.25 per day for first year; $2.50 after. Freight Flagmen $1.75 per day for first year; $2 after. Freight Brakemen, $1.60 per day for first year; $1.75 after. Yard Conductors and Brakemen are paid the same rate as on the road. June 29, 1892.

*Not official.

WISCONSIN CENTRAL LINES.

1. *Passenger Conductors:* (*a.*) Passenger Conductors between Chicago and Stevens Point and Menasha, or regular trains Nos. 1, 2, 3, 4, 5, 6, 7 and 8, shall run first in first out, and shall receive $110 per month; ten crews.

(*b.*) Between Stevens Point, Eau Claire and Minneapolis on trains Nos. 1, 2, 3, 4, 7 and 8, shall run first in first out, and shall receive $110 per month; seven crews.

(*c.*) Between Abbotsford, Bessemer and Ashland on trains Nos. 11, 12, 17, 18, 19, 20, 21 and 22, shall run first in first out, and shall receive $110 per month; four crews. During the time from March 15th to June 1st of each year an extra crew is to be put on; provided, in the judgment of the Superintendent the business requires it. Nos. 5 and 6 between Chicago and Menasha, and Nos. 7 and 8 between Stevens Point and Eau Claire are to be classed as through trains. The present time card is to govern the basis on which this schedule is made.

(*d.*) Any additional trips, such as picnic or special train, etc., are to be paid for as per above schedule, 100 miles or less to constitute a day. All runs of 25 miles or less will be counted as one-fourth of a day. All other passenger Conductors shall receive $100 per month, except on Twin City Belt Line, where pay will remain as at present.

(*e.*) Crews on regular assigned runs making extra mileage are to be allowed for all extra work done, at the above rate.

(*f.*) Each Conductor on through run is to be allowed two Brakemen regularly between Chicago and Minneapolis, except on trains 5 and 6, between Oct. 1st and April 1st, when only one will be allowed on these runs, and except on Nos. 7 and 8, north of Stevens Point; provided, that on trains 1, 2, 3 and 4, north of Stevens Point, the Superintendent may put on five Flagmen instead of two regular Brakemen to each crew, without extra allowance.

2. *Passenger Brakemen:* All passenger Brakemen shall receive $50 per month, regardless of the runs they are on, and extra allowance, same as Conductors' schedule.

3. (*a.*) *Freight Service:* Through freight, Conductors, $2.90 per day, ten hours or less, 100 miles or less, 29 cents per hour; Brakemen, $1.95 per day, ten hours or less, 100 miles or less, 19½ cents per hour; except on the Ashland division, where pay will be at rate of 3 cents for Conductors and 2 cents for Brakemen, per mile.

(*b.*) Way freights, Chicago and Waukesha; two crews and three Brakemen; an extra crew to be put on when business warrants, Superintendent to decide. Conductors, $90 per month; Brakemen, $60 per month. Waukesha and Oshkosh, two crews, two Brakemen. Conductors, $85 per month; Brakemen, $57.50 per month. Oshkosh and Stevens Point, two crews, three Brakemen. Stevens Point and Irvine, three crews, three Brakemen. Irvine and St. Paul, same as now, two crews. Abbotsford and Mellen, three crews, three Brakemen. Conductors, $85 per month; Brakemen, $57.50 per month. Ashland and Bessemer, one crew, with same number of Brakemen as at present. Conductors, 3 cents per mile; Brakemen, 2 cents per mile. Twenty-six or twenty-seven days or less constitute a month, provided the crew makes all its regular runs; extra for mileage made on lay-over days and Sundays, at through train rates.

(*c.*) Conductors now employed on Chicago and Milwaukee divisions as such will receive $2.80 per 100 miles, eight miles to be added to the mileage of each of these two divisions, making Chicago division 106 miles, and Milwaukee division 160 miles. All Conductors promoted on these two divisions after the date of this schedule taking effect shall receive $2.90 per 100 miles, actual mileage, 100 miles to be allowed for the Chicago division. Brakemen to receive $1.95 per 100 miles, same computation.

(*d.*) On Portage branch trainmen will be paid through freight train rates when making 100 miles or less (on extra trains), which will constitute a day; when making over 100 miles actual mileage to be counted. This rule does not apply to regular trains, which will be allowed, as at present, 100 miles over the branch.

(*e.*) Work trains: Conductors will receive $85 and Brakemen $57.50 per month. Twenty-six days to constitute a month, and twelve hours or less constituting a day's work. All over twenty-six days is to be paid for at same rate, and all over twelve hours to be paid for at through train rates. Trainmen will be allowed mileage made. going to or from work, when handling freight, at through train rates.

(*f.*) Overtime in road service shall be paid for at the rate of ten miles per hour on basis of rate and classification. Overtime shall begin after ten hours in service. In computing all overtime, thirty minutes or over will be counted as one hour after first hour. On all through freight runs of over 100 miles, Conductors and Brakemen shall be paid for all mileage made on each run, and in addition to actual mileage overtime shall be allowed and paid them on the basis of ten miles per hour. This does not apply to way freights.

(*g.*) Local crews will not be required to do construction work, loading or unloading material, to exceed one hour on each trip, and if so held they will be paid at overtime rates while engaged strictly at this work.

4. (*a.*) Trainmen held in yards or terminals waiting for trains or engines beyond the time train was specified or due to leave, will be allowed and paid for each hour held, at rates for overtime, provided train is held one hour or more.

(*b.*) Trainmen required to remain on duty with their trains after arrival at terminal stations one hour or more. shall be paid therefor at overtime rates.

5. When time is not allowed as per Conductor's daily time slip, it shall be returned at once with the reason for not allowing the time.

6. (*a.*) When trains for which men have been called are abandoned, they shall be allowed not less than one-fourth day, and stand first out; provided they are not again required for service within two and one-half hours from time first specified to leave, in which case they will be paid overtime, as per rule governing time before starting.

(*b.*) Trainmen when required to do switching at terminals will be paid for such service at schedule rates for overtime.

7. (*a.*) Trainmen will be called as nearly as practicable one hour and fifteen minutes before leaving time of train. The Caller will have a book in which trainmen will register their names and the time when they were called.

(*b.*) There will be one or more Callers at all division terminals, except Rugby Junction and Abbotsford, to call trainmen for all trains or runs, except on passenger trains between the hours of 6 a. m. and 10 p. m.

(*c.*) After sixteen hours of continuous service, or more, trainmen will be entitled to and allowed eight hours' rest at terminals, provided they so desire and give timely notice thereof, except in cases of washouts, wrecks and other similar emergencies.

8. (*a.*) In making up trains yardmen shall put all air cars on the head end of train and next to the engine when practicable.

(*b.*) At terminal stations where switch engines are stationed, yardmen shall ascertain where trains are and let all trains into the yards when practicable to do so.

9. All allowances made to regular trains will be made to extra trains.

10. (*a.*) On all turn-arounds or short runs, switch engines and crews are to make up trains where switch engines are stationed, except on special order of Superintendent.

(*b.*) On turn-arounds or short runs, where trainmen make up their own trains, they shall be paid for such time doing this work at overtime rates, thirty minutes or over to count as one hour.

(*c.*) When trainmen are required to shovel coal from cars, shed or platform, they will be paid for same at rate of six cents per ton, dividing this between the men employed.

11. (*a.*) Trainmen dead-heading over the road in Company's service will receive half mileage, provided that not less than full mileage be allowed where no other service is performed same date; full mileage to be allowed when dead-heading on freight trains. New men employed will receive no pay dead-heading to work.

(*b.*) In ordering crews the first crew out shall run the train, the second crew dead-heading when such service is required; the crew dead-heading being ahead of the crew with which they dead-headed on reaching the terminal of that run.

12. (*a.*) When held as witnesses for the Company, trainmen and yardmen will be paid schedule rates, one day or 100 miles for each calendar day.

(*b.*) Allowances for necessary expenses will be made when on Company business. Time held attending court is to be certified to by the Company's attorney.

13. Freight trainmen will be allowed full freight train rates and mileage for handling passenger trains or passenger equipment. When more than one round trip is made on regular passenger runs, passenger Conductors' schedule is to govern the pay.

14. (*a.*) When good cause is shown for doubling hills, actual mileage will be allowed.

(*b.*) Any trip to and from the stock yards by Chicago division crews, or train crews, will be estimated at ten miles per hour.

15. Whenever a Conductor is sent over the road with an engine without a train or caboose he shall receive pay of a through freight Conductor.

16. The right to regular runs and to promotion will be governed by merit, ability and seniority. Everything being equal the Conductor or Brakeman longest in the service will have the preference. The Superintendent is to be the judge of the qualifications. Nothing in this article shall be construed as preventing the Company from employing experienced men from other roads, or promoting them from the ranks of the Brakemen, when the good of the service requires it. Experienced men to be construed as those who have had at least one year's experience as a Conductor. None who are known to use liquor as a beverage will be selected.

17. Freight Conductors will be promoted to passenger trains according to their ability and age of continuous service on their respective divisions; the question of age and ability to be determined by the Superintendents. No Conductor will be employed as a passenger Conductor unless he has had one or more years of experience as a freight Conductor.

18. Trainmen will rank from the date they are employed, and in the event of there being a surplus of men, the oldest in the service and married men on their respective divisions shall have the preference of employment. This is to be decided to the best interests of all concerned.

19. No more men are to be employed in the through freight service than are necessary to do the work and earn a reasonable monthly compensation of not less than 2,600 miles, at the schedule established. Whenever in the judgment of the trainmen there are too many crews, a committee of not less than three Conductors and two Brakemen, in good standing, employed on the division, may call the attention of the Trainmaster or Superintendent to such surplus of men, when the matter will be fully investigated, and if the conditions are found to warrant it, will be remedied, it being always understood that men will be retained under seniority of rights, as provided for in Article 18.

20. Conductors and Brakemen charged with offenses involving either suspension or discharge, shall have a full investigation within a reasonable time, which, except in extreme and unavoidable cases, shall not exceed five days. If, after investigation, the Conductor or Brakeman is found blameless, he shall be immediately reinstated and receive full pay for all time lost on account of such suspension or discharge. Trainmen charged with offenses involving either suspension or discharge, excepting in cases involving fraud or dishonesty, will be advised of the offenses in writing. All parties concerned will be present at the investigation.

21. It is the rule and intention of the Company to run through freight crews first in first out. But circumstances may arise where this should be changed and the Company reserves the right to do so. For instance, it may be deemed advisable to run certain crews upon certain designated trains, and the Company must be at liberty to arrange such matters for its best interests.

22. (a.) Conductors in charge of trains will be held responsible for their safe management, and shall have the right and power to place their Brakemen as their best judgment may dictate, so long as it does not conflict with the book of rules; but nothing in this clause shall give the Conductor the right to discriminate against an old Brakeman. All things being equal the oldest Brakeman shall have the preference to the rear end.

(b.) In any case where a Brakeman fails to obey orders of a Conductor he shall be suspended or discharged, as the case may require, upon a thorough investigation by the proper officials.

(c.) No Conductor shall be required to take out more than one inexperienced Brakeman on any train.

23. Brakemen who have never worked on a freight train shall work at least one year on a freight train before they will be entitled to an examination for promotion to a freight Conductorship.

24. No fines shall be imposed on a Conductor or Brakeman for damages.

25. There shall be no discrimination against any employe of the Company on account of being a member of any of the railway organizations.

26. (a.) When trainmen or yardmen leave the service of the Company they shall be given letters stating the time of service, in what capacity or capacities employed, and cause of leaving the service.

(b.) Letters shall be given three days from application, providing the men shall have worked on the division thirty days or over, and shall be signed and stamped by the Division Superintendent.

27. Trainmen or yardmen who have been discharged, and who upon further investigation are found to have been unjustly dealt with, will be reinstated, provided the matter is settled within two months from the time of discharge; otherwise, if re-employed, they shall rank as new men on the road or in the yard.

28. The train now on the Marshfield branch, and trains Nos. 229 and 230, between Rugby Junction and Milwaukee, are to be known and classed as local trains, and will do the same work as at present.

29. On the Eau Claire branch runs Conductors are to receive $85, and Brakemen $50 per month.

30. (*a*.) This agreement on the part of the Company will be observed by all concerned. The signing Conductors and Brakemen agree, for themselves and associates, to do their part toward a faithful observance of the same, and should a real or imagnary grievance arise from any cause, will select a favorable opportunity to present the same to the proper authority.

(*b*.) All previous agreements are hereby abolished. This schedule shall not be altered or amended except by mutual consent.

WISCONSIN CENTRAL LINES, NORTHERN PACIFIC R. R. CO., Lessee.
For Order of Railway Conductors: G. CAMPBELL,
E. HAMILTON, Chairman.   General Superintendent.
IRA YANTIS.   Approved: S. R. AINSLEE,
PETER McHUGH.   General Manager.
For Brotherhood of Railroad Trainmen:
H. L. CAMERON, Chairman, L. T. KANE, T. GRAY, O. OSTERMYER.
March 1, 1892.

ZANESVILLE & OHIO RIVER RAILWAY COMPANY.

Passenger Conductors, $70 per month, 150 miles per day. Passenger Brakemen, 1 cent per mile, 150 miles per day. Baggagemasters, $50 per month, 150 miles per day. Freight Conductors receive $2.50 and $2.75 per day and run 75 miles. Freight Brakemen receive $1.60 and $1.80 per day and run 75 miles. We employ no Switchmen or yardmen, the crews doing their own switching. At the Zanesville terminus we occupy the C. & M. V. passenger and freight depot and their yard engine does the switching.
May 16, 1892.   J. HOPE SUTOR, General Manager.

CHICAGO & ERIE RAILWAY.

1. The pay of Conductors on through passenger trains will be two cents per mile, and one cent per mile for dead-heading on Company's business. Baggagemen will receive one cent per mile, and one-half cent per mile for dead-heading. Brakemen on through passenger trains will receive 9-10 cents per mile. Trains 9 and 10, milk run, (run every day in the month, 140 miles per day,) Conductors will receive 2 cents per mile, Baggagemen will receive $53.00 per month, and Brakemen $50.00 per month. Trains 3 and 12, the Flagman will receive $50.00 per month.

2. Through Freight Conductors will receive 2 9-10 cents per mile. Brakemen will receive 1 98-100 cents per mile, 80 to 100 miles to constitute a day's work. All over 100 miles, Conductors to receive 2 9-10 cents per mile, and Brakemen 1 98-100 cents per mile; except that for five hours or less service 50 miles or one-half day be allowed. On runs of more than 50 miles, or less than 80, actual mileage will be allowed.

3. The Conductors on all local freights will receive $84.00 per month, and local Brakemen will receive $54.00 per month. After 14 hours on duty overtime will commence. Conductors will be allowed 27¼ cents per hour, and Brakemen 17¼ cents, time to be counted from leaving time of trains, 30 minutes or more to be counted one hour, less than 30 minutes not to be counted.

4. Conductors of work or construction trains will receive $2.90 per day, 50 to 100 miles, or 5 to 12 hours to constitute a day's work.

5. Conductors who are required by order of a superior officer to dead-head over any division on business of the railway, shall receive one-half regular pay per day for time spent, and for attending court as witnesses at the request of the railway, shall receive $2.90 per day, and $1.00 per day for expenses. Brakemen will be allowed one-half regular pay per day for dead-heading over any division on business of the railway, and for attending court as witness at the request of the railway, will receive $1.98 per day, and $1.00 per day for expenses.

6. All through freight Conductors will, when practicable, be assigned to divisions to run first in first out on the divisions to which they are assigned. The right to the regular runs will be governed by their ability and seniority, all other things being equal.

7. When a Conductor or Brakemen has been taken off his run for cause, an investigation will be held at as early a date as possible, and within 10 days or less, unless circumstances intervene to prevent. The right of any employe is recognized to personally appear before the proper officers and present grievances for a hearing, and adjustment without prejudice. It is not deemed necessary to have a second party appear in behalf of the accused during the investigation.

8. No greater number of freight crews shall be employed than can reasonably be expected to make at least 2,500 miles per month; and any Conductor who has been on duty 15 consecutive hours shall have at least 6 hours rest before going out again, unless he goes voluntarily. Same rule applies to Brakemen.

9. The Conductors and Brakemen not to be called for duty until a reasonable time before the train is to leave. It would be impossible for all crews to be called just one hour before leaving time, on account of the great diversity of places the Caller would have to visit to call the men. In case a Conductor and Brakeman are called for a train and the train is annulled, the Conductor shall receive 27½ cents per hour and Brakemen 17½ cents, for time on duty, and shall stand first out. After being on duty 13 hours on East Division, and 14 hours on Western Division, overtime will commence at the rate of 27½ cents for Conductors and 17½ cents per hour for Brakemen. In computing time, any fraction of an hour less than 30 minutes will not be counted, over 30 minutes will be counted one hour. Overtime to commence from leaving time. Trainmen to strictly observe the rule to be on hand 30 minutes before leaving time.

10. All Officers, Conductors, Engineers, Firemen and Brakemen will observe strict courtesy of manner in their intercourse with each other and with all other employes.

11. Employes will not be dismissed from the service of this Company on account of serving on Grievance Committees.

12. In case of damage to the property of the railway, the offending person shall be subject to suspension, equitable fine, or dismissal, as the necessities of the case may demand, time of suspension not to exceed in money value the amount of the fine.

13. Local cars to be set out will be placed in the head end of trains on through freight. It is the intention of this Company as soon as consistent with the financial condition of the road, to place air brakes on all its mogul engines. It is not considered that the putting on of the third Brakeman on mogul trains is necessary for the service.

14. Uniformity of height of cars next to engines and cabooses is regarded important, and will be carried out as often as may be consistent without unnecessary switching to obtain the result. Approved as above:
March 1, 1890. G. M. BEACH,
General Manager C. & A. Ry.

SUPPLEMENT.

On and after April 1st, 1892: Increase the pay of Brakemen on through passenger trains one mill per mile, making the future rate ten mills instead of nine mills per mile. Increase the pay of Brakemen on trains 13 and 14, one mill per mile, making the future rate nine mills instead of eight mills per mile. Increase the pay of Baggagemen on the North Judson and Chicago run, $2.00 per month, making the rate $55.00 instead of $53.00 per month as at present; Brakemen on the North Judson and Chicago run, $55.00 instead of $50.00 per month as at present. J. C. MOORHEAD,
April 2, 1892. General Superintendent.

CHICAGO & EASTERN ILLINOIS RAILROAD COMPANY.
OPERATING THE CHICAGO & INDIANA COAL RAILWAY.

Through Passenger Runs: Conductors, $100 per month; Baggagemen, $57.50 per month; Baggagemen joint with Express Company, $60 per month; passenger Brakemen, $48 per month. Crews assigned to regular runs will be paid extra for any service performed outside of their regular runs at the regular rates for class of service performed.

Short Passenger Runs: Watseka and Terre Haute, Conductors $90, and Brakemen $50 per month. St. Louis division, Conductors $90, and Brakemen $50 per month. Suburban, including Momence and Chicago, Conductors $95, and Brakemen $52.50 per month, and Flagmen $45 per month.

Local Freight Runs: Conductors $85, and Brakemen $57.50 per month. All local freight runs to have three Brakemen, except Terre Haute and St. Louis divisions, which will have what is called the Swingman, who will receive $60 per month. Cissna Park, Conductors $75 per month, two Brakemen $50 per month each. Extra road service rendered by local train crews shall be paid for at the regular rate for class of work performed.

Through Freight Runs: On all through runs of 100 miles or more, Conductors shall receive 3 cents and Brakemen 2 cents per mile for the entire distance run. All coal runs between Danville and Grape Creek shall receive, Conductors $80 per month, and Brakemen $55 per month. Freight trains will be allowed three Brakemen when the work requires it, the Superintendent of Transportation or Trainmaster to be the one to decide when this is necessary. Through freight runs on Terre Haute division to be based as follows: Danville to Terre Haute and return, and Danville to Brazil and return, to constitute a trip same as through freight on longer divisions and based on 12 hours for a day's work. Conductors to receive 3 cents per mile, and Brakemen 2 cents per mile. Where trains are run from Danville to Terre Haute and return, or from Danville to Brazil and return, one way local and return on through freight, time is to be computed on the basis of 13 hours; on the same runs where trains are run both ways as local freight, time to be computed on the basis of 14 hours, and overtime to be allowed at the rate of 30 cents per hour for Conductors and 20 cents per hour for Brakemen, after 12 hours on through freight, 13 hours on local and through freight, and 14 hours on local freight. Freight Conductors promoted from Brakemen shall receive two-tenths of a cent per mile less than regular rates for the first year's service. Freight Conductors having regular crews will not be called upon to take extra runs when an extra Conductor can be obtained. Clinton Mine run to receive, Conductors $85 per month, and Brakemen $57.50 per month; overtime after 12 hours. Turn-around trips between Chicago and Momence will be paid as follows: Conductors, first-class, $3.50, second-class, $3.25; Brakemen, $2.30 round trip, overtime to be allowed after six hours each way. Short runs not otherwise specified, where mileage is 50 miles or less, will be allowed 50 miles; over 50 miles and less than 100 miles to be allowed 100 miles, provided no other mileage is made on that same date. If aggregate mileage made on any date equals or exceeds 100 miles, actual mileage will govern; dates to begin and end at midnight, and each trip to date from starting time.

Work Trains: Conductors of work trains shall receive $3 per day, and Brakemen $2 per day.

Crews Running Light: Crews running light shall receive two-thirds of regular through freight pay.

Pilots: Conductors piloting engines over the road shall receive freight Conductor's pay for such service.

Dead-head Trips: Freight crews required to make dead-head trips shall receive one-half the rate for the class of service which requires such dead-head trip.

Crews Attending Court: Trainmen attending court on the Company's business will be allowed regular pay.

Overtime: All over 12 hours on through freight or work trains, and 14 hours on local freight trains, will be paid for as overtime at the rate of 30 cents per hour for Conductors and 20 cents per hour for Brakemen, provided that such overtime is not the fault of such Conductor or Brakeman. Trainmen required to remain on duty after arrival at terminal station will be allowed yard delay time for all such time on duty. Fractions of an hour less than 35 minutes will not be counted; over 35 minutes and less than 60 minutes to be counted an hour.

Rest: Trainmen, after continued service of 16 hours or more, shall take sufficient rest before they are again called for service, except in cases of wrecks or similar emergencies. Trainmen living within one mile of yard offices to be called up to go out as near as practicable, two hours before the time they are expected to leave; the Caller to have a book in which the trainmen shall register their names and time called. Any Conductor or Brakeman failing to respond after being thus called shall be liable to suspension or discharge, as the General Superintendent or Superintendent of Transportation may determine. Their time will begin two hours after they sign the Caller's book, unless they go on duty sooner. When trainmen are called for a train, and the said train is afterward annulled, the Conductor shall receive 30 cents per hour and the Brakeman 20 cents per hour for the time held, and shall stand first out. Trainmen will be notified when time is not allowed as per time slip, and the reason why it was not allowed.

Trainmen Taken Off Run: If a trainman is relieved from duty for any cause, he shall be granted a thorough investigation, hearing and decision within five days, at which investigation he shall have the right to be present, and to have another Conductor or Brakeman, as the case may be, of his own selection, to appear to speak for him, and shall have the right to appeal from the local to the general officers of the road, and a decision in five days after presenting his appeal, and in case such decision is not made within five days on such appeal, one-half pay shall begin and continue until such decision is made.

Promotions: Trainmen will be in line of promotion according to their time of service, dependent upon their general good conduct and the faithful discharge of their duties, and their ability to assume increased responsibilities, the Superintendent of Transportation to be judge of such qualifications. The Railroad Company has the right to employ one Conductor to one Brakeman promoted. Promotion in the train service to be confined to the ranks of train employes as above. When practicable, Conductors and Brakemen shall be assigned to regular runs. On all freight trains except local freight trains, they will run first in first out, unless the service requires it otherwise. The right to regular runs will be governed by merit, ability and seniority. Everything being equal, the Conductors and Brakemen longest in faithful service will have the preference. When the freight traffic is so light that the crews in service are not able to make reasonable wages, crews will be taken off, beginning with the youngest men, until the crews left in service are able to make reasonable wages. Conductors taken off under this rule will be given preference as Brakemen, and again placed on their runs when business demands an increase of crews.

CHICAGO & EASTERN ILLINOIS RAILROAD COMPANY,
For the Order of Railway Conductors: CHAS. H. ROCKWELL,
W. M. BELL, Chairman.   General Superintendent.
S. P. NOEL,
FRED SMITH, Secretary.
For the Brotherhood of Railroad Trainmen:
CHAS. J. KNIERIM, Chairman, J. SCHOOLCRAFT, C. A. ISBELL, Secretary
July 15, 1892.

CHICAGO GREAT WESTERN RAILWAY COMPANY.

1. Rate of compensation for passenger Conductors on main line trains, $115 per month. Brakeman, $55 per month. Nine Baggagemen between Minneapolis and Chicago, $65 per month. Present rates in effect on Waverly and other branch lines, also Savannah suburban service, to remain the same as at present. When crews on daily runs exceed the monthly mileage of such runs they shall be paid pro rata. Crews running on local passenger trains may be used for extra serivce when required without extra compensation, provided they do not exceed the mileage made by crews on daily runs. When such mileage is exceeded extra compensation will be allowed at regular rates. In filling vacancies in the ranks of passenger Conductors the freight Conductor longest in continuous service of the company on division or divisions now established as passenger divisions shall be selected if qualified.

2. *Through Freight Service.*—Conductors and Brakemen shall be paid at the rate of 3 and 2 cents per mile respectively. One hundred miles or less, ten hours or less, shall constitute one day's work. All over 100 miles or over ten hours to be paid pro rata. All doubles of less than 85 miles, if made within fourteen hours, actual mileage will be allowed. If not doubled within fourteen hours, one day each way will be allowed. (This in no way to conflict with first paragraph of this Article.)

3. The actual number of days in any calendar month, exclusive of Sundays, will constitute one month's work for any specified month in local or work train service. All mileage over and above the regular monthly mileage to be paid for at regular freight train rates.

4. *Local Freight Service.—Chicago Division:* There shall be placed upon this division four regular freight crews: Between Robey street and Byron two crews, to consist of one Conductor and three Brakemen each; between Byron and Fair Grounds, two crews to consist of one Conductor and two Brakemen each.

Dubuque Division: Upon this division there shall be three regularly assigned crews consisting of one Conductor and three Brakemen each.

St. Paul Division: Upon this division there shall be two regularly assigned crews consisting of one Conductor and three Brakemen each, regular freight train mileage to be allowed.

Des Moines Division: Upon this division there shall be three regularly assigned crews, to consist of one Conductor and three Brakemen each.

St. Joseph Division: Upon this division there shall be three regularly assigned crews, to consist of one Conductor and two Brakemen each.

The compensation for local freight trainmen shall be $90 for Conductors and $60 for Brakemen, per month. (St. Paul division excepted, as per third paragraph of this Article.)

5. *Overtime:* In computing overtime on several divisions, overtime will be allowed after the expiration of the following hours: On the Chicago division, 17 hours; on the Dubuque division, 12 hours; on the St. Paul division, 13 hours; on the Des Moines division, 13 hours; on the St. Joseph division, 15½ hours; on the Kansas City division, 10 hours. In computing overtime no fraction of an hour less than thirty minutes to be considered; thirty minutes and over constitute one hour. In case any regular or extra freight train is required to do construction work, such as unloading Company material mileage will be allowed at the rate of ten miles per hour for all time over one hour so delayed.

6. *Work Train Service:* Compensation for work train crews will be $90 for Conductors and $60 for Brakemen, per month, twelve hours or less to constitute one day's work

All time over twelve hours will be paid pro rata. Crews will not suffer any reduction in salary on account of train not working when held for duty between division terminals.

7. *Switching Service:* When trainmen are required to do switching at terminal and turn-round stations they shall receive compensation for such service at road rates, viz.: ten miles per hour, no allowance to be made for less than thirty minutes.

GENERAL RULES.

1. Freight trainmen assigned to passenger service not exceeding one round trip will be allowed regular freight rates. For handling passenger equipment freight train rates will govern.

2. It is the rule of the Company to run crews first in first out. This rule, however, cannot be rigidly carried out at all times, and the proper officers of the Company will vary therefrom only in case of an emergency. Everything being equal, the oldest Conductors and Brakemen in the service of the Company will have choice of runs upon their respective divisions. In case, however, the oldest man declines to take the run to which his age in the service entitles him, the man superseding him to be ahead of him in line of further or future promotion.

3. Freight trainmen will be called at division terminal stations by a train Caller, who will be provided with a book in which the men called will register their names, together with the time they are called. The district within which trainmen will be called will be established by the Division Superintendent. This will not apply to Kansas City terminal and branch runs.

4. The working time of all freight trainmen will commence from the time the train is ordered to leave.

5. Whenever freight trainmen are called and for any reason, other than their own action, do not go out and are held on duty less than five hours, they will be allowed fifty miles. If held on duty over five hours they will be allowed ten miles per hour for all time so held. Crews released after being held seven and one-half hours or less stand first out; when held over seven and one-half hours, and are then released, they will go behind all crews at that point.

6. Crews of wrecking trains will be paid mileage for all mileage running to and from a wreck and, in addition, overtime rates for all hours used at wreck.

7. Conductors, Baggagemen and Brakemen will not be suspended nor dismissed from the Company's service without just cause. In case of suspension or dismissal, if an employe thinks his sentence unjust he shall have the right, within ten days, to refer his case by written statement to the Division Superintendent. Within ten days after the receipt of this notice his case shall have a thorough investigation, at which he may be present if he so desires. In the event of it not being to the convenience of the Company to have present the party making the charge, written statement of the absentee will be considered sufficient. In case of intoxication or insubordination dismissal will follow without hearing. In case suspension or dismissal is found to be unjust he shall be reinstated and paid for all time lost.

8. When freight traffic is so light that crews cannot make regular wages (about 3,000 miles per month) crews will be taken off, in the order of promotion, until crews remaining are able to make about that amount. Conductors thus reduced shall, as far as practicable, be given preference as Brakemen until such time as the increase of business warrants their reinstatement as Conductors. This not to include crews assigned to regular runs. Every employe should understand that it is his privilege and duty to make a written appeal to his Superintendent whenever, by promotion, reduction or assignment, he deems that injustice has been done him.

9. When attending law suits, at the Company's request, full time will be allowed; expenses paid when away from home stations.

10. When a change of divisions or train runs requires trainmen to change their places of residence they will be furnished free transportation for their families and their household goods.

11. Trainmen leaving the service of the Company shall be given, by the proper officer, a letter stating time of service, capacity employed in and cause for leaving; said letter not to be given unless the party has been employed on the division six months or more.

12. Any trainman after continuous service of sixteen hours or more shall, upon a written or telegraphic notice upon Trainmaster or Division Superintendent, be entitled to eight hours' rest before he is again called for service, except in cases of wrecks, washouts or snow blockades, and providing also that such notice is given prior to or at the expiration of any run. The crews following will have the right to run around any crew lying over for rest. Crews will not be released between division terminals.

13. Trainmen dead-heading over the road on Company business, on passenger trains, will be paid half regular freight train rates. When dead-heading on freight

trains full rates will be allowed. When necessary to dead-head crews on freight trains the first crew out will run the train and the second crew dead-head, the crew dead-heading to stand ahead of the crew running the train on arrival at terminal point.

14. Whenever a trainman is transferred from his department by the request of the Company, he does not forfeit his rights in the department he leaves.

15. A trainman being suspended shall be notified in writing, which shall plainly state length of time suspended and cause therefor.

16. When time is not allowed as per Conductors' daily time slips they shall be returned at once, stating cause.

17. In line of promotion two Brakemen will be promoted from rank of Brakeman, according to age on respective divisions and their ability to assume the duties of Conductor. For every two Brakemen so promoted one Conductor may be hired or promoted from the rank of Brakeman regardless of age in the service. Any Conductor so hired or promoted shall have had at least one year's experience on a steam surface railway as Conductor and shall be required to pass such examination as the rules of this Company may require.

18. If, for any cause, a Conductor is unable to take out his crew an extra Conductor shall be furnished as soon as possible.

19. In case of any change in the present division terminals the established runs will be changed by the officers of the Company, when in their judgment it will serve the Company's interest to do so.

20. Actual mileage will be allowed for doubling hills.

21. When reasonable notice has been given, members of grievance committee will be granted unlimited leave of absence when on committee business. Transportation will be granted to grievance committees to any point of meeting on this system, upon application to Division Superintendent.

22. When pilots are used they will be paid regular through freight Conductors' rate.

23. The necessary officers and trainmen will be furnished with copies of this schedule.

24. No departure from the provisions of this agreement will be made by any party thereto without reasonable notice of such a desire, in writing, having been served upon other parties thereto. The articles enumerated constitute in their entirety an agreement between the Chicago Great Western Railway Company and its Conductors, Baggagemen and Brakemen.

J. A. KELLY,
E. H. RIGGS, Chairman for the Conductors.
A. J PATERSON, Chairman for the Trainmen.
D. McNAB,
B. F. EGAN,
J. BERLINGETT,
Approved: JNO. M. EGAN,
General Manager.
December 1, 1892.
Division Superintendents.

CHICAGO & NORTHWESTERN RAILWAY COMPANY.

PASSENGER TRAINMEN'S SCHEDULE.

1. *Compensation:* Extra compensation shall be allowed Passenger Trainmen for all mileage made in excess of their regular runs, except on suburban trains, and where the mileage is less than 2,600 miles. Passenger Trainmen called upon to do freight work will receive the same compensation as men in freight service. When a Passenger Conductor is taken off his regular run to run specials, or extras, he shall receive 3 cents per mile for such service. When a Passenger Conductor doubles for such Conductor, taken off his regular run, he shall receive such compensation as such Conductor would receive, in addition to his regular salary. No deduction shall be made for any time lost on account of snow blockades or washouts. On divisions where extra Passenger Conductors are employed, their pay shall be $100.00 per month, and they shall not be called upon to do freight work. Milk Conductors will be paid $55.00 per month.

2. *Rights and Privileges of Passenger Trainmen:* No rights heretofore enjoyed by Passenger Trainmen shall be abrogated. The rights of Passenger Baggagemen and Brakemen commence on the day of their first trip, and they shall have the choice of runs to which their age as Brakemen or Baggagemen entitles them, provided they are morally and intellectually fitted for it in the opinion of their Superintendent. Passenger Brakemen will be promoted to the position of Baggagemen in their regular order where they are competent, the Superintendent of the Division to be the judge. Extra Passenger Brakemen will be promoted to regular runs according to date of their first trip in passenger service, and the compensation for such service will be the same as the Brakemen would receive for whom they run. Passenger Trainmen will be allowed to lay off on account of sickness of themselves or their families, to serve on committees or for other good and sufficient reasons, providing due notice is given the proper officer,

that their places may be filled. Any Passenger Trainman having been absent to exceed six consecutive months, thereby forfeits all rights with the Company, except in case of sickness, or where leave of absence has been granted. No leave of absence will be granted to exceed one year, nor re-instatements made after one year's continuous absence, except in case of sickness. Where passenger crews run over more than one freight division, the oldest Passenger Trainmen will be considered as entitled to promotion to passenger runs as above. Nothing in this article shall be considered as preventing the Company from employing experienced men when the service requires it. When a Passenger Trainman leaves one division of his own accord, to work on another division, he will be considered a new employe, but should he be transferred by order of the Company, the same right he possessed on the first division will be retained on his return. The employment of Brakemen and Baggagemen is placed in the hands of the Division Superintendent, but Brakemen will in all cases be placed as Conductor's best judgment may dictate.

FREIGHT TRAINMEN'S SCHEDULE.

1. *Rates and Grades:* There shall be two grades of Freight Conductors established, and the compensation shall be as follows: (a) For the first year's actual service after promotion from a Brakeman, $68.00 per month. (b) For the second year's service, and thereafter, $78.00 per month. There shall be two grades of Freight Brakemen established, and the compensation shall be as follows: (a) For the first three months of actual service, $45.00 per month. (b) For all service thereafter, $52.00 per month. Conductors of way freight trains will be paid $85.00, and Brakemen $60.00 for 2,600 miles or less, made in any one month. All mileage made in any one month in excess of 2,600 miles will be paid for extra at the rate of 3¼ cents per mile for Conductors and 2 3-10 cents per mile for Brakemen. (a) Conductors on work trains will be paid not less than $85.00 and Brakemen $55.00 per month of 26 days, 10 hours or less to constitute a day's work, providing crews are not called for further duty the same date. All time made in excess of 10 hours will be paid for at the rate of 3¼ cents per mile for Conductors and 2 1-10 cents per mile for Brakemen. (b) Work Train Conductors having charge of gangs of men and acting as foreman will receive $15.00 in addition to the $85.00 per month. The pay of crews on mixed trains shall be computed at freight rates. Freight Conductors temporarily in passenger service will be paid freight mileage. Temporarily is construed to mean anything less than one month. One month and over will be paid for at passenger rates. In no case, however, shall an extra Conductor receive more pay for a part of a month than the regular Conductor would have received for the whole month, even should the mileage exceed the amount of a full month's pay. Trainmen attending court under instructions from the Company will be paid 100 miles per day and living expenses while away from home.

2. *Rules for Computation:* The monthly compensation is to be based on a mileage of 2,600 miles or 26 days per month, and any excess over this mileage made by Freight Trainmen will be paid for in the same proportion as the monthly compensation is to 2,600 miles. If the mileage of a Freight Trainman falls below 2,600 miles in any one month, and he has been ready for service, losing no time on his own account, in such cases full time for 2,600 miles shall be allowed. The first year's service is to consist of 12 calendar months. Should it become necessary to reduce the force on account of decreased business, and the Conductor still remains in the employ of the Company as Brakeman, his promotion is to date from the time he made his first trip as Conductor, and he shall receive the highest rate paid Brakemen. Freight Trainmen will be notified when time is not allowed as per trip report. Brakemen who are laid off on account of decreased business will be reinstated and hold their rights as per Article 8, provided they report for work when wanted.

3. *Extra Mileage:* All Freight Trainmen on regular runs will receive compensation for extra mileage made outside of their regular runs. All runs of less than 100 miles shall be computed as one day's work, provided the men do not go out again the same day, except on branch runs where the mileage is less than 60 miles per day, where the Company reserves the right to make special agreements with its Trainmen as to the compensation they shall receive. Where crews are required to double hills, such crews will be allowed the extra mileage made. All crews going through to Union Stock Yards will be paid at the rate of 15 miles per hour. This work to be considered as extra work, Western Avenue being considered a terminal for all freight runs on the Galena Division and Mayfair on the Wisconsin Division.

4. *Delayed Time:* Trainmen will be called, as nearly as possible, one hour before the leaving time of their trains. They will be paid for all delayed time at terminal stations, provided the delay exceeds one hour. They will also be paid for all delayed time between terminal stations in case of accidents, washouts, snow or unloading or loading material, provided no claim will be made unless there is a full hour's delay, or if train arrives at its terminal on time. All delayed time will be paid at the rate of 10

miles per hour. When trains for which men have been called are abandoned, men will be paid for the time held between times, should the time exceed one hour. Where trains are delayed for which men have been called, delayed time will be allowed at rates governing the same, commencing from the time the train is scheduled to leave. No time will be allowed unless there is a full hour's delay.

5. *Dead-head Time:* Trainmen will be allowed 10 miles per hour for dead-heading on passenger trains. All other dead-heading shall be computed as actual miles run. When freight crews and way-cars are ordered dead-head, the crews shall accompany their way cars. In ordering crews, the first crew shall run the train, the next crew dead-heading, when such service is required, said crew being ahead of the crew with whom they dead-head, on reaching the terminal of that run.

6. *Switching Service:* If Freight Trainmen are required to do switching at terminal stations, either before leaving or after arriving at such terminal, they will be paid extra for all such switching at the rate of 10 miles per hour. Less than 45 minutes will not be counted; 45 minutes and less than one hour will be counted one hour. It is to be fully understood that freight crews will not be called on to do switching where switch engines are employed, except in cases of absolute necessity.

7. *Discipline:* In case of dismissal or suspension of a Trainman by any one below the Division Superintendent in rank, he shall have the right to appeal to the Division Superintendent for a full and impartial investigation. Should the Division Superintendent fail to adjust the case, the Trainman may appeal to the General Superintendent or the General Manager. No fault shall be found with a Trainman who refuses to go out on account of needed rest. When a Freight Trainman is taken from his run for an alleged fault, an investigation shall be held ordinarily within three days. Where more than three days elapse, he shall, if found innocent, receive pay for all the time lost after the third day. No punishment to be fixed without a thorough investigation. No member of the Trainmen's Order shall be suspended or discharged on account of representing a committee.

8. *Trainmen's Rights and Privileges:* No privileges heretofore enjoyed by Freight Trainmen shall be abrogated. Conductors shall have the right to object to Brakemen for cause, and when objections are sustained by facts, they will be furnished other men. In the choosing of runs by Freight Brakemen, it shall be fully understood that it shall be considered no choice in runs, running first in, first out. When Trainmen have been in the service of the Company for three months or more, and leave the service, they will, if desired, be furnished a letter stating the time and kind of service, and whether leaving on account of resignation or dismissal. Trainmen will not be required to pay fines on account of breakage. When a change of a division or train run requires men to change their place of residence, they will be furnished free transportation for their families and household goods. Trainmen will be allowed to lay off on account of the sickness of themselves, their families, to serve on committees, or for other good and sufficient reasons, provided due notice is given to the proper officers, so that their places may be filled with other men. This does not permit Trainmen to leave the division on which they are employed without permission from their Superintendent. Any Trainman having been absent to exceed six consecutive months, thereby forfeits all rights with the Company, except in case of sickness, or where leave of absence has been granted. No leave of absence shall be granted to exceed one year, nor re-instatements made after one year's continuous absence, except in case of sickness. The rights of a Conductor commence on the day of his promotion, and he shall have the choice of runs to which his age as Conductor entitles him, providing he is intellectually and morally fitted for it in the opinion of his Superintendent. The rights of a Brakeman commence on the day of his first trip, and he will have the choice of runs to which his age in the service as Brakeman entitles him,—merit and competency being equal in the judgment of the Conductor. The employment of Brakemen is placed in the hands of the Division Superintendents, or their representatives; but Brakemen will, in all cases, be placed as the Conductor's best judgment may dictate. If a Brakeman transfers from either the Freight or Passenger Department to the other, he forfeits all rights in the Department which he leaves, and will be classed as a new employe,—except in case of disability. In examining men on the Book of Rules for promotion to Conductors, the oldest Brakemen must have the preference, merit and competency being equal. The Company reserves the right, however, to hire Conductors outside of the employes of the Company, should the service demand it. Where passenger crews run over more than one Freight Division, the oldest Freight Conductor on either division will be considered as entitled to promotion to passenger runs as above. Nothing in this article shall be considered as preventing the Company from employing experienced men when the service requires it. Conductors having charge of trains will be held responsible for their safe management, and shall have the right to place their Brakemen as their best judgment may dictate. When a Trainman leaves

one Division, of his own accord, to work on another Division, he shall be considered a new employe, but should he be transferred by order of the Company, the same rights he possessed on the first Division shall be maintained on his return to the same.

9. *Calling of Men:* A book shall be kept in the Train Dispatcher's office, showing the name of each Trainman and his residence. Superintendents shall agree with their men on certain limits within which men shall be called to take their trains, where call boys are provided. Call boys shall be provided with a book in which Trainmen shall register their names and the time they are called. Trainmen shall also register in a book kept for that purpose in the Train Dispatcher's office, or other designated place, 30 minutes before the trains are due to leave.

10. *Running of Crews:* On other than assigned runs the crews will run first in first out.

11. *Way Freights:* All trains loading or unloading way freight, or doing station switching, shall be classed as way freights, and crews shall receive compensation accordingly. This shall not be construed to apply to through trains setting out or picking up car loads, or handling small lots of local freight, in case of emergency.

12. *Turn-arounds:* Turn-arounds shall be considered as follows: All runs turning at intermediate points on the same date.

SWITCHMEN'S AND YARDMASTERS' SCHEDULE.

1. No privileges heretofore enjoyed by Switchmen and Yardmasters shall be abrogated.

2. Twenty-six days to constitute a month's work, ten hours a day. Overtime to be paid for at the same rate. Crews working from 12 o'clock noon to 12 o'clock midnight, or part day and part night, will receive stipulated wages for night crews. Day crews and night crews to be allowed one hour between 11:30 a. m. and 1:00 p. m., and between 11:30 p. m. and 1:00 a. m., respectively, for eating. If required to work later than 1:00 p. m. or 1:00 a. m., as the case may be, 30 minutes will be allowed for dinner and compensation will be allowed for the full hour, 30 minutes of which has been consumed in eating. All Foremen of switch engines will be furnished with time report book, Form 170, and should any time be not allowed by Yardmaster, the same report will be sent back to Foreman.

3. In case of dismissal or suspension of a Switchman, by any one below the Division Superintendent in rank, he shall have the right to appeal to the Division Superintendent for a full and impartial investigation, and should the Division Superintendent fail to adjust the case, he may appeal to the General Superintendent.

4. When a Switchman is suspended, he shall be notified the day his suspension takes place, and such notice shall plainly state the length of time of suspension, and for what cause.

5. Merit and competency being equal, the Yardmaster to decide, the oldest Helper shall be eligible to any vacant Foremanship, and the oldest Foreman shall be eligible to the position of Assistant Yardmaster. If the promotion is accepted, and the man does not prove satisfactory, he may be reduced to his former position or dismissed from service at the discretion of the Yardmaster. Superintendents shall designate such of their Assistants (Trainmasters, Agents or Yardmasters) as shall employ Switchmen temporarily, it being distinctly understood that no Switchman shall be considered permanently in the service until his application blank has been approved by his Superintendent. Yardmasters will have authority to suspend or dismiss Switchmen from the service, it being understood that men so dismissed shall have the right to appeal to the Superintendent within three days, if circumstances warrant, and if reinstated shall be entitled to full pay for time lost.

6. Switchmen will be allowed to lay off on account of sickness of themselves, their families or for other good and sufficient reasons, provided due notice is given to proper officers, so that their places may be filled with other men, and when reasonable notice has been given, members of the grievance committee will be granted unlimited leave of absence while on committee business

7. Switchmen leaving the employ of the Company without leave of absence forfeit all right with the Company after 60 days, except in cases of sickness of themselves or families. No leave of absence shall be granted to exceed 60 days, nor reinstatement made after 60 days' absence, except in case of sickness.

8. When a Switchman leaves a division of his own accord, he shall not be reinstated, but should he be transferred by order of the Company or laid off on account of decreased business and returned on increase of business, the same rights he possessed on the first division shall be maintained on his return to the same.

9. When Switchmen leave the service of the Company they shall be given letters stating time of service, in what capacity employed and cause for leaving the same; said letters to be given within a reasonable time, provided they have worked on the division 90 days or more, and to be signed and stamped by the Superintendent of the division.

10. The rights of a Switchman commence on the date of entering the service, and he will have the choice of work to which his age in the service as a Switchman entitles him, and he will be in line of promotion according to his term of service, merit and competency being equal in the judgment of the Yardmaster and Superintendent.
Approved: J. M. WHITMAN,   S. SANBORN,
              General Manager.   General Superintendent.
October 1, 1892.

CHICAGO, ROCK ISLAND & PACIFIC RAILWAY.

BRAKEMEN'S SCHEDULE.

1. On lines east of the Missouri river four freight Brakemen shall be promoted from the rank of Brakemen according to age of service on their respective divisions and their ability to assume the duties of Conductor. For every four Brakemen so promoted, one Conductor may be hired or promoted from the rank of Brakeman, regardless of age in service. On lines west of Missouri river, two freight Brakemen shall be promoted according to age in service on their respective divisions and their ability to assume the duties of Conductor. For every two Brakemen so promoted, one Conductor may be hired or promoted from rank of Brakeman, regardless of age in service. Any Conductor so hired or promoted shall have had at least one year's experience as Conductor on steam surface railway, and shall be required to pass such examination as the Company requires. When a Brakeman is called for examination and should fail to pass said examination, and feel that an injustice has been done him, he can call any disinterested party that he wishes and in the presence of the Superintendent of the division be again examined.

2. Brakemen will not be dismissed or suspended from the Company's service without just cause. In case of suspension or dismissal, if the employe thinks his sentence unjust, he shall have the right, within ten days, to refer his case by written statement to the Division Superintendent. Within ten days from the receipt of said notice his case shall have a thorough investigation by the Division Superintendent, at which he shall be present. In case he shall be dissatisfied with the result of said investigation, he shall have the right to appeal to the General Superintendent and to the General Manager. In case the suspension or dismissal is found to be unjust, he shall be reinstated and paid for all time lost.

3. Any Brakeman upon being promoted to a Conductor shall be considered competent to run trains on any part of the system or any of its leased or operated lines.

4. Time consumed in switching at terminal or turn-around points will be computed as overtime.

5. Crews dead-heading under orders will be paid one-half their regular rate; provided, that crews dead-heading perform no other service that date, will be paid full rate for 100 miles.

6. Trainmen attending court at the request of the Company, if on assigned runs, shall be allowed full time; and when in irregular service, 100 miles per day until ordered to resume work in the department in which they are employed, and allowed all legitimate expenses while away from home.

7. Doubling trains or double-headers shall not be allowed.

8. Delayed time on leaving terminal, crews will be paid for actual time delayed, it being understood that one full hour must expire before overtime will be claimed. On arriving at terminals crews will be paid for actual time delayed.

9. On all freight runs of 100 miles or less, requiring more than ten hours to make the trip, overtime will be allowed at the rate of ten miles per hour. On all freight runs exceeding 100 miles, overtime will be allowed for all time consumed to make the trip in excess of an average rate of speed of ten miles per hour at the above rate.

10. Freight train crews will be allowed regular freight rate for handling passenger trains or passenger equipment.

11. There shall be regularly assigned crews on all local and switching main line trains, and three Brakemen to each crew. Trains loading or unloading way freight shall be termed local trains. All other main line crews will be run first in first out.

12. Brakemen called to make a trip shall be paid (provided the train is afterward annulled) for three hours' time, on the basis of the pay they are receiving, and stand first out.

13. When crews make turn-around runs of less than 100 miles, 100 miles will be allowed. When making doubles, the single of which is less than 100 miles, and the double more than 100 miles, will be allowed 200 miles should the double consume to exceed sixteen hours.

14. Twelve hours or less shall constitute one day's work; in work train service, twenty-six or twenty-seven days per calendar month shall constitute a month's work. In work train service crews paid on basis of calendar month will not have their pay reduced on account of national holiday in case their train does not run. There shall be two Brakemen on each work train crew. Work train Brakemen shall receive $60 per month.

15. Crews will be furnished coupon mileage book from which mileage and overtime slip will be sent in to Trainmaster, and stub retained by Conductor for reference.

16. In ordering crews, when dead-heading is required, the second crew will run the train, the first crew will dead-head, and on arriving at terminal stations will stand ahead of crew with which they were dead-headed.

17. Where crews are compelled to double hills they will be allowed actual time consumed.

18. There shall be no greater number of crews employed on each division than can make 3,500 miles per month; except on Illinois division, where no greater number of crews shall be employed than can make 4,000 miles per month.

19. Brakemen will not be required to chain up cars or perform other duty of car repairer, unless such cars contain stock or perishable goods.

20. A Caller shall be provided at all divisions and terminals, who shall call trainmen within the radius of one mile from calling station, and shall be provided with register book in which each trainman shall sign his name, time of calling, number of train and time of leaving, for which he is called. As near as practicable, the trainmen will be called one hour before leaving time. The pay of trainmen shall begin from the time the train is ordered for, as shown on order of calling, and continue to the time of arriving at the end of the run.

21. When a change of division or train runs require trainmen to change their residence, they will be furnished free transportation for their families and household goods, and if discharged from the Company's service after so moving, they shall be furnished free transportation for their families and household goods to their former place of residence.

22. Whenever complaint is made against a trainman, it shall be done in writing with the informer's name attached, and a complete copy shall be furnished to the one against whom complaint has been made, and when a trainman is suspended he shall be notified in writing the day his suspension takes place, and it shall plainly state the length of time suspended and for what cause. When so suspended his time shall be his own.

23. When trainmen leave the service of the Company they shall be given letters stating time of service, in what capacity employed and cause for leaving service. Said letters to be given within five days from leaving Company's service. Said letter to be signed and stamped by the Superintendent of the division.

24. At all terminal yards trains will be made up by yard crews and cabooses and engines attached, and on arrival of trains at terminal stations engines will be taken from train by yard crew.

25. When it becomes necessary, caboose will be set in convenient place for drawing supplies and scrubbing out.

26. Trainmen will not be required to coal up engine except in case of emergency, when two hours overtime shall be allowed at schedule rate. Crews required to load or unload stock, or do construction work, shall be allowed actual time consumed, at schedule rate.

27. When Brakemen are held in for snow plow service they will be allowed the regular rates they are receiving for each day of twenty-four hours they are so held subject to orders, and on the basis of ten hours and ten miles per hour.

28. Seniority in service as Brakeman shall hereafter govern in all choice of runs, it being understood that the rule to be generally pursued does not permit of transferring an employe from one division to another, to the detriment of the division employe. The future choice of runs shall be based on this principle.

29. Regular trainmen employed on Illinois division shall be supplied with passes between Blue Island and Van Buren street, Chicago.

30. On Illinois division there shall be regular crews on all local or switching trains or trains doing such work, as trains Nos. 33 and 35, and their divisions not to exceed 110 miles.

31. Trainmen required to pilot engines over the road shall be allowed Conductors' rate of pay.

32. The Company to furnish all badges and buttons for uniform use to Baggagemen and Brakemen in train service. There shall be one white Brakeman for each

three cars or less, in passenger service; each passenger train in excess of three cars will be furnished with two white Brakemen, and Brakemen employed in passenger service shall have been employed in freight service at least one year as freight Brakeman.

33. Crews running over joint track will receive pay as per schedule of track run over.

34. When overtime or mileage for Brakemen has been sent in by Conductors and been refused by Trainmaster or Division Superintendent, it shall be returned to the Conductor and accompanied by a plainly written statement why such overtime or mileage has been so refused.

35. When reasonable notice has been given, members of the general grievance committee will be granted unlimited leave of absence when on committee business.

36. When trainmen leave the service of their department of their own accord, they shall not be reinstated. Leave of absence shall not be granted for more than 90 days, except in case of sickness or disability.

37. All vacancies occurring in the baggage runs shall be filled from the ranks of the eligible and competent passenger Brakemen; the oldest passenger Brakemen in the service to have the preference on all extra or special passenger runs on their respective divisions.

38. When it becomes necessary for the Company to increase the force of trainmen on any of the various divisions, experienced trainmen shall have the preference. Crews will not be made up of men who have not had acquaintance with the division on which they are to run.

39. Trainmen will be allowed eight hours' rest after sixteen hours' continuous service, provided proper notice is given at the end of such run, except in case of emergency.

40. The following rate of pay will be allowed passenger and freight Brakemen: Freight Brakemen: Local, 2¼ cents per mile, overtime 25 cents per hour; through freight, 2 cents per mile, overtime 20 cents per hour. Passenger Brakemen: Through express, 4,000 to 6,510 miles per month, $60 per month; main line, local or dummy runs, 2,600 to 4.000 miles per month, $55 per month; short and branch runs, 2,600 miles or less per month, $45 per month. Brakemen of passenger trains must make during the month the minimum of mileage established, else they will drop back to the pay established for Brakemen making an equal mileage. Extra mileage over the maximums here established for passenger Brakemen will be paid for at proportionate rates. Freight Brakemen on all branches where mileage is less than seventy miles per day will receive $45 per month. When mileage is more than seventy and less than 100 miles, will be allowed 100 miles per day at 2 cents per mile. Where runs exceed 100 miles per day actual mileage will be allowed at 2 cents per mile.

SWITCHMEN'S SCHEDULE.

1. It shall be arranged to give Switchmen their dinner hour between 11 o'clock A. M. and 1 o'clock P. M., and when it occurs that the necessities of business prevent a Switchman from using the hour assigned him for dinner, he shall be paid extra for such overtime at the rate per hour he is receiving.

2. Twenty-six days constitute a month, and ten hours constitute a day or a night's work. All over this is extra, and will be paid for at the regular rate the Switchmen are receiving. Time in yard service will not be counted as train service, nor vice versa.

3. Crews commencing work at 1 o'clock P. M. and working until 12 o'clock midnight shall receive night men's pay.

4. The Chicago scale of wages is as follows: Day Foremen, $70 per month; day Helpers, $65; night Foremen, $75; night Helpers, $70. At points not paying Chicago scale of wages, at present the rate of wages will be five per cent less than the Chicago scale.

September 1, 1892.

E. ST. JOHN,
General Manager.
W. I. ALLEN,
Assistant General Manager.

INTERNATIONAL & GREAT NORTHERN RAILROAD.

This memorandum, made this 15th day of September, 1891, will govern all Superintendents, Trainmasters and other officers in the service of the International & Great Northern Railroad Company in the discipline and control of all Conductors, trainmen and yardmen in the service of said Company, and will constitute a letter of instructions in all matters herein stated. Hereafter, in the employment of Conductors, Brakemen and yardmen in the service of the above Company, Trainmasters are hereby instructed to employ none but sober, reliable and competent men for this service, and all such employes will be directly responsible to and subject to the orders and control of Trainmasters and Yardmasters at all times and in all matters pertaining to their duties. No other subordinate officer will be allowed to interfere in the discipline and control of these employes, but Brakemen will obey instructions from their Conductors while on duty. The following regulations and schedule of pay will govern Conductors and Brakemen on the International & Great Northern Railroad on and after September 15, 1891.

1. Conductors and Brakemen will not be dismissed nor suspended from the Company's service without just cause.
2. No Conductor or Brakeman will be discharged or suspended without a fair and impartial investigation; in case they are found innocent they will be reinstated and be paid half time. His case will have a thorough investigation, within ten days, by the proper officers of the Railroad Company, at which he may be present if he so desires and produce any witnesses he may be able to secure.
3. All employes will be regarded in the line of promotion, dependent upon the faithful discharge of duties, capacity for responsibility and term of service, and where one Conductor is hired two Brakemen are to be promoted.
4. Every employe will understand that it is his duty and privilege to make written or personal appeal to his superior officer whenever, by promotion, reduction or assignment, he deems any injustice has been done him.
5. Employes dead-heading on Company's business will be paid for actual time lost and, when necessary to leave home, hotel expenses not to exceed $2 per day, and traveling expenses will also be paid by the Company.
6. Passenger Conductors are to be paid $100 per month, and passenger Brakemen $55 per month.
7. Conductors and Brakemen running through freight trains will receive 3 and 2 cents per mile respectively; 100 miles or less to constitute a day's work. Train crews will be allowed same mileage for short runs as engine crews.
8. All time consumed in making any one trip on these trains in excess of the time necessary to complete the trip at an average rate of ten miles an hour will be paid for as overtime, overtime to begin thirty-five minutes after. Conductors will be paid 30 cents and Brakemen 20 cents per hour for overtime.
9. Certain freight trains will be designated to do the local work. The way freight and other local work to be put on these trains. A. R. T. or other perishable local freight to be unloaded by through trains, when necessary, and overtime of one hour or more paid for, at overtime rate, in addition to time used in making the trip.
10. When necessary to put three local crews on Taylor or San Antonio sections, the pay of Conductors will be $90 per month and Brakemen $60 per month, and overtime to be allowed if any made. Three Brakemen to each crew, and trains to run daily except Sunday.
11. Conductors or Brakemen will be allowed to lay off on account of sickness of themselves or their families, or other good and sufficient reason, of which the proper official will be the judge, provided due notice be given proper official so that their places may be filled with other men.
12. In ordering crews for dead-heading the first crew out will run the train, the crew dead-heading will on arrival at terminal station go out ahead of the crew with which they dead-headed. Crews dead-heading under orders will be paid full pay; full time to be allowed for light trains. Conductors will be notified when time is not allowed as per this rule.
13. The rights of Conductors will commence on the day of their promotion, and they will have the choice of runs of which their age and merit as Conductor entitles them.
14. Employes will not be required to pay for supplies used in the discharge of their respective duties; excepting for switch keys, and the charge for them will be limited to $5, and for one white lantern and one Bishop coupler, for which will be charged $1 each, such amounts to be collected at termination of service if employe fails to return the articles drawn.
15. The practice will be that no train or engine will be run on the road without a Conductor or Pilot, who will receive 3 cents per mile. An employe cannot count promotion on account of piloting engines.
16. The Company will issue to some responsible person a pass book for the transportation of Brotherhood men, who show traveling card correctly stamped, with lodge number and seal. And person to whom pass book is issued will take name of person who presents such card, with number of lodge issuing the card and the date same was issued. When the Company finds it necessary to remove an employe to another division it will furnish said employe free transportation for himself and family.
17. Trainmen required to remain on duty over thirty minutes with their trains, on arriving at terminal station, will be paid at the rate of ten miles per hour as overtime.

18. Construction or work trains to be paid as follows: Conductors, $3.60 per day; Brakemen, $2.40; twelve hours to constitute a day's work. If extra service, overtime to be allowed as follows: Conductors 30 cents and Brakemen 20 cents per hour. When Conductor acts as foreman of construction or work train he shall receive $25 per month additional.

19. The use of intoxicating liquors or visiting saloons while on duty will be met with dismissal.

20. When crews are called and from any reason not their own fault they fail to go out, they will be paid as follows: If held on duty less than five hours they will be paid one-half day and stand first out, if held five hours or more they will be paid one day and go out behind other crews at that point; it being understood that in case crews go out within five hours time while on duty said time will be recorded from the time they were called.

21. Trainmen will be called within three-fourths of a mile of main line division or terminal stations by train Caller, who will always be provided with a book in which the men called will enter their names, together with the time they are called. The time of trainmen will begin one hour from the time they are called.

22. Trains leaving terminals having empties or loads to be distributed, except trains having empty coal or flat cars, will have them switched ahead in station order, and sufficient air to handle trains when practicable.

23. No Conductor or Brakeman will be required to coal an engine, except in cases of emergency; when necessary to coal engines Brakemen will be allowed twenty miles for same.

24. In employing trainmen experienced men will be employed in preference to others, when they can be had.

25. Conductors will not be required to register their trains in consist books at terminals or other stations, except at Milano, Hearne, Troupe, Tyler, Trinity and Willis, but will be required to make a consist of their trains only.

26. Yard limit board will be protection for rear end of all trains within yard limits.

27. Freight crews pulled off of regular runs to run special passenger or pay car will be paid regular freight rates.

28. When an employe is discharged or leaves the service of the Company he will not be held waiting for his time over five days. Should such person be held beyond the expiration of five days he will be paid for time, at overtime rates, as well as his expenses.

29. The Laredo section to be considered as a promotion, and men from the San Antonio section to be promoted thereto according to their age. Brakemen on Laredo section to be promoted to San Antonio section according to their age.

30. One-half of the passenger Conductors between San Antonio and Palestine will be appointed from the San Antonio section. Longview to Palestine to have two passenger Conductors, and Palestine to Galveston to have four passenger Conductors on through trains.

31. Extra Conductors to be classed the same as regular Conductors, the oldest extra Conductor to have preference, his age to rank from the day he is promoted. Service as Yardmaster or switching, running baggage car or braking on passenger trains not to be considered in making promotion in freight service.

32. Yardmen will not be required to coal up their engines.

33. No change in these rules and regulations will be made without thirty days notice.

T. G. GOLDEN,
For the Order of Railway Conductors: General Superintendent.
W. H. TURNER, T. G. BUNN, W. C. GALLOWAY.
For Brotherhood of Railroad Trainmen:
J. R. EDWARDS, P. H. CORRIGAN, J. H. DAVIS.
September 15, 1891.   Approved: T. M. CAMPBELL, Receiver.

INDEX.

[When two schedules for the same road or system appear, the Index will designate the latest; several schedules were received after the first part of the book went to press. The schedules governing Engineers and Firemen, and published in connection with those governing trainmen, were not secured by the Brotherhood of Railroad Trainmen nor the Order of Railway Conductors, but are published at the request of the officials of the road or system.]

	Page.
Addison & Pennsylvania Railway	3
Alabama Great Southern Railroad Company (C. N. O. & T. P.)	62
Alabama & Vicksburg Railway Company (C. N. O. & T. P.)	62
Annapolis & Baltimore Short Line Railroad	3
Atchison, Topeka & Santa Fe Railroad	3
Atchison, Topeka & Santa Fe Railroad — Supplement	19
Atlantic & Pacific Railroad Company, Western division (Santa Fe system)	7
Atlantic & Danville Railway	19
Baltimore & Lehigh Railroad Company	20
Baltimore & Ohio Railroad, Philadelphia and Main Stem divisions	20
Baltimore & Ohio Railroad, Trans-Ohio division	21
Baltimore & Ohio Railroad, Pittsburg & Western division	23
Baltimore & Ohio Southwestern Railroad Company	25
Belt Railway Company of Chicago	37
Bennington & Rutland Railway	28
Boston & Maine Railroad	28
Burlington & Missouri River Railroad in Nebraska (C. B. & Q. system)	48
Calumet & Blue Island Railway Company	28
Canadian Pacific Railway Company, Pacific division	28
Canadian Pacific Railway Company, Western division	31
Central Railroad of New Jersey and leased lines	31
Charleston, Cincinnati & Chicago Railroad	31
Chesapeake & Ohio Railway Company	34
Chicago & Alton Railroad Company	35
Chicago & Alton Railroad Company — Supplement	29
Chicago & Eastern Illinois Railroad Company	38
Chicago & Eastern Illinois Railroad Company — Later	178
Chicago & Erie Railway Company	177
Chicago & Erie Railway Company — Supplement	178
Chicago & Indiana Coal Railway	35
Chicago & Indiana Coal Railway — Later	178
Chicago & Northwestern Company	37
Chicago & Northwestern Company — Later	182
Chicago & Western Indiana Railroad Company	37
Chicago, Burlington & Quincy Railroad	44
Chicago, Burlington & Kansas City Railroad (C. B. & Q. system)	51
Chicago Great Western Railway Company	54
Chicago Great Western Railway Company — Later	180
Chicago, Milwaukee & St. Paul Railway	54
Chicago, Rock Island & Pacific Railway	56
Chicago, Rock Island & Pacific Railway — Later	186
Chicago, St. Paul, Minneapolis & Omaha Railway Company (Northwestern line)	42
Choctaw Coal and Railway Company	62
Cincinnati, New Orleans & Texas Pacific Railway Company (Queen & Crescent route)	62
Cleveland, Cincinnati, Chicago & St. Louis Railway Company (Big Four route)	65
Cleveland, Lorain & Wheeling Railway	69
Colorado Midland Railway, First division (Santa Fe system)	15
Colorado Midland Railway, Second division (Santa Fe system)	17
Columbus, Hocking Valley & Toledo Railway	70
Columbus, Shawnee & Hocking Railway Company	71
Cornwall & Lebanon Railroad	72
Delaware & Hudson Canal Company	72
Delaware, Lackawanna & Western Railroad Company	72
Denver & Rio Grande Railway Company	73
Des Moines, Northern & Western Railway Company	75
Duluth & Iron Range Railroad Company	77
Duluth, South Shore & Atlantic Railway	77
Duluth, Watertown & Pacific Railway (Great Northern line)	81
East Tennessee, Virginia & Georgia Railway (C. N. O. & T. P.)	62
East Tennessee, Virginia & Georgia Railway	79
Elgin, Joliet & Eastern Railway Company	80
Fall Brook Coal Company	80
Ferrocarril Mexicano del Norte	81
Ferrocarril Mexicano del Sur	81
Flint & Pere Marquette Railroad	81
Fort Worth & Rio Grande Railway Company	81
Fremont, Elkhorn & Missouri Valley (Northwestern line)	44
Galveston, Harrisburg & San Antonio Railway Company (Southern Pacific company)	144
Great Northern Railway	81
Gulf, Colorado & Santa Fe Railway (Santa Fe system)	10
Gulf, Western Texas & Pacific Railway Company (Southern Pacific company)	144
Hannibal & St. Joseph Railroad (C. B. & Q. system)	51
Houston & Texas Central Railway Company	82

Illinois Central Railroad Company.. 82
Indianapolis, Decatur & Western Railway... 85
Intercolonial Railway of Canada... 85
International & Great Northern Railroad... 86
International & Great Northern Railroad — Later.. 188
Interoceanic Railway of Mexico, Limited.. 86
Iowa Central Railway Company.. 86
Jacksonville Southeastern line.. 86
Kansas City Belt Railway Company... 87
Kansas City, Fort Scott & Memphis Railroad Company, and associated companies west of the Mississippi river.. 87
Kansas City, St. Joseph & Council Bluffs Railroad (C. B. & Q. system)............ 51
Kentucky & Indiana Bridge Company.. 89
Kentucky Midland Railway... 89
Knoxville & Ohio Railroad (E. T. V. & G. system).. 79
Lake Erie & Western Railroad Company... 90
Lake Shore & Michigan Southern Railway Company... 91
Lehigh & Hudson River Railway Company... 91
Louisiana Western Extension Railroad Company (Southern Pacific company)... 144
Louisville & Nashville Railroad Company... 91
Louisville, New Albany & Chicago Railway Company... 98
Louisville Southern Railroad (East Tennessee, Virginia & Georgia Railway, lessee)... 62
Memphis & Charleston Railroad (E. T. V. & G. system)...................................... 79
Michigan Central Railroad Company... 100
Milwaukee, Lake Shore & Western Railway Company (Northwestern line)....... 42
Missouri, Kansas & Texas Railway... 103
Missouri Pacific Railway Company... 106
Mobile & Birmingham Railway (E. T. V. & G. system).. 79
Mobile & Ohio Railroad Company.. 110
Montana Union Railway Company.. 114
Nashville, Chattanooga & St. Louis Railway... 115
New Orleans & Northeastern Railroad Company (C. N. O. & T. P.)................... 62
New York & New England Railroad Company.. 119
New York & Northern Railway Company.. 119
New York, Chicago & St. Louis Railroad Company (Nickel Plate)...................... 119
New York, Texas & Mexican Railway Company (Southern Pacific company)... 144
Northern Pacific Railroad Company... 121
Ohio & Mississippi Railway Company... 124
Ohio Southern Railroad Company.. 127
Omaha & St. Louis Railway Company).. 127
Pennsylvania Lines, west of Pittsburg — Northwest system, P. Y. & A. division... 127
Peoria & Pekin Union Railway Company... 128
Pittsburg & Lake Erie Railroad Company.. 128
Pittsburg & Western Railway (B. & O. system).. 23
Pittsburg, Cincinnati, Chicago & St. Louis Railway Company — Southwest system, Logansport div... 128
Pittsburg, Shenango & Lake Erie Railroad Company... 129
Quincy, Omaha & Kansas City Railway... 129
Richmond & Danville Railroad Company, and leased lines................................. 129
Richmond, Fredericksburg & Potomac Railroad Company.................................. 131
Rio Grande Southern Railroad Company... 131
Rio Grande Western Railway Company.. 132
Sabine & East Texas Railway Company (Southern Pacific company)................ 144
St. Joseph & Grand Island Railroad Company, and operated lines..................... 132
St. Louis & San Francisco Railway (Santa Fe system)... 13
St. Louis, Iron Mountain & Southern Railway Company (Missouri Pacific)...... 106
St. Louis, Keokuk & Northwestern Railroad (C. B. & Q. system)....................... 51
St. Louis Merchants Bridge Terminal Railway... 134
St. Louis Southwestern Railway Company... 134
St. Louis Southwestern Railway Company of Texas.. 138
St. Paul & Duluth Railroad... 142
San Antonio & Aransas Pass Railway.. 142
Savannah, Americus & Montgomery Railway.. 142
Seattle, Lake Shore & Eastern Railway Company... 142
Sioux City & Pacific Railway Company (Northwestern line).............................. 44
South Carolina Railway... 143
Southern Pacific Company, Atlantic system... 144
Southern Pacific Company, Pacific system and lines in Oregon......................... 148
Tampico Route (Companyia del Ferrocarril de Monterey al Golfo Mexicano).. 154
Terminal Railroad Association of St. Louis... 154
Texas Central Railway.. 154
Texas & New Orleans Railroad Company (Southern Pacific company)............. 144
Toledo & Ohio Central Railroad Company.. 155
Toledo, Ann Arbor & North Michigan Railway Company................................... 154
Toledo, Peoria & Western Railway.. 157
Toledo, St. Louis & Kansas City Railroad Company... 15,
Tyler Southeastern Railway Company... 138
Union Pacific System... 163
Valley Railway Company.. 169
Vandalia Line... 171
Vicksburg, Shreveport & Pacific Railroad Company (C. N. O. & T. P.)............. 62
Wabash Railroad Company... 171
Western & Atlantic Railroad (N. C. & St. L.)... 115
West Virginia Central & Pittsburg Railroad.. 174
Willmar & Sioux Falls Railway (Great Northern line)... 81
Wisconsin Central Lines.. 174
Zanesville & Ohio River Railway Company.. 177

www.ingramcontent.com/pod-product-compliance
Lightning Source LLC
Chambersburg PA
CBHW032133160426
43197CB00008B/622